ENGLISH WORKERS AND THE COMING OF THE WELFARE STATE 1918–1945

A thirty-five volume facsimile series
documenting the debate over the role of government
in the lives of the English people

Edited by F.M. Leventhal
Boston University

A GARLAND SERIES

MEN WITHOUT WORK

A Report Made to the
Pilgrim Trust

Garland Publishing, Inc.
New York & London
1985

For a complete list of the titles in this series
see the final pages of this volume.

This facsimile has been made from a copy in
the Yale University Library.

First published in 1938 by the Cambridge University Press.
Reprinted by permission of the Cambridge University Press.

Library of Congress Cataloging in Publication Data
Main entry under title:

Men without work.

(English workers and the coming of
the welfare state, 1918–1945)
Reprint. Originally published: Cambridge :
University Press, 1938.
Includes index.
1. Unemployed—Great Britain. 2. Great Britain—
Social conditions—20th century. 3. Social service—
Great Britain. I. Pilgrim Trust (Great Britain)
II. Series.
HD5765.A6M46 1985 331.13′7941 85-13069
ISBN 0-8240-7619-2 (alk. paper)

Design by Bonnie Goldsmith

The volumes in this series are printed on
acid-free, 250-year-life paper.

Printed in the United States of America

MEN WITHOUT WORK

LONDON
Cambridge University Press
BENTLEY HOUSE, N.W. 1

NEW YORK · TORONTO
BOMBAY · CALCUTTA · MADRAS
Macmillan

TOKYO
Maruzen Company Ltd

MEN WITHOUT WORK

A Report made to the Pilgrim Trust

WITH AN
Introduction by the
ARCHBISHOP OF YORK
and a Preface by
LORD MACMILLAN

CAMBRIDGE
AT THE UNIVERSITY PRESS
1938

PRINTED IN GREAT BRITAIN

CONTENTS

CONTENTS

PREFACE

FROM the outset the Pilgrim Trustees have felt that they could not better give practical effect to the intentions of the generous founder of their Trust than by devoting a substantial part of the available income to the alleviation of the social consequences of the malady of unemployment which in these days so grievously afflicts the body politic. But, confronted as they have been with innumerable applications for assistance to schemes of all kinds designed to this end, the Trustees have sometimes had the misgivings which must assail all who have the privilege of distributing funds for philanthropic objects and they have been anxious to obtain the best guidance which would ensure that their grants really did good.

Consequently, recognising that a sound diagnosis is the essential prerequisite of sound treatment, the Trustees welcomed the suggestion that an investigation, sympathetic but thorough, should be made of all the symptoms, moral, social and economic, of unemployment and a critical survey undertaken of the modes of treatment hitherto devised. Here, in this volume, will be found the results of this investigation and survey. I do not hesitate to say that all students of social science will share the gratitude of the Trustees to those who have so competently fulfilled a task full of difficulty. While the Report has the objectivity appropriate to a piece of scientific research, it should never be forgotten that the inquiry was concerned with the actual experiences, too often the sufferings, of human beings and that the formal arrays of figures in the statistical tables which have been compiled relate to living men and women, not to abstractions. It is to the credit of the compilers of this volume that they have never lost sight of this human aspect of the problem.

We are all, statesmen, economists and ordinary citizens alike, puzzled by the intractable problem of unemployment and our bewilderment is apt to be increased rather than diminished by the constant output of writing on the subject. It is probably just because we are none of us, not even the most self-assured, quite certain in our own minds as to what should be done that we seek to salve our consciences and condone our inefficacy by the institution of innumerable committees and inquiries and the writing of innumerable reports. But this volume is not a contribution to the literature of escape. It is a manual of facts for the enlightenment and guidance of those who desire to address themselves to practical measures.

It is right to make it clear that the Pilgrim Trust is not responsible for the views expressed in these pages. The Trustees have neither directly nor indirectly sought to influence the investigators in the performance of their task and the Report is printed exactly as it was received. But, this disclaimer made, the Trustees believe that the Report, by its fresh, humane and independent treatment of its subject, makes a contribution of real value to the understanding of the conditions and the problems of the long unemployed in this country and as such my colleagues and I commend it to the study of our fellow citizens.

MACMILLAN

6 *February* 1938

INTRODUCTION

In 1933, when unemployment was still at its worst, I invited a group of people to consult with me about the problem. As a result of the consultations and enquiries which took place, the Committee which I had formed became convinced that there was need for a far more thorough investigation of the work that could be done by voluntary societies for the unemployed, an investigation which must inevitably involve an enquiry into the effects of unemployment and the real needs of the unemployed man. We found that the Pilgrim Trustees were also concerned that such an enquiry should be made, partly in order to aid them in a wise allocation of their funds, so far as these were used to finance pioneer enterprises.

They agreed therefore to finance such an enquiry and invited certain members of my Committee to be responsible for conducting it, together with one or two additional members nominated by the Pilgrim Trust. The Committee thus formed was composed of the following: the Bishop of Chichester, the Master of Balliol, Miss Iredale, Dr Thomas Jones, Sir Walter Moberly, Dr J. H. Oldham and Sir Edward Peacock, with myself as Chairman.

The Committee was fortunate in securing a capable band of investigators to carry out the enquiry. Throughout the enterprise, the secretary of my own former unemployment Committee, Miss Eleanora Iredale, has acted as Secretary to this Committee. She has been the initiator of all its activities, and also a member of the team. In addition to sharing the whole burden to the full, she devoted special attention to that part of the enquiry which relates to women's unemployment. The others who took part in the enquiry were Mr W. F. Oakeshott, Mr A. D. K. Owen, Dr H. W. Singer and, at a later stage, Dr Wagner. Mr Oakeshott, a master at Winchester College, was, on the initiative of the Headmaster, Mr S. Leeson, generously given a year's leave of absence, later extended to four terms. Mr Owen was Secretary of the Civics Section of Political and Economic Planning and Mr Israel Sieff, their Chairman, most kindly released him for this purpose. Dr Singer is an economist of

Bonn and Cambridge Universities, and Dr Wagner a psychologist who took part in the well-known survey of unemployment carried out in Marienthal. One distinctive feature of the enquiry lies in the fact that, though the team included specialists, the whole team shared fully the work of the sample and the drafting of the Report.

It was evident that a satisfactory estimate of the value of work undertaken among the unemployed must begin with a fairly exact account of the unemployed themselves. For what was good for those of one type might be useless for those of another. In this part of the undertaking our investigators received invaluable help from the officials of the Unemployment Assistance Board, and here I should like to interject a word of warm appreciation of the spirit displayed and the methods followed by the Board and very many of its officers in the discharge of what is essentially a great social service, but might easily appear to its own beneficiaries as a bureaucratic machine. Every effort is made to render its activities not only humane but human; and the results are beginning to be apparent. Most valuable help and advice were also given to us by the Ministry of Labour at Whitehall and in the local Exchanges.

While this enquiry into the question: Who are the unemployed? was taking place, there was always in mind the further question of the scope and effectiveness of voluntary work among them. This has now assumed such proportions that no work dealing with unemployment from a human standpoint could afford to neglect it, but for us it was obviously a matter of central importance. Any just appreciation of it, however, must be based, on a knowledge of the types of local unemployment and of the needs which these create. The two questions are closely bound up with one another. Indeed the subject-matter of the Report is essentially a single whole and it is impossible to consider the effectiveness of any of the voluntary enterprises without first understanding the situation with which they are faced and the peculiar problems, physical, psychological and moral, to which unemployment gives rise.

The Report represents a new approach to the problems created by unemployment, and one which I am persuaded gets much closer to the real difficulties than a purely economic approach could have done. We have become accustomed to a high degree of unemployment and are inclined to be secure in the feeling, partly justified by the facts, that unemployment is "well in hand" so far as the authorities are concerned, and is not impairing seriously the prosperity of the country. The Report shows the existence of such a state of affairs that acquiescence in existing activities as a policy for the present cannot be tolerated, and as a policy for the future may be exceedingly dangerous. Again, prolonged unemployment must reduce those who are exposed to it to a common minimum level. This fact will affect the skilled man who has previously had a good wage differently from the man who has had nothing but casual or unskilled work and who may never have earned very much more than he now receives. If this is so, the appropriate method of helping them must almost inevitably be different. The Report shows that prolonged unemployment creates a number of difficulties which cannot be ignored. Because the issues raised are largely personal, they are easily understood. We can deal with them from a personal as well as an administrative point of view, and herein lies the importance of knowing and understanding the place and possibilities of voluntary effort in relation to the actual difficulties of the unemployed themselves.

The investigation had to be limited in scope if it was to be thorough and scientific. It was in fact limited to the effects of "long unemployment", according to the accepted definition of that term, i.e. unemployment continued for more than a year. In this connexion it must be noted that the reduction of the number of the unemployed resulting from the improvement of trade does not bring with it anything like a proportionate reduction of "long unemployment". Those who fell out of work recently, or who have been intermittently employed, are reabsorbed into industry as better times return; but this does not happen in at all the same degree with the "long unemployed". Here it would seem that we are confronted with a problem new in character, at any rate on the scale which it exhibits now; it is not only a question of an economic burden to be carried by the country, but of a real danger of moral decay.

I am convinced that the investigators have produced a piece of work as important as it is interesting. Much of it is novel, even to those most expert in the subject. And it is a genuinely human document, which being readable as well as scientific, may well win the attention of a large public. The Pilgrim Trust deserves the gratitude, not only of the Committee and of the investigators, but of all men of good will for making possible its publication.

The investigators have received valuable help in planning the enquiry, in consultation during its progress, in reading and commenting on the draft of the report and in many other ways from Sir William Beveridge, Mr Henry Brooke, Mr D. Caradog Jones, Professor A. M. Carr-Saunders, The Rev. Henry Carter, Mr John Dale, Mr Ronald Davison, Miss Dorothy Elliott, Dr R. D. Gillespie, Mr Claude Guillebaud, Professor N. F. Hall, Professor John Jewkes, Miss D. C. Keeling, Mr E. C. Lascelles, Dr Leishman, Mr Godfrey Lloyd, Miss Janet McCrindell, Mr S. H. Mackintosh, Dr J. J. Mallon, Dr Henry Mess, Mr S. Myers, Mr John Newsom, Mr William Noble, Mr E. C. Ramsbottom, Mr E. A. G. Robinson, Mr Wright Robinson, Mr B. Seebohm Rowntree, Sir Arthur Salter, Mrs J. L. Stocks, Mr F. D. Stuart, Professor R. H. Tawney, and Dr Brinley Thomas. None of these is of course committed in any way by what is said in the Report. Acknowledgement must also be made of the help received from many representatives of the National Council of Social Service. Not only have their headquarters given generous help, but the many contacts with their local representatives and with the Wardens of the Colleges for Adult Education were invaluable. It is impossible to mention by name the very many others who in the course of the enquiry gave valuable assistance and advice, but I should like to acknowledge the untiring secretarial help given by Miss Dorothy Calvert to Miss Iredale and her fellow investigators.

WILLIAM EBOR:

BISHOPTHORPE, YORK
3 *February* 1938

Part I

FACTS AND FIGURES

(i) THE AIMS OF THE STUDY

UNEMPLOYMENT has been since the War one of the greatest social problems in this country, and one which, on account of the poverty and distress associated with it, and of its effects on character and personality, cannot fail to interest those who care for their fellow men. Hitherto it has been impossible to say accurately what its effects on body and mind may be, and, apart from Mr Bakke's brilliant study of the unemployed man, which appeared in 1932, no general estimate based on extensive observation has been made. Until we know something of these effects, we can scarcely hope to deal with them successfully, and the object of this enquiry has been, first, to find out something about them, and secondly, to consider in the light of that knowledge the efficacy of the various efforts (both statutory and, in particular, voluntary) which are being made to deal with them.

The methods adopted in the enquiry were due primarily to suggestions made by the late Professor Daniels of Manchester, and Sir William Beveridge. The former pointed out that no satisfactory answer could yet be given to the questions: Who are the unemployed? What kind of men are those who are out of work, and why has the disaster of unemployment overtaken these and not others? Sir William Beveridge suggested that the crux of the matter was long unemployment, and that if we took a sample and interviewed in their homes something like 1,000 of the long unemployed, it ought at least to suggest what types of men were those who had been out of work for long; whether it was only the industrial misfits, with those who were too old for work and those who were work-shy, or whether there was a real problem of waste; of material, potentially good, which was rotting for lack of use. It would show what connexion there was between a man's previous employment history and unemployment, and might provide some information as to the attitude towards possible re-employment of the long unemployed. It might even throw some light on the question whether unemployment was affecting what, for want of more sharply defined words, we may call their standards and values, and whether the opportunities which unemployment provides of developing leisure activities were being used—if indeed they can, under present conditions, be used at all.

The technique of taking such a sample is familiar to statisticians and administrators, but perhaps not so familiar to the general public, and it is explained in detail in an early section of this report. In this enquiry it was decided to study the long unemployed, whom we defined for our purpose as those who had had not more than three days' continuous work in the year previous to the sample date, in six towns, the local differences of which might, when taken together, be expected to form a fairly representative picture of unemployment. These were Deptford, Leicester, the Rhondda Urban District in South Wales, Crook in County Durham, Liverpool, and Blackburn. There are aspects of long unemployment which are not adequately illustrated by the situation in these towns, and in some directions it was possible to collect additional material elsewhere. The selection of cases was made at random, in these various areas, from the live register of the Unemployment Assistance Board, which is responsible for the maintenance of the long unemployed.[1] We did not attempt to deal exhaustively with the group of unemployed who were not qualified to draw unemployment assistance at that time (owing to the fact that they had not previously worked at an insurable occupation) but depended on public assistance for maintenance. In two of the six places visited we were able to learn enough of this group to provide some comparison with those in the sample. One cogent reason why more could not be done was lack of time.

[1] In Appendix III (p. 416) an account will be found of the various statutory agencies dealing with unemployment. The difference between Unemployment Insurance, Unemployment Assistance, and Public Assistance is there explained.

The form of record card used is printed in Appendix II (p. 413). It was planned to contain on one side details of age, occupation, composition of family, family income and regular outgoings, and employment record (the latter taken, after visits had been made, from records in the Employment Exchanges), while on the other side there were the more personal details, such as the man's appearance, his intelligence, his and his family's health, the domestic standards of his household, the "atmosphere" of the family so far as it could be judged, the man's employability and attitude towards possible employment, his attitude towards industrial transference and training, his relations with the social institutions of his neighbourhood, including the unemployed clubs, and his leisure. In most instances some particular aspects of the case proved to be specially interesting and were written up fully, while others were omitted; but taken as a whole the results give a vast amount of information on most of the problems which we set out to investigate. References to the numbers of effective visits in some of the tables given (e.g. pp. 197, 432) indicate the number of visits where information relevant to the particular topic discussed was obtained.

There are two features of this method which deserve further remark. One is that it has made it possible to form a picture of the effects of unemployment on the ordinary man. This proved to be very different from the picture which would have been given if we had only come into contact with unemployed men through the unemployed clubs, for in many places the clubs appeal only to a section of the unemployed. The second is that whereas the sample method has been employed many times before to the study of different aspects of unemployment, there has not been before in this country, so far as we are aware, an application of the method so widely as we applied it, in the effort to obtain not only statistical information, but an insight into the minds and feelings of the men we visited. The degree of success which was attained exceeded our expectations. Though we had our failures and a few doors were slammed in our faces, it was noticeable that the majority of men interviewed, and their wives also, talked readily. They often said that they had never before had such an opportunity as these interviews gave, for talking over their problems and relieving their minds by "telling someone about it all", and each one of us is the richer by some personal friendships as a result.

The Unemployment Assistance Board generously put at our disposal their register for the selection of a sample of long-unemployed cases which would satisfy recognized statistical tests as being unbiased. We were also helped in the selection of the six towns, where, as explained later, the sample was carried out, by the statistical authorities in the Board and the Ministry of Labour. The records of the Unemployment Assistance Board and of the Labour Exchange are confidential, as are the records of our talks with the men. Though the sample was taken from the register of the Unemployment Assistance Board, no names or addresses appear on our record cards, only guide numbers. It was surprising how willing men were to talk to strangers with no introduction save a letter signed by ourselves, stating that we were interested in unemployment, a letter which in the later stages of the sample was discarded as unnecessary. We believe that in a great number of instances their confidence was won, and that it has been respected.

It is hardly necessary to add that in interviews of this kind subjective factors are likely to influence the result. We are aware of this, but the number of those who undertook the visits, which were all made by those directly concerned in drawing up this report, was sufficiently small for it to be possible to isolate some at least of these factors in the records and to make allowances for them. Many of the questions we discuss cannot be measured or stated in terms of figures, but they are none the less important, and where generalizations are made in the report, they are made, not on the basis of individual instances, but of a group of cases about which we are in substantial agreement.

Thus the report has some claims to be taken as a picture of the situation as a whole. Each of the men interviewed represents many others, for even the isolated cases of long unemployment in our London borough have their counterparts in other parts of London and in many of the prosperous towns of the south of

England. Where we talk of problems by tens, it means that these problems exist in thousands. To the situation in each of our areas the situation of some place, or places, elsewhere corresponds. It is only when the greatness of these problems, in numbers as well as in complexity, is understood that their urgency can be recognized. The homes we visited are like 300,000 others. Our only justification for intruding on the privacy of these hundreds of unemployed will be if it has made possible such an analysis of their real needs that something more can be done to meet them.

(ii) LONG UNEMPLOYMENT BEFORE THE SLUMP

In November 1936, when the sample enquiry was undertaken, a cycle of three years' growing depression, followed by four of recovery, had just been completed. In November 1929 the economic life of the country had been for some time in a state of equilibrium. These were not years of real prosperity, though they appeared so in the light of the "great depression" that was going to follow. Of ten English workers willing to contribute their share to national production, only nine were doing so at any time during that period. The tenth man was registered at an Employment Exchange as looking for work. Thus, of Great Britain's working population insured against the risk of unemployment,[1] gradually increasing from 11,000,000 men and women to 12,000,000, rather more than 1,000,000 were involuntarily out of work. This state of affairs, though puzzling to the mind of those used to the "good old times" before the War (and, incidentally, before disturbing figures of unemployment began to be officially published), had gradually come to be accepted as a normal state.

There was no considerable section of the population which was permanently "tenth man". In February 1930 when the depression had already begun to make itself felt and the number of unemployed had risen to 1,500,000, only 131,000 of this number had failed, between February 1928 and February 1930,

[1] About three-quarters of the total working population in a social sense, but representative for nearly the whole *industrial* working class.

to make at least thirty contributions to the Unemployment Insurance Scheme, while the number of people who had had no work at all during this time was again very much smaller. In September 1929, of a total unemployed army of 1,150,000 people, only 53,000[1] (less than 5%) had been continuously out of work for a year or more. Apart from this small stagnant pool, we must think of pre-depression unemployment as a fairly rapidly moving stream. A figure of 53,000 means that in a typical middle-sized community of 40,000 people there were not more than some fifty long-unemployed men and women. The percentage of the total industrial population which persistently failed to get absorbed into employment (less than ½%) was the same as that which we found seven years later in the most prosperous of our six towns, the Borough of Deptford. Although there is no information whatsoever available about the composition of this small number of long-unemployed men in 1929, because no one bothered about a problem of this extent, some light may be thrown on who the long unemployed were before the depression by the description which will be given of long unemployment in Deptford, and the reader who tries to imagine pre-depression conditions in the light of our Deptford study will not be very far wrong.

There are reasons for thinking, however, that even the situation as we found it in Deptford was worse than that of the normal community in 1929. Of the 53,000 unemployed for more than a year at that time, not less than 38,000[2] were coal-miners, most of them thrown out of work in the 1926 lock-out and never reabsorbed. The problem in 1929 was thus mainly a localized abnormality of coal-mining districts dependent on mines abandoned or permanently closed. In all other industries taken together, the number of long unemployed shrinks to the small figure of 15,000 and the number of long-unemployed families in our

[1] This figure is not official, but an estimate is made to show the problem of the following enquiry in its economic perspective, as one of the last depression. The estimate is based on a Ministry of Labour sample enquiry conducted at that time, involving 10,000 unemployed. It is probably correct within a small margin of error.

[2] This figure again is not official, but is an estimate made for this report.

normal community of 40,000 people, if it does not happen to be a mining community, shrinks from 50 to 15, unnoticeable, and an easy object for individual help and supervision.

(iii) DEPRESSION AND RECOVERY

Within three years of the beginning of the depression the number of unemployed had risen from 1,281,000 in the last quarter of 1929 to 2,757,000 in the last quarter of 1932. There were four men for every three available jobs. 60 % of all workers in shipbuilding and allied industries were out of work, 46 % of all workers in the iron and steel industries. As the depression went on, the number of men and women out of work for a year or more increased even more rapidly than the general tide, as more and more men who had been thrown out or temporarily stopped work by firms closing or contracting failed to get work and began to be reckoned as long unemployed.

At the beginning of 1932 the number of long-unemployed[1] men alone passed the 300,000 mark, and during that year, when the depression gradually spent its force and not many more men were turned out of work afresh, the number of long-unemployed men continued to increase rapidly, passing the 350,000 mark in the summer of 1932, the 400,000 mark in autumn, and the 450,000 mark early in 1933. Their number continued to increase right into the summer of 1933, when the general tide of unemployment had already definitely begun to recede.[2]

In July 1933 the total number of long-unemployed men and women was over 480,000. Of 100 men queuing up at the Exchange in September 1929, only 5 or 6 had been persistently unemployed. Of 100 men queuing up three years later, when the depression was at its worst, 20 had had no work for a year or more. In the middle of 1933, when the last of the men thrown out by the depression and not reabsorbed had passed on into the

[1] By "long unemployed" we shall from now on mean men continuously unemployed for more than a year.

[2] The numbers of long-unemployed women follow a rather different course, but mainly for administrative reasons with which we are not concerned here.

long-term class, 25 of every 100 unemployed had had no work during the last year. Instead of 50 families in our "average community" there was now a crowd of 480 families. A social problem of the first order had arisen. We have seen that, with the exception of some mining districts, it was wholly a creation of the economic depression. The question was whether recovery would undo what the depression had done, and whether the new problem was thus going to be automatically solved.

The three years of depression had already been followed by four years of recovery when the sample of long unemployment which forms the basis of this report was taken. Thus it illustrates a state of recovery which had progressed considerably both in duration and extent, though it was by no means yet completed; for the year which has passed since it was made brought continued recovery, and we found a considerable number of long unemployed in work again when they were visited in the course of the six months following the sample date. The problem that we saw and now describe is, therefore, what was left by the great depression. Some of these long unemployed may still be absorbed into normal industrial society, but they have failed to be reabsorbed for a long time, during which expanding industrial activity has brought back to work many unemployed and has absorbed many newcomers as well. Economic forecasts are uncertain, though perhaps less so than they used to be. Conditions during the slump showed that the industrial system can fare worse than when we analysed its least used resources of labour in 1936, and subsequent improvements have shown that it can fare better. We may perhaps say that by November 1936 a stage had been reached which represented fair prosperity for the country as a whole under post-War economic conditions.

Of the rise in unemployment from 1,281,000 to 2,757,000 persons between the last quarters of 1929 and 1932, a great portion has been made good in the four following years. In the last quarter of 1936, 1,621,000 persons were out of work. Of 100 men and women thrown out of work between 1929 and 1932, the great majority, 77, have returned to employment, if we neglect for the moment those who died, those who retired with an Old Age Pension, or the women who withdrew from the labour market into family life. By the third quarter of 1937 the majority of the remaining 23, namely 17, had returned to employment as well. But, in this recovery, what had become of the long-unemployed man, this new phenomenon of the depression?

We saw that before the depression (September 1929), among 100 men queuing up at the Exchange, there would have been no more than five or six who had not had work for a year past, and we noticed the rapid rise of this figure to 20 at the depth of the depression, and to 25 in the summer of 1933 when firms had ceased to close down, but the last batch of dismissals during the depression had increased the number of long-unemployed men to the new high level of 460,000. When the recovery took place, the proportion of long unemployed did not go back to the old level; it did not even show a tendency to decline again, but it went on increasing.

During the first year after the peak in the summer of 1933, the actual number of men out of work for a year or more fell considerably. It had dropped by 90,000 to 370,000 in October 1934, and at that date we would have found 24 long-unemployed men among 100 registering at the Exchange, and some optimistic observers might have thought that unemployment might both return to its old level, and, in the process, revert to its old character as mainly an industrial turnover of human labour, a fairly rapidly moving stream with only small stagnant pools here and there. But the following year, from October 1934 to October 1935, showed that nothing of the sort was going to happen. While the recovery went on rapidly and the total number of unemployed men fell by a considerably larger number than the year before, the number of the long unemployed remained nearly stationary, declining by a bare 10,000 to 360,000, so that in the autumn of 1935, 26 out of 100 men at the Exchange had been out of work for a full year or more.

In the following year (that preceding our enquiry), from autumn 1935 to autumn 1936, with industrial activity growing apace, the number of long-unemployed men went down again by another 60,000 to just under 300,000.[1] But the proportion they bore to the whole did not change, and there were still 26 men out of 100 unemployed. During the year following the sample, the time during which the data for this report were collected, the number of long-unemployed men continued to decline, and a fall of about 65,000 in nine months brought the total down to 265,000 men.[2] But the proportion had now risen, and there were, in August 1937, 27 men out of 100 unemployed.

Thus a majority of workers, turned out of their jobs during the first three years of the seven years' cycle between November 1929 and 1936, had got back during the following four years, but for every 100 men who had become long unemployed between 1929 and the depth of the depression, only 39 had managed to get out of that class again. In addition, the problem had ceased to be so predominantly one of the coal industry since, in our average non-coal-mining community of 40,000, the number of long-unemployed families had risen sharply from 15 to 220. Recovery had failed to solve the problem. On the contrary, as the unemployment figures fell, its seriousness became more and more obvious.

Another analysis of the unemployment figures will help to show what has happened. For this purpose we will consider four different categories of unemployed: (*a*) the man just out of work, who has been out for less than three months; (*b*) the short-term unemployed (three to six months); (*c*) the middle-term unemployed (six to twelve months); and (*d*) the long-term unemployed (over one year). These categories represent, of course, quite different types of problem. Many of those in category (*a*) would not be reckoned in some countries as unemployed at all. The docker who works regularly those days of the week when ships come in and is idle the rest of it appears

[1] To this figure there should, however, be added an, at that time, unknown total of able-bodied long-unemployed men in receipt of neither assistance nor insurance payments. A few months later when this category was brought into the scope of official statistics, their number turned out to be about 30,000. The real number of long unemployed at the time of our count was, therefore, about 330,000.

[2] The 30,000 newcomers had by now been included in the official figures.

then in the unemployment figures, as does the factory worker who is temporarily stopped perhaps because of a shortage of raw materials, but will start again as soon as new supplies arrive. Others in this category, whose unemployment does not necessarily represent any problem, are the labourers who move from one job to another with intermittent short spells of unemployment between them, possibly rather longer (for example, if the man is a builder's labourer) in winter than in summer; or the miners, who in some pits are regularly stopped for two or three weeks at certain times of the year; or the workers in the Potteries who work only four days a week; or again, the skilled men who will be snapped up a few days after they become available. Those in categories (*b*) and (*c*) are a somewhat different proposition. Some of them are in transition from one permanent job to another, but many of them are the "very casual" workers in receipt of Unemployment Assistance who are hardly distinguishable from those in category (*d*). The man who gets work only every Christmas for the Post Office in the rush, for instance, will be grouped, not among the long unemployed, but for most of the year in categories (*b*) and (*c*). Many men in these categories are thus virtually long unemployed, presenting the same sort of problem as those to whom the sample was limited, while a few (including those former long unemployed who have had a fairly recent spell of "relief work" organized by the local councils) are actually on their way to join the long unemployed.

If we compare the numbers in these four categories of unemployed men at the time the sample was taken with the highest numbers ever reached during the past depression, the proportions are as follows:

TABLE I

	In-and-out	Short term	Middle term	Long term
Depression	100	100	100	100
1936	52	34	32	65

Thus in the present period of recovery the band of unemployment tends to broaden at both ends. The two types of the in-and-out and of the long unemployed tend to emerge more and more clearly as two separate classes, separated by a narrowing band of unemployed somewhere between these two states. The reasons why these two groups fail to decline to the same extent as the middle groups are, of course, entirely different in the two cases. Among the ins-and-outs, the majority are not now men who are entering on a long spell of unemployment, as it was some six years ago, but it is now the normal turn-over of industry which, with the present organization of industry at least, cannot go below a certain figure, and is, moreover, a sign of industrial activity rather than industrial depression.

The failure of the long-unemployed group to decrease proportionately is due to difficulties of reabsorption: industry, for some reason, is clearly reluctant to draw on this reserve to provide for its expansion or there is some other obstacle such as personal factors in the men themselves. The decline of the middle groups means that those who are being turned over by industry nowadays are not to any comparable degree exposed to the danger of passing into the ranks of the long unemployed, for in the time of the slump it was those passing through the two middle groups, rather than those of the "very casual" type, that formed the bulk of their numbers. It becomes increasingly apparent that the present practice followed in the official statistics of grouping together in one figure the turn-over of industry and the unemployed, who are now chiefly long unemployed, is no longer satisfactory. This enquiry is based on the recognition that the economic, social, administrative and political problems raised by the existence of the ins-and-outs and the long unemployed are by nature essentially different.

That the unemployed are grouping themselves everywhere into these two classes, the in-and-out and the long unemployed, can be seen from a study of the six towns in which the present enquiry has been conducted. As we later attempt to show, economic, industrial, social and other conditions varied as widely as six towns can vary. But a comparison of the 1932 and 1936 unemployment register in these six places[1] shows that every-

[1] September figures which were kindly supplied by the Ministry of Labour

where the same tendencies could be observed. Total unemployment had fallen to a varying degree. Out of every 100 men and women at the Exchanges in 1932, there have dropped out, by 1936, by finding local employment or employment elsewhere:

In the Borough of Deptford ...	62
In the City of Leicester ...	40
In the City of Liverpool ...	29
In Blackburn C. B.	37
In Crook, Co. Durham ...	44
In Rhondda U.D.	23

Thus in Deptford nearly three times as many people dropped out of the queue of 100 as did in the Rhondda U.D. But whatever the number of men dropping out, among the remainder there was a higher proportion of long-unemployed men than among the swollen queues of 1932. Among 100 men and women in the queue there were the following long unemployed:

TABLE II

	1932	1936
Deptford	4	6
Leicester	4	11
Liverpool	19	23
Blackburn	37[1]	38
Crook	46	56
Rhondda	33	63

The conclusion to be drawn from this table is inevitable. The reasons, or at least some of the reasons, why long unemployment fails to go down to the 1929 level cannot be identified with conditions in certain districts or certain industries, or with differ-

[1] The comparatively high number of long-unemployed men and women in Blackburn for 1932 is explained by the fact that as the depth of the depression was reached much earlier in the cotton industry than elsewhere, the "last wave" of dismissals had already swollen the long unemployed, whereas this was not so in other industries by September 1932.

ences in the extent of industrial recovery. There is a "hard core" of long unemployment which will not be resolved by recovery alone, in every town of this country, however prosperous, however diversified its range of industries, or however much its main industry benefits from industrial trends, and wherever it is situated. The problem is of increasing social importance throughout the country and is not entirely bound up with the problem of economic activity and depression. This is one of the main reasons for the inclusion of two prosperous places in the study.

A further conclusion is to be drawn from Table II. Everybody knows that there are at present in England prosperous districts and "depressed areas". The case of a prosperous district is described by conditions in Deptford, where about 7% of the industrial population were unemployed in November 1936; the Rhondda U.D. is part of a depressed area, and 35% of the industrial population were out of work. Table II suggests that this description is inadequate to describe the difference in conditions. Not only are the number unemployed in Deptford very much smaller (in proportion to the working population) than they are in the Rhondda, but they represent entirely different types of unemployment. Only 6% of the Deptford unemployed were long-unemployed men, but 63% in the Rhondda. The inclusion of the ins-and-outs in the unemployment figures must produce an entirely false picture of the differences in unemployment conditions in various parts of the country. Between prosperous and depressed districts there are two differences. The queues in the Rhondda are far longer than in Deptford, for example, and at the same time among them the proportion of "really" unemployed men is far higher. Among every 1,000 workers, 4 in Deptford, but 280 in the Rhondda have failed to get a job for at least a year. This gives an idea of the unevenness in the distribution of the long unemployed over the country. The difference between a prosperous and a depressed area is thus not in the neighbourhood of 1 : 7, but of 1 : 70. In a depressed community there are 70 long-unemployed men, where in a prosperous community of the same size there is one.

This is the proportion that should be kept in mind when comparing the reports from prosperous and depressed places in the following parts.

It will perhaps be useful to have a table (Table III) showing the number of long unemployed per 1,000 workers for all the six places which will be described in the following part:

TABLE III. SEPTEMBER 1936

	Of 1,000 workers	
	Recorded as Unemployed	Unemployed for a year or more
Deptford	67	4
Leicester	74	8
Liverpool	257	59
Blackburn	295	112
Crook	336	188
Rhondda	445	281

A comparison of Table III with Table II shows that there is a well-marked general tendency which it is always important to have in mind when thinking of prosperous and depressed communities. As the queues become longer, at the same time their composition changes. It is not simply an enlargement of the old queues with all their elements reproduced. The longer queue has, almost always, a far greater proportion of long-unemployed men.

These six places, though each has its individual characteristics, each stand for a vast district of the country and the 300,000 long-unemployed men and women are distributed very unequally over the country as a whole. Thus we can divide England and Wales into seven broad regions, of which the first four are prosperous in the sense that the queues at the Exchanges are smaller, and the last three suffer from a much heavier burden of unemployment. Table IV deals with the 275,000 long-unemployed men, in England and Wales only, for a date in June 1936. The first column shows the total length of the queues in relation to the working population, the second column shows the composition of the queues and confirms the tendency we have just pointed out, and the third column gives an idea of the inequality in the distribution of long unemployment over the country.[1]

The figures in the last column had to be obtained in a somewhat roundabout way, but they are none the less reliable (within a small margin of error).

TABLE IV. SUMMER 1936

Division	Total insured working population (men and women)	How many of 1,000 men stand in the queue	Percentage of queues that are long unemployed	How many of 1,000 workers are long unemployed
		I	II	III
South-east	1,126,000	62	6	4
London	2,562,000	76	7	6
South-west	960,000	89	12	11
Midlands	2,008,000	101	22	22
North-west	2,150,000	186	23	46
North-east	2,104,000	212	26	57
Wales	611,000	322	37	123

Table IV deserves careful study, for the third column shows us where the bulk of the long unemployment in this country is concentrated. If it is compared with the corresponding table for the six towns of this enquiry, it will be seen that Deptford is typical for conditions in London and the South-east, Leicester for conditions in the South-west and the Midlands (although it fails to represent the more depressed parts of the Midlands),[2] Liverpool is fairly representative of the North-west, but

[1] Here again we find that the "temporarily unemployed" are much more equally distributed over the country as a whole, and see again at a glance that they are not indicative of real differences in the unemployment situation which their numbers only tend to obscure. Of 1,000 workers, there were "temporarily unemployed": South-east 36, London 46, South-west 52, Midlands 53, North-west 85, North-east 107, Wales 134. Compare this with the distribution of the long unemployed in column III of Table IV.

[2] In parts of which there is very heavy unemployment. Kidsgrove, for example, is one of the hardest hit towns in this country.

Blackburn is a "black spot" there, and so is Crook in the North-east, and the Rhondda fails, of course, to represent the "bright belt" of Wales. The reader who studies the preceding tables will be conscious of the qualifications on this account with which our general conclusions later on will have to be read. At the same time, it will be a reminder that in thinking of unemployment we should beware of imagining (as might be suggested by the terms "depressed areas", "prosperous South England") wide areas within which conditions are uniform and which are fairly clearly marked off against other regions with another uniform level. On the light or dark background of prosperity or depression, there are innumerable patches of a still brighter light, or perhaps a sombre dark on light, or of an even intenser dark or of light patches within a sea of black. Table IV should, therefore, be understood as the ground colours of a very patchy picture. The importance of these patches in the general picture, and the tenacity with which they remain where they are is too little known.[1]

We now know something about the question: where do the long unemployed live? The second question for which official statistics, modified by certain other information, provide an answer is: to which industries do the long unemployed belong? In order to reach the answer given below we have eliminated certain categories in the official figures, and in particular "Public Works Contracting". This item consists almost entirely of men who have been long unemployed and have been given spells of Council work on the roads, or in some other similar form. Their industrial history shows that they really belong to one or other of the heavy industries, coal-mining or ship-building, or whatever it may be; and here they are classified under these original occupations, which can reasonably well be estimated.

The facts, for June 1936, were as shown in Table V. The major industries which contribute most heavily to the queues of unemployed men can be clearly seen from this table, and the close connexion between long unemployment and

[1] For further details, see Dr Singer's first Interim Report, "Local Differences in the Incidence of Unemployment."

TABLE V

	Men only	How many per 1,000 workers were unemployed for a year or more in the summer of 1936
1	Coal-miners	123
2	Ship-builders and repairers	95
3	Cotton workers	67
4	Seamen	59
5	Pig-iron and Iron and Steel workers	57
6	Pottery and Earthenware workers	54
7	Workers in Textile Bleaching, Dyeing, etc.	37
8	Waiters and other workers in Hotels, Public-houses and Restaurants	33
9	Gas, Water and Electricity workers	33
10	Boot and Shoe workers	31
11	General Engineering	31
12	Dock and Harbour workers	27
13	Workers in Distributive Trades	27
14	Workers in Bread, Biscuits, Cakes, etc.	26
15	Workers in Tailoring firms	25
16	Builders and Building labourers	24
17	Furniture workers	21
18	Printers, Bookbinders	14
19	Workers in Motor Vehicles, Cycles, etc.	10
	All workers	41

industrial decline is obvious. Indeed (though it does not, of course, appear in Table V) at least 40% of the long unemployment throughout the country is concentrated in the four basic and (in the post-War period) structurally declining industries, coal-mining, ship-building, iron and steel, textile manufacture.

Table V shows that the long-unemployed men are just as unequally distributed over the various industries as they are over the various regions. In fact, the major industries are, in their location, distinctly associated with a certain region, and the regional and industrial inequality of the length of queues of long-unemployed men is, therefore, partly the same thing, only described from a different angle.

The additional fact which makes the queues in towns with

hard-hit main industries even longer than the purely industrial factor would explain, is that unemployment in the major industry tends to produce secondary unemployment (partly through a fall in purchasing power, and partly through emigration) in such groups as Building, Gas, water, electricity, and Distributive trades, Hotels, public-houses and restaurant services, etc. Table VI is given to enable the reader to form an opinion of the part this factor plays in differences of length in the unemployment queues of the various regions.

TABLE VI

Region	Figures based on conditions in	How many per 1,000 workers connected with the building industry were long unemployed in June 1936
London	Deptford	15
South-east	,,	13
South-west	Leicester	14
Midlands (prosperous part)	,,	18
North-west } The more depressed parts	Liverpool, Blackburn	50
North-east } The more depressed parts	Crook	54
Wales } The more depressed parts	Rhondda	165

These figures are not claimed as entirely accurate, but they are again estimates based on whatever material we could secure for our six places to throw light on this question. The general lesson from Table VI, however, is beyond doubt, though details may be open to question. Within the range of secondary industries long unemployment is so unequally distributed for each that what is a prosperous industry in some parts is a depressed industry elsewhere. It is, therefore, only half of the story to say that the concentration of long unemployment is due to the different industrial occupations of workers in different districts. It is a true causal analysis: it explains why the queues of long-unemployed men in the Rhondda are so much longer than in Deptford. But it does not describe who it is that stands in the longer queues in the Rhondda.

A third important fact in the degree to which a man is exposed to the danger of long-continued unemployment, apart from the place where he is living and the industry in which he was working, is his age. On this point reasonably accurate information can be given, thanks in particular to information supplied by Sir William Beveridge.[1] Table VII shows unmistakably that the difference as between age groups is not smaller than that between regions and industries.

TABLE VII. JULY 1935

Age group	How many per 1,000 workers of that age have been out of a job for a year or more
18–20	7
21–24	29
25–34	31
35–44	42
45–54	54
55–59	80
60–64	105
18–64	41

There are prosperous age groups and depressed age groups just as much as there are prosperous and depressed districts and prosperous and depressed industries. It will be seen that the risk of long unemployment rises suddenly at 21, then rises fairly gradually to the age of 55, where there is another sudden jump. Not less than 12 years of life separate the average employed worker (about 32 years in 1935) from the average long unemployed (44 years).

Sir William Beveridge shows that it is specifically the risk of *long* unemployment to which the older men are exposed.

[1] "An analysis of Unemployment", *Economica*, February 1937.

Among the newcomers to the queues we find young men in similar, or even greater numbers than the old men. The difference is that the older a man, the truer it becomes: once in the queue, ever in the queue. That things have not worked in favour of the elderly men and that reabsorption into employment continues to favour the younger men, is more than a general impression. In the year preceding our enquiry, the number that managed to find work, or at least to leave the queues[1] is given in Table VIII.

TABLE VIII

Age group	How many per 100 men left the queue between Nov. 1935 and Nov. 1936
18–20	32
21–24	23
25–34	20
35–44	14
45–54	14
55–59	10
60–64	6

It can, therefore, be said with certainty that the difference in the degree to which various age groups are exposed to the risk of long unemployment in November 1936 was even more marked than that suggested by Table VII. A fairly safe guess of how the 300,000[2] long-unemployed men in Great Britain were distributed among the various age groups at the date of our count is shown in the following table. These figures have been worked out by assuming that the proportions of men dropping out of the queue at various ages bore the same relations to each other in the case of the long unemployed as in that of the total queues (as shown in Table VIII). This enables us to transcribe the count

[1] This figure, of course, includes, besides the long unemployed, the industrial turn-over, the ins-and-outs, the short- and middle-term unemployed.

[2] Excluding the 30,000 men in receipt of Public Assistance, later taken over by the U.A.B.

of the summer 1935 to conditions prevailing in November 1936, and the result (Table IX) can be relied upon to be not very far out, that is to say, perhaps by a few hundreds, but not by thousands.

TABLE IX

LONG-UNEMPLOYED MEN: NOVEMBER 1936

Age group	How many	How many per 1,000 workers at that age	How many of 100 men in the queue were long unemployed
	I	II	III
18–20	3,900	5	9
21–24	23,500	21	19
25–34	59,900	23	23
35–44	60,400	34	27
45–54	66,000	44	30
55–59	49,700	69	34
60–64	43,600	97	38
All	307,000	32	26

Again the jumps at 21 and at 55 in Column II are well worth noting. The risk of remaining out of work once you fall out increases with age, and this fact, to which Sir William Beveridge has drawn attention, emerges very strikingly from a study of the last column; and the risk increases with a remarkable regularity.

We have also just seen[1] that during the year preceding our enquiry (November 1935 to November 1936), the chances of a man of 62 getting back into employment once he had become unemployed were only a fifth of those of a youth of 19, a third of those of a man of 30, and a half of those of a man of 50. At the same time, however, it can be shown that as recovery went on, the chances of the elderly men, though still constantly handicapped, improved somewhat as the scarcity of younger or experienced men in certain districts and industries increased.

A study of Table X shows how recovery has gradually "leaked through" to the older men and diminished their disadvantage in

[1] Cf. Table VIII above.

TABLE X. AGE DISTRIBUTION OF 1000 MEN REABSORBED INTO EMPLOYMENT[1]

Age group	(1) Between May and Nov. 1935	(2) Between May and Nov. 1936	(3) Column 2 in % of column 1
18–20	131	103	78
21–24	186	165	89
25–34	320	319	100
35–44	164	175	107
45–54	139	155	112
55–64	57	83	146

getting back to work. That this disadvantage is still tremendous and that age continues to be a no less important factor than geography and industry will be clear to anybody who studies the following pages.

Certain information is available which throws light on the duration of unemployment within this group of chronically unemployed men. Table XI shows how many of the long-unemployed men were unemployed for various periods; the figures were taken in the summer of 1935 and the summer of 1936.[2]

TABLE XI. IN GREAT BRITAIN

	Men between 18 and 64, continuously unemployed for					
	1–2 years	2–3 years	3–4 years	4–5 years	Over 5 years	Total
Summer 1935	137,000	81,400	65,800	52,500	30,000	366,700
Summer 1936	119,600	65,400	46,100	41,000	52,900	325,000

[1] Table X is not strictly accurate, because disappearance from the Exchange Register, on which the figures are based, is not the same thing as re-employment. Leaving the queue includes not only finding work, but also dying or retiring, of which the chance is greater for the older men, and the table therefore exaggerates somewhat the proportion of older men reabsorbed. The difference between the two years, however, is clear.

[2] The figures were very kindly supplied by Sir William Beveridge.

Table XI draws attention to a fourth important factor in unemployment. Between the summer of 1935 and the summer of 1936, although the total number of long unemployed declined by over 40,000 (or 11–12%), the number of very long unemployed (over five years) increased by nearly 23,000 (or 77%). It is evident that this hard core of long unemployment carries within itself another hard core of very long unemployment which proves even more obstinate to re-employment than the hard core itself. In the summer of 1935, out of 100 long-unemployed men 8 were very long unemployed, but within a year this number had doubled to 16. It is a vivid reminder of the changed conditions when it is realized that in 1936 the number of men who had been without work for fully five years was the same as the number of men before the depression who were unemployed and had been without work in the previous year. The "hard core within the hard core" in 1936 was the same size as the total hard core of 1929. Evidently this "hard core within the hard core" consists of thousands of men who are being passed on from year to year and finally accumulate in that remotest of all backwaters, "five years or more out of work".

It seems desirable to get a clearer insight into the working of this paradoxical fourth factor; that long unemployment tends to be self-generating, and that the longer a man stands in the queue, the less likely he is to get out of it again; and that long unemployment (in addition to age, a home in a depressed district, and connexion with a contracting industry) is in itself a bar to re-employment. If we neglect (as we can reasonably do over the comparatively short period of one year) deaths and other reasons for being struck off the Register at the Exchange—reasons such as becoming an Old Age Pensioner, becoming unfit for work, etc.[1]—we may say that those men who were not passed on from, e.g. the two to three years' group in 1935 to the three to four years' group in 1936 found their way back to work, however temporary. On this basis we can find the proportions of those men, out of work for various long periods in the

[1] This omission will not vitiate the *comparison* between the various classes of unemployed men to any appreciable extent.

summer of 1935, who found work or remained unemployed in the next year. The result (Table XII) is worth keeping in mind.

TABLE XII

100 men out of work in the summer 1935, for	Found some work in the subsequent year	Remained unemployed
1–2 years	52	48
2–3 years	43	57
3–4 years	38	62
Over 4 years	36	64

It would be interesting and would throw much-needed light on the social forces making for prolonged unemployment to know something about the incidence of long unemployment in different grades of occupation within the principal industries and for the country as a whole. What is known about that we owe to Mr Colin Clark, who could do no more than measure the incidence of *total* (not long) unemployment in 1931, when the last Census of Occupations was taken. His results are most remarkable,[1] and we reproduce them (Table XIII) for the four grades of workers most likely to be covered by the Compulsory Unemployment Insurance Scheme.

TABLE XIII

	How many per 1,000 workers in each grade of work were unemployed in 1931
Unskilled manual workers	305
Skilled and semi-skilled manual workers	144
Personal service workers, barbers, waiters, etc.	99
Salesmen and shop assistants	79

The variations of Table XIII lend force to Mr Clark's conclusion that "a large, and perhaps increasing, proportion of

[1] Colin Clark. *National Income and Outlay*, p. 46.

unemployment is accounted for by a relative oversupply of the more untrained types of labour". Bearing in mind the results of some previous examinations of general unemployment figures it seems not unreasonable to assume that the differences in the degree to which workers in various grades are exposed to *long* unemployment are even more pronounced than the table suggests. It is, however, important to remember that the table says nothing about the reasons for this higher exposure of the unskilled worker. Is it because the semi-skilled and skilled man is mainly to be found in the expanding industries, or is it true for each individual industry that a higher degree of skill diminishes the risk of unemployment, or is it a combination of both? Probably the last of the three, but we simply do not know; this is one of the worst gaps in our knowledge of the factors behind long unemployment.

As all other information on this point is lacking, it may be a good thing to anticipate here again the conclusion derived from our sample, which is now to be described. If this sample is in any way representative of the two main grades in the English working population, and on the assumption that the proportion of the two grades has not changed violently since 1931, Mr Colin Clark's conclusion is fully confirmed.

TABLE XIV

	How many of 1,000 workers are long unemployed
Unskilled manual workers	81
Semi-skilled and skilled manual workers	27

(iv) THE SAMPLE INTRODUCED

The personal staff, time and money at the disposal of the enquiry were limited. Furthermore, it was clear that a real answer to the question: "Who are the long unemployed?" could not be provided on the basis of second-hand information but required personal contacts. The only way to make these provide an answer was to represent the long unemployed as a whole by a sample, large enough to reflect the important divisions within that whole and small enough to make it possible for the four of us to learn something about the social, psychological, and human problems to which continued unemployment gives rise. Long unemployment, as we shall have reason to see, is one of those social problems where cause and effect are inextricably mixed—where, for instance, long unemployment may itself make a man unemployable. We had therefore to see something of the personal causes, as well as the effects of unemployment, and to try in some degree to disentangle them.

The device of a sample is based on the fact, demonstrable in mathematical terms, that if some information about a very large population is wanted, there is no need to examine the whole population, but from a certain comparatively small selection of it conclusions can be drawn that are valid for the whole, within certain fairly narrow limits of sampling errors—provided only that every conceivable bias in the selection of the sample is excluded. If that condition is fulfilled, knowledge of a part of the whole is not only better than nothing, but it is practically the same as knowledge of the whole.

The sampling principle had to be modified to meet the special requirements of the case. First, there had to be a selection of places. To take an ideal sample would be to write the names of every long-unemployed man on a scrap of paper, throw the 300,000 of them into a ballot box, and visit 1,200 drawn from it. Not only was this course not practicable, but in this way one of the most important parts of the study would have been lost: the differences in local "colour" and their influence on the situation of long-unemployed men and women. We might perhaps have left the selection of places to chance. But the number of places we could consider visiting was so small that the result of an accidental choice might have been quite unrepresentative for the country as a whole. And the choice of the place in which the enquiry had to be conducted was too decisive, for the measure of insight the investigators might hope to get and for the value their observations might have, to be left to any kind of accident. Sampling principles were observed, therefore, for the selection of cases of long unemployed within the six towns of the sample, but the selection of the six towns themselves was deliberate.

Selection means elimination of alternatives sometimes very attractive. In this case it meant sacrificing the hope of representing fairly every shade of local conditions. We could undertake no more than six local studies; and it was decided with regret that these six places must be in England and Wales, in spite of the strong claims of Scotland. The selection was finally governed by the decision to include two prosperous towns, two with a fair amount of employment but also fairly high unemployment figures, and two places in specially distressed areas. The six towns selected have already been mentioned: the Borough of Deptford, the City of Leicester, the City of Liverpool, the County Borough of Blackburn, the Township of Crook (Co. Durham), the Urban District of Rhondda. Their main qualifications for passing the test of selection successfully can be described briefly as follows.

Deptford we took to represent London and the South-east. It is very prosperous and unemployment is small. The range of occupations both within and outside the borough is large, and there is also much casual labour employed in the South London docks. It illustrates too the problem of the metropolitan worker, and though slum clearance is proceeding rapidly, there is still bad housing and high rents. One of the Midland manufacturing towns clearly had to be included, and Leicester, prosperous and steadily progressing, was chosen. It is not in the chaotic phase of development which rapid expansion has brought to some other Midland towns. It is an old city, with long-established traditions of social service, and has a fairly wide range of industries with boot and shoe manufacture and hosiery as the chief. It also has a substantial degree of women's employment.

Liverpool picked itself, a port with a past of great prosperity but suffering from prolonged depression as southern ports compete more and more successfully with it. In spite of heavy unemployment, Liverpool still has a fairly large range of working industries, and there is a large amount of casual labour for workers and seamen. Trade Unions are on the whole weak, wages low, and there are what may be called long-standing pauper traditions. Housing, though here too enormous improvements have been recently effected, is still in many ways bad, and alone of the six places chosen it has a very large proportion of long-unemployed young men. As in Glasgow, the Irish element is important, and is partly responsible for the large families that are characteristic of the Liverpool working-class population. Blackburn was chosen as a Lancashire cotton town, typical for the whole cotton area. It is mainly dependent on this one industry, but in spite of heavy unemployment, it is not doomed, and recently there has been a definite recovery. Here we were to come in contact seriously with the problem of long unemployment among women as well as men.

Of the two places in the Special Areas, Crook is a small mining community in south-west Durham, an area that has for some time been considered as doomed and without an industrial future. It depends on one single declining industry. The lack of amenities from which it suffers has to some extent been remedied by intensive social service work. The Rhondda lies in the most important of the Special Areas. It has depended, like Crook, on a single industry, coal-mining, and presents a variety of conditions ranging from the "doomed" villages at the head of the valley where the coal is worked out to communities within the radius of the new trading estate. It has a marked Welsh cultural background. A generation ago it was exceedingly prosperous, and Trade Unions are strong. There has been a heavy emigration of young men, but it is still known as a politically alive district, and is one in which remarkable social service work has been done.

It may be said that we have had no reason to regret the choice. A strong claim might have been made for including, had it been possible, a Yorkshire steel town with about 15% of its insured population unemployed, among them a fair number of young men, or one of the small, isolated, very depressed communities outside the Special Areas and not associated with the coal industry—such as Kidsgrove, in the Potteries. But the results of the sample can be taken to illustrate fairly the situation in the country as a whole. For in so far as the sample, taken as a whole, fails to give to the major divisions among the long unemployed their precisely proportionate share, this does not mean that conclusions drawn from the sample are biased in the same way as the sample itself. The necessary allowances and corrections can be made by attaching their due weight to these major groups. Extensive use has been made of this method of checking the representative character of the sample to prevent the selection of the towns from giving a bias to the picture of the general situation.

Though chance was eliminated from the selection of the towns, it was given free play for the choice of the long-unemployed cases within them. Every long-unemployed man and woman in these six towns, who was, on 23 November 1936 (the "zero hour" of the Enquiry) registered in the "Live File" of the Unemployment Assistance Board, had an equal chance of entering the sample; and there was no deliberate selection whatsoever. We wanted to avoid getting a selected type of long-unemployed persons. It should, however, be kept in mind that the principle of Selection as against that of Chance operated in two directions even after the towns had been chosen.

The first was the definition of long unemployment. No one was admitted who had done more than three continuous days of ordinary work between 23 November 1935 and the same day in 1936. "Ordinary work" was work done for remuneration whether for private firms, on Council or Government schemes, or on an individual's own account. We did not, however, consider as a bar to entry in the sample (*a*) work acknowledged by the Unemployment Assistance Board to be a "subsidiary occupation", e.g. a man working as a cinema porter from 8 to 10.30 p.m., or a woman working as a charwoman twice a week for two hours; (*b*) work not done for remuneration, e.g. voluntary work in the "amenity" schemes or in social service schemes for a weekly food voucher; (*c*) work in a Government Training Centre, Instructional Centre, Domestic Training Centre, etc.; (*d*) any short spell of work of a strictly temporary emergency and auxiliary nature. The definition used in the sample corresponds on the whole to the common-sense description of no work.

In another way also the sample represents something different from a chance sample in that it was taken from the Register of the Unemployment Assistance Board. The facilities allowed by the Board and the difficulties in the way of similar access to the other sections of the long-unemployed population, together with the fact that the Board is the representative body on which the overwhelming majority of the long unemployed rely for their maintenance,[1] determined this choice; but it should be remembered that the "lower tenth" of the unemployment register who were not maintained by the Board's allowances at the time of the sample, but by Public Assistance, are not represented in the general sample, and that there is a similar omission consisting of a small number of men still carried by Unemployment Insurance, these representing, as it were, an "upper tenth".

The number of visits possible for us, limited since each involved a written record often of considerable length, fortunately represented something like the minimum number that could be expected to give a satisfactory picture of the situation in the towns investigated and, through them, of the various problems with which those who come into contact with the unemployed are concerned. The figure which these various considerations suggested was one slightly in excess of a thousand cases, with a total of effective visits slightly under a thousand. As we were able to find out certain details about the employment record, etc., of the sample cases, even where an effective visit was not made, these details could be used to strengthen the results in some directions. The completed sample contained 1,086 persons, 938 men and 148 women, while when the field work was completed, we found that about 880 persons (760 men and 120 women) had been successfully visited.[2] Of the persons in the sample, 14% were women, as against only 6% of all long-unemployed persons in the country as a whole. The reason why the sample includes this large proportion is that family employment and unemployment among women was one of the special problems we set ourselves to study. To do this we had to include a town with many unemployed women (Blackburn), and within that town the number had to be sufficiently large to allow general conclusions. This is an instance of what has been

[1] See below, Appendix III.

[2] This figure does not include the additional visits made, e.g. in Liverpool, to unemployed not on the register of the U.A.B. Where records of such visits are used in this report, it is specified they were not made in the ordinary course of the sample.

said already, that the main consideration was not to get as near as possible to an ideal sample of the long unemployed population. As the problem of the long-unemployed woman is completely different from that of the long-unemployed man, it has seemed best to treat this in a separate section. Here we are concerned with the men only, and the information derived from the 938 men in the sample and the 760 talks with them which have been recorded by the investigators.

The sampling proportion in each of the six towns was determined by five considerations: (1) the total of possible visits; (2) the numbers of long unemployed in each place; (3) the minimum number of cases and visits in each place necessary for any conclusions as to the situation there; (4) the extent to which the type of place and its main industries represented aspects of the general situation elsewhere also; (5) the importance of the particular problem which each of the six places was intended to illustrate. These considerations worked in such a way as to make the number of cases in each place increase with the number of long-unemployed men in that place, but the increase in the sample numbers is proportionately much smaller.

TABLE XV. SAMPLING PROPORTION AND NUMBER OF CASES

	No. of long-unemployed men, Nov. 1936	Sampling proportion	Number of cases in sample
Deptford	92	1 : 1	92
Leicester	*c.* 450	1 : 5	89
Crook (Co. Durham)	*c.* 800	1 : 7	119
Blackburn	*c.* 3,000	1 : 25	123
Liverpool	*c.* 9,500	1 : 35	273
Rhondda U.D.	*c.* 10,000	1 : 40	242
Total	*c.* 23,850	*c.* 1 : 25	938

Before considering what new light has been thrown on long unemployment by this sample, it is useful to test its accuracy in bringing out the factors of place and age as operative in creating long unemployment. Here the sample results can be checked by official figures and the validity of the sample thus tested.

TABLE XVI. DEPRESSED AND PROSPEROUS DISTRICTS IN THE SAMPLE AND IN OFFICIAL FIGURES

	Per 100 long-unemployed men, 14 Dec. 1936	Represented in the sample by	Per 100 men in the sample
London and South-east	6 } 20	Deptford	10 } 20
Midlands and South-west	14 } 20	Leicester	10 } 20
North-west and North-east	57	Liverpool, Blackburn, and Crook	54
Wales	23	Rhondda	26

It can be seen that the sample is a fair picture of the distribution of long-unemployed men for those three regions in which Table XVI has been arranged: the South and Midlands contain one-fifth both of the total long unemployed and of the men in our sample, the English North rather more than one-half, and Wales one-quarter. Seen like this, no further adjustments seem to be needed before applying the sample figures to the elucidation of the situation as a whole. But this happy state of affairs is to some extent fallacious. Table XVI shows that within the prosperous South and Midlands group, London and the South-east have more, the Midlands and the South-west less than their due share. What it does not show[1] is that, within the northern group, the North-west has more than its due share, and the North-east correspondingly less; in the sample only 23 % of the total for the North is in the North-east, whereas actually the proportion is 57 %. That the shares of the three regions are fair is thus to some extent a balance of vices. Adjustments will be made for this where necessary, but wherever conditions in the South, North, or Wales seem to be sufficiently homogeneous to warrant

[1] Because for its date, which practically coincides with "zero hour" of the sample, owing to a reshuffling of areas no separate figures for the North-west and the North-east are available, but only an aggregate for the North.

it, it may be useful to invoke this virtue of the sample, in spite of its superficial character.

The "Special Areas" outside Scotland[1] are represented in the sample by Crook and the Rhondda U.D. At the time of the sample, out of 100 long-unemployed men in England and Wales, 42 were living in these special areas. Out of 100 men in the sample, 39 were living there. Thus the sample is far from being biased in the direction of another Special Areas Enquiry. On the whole, the proportions of Crook and the Rhondda, taken together, in the tables and figures of this report, will give a fair, if anything slightly understated, picture of the proportion of men to whom the special conditions and the legal and administrative facilities of the Areas apply.

Fairly reliable information as to the age distribution of the 250,000 long-unemployed men in England and Wales in November 1936 can be given by the method described above.[2] A comparison of the sample distribution with the actual figures brings out an important feature of the sample.

TABLE XVII

	(1) England and Wales. Actual figure	(2) England and Wales. Sample magnified	(3) The 936 men in our sample
18–24: "very young"	22,800	13,600	51
25–34: "young"	49,900	48,400	181
35–44: "middle-aged"	50,400	60,100	225
45–54: "elderly"	55,100	55,800	209
55–64: "old"	71,800	72,100	270
	250,000	250,000	936[3]

In three of the five age groups there is a close correspondence between the actual number and the proportion in the sample. But the sample as a whole clearly does not contain a due pro-

[1] These are South Wales, Durham and Tyneside, and West Cumberland. The boundaries of these areas have been frequently criticized, and there would be a case, e.g. for including Blackburn within a Special Area; see "Readjustment in Lancashire", by members of the Economics Research Section of Manchester University.

[2] See p. 29. [3] In two cases, age was not stated.

portion of young men under 25, and correspondingly over-emphasizes the 35–44 years group. The reason for this is that two of the six towns are prosperous (in which case, broadly speaking, young men are not long unemployed), and that the others are declining towns from which, with the exception of Liverpool, young men have tended to migrate. The comparatively small number of young men is caused by the omission of places with a more average degree of unemployment, a natural omission, but one that will have to be kept in mind in judging the results of the sample for the condition and problems of this youngest age group. Whereas the total sample contained one out of 270 long unemployed, it contains only one out of 450 of the very young men.

Once this defect has been understood, we can allow for it, and on the basis of the sample, we can now estimate the regional distribution of the various age groups. In Table XVIII the inaccuracies of the sample have been corrected on reasonable assumptions:

TABLE XVIII

	Of 100 long-unemployed men in each age group there live in			Estimated actual numbers of long-unemployed men		
	South and Midlands	North	Wales	South and Midlands	North	Wales
Very young	6	67	27	1,400	15,300	6,100
		94 (North and Wales)				
Young	7	68	25	3,500	34,000	12,400
		93 (North and Wales)				
Middle-aged	11	68	21	5,800	34,000	10,600
		89 (North and Wales)				
Elderly	20	52	28	11,100	28,500	15,500
		80 (North and Wales)				
Old	32	50	18	22,900	35,900	13,000
		68 (North and Wales)				
Of 100 workers	58	37	5	44,700	147,700	57,600

Table XVIII clearly shows that the distribution of the older long unemployed is much more even over the country, and more in accordance with the distribution of the working population, than is the case for the younger men.

A comparison of the age composition of the long unemployed in South England and the Midlands with those in Wales is particularly instructive. For 100 long unemployed in the South and Midlands in each age group, there are in Wales:

Very young	434
Young	357
Middle-aged	186
Elderly	139
Old	57

Age comes in as an important operative factor in South England and the Midlands,[1] and tends to counterbalance the enormous differences in the numbers of the long unemployed in various parts of the country and to make it more similar to the distribution of workers. The working of this process can be seen from Table XIX.

TABLE XIX. (ESTIMATED) NUMBER OF HOW MANY PER 1,000 WORKERS ARE LONG UNEMPLOYED, AT VARIOUS AGES, IN THE THREE MAIN REGIONS

	South and Midlands	North	Wales
Very young	1	18	53
Young	2	32	86
Middle-aged	5	46	107
Elderly	12	47	190
Old	34	83	220

This is a table of great importance. The columns, read from top to bottom, show the universal presence of the age factor in

[1] The table probably tends slightly to exaggerate the operation of the age factor, because the age composition of the South and Midlands unemployed is partly derived from the age composition in Deptford, where the existence of a big L.C.C. lodging-house tended to attract, to some extent, elderly and old unemployed from outside.

the South, North, and Wales alike, and bring out the striking fact that there is a practical absence of long unemployment[1] among very young and young workers (up to 34) in the South and Midlands. The table shows clearly that the age factor is relatively more important where, in general, long unemployment is lower. If we compare the risk run by a middle-aged worker (35–44) of being out of work for a long period with that run by a very young man, we find that it is five times as high in the South, three times as high in the North, and twice as high in Wales, and a similar comparison between old and young shows even greater differences. If we compare the risk of being unemployed for a long period run by the worker in Wales with that in the South, we find that it is fifty-three times as high for the very young worker (18–24), forty-three times for the young (25–34), twenty-one times for the middle-aged (35–44), sixteen times for the elderly, and only six times for the old.

We may see in this table the overlapping between the "depressed age" and "depressed place" factor. Though long unemployment is higher in the North than in the South, among the old workers in the South it is higher than among both the very young and young workers in the North. The old workers in the North are more exposed to the danger of long unemployment than the very young workers in Wales, and only very slightly less than the young workers there. There is, however, no overlapping between the South and Wales; even the old worker in the South is less likely to be long unemployed than the very young in Wales.

Even more important, however, is the distinction suggested by this table between two types of long unemployment. In the prosperous regions like Deptford and Leicester with unsatisfied demands for labour, there are still appreciable numbers who fail, for a year or more, to obtain any work at all: each is out of work

[1] As defined for the sample. On the other hand, there are considerable numbers of young men with very poor employment records on the U.A.B. registers in London and elsewhere. The latest U.A.B. report showed that approximately a quarter of the U.A.B. register in London belong to the age groups "very young" and "young". More will be said of this later when we consider the problem of the younger men separately.

for individual or personal reasons, and the problem they represent may be described as "residual", since they remain unemployed even when there are places waiting to be filled. The description later given of the sample in Leicester will show that it is unjustifiable to assume this residuum to be entirely unemployable or work-shy, but it remains true that the cause of unemployment is personal rather than economic. In Appendix I we show that it can be distinguished in various ways from the bulk of the long unemployed in the other four places of the sample, for whose state we use the term "industrial" unemployment. They are men whose unemployment is due in the first place to industrial and not personal causes.

In the less prosperous districts, however, there must obviously also be individuals unemployed for personal reasons. In what has been written below we assume that this type of unemployment, being personal, will form the same proportion of all the insured population in each region, irrespective of its prosperity or depression. On this assumption an estimate of the total residual long unemployment in the country has been made.[1] On this basis, Table XX has been prepared.

TABLE XX. "RESIDUAL" LONG UNEMPLOYMENT IN ENGLAND AND WALES, NOVEMBER 1936

	Number	Risk How many per 1,000 workers (in the whole country)	Age distribution %
Very young	2,400	1	3
Young	6,000	2	8
Middle-aged	10,000	5	13
Elderly	19,400	12	25
Old	39,500	34	51
Total residual long unemployment	77,300	10	100

[1] It must be borne in mind that this estimate of residual unemployment is particularly affected by the fact that the sample omitted the P.A.C. cases of long unemployment on the register; see above, p. 21.

A similar table (Table XXI) for industrial unemployment in the North and in Wales has also been prepared.

TABLE XXI

	Number	Risk How many of 1,000 workers (in the whole country)	Age distribution %
Very young	20,400	9	12
Young	43,900	15	25
Middle-aged	40,400	20	23
Elderly	35,700	22	21
Old	32,300	28	19
Total industrial unemployment	172,700	22	100

It is remarkable how the different age groups split up into a residual and an industrial problem. This can be seen from a comparison of columns 3 of Tables XX and XXI. The highest proportion among the residual unemployed is of the old men, and the numbers increase steadily from the young group to the old group. Among the industrially long unemployed, however, we find that the highest proportion is among the young men, the numbers decreasing steadily, though slowly, from the young group to the old group. From a comparison of columns 2 in each table it can be seen that the risk of industrial unemployment increases only very slowly with age; this is natural, as industrial decline strikes certain districts and industries irrespective of the age structure of the population. The increase in risk evident in the second column of Table XXI is due to the fact that there is a possibility of younger men escaping industrial unemployment without fear of becoming residually unemployed somewhere else; whereas, for the old men there is not this possibility. These points, which are of fundamental importance for understanding the situation, may be summarized as follows:

TABLE XXII

	Number of long unem-ployed	Residual problem	Industrial problem	Of 100 long unemployed	
				Resi-dual	In-dustrial
Very young men	22,800	2,400	20,400	10	90
Young men	49,900	6,000	43,900	12	88
Middle-aged men	50,400	10,000	40,400	20	80
Elderly men	55,100	19,400	35,700	35	65
Old men	71,800	39,500	32,300	55	45
All workers: England and Wales	250,000	77,300	172,700	31	69

This result also serves to stress the importance of the personal element in unemployment (which, as we shall see, enters very largely into the residual problem) which is not due to industrial depression. It will be noticed that the size of this group of the long unemployed is considerably in excess of the total number of long-unemployed men seven years before, in 1929.[1] Over 30%[2] of the present long-unemployment problem must be considered and treated largely as a personal problem. What this means will be shown in the following parts. This result is a justification for carrying out the enquiry in prosperous as well as in depressed towns. There are two particular reasons why the importance of the residual element has not been sufficiently grasped: (1) the concentration of interest on the hard-hit and "special" areas where the residual element in long unemployment is thickly overlaid by the industrial, although it is there all the same; (2) the much smaller proportion of residual unemployment

[1] This remains true even if the increase in scale of industry and in working population is taken into account.

[2] This figure is probably slightly in excess of the true figure because of the spots in the South and Midlands where there is still industrial depression and where some part of the unemployed should have been classified as industrial. Against this, however, must be set the fact that some parts in the North and Wales are free from industrial depression, and so no part of their unemployment should have been attributed to the industrial factor.

among the industrially and also, on the long view, socially more important very young, young, and middle-aged workers (under 45), where the importance of the personal element is much lower, accounting for only 15% of the total.

But not only is the residual problem even for these men under 45 a formidable one—some 18,000–19,000 men with their dependents; from any other but a long-run industrial view, it is impossible to deny that the elderly and old long unemployed are a very serious social and humanitarian problem, a large part of which is, as we shall see, personal and unconnected with the state of industrial activity.

Perhaps the most important contribution which our sample can make towards increasing our knowledge of facts and figures of long unemployment is a separate treatment of these two groups, the residually and industrially unemployed, with regard to the three main factors determining life and outlook of an unemployed man—his age, marital state, and employment value. The analysis of the two last factors will be found in Appendix I, "Residual and Industrial long unemployment". There is defined the numerical extent of the problems thrown up by the sample visits, and the economic aspects of long unemployment bound up with the employment value of the long unemployed, are treated in detail. The assessment of the employment value of the long unemployed shows also significant differences as between the two types and the various age groups, and gives an indication of the social waste of long unemployment.

Apart from this extension of our knowledge of "who are the long unemployed", there are two questions on which further classification becomes now possible on the basis of the sample. The first is concerned with the duration of long unemployment, the second with the social circle of long unemployment, of which the men in the queue are but a sector.

It has already been said that time is a factor behind long unemployment, perhaps less powerful and less obvious than space, but by no means negligible. The following figures (Table XXIII) separate long unemployment by periods for the Special Areas and elsewhere:

TABLE XXIII

England, Wales and Scotland	Total	1–2 years	2–3 years	3–4 years	4–5 years	Over 5 years
Special Areas	105,000	32,000	19,400	14,700	15,300	23,600
Per 100	100	30	18	14	15	23
Rest of Country	222,000	87,600	46,000	31,400	27,700	29,300
Per 100	100	40	21	14	12	13

These figures refer to the summer of 1936, a few months prior to the sample date. The contrast which they show is clear. The average period from the last job was about three years and two months for the long unemployed in the Special Areas and two years five months elsewhere. What happens is that as we compare separately groups of long-unemployed men at various periods from their last job, we find that the proportion concentrated in the areas with heavy unemployment increases steadily and with great regularity.

TABLE XXIV. HOW MANY OF 100 LONG UNEMPLOYED AT VARIOUS PERIODS FROM LAST JOB LIVE IN SPECIAL AREAS AND ELSEWHERE

	1–2 years	2–3 years	3–4 years	4–5 years	Over 5 years
Special Areas	27	30	32	37	45
Elsewhere	73	70	68	63	55

Thus, in areas with heavy long unemployment we find not only longer and differently composed queues of long-unemployed men, but we also find the long-unemployed men stand for a longer time in the queue. What is true of the queues in general, that with rising unemployment there is also a rising proportion of men who are in the queue for a considerable time, is also true for the long-unemployed queues, that with a lengthening of the queue the duration of unemployment increases too. This suggests that even the number of 1,000 workers being unemployed for a year or more is not yet a real indication of the tremendous differences in unemployment conditions existing at present in this country. A difference between 4 out of 1,000 workers long unemployed in Deptford and 281 in the Rhondda seems considerable enough, but in addition to that, the average long-unemployed man in Deptford has faced fifteen months of continuous unemployment, whereas the average long-unemployed man in the Rhondda has faced no less than fifty-six months, nearly a full five years. Any measure which takes this into account will show a difference in the importance of long unemployment in a really prosperous town like Deptford and a depressed township like the Rhondda of 1:260. For every year of long unemployment that is suffered among Deptford workers, there are 260 years among the same number of workers in the Rhondda.

The sample shows, however, that the rule that "the duration of long unemployment rises with its extent" is not without exceptions, and that much depends on the actual local situation. In a very large town like Liverpool with a port offering all kinds of occasional jobs and where many of the unemployed are young, the average distance from the last job is smaller (thirty-one months) than in Leicester (thirty-two months) though the latter has a much smaller burden of long unemployment.[1]

Finally it is clear that the social importance of long unemployment cannot be measured by the queues alone, but must be considered in terms of homes. On the man in the queue there may depend a large family at home which is, perhaps, more affected than he is himself by his state of prolonged unemployment. The sample enables us to count in homes. The social importance of long unemployment may be defined in a wider or in a narrower sense. In a wider sense it concerns the people living in the same household with a long-unemployed man; and in the narrower the persons who are dependent on him for their

[1] Cf. Part II. Liverpool, p. 88.

maintenance (mainly wife and children in so far as they have no earnings or assistance in their own right). On this question we may safely draw conclusions from our sample which included both towns with high birth-rates, Liverpool, and low birth-rates, Blackburn; one town where the wife is not usually dependent on her husband, Blackburn, and five towns where she usually is. The number of people living in the same household with the 250,000 long-unemployed men in England and Wales, and directly affected by long unemployment, is approximately 875,000;[1] equal to the population of Liverpool. A measure of much more real significance is, however, the social circle of the unemployed men themselves and the people who are directly dependent on them for their maintenance. This social circle consisted of 600,000 persons; more than the population of Sheffield.

The importance of the various age groups of long-unemployed men varies greatly if we are considering this additional group of their dependents.

TABLE XXV

	Total number of long-unemployed men in the queues	Total number of dependents at home	Number of dependents at home per 100 men in the queue
Very young	22,800	14,400	63
Young	49,900	100,300	201
Middle-aged	50,400	143,900	285
Elderly	55,100	91,200	166
Old	71,800	61,100	85
All	250,000	410,900	164

Here is a new and different aspect of the age factor. Among the queues we have seen a steadily increasing number of men in the higher ages. Among the dependents at home, however, we

[1] This figure includes the unemployed men themselves, but it makes an allowance for the cases of overlapping where there are two long-unemployed men in the same household.

see a marked cycle with the highest number of dependents in the middle-aged group:

TABLE XXVI

	(a) In the queues alone	(b) For the dependents at home alone
Very young	9	4
Young	20	24
Middle-aged	20	35
Elderly	22	22
Old	29	15
	100	100

However much imagination we may apply to the men in the queues, from however many different angles we may have examined them, we should always remain conscious of the fact that only for the very young and the old men are the majority of persons affected by long unemployment to be found in the queues at all. For the men aged 25–34 the proportion is less than one-third, for the middle-aged men not much over one-quarter of all persons affected. Beyond the man in the queue we should always be aware of those two or three persons at home whom he has to support. This is the justification for the view underlying this report, that no examination of long unemployment is possible which does not include those "shadows behind the queues", the women and children at home, and the economic problems of family life and dependence in unemployed families.

And there is, finally, that supremely important aspect of long unemployment, that its conditions determine the lives of innumerable members of the younger generation on which the future, industrial and otherwise, of our society depends. In this respect, for certain reasons, our sample would rather minimize the extent of the problem, but even so, it is safe to say that at the date of the sample, in a time of comparative prosperity, there were in England and Wales 270,000 children under 14 years growing up in homes where unemployment had become a permanent state and was moulding minds and lives in ways which the later parts of this report will try to describe. Long unemployment cannot be analysed by thinking of and examining the 250,000 men; it is also a problem of 270,000 young children, and of the 170,000 wives of these men, whose burden is perhaps the heaviest of all. For all this, and that is what the coming report is mainly about, the description given in this chapter is a starting-point.

Part II

THE SAMPLE STUDY

A. *UNEMPLOYMENT IN THE SIX TOWNS*

RESIDUAL UNEMPLOYMENT

Leicester and Deptford

(i) LEICESTER

It is often said that there is at present no serious problem of long unemployment outside the Special Areas. There are "black spots" in many parts of the country outside the Special Areas where unemployment is as intense as it is within them. But we were anxious to discover what long unemployment meant in places that are by accepted standards prosperous. When factories and wharves are working to capacity, are there still men perpetually out of work? If so, is it only those who could not work; and is unemployed only a courtesy title for them? Or is it those who do not want work? To answer this question, what the residual unemployment problem in a prosperous place might be, it was decided that two prosperous districts, one Leicester, and the other the London Borough of Deptford, should be included in the sample. The residual problem underlies the situation even in those districts where unemployment percentages are high, and we begin our account of the sample therefore with an attempt to describe it as it appeared in these two places.

Leicester claims to be the most prosperous city in England. Certainly it has the most prosperous air about it of any of the places we visited, for though, on the figures, Deptford is in some respects more prosperous, it has not the rich business population which is so much in evidence in Leicester. Yet under the sample definition of long unemployment—unemployment for over a year with not more than three days' consecutive employment within the period—there are something like 500 long unemployed, about 150 of whom have been out of work for not one year but five, and the official figures for those unemployed for a year or more in November 1936 in Leicester were nearly 900. This number includes young as well as old, and it includes workmen of the best type who need work desperately and who find it impossible to reconcile themselves to long unemployment. Leicester is a city where light industries (in particular the manufacture of hosiery and of cheap boots and shoes) predominate, and where a large proportion of the labour employed is women and girls (72,701 men to 49,074 women, according to the 1931 census). We may take conditions there to be typical of other great cities also, where the modern type of light industry is established, and which have reached the peak of their prosperity during the last few months. Our task was to look below the surface of this prosperity and discover what was the unemployment problem that it concealed. What we saw may not look impressive when it is shown in percentages. But if we consider it in terms of numbers, it is a different matter, and considered (as we could not avoid considering it) in terms of human values, different again. We reckon that in Birmingham, Northampton, Coventry, Nottingham, Derby and Leicester there are over 5,000 long unemployed in the terms of the sample definition. If we can take the Leicester figures as typical, something like a fifth only of this number are not fit for ordinary employment again, while well over half the remainder are fit for their old jobs if only those jobs were still there for them. Thus we may reckon in these six towns perhaps 3,000 fully employable men who have not had more than an hour or two working during the last twelve months, and 1,000 more who could be fitted into employment if light employment were available. This is the "residual problem" in some of the big manufacturing cities.

It soon became apparent that the manufacturing town, as exemplified by Leicester, presented different features from those of Deptford, the other prosperous town, where the most important occupation, numerically speaking, is "transport and communications", mainly dock work. In Liverpool the situation in this respect is comparable rather to Deptford, for a seaport always needs a large volume of casual labour, and Liverpool is no exception. The figures of the sample in these three places, analysed by the character of employment, are as follows:

TABLE XXVII

	Minor commercial	Skilled	Semi-skilled	Unskilled	Sub-marginal
Deptford	6	2	15	63	4
Leicester	3	7	46	30	1
Liverpool	9	14	·89	141	1

In Liverpool the proportion of unskilled unemployed workers is not so great as the proportion in Deptford, but much greater than the proportion in Leicester, where, as the table shows, well over half the long unemployed are semi-skilled men—factory workers, or those whose work has always been connected with some one particular industry. Considerably more than half of these semi-skilled men in Leicester had at one time been employed in the shoe or in the hosiery industry. In recent years technical changes in these industries are said to have become increasingly rapid.[1] A machine becomes out of date in a few years, and if the man who is working it is not as young as he was, he does not get taken on to work its successor. Moreover, new machines in most instances make the work much simpler than it used to be, so that they can be worked by women or boys or girls as easily as and more cheaply than they can be worked by men. The real residual unemployment is to be seen in factory towns only among the women. In spite of the large numbers of women employed in Leicester (where to every three men in employment there are more than two women in employment), long unemployment among women numbered less than a

[1] This was suggested to us on the spot by several competent observers. There is reason to think, however, that it is not true of industry as a whole.

tenth what it numbered among men. The women who were out of work and were drawing assistance were those who could or would not work, crippled or nervy or approaching pensionable age.[1] This fact must be borne in mind later when the relation between wage levels and unemployment assistance is considered. For the present we only point out that the negligible degree of women's unemployment in Leicester is a clear indication of the extent to which unemployment is bound up with the question of wages, and shows what the residual problem in Leicester ought to be.

Another feature of this unemployment among semi-skilled workers, which the sample brings out, is its close relation to the trade cycle. Thus in Deptford, where the character of long unemployment was mainly unskilled, only 3% had had no work for five years or more and thus dated back to the time of the slump. In Leicester the figure was 31%, and might reasonably be put considerably higher if those were reckoned who had been thrown out of permanent employment at that time, and have had only occasional short spells of work since. The analysis given in Part I of this report has already shown that, broadly speaking, long unemployment is the legacy of the trade depression, and the Leicester situation fully bears out this contention.

A few actual instances will help to show the nature of the Leicester situation more clearly. The first is a "clicker" in the shoe trade. His occupation is a skilled one, for the clicker cuts out the "uppers" of the shoes from the skins, and it is a good sight to see how the skilled clicker avoids waste in cutting, and fits the strongest parts of the skin to those parts of the shoe where strength is most needed. This man's only fault was his age, 57, for he was intelligent and fit, and looked ten years younger than he actually was. He had had a few odd weeks' work in the last

[1] This does not necessarily represent the whole amount of women's unemployment, as many women not eligible for benefit or assistance drop out of the records, because they do not register at the Exchanges. In some towns in Lancashire, a number of women continue to pay Trade Union subscriptions who used to work and would work again if opportunity arose, but who are not included in the unemployment figures.

five years, working in place of men who fell sick. Up till 1932 he had been in regular work, forty years with the same firm. He and his wife were living in exceptionally clean rooms, but one of the things they felt most about unemployment was that they had had to move from their house, the rent of which had been 17*s.* a week, to go into lodgings at 10*s.* He says he is constantly told at the Exchange that it is no use his applying for a job, and trade union officials with whom we talked confirmed this. When a man gets out of work in the boot and shoe trade, if he is over 50, there is little hope of his getting back again. In fact his trade is virtually closed to him. What is he to do? "Caretaker?" he asked. "But I've had no experience of furnaces or boilers. Clerk? I'm not bad at figures, but I've no experience of the work. Outside work? I haven't the physique for it." They know hardly anyone in the neighbourhood now that they have moved. "We've always tried to keep our troubles to ourselves", said his wife. "Sometimes I wonder whether we've not kept to ourselves too much, whether things might not have been easier if we'd been able to tell other people about them." Incidentally the case shows us for the first time, and in an acute form, that isolation which unemployment in the big cities brings in its train.

It would not be difficult to multiply instances. There was a man of 59, a shoe finisher, whose employment record showed that his qualifications were high. He had actually had a telegram recently from the Exchange to send him for a job, but when he got to it he was turned away as too old. He had been stopped owing to shortening of staff—"rationalization". He attributed unemployment to the "genius of man getting the mastery" and the introduction of one patent machine after another. His job, he said, had now been highly simplified and was done by a machine that a lad could work. What he felt most was the monotony of it all, "day after day, year after year the same thing. There are thousands of us, and our only future is the old age pension." Another man, the same age, a shoe laster with a record of thirty-seven years' service with one firm, had been stopped similarly on account of age, with a hundred others.

Once again rationalization was the reason, and here too it was those with the long records of service that were hit by it. The moment he was stopped he knew that he would never work again, and the Clerk at the Labour Exchange put it bluntly to him. "You belonged to a Federation shop. Now I've been told not to send anyone for work in a Federation shop who's not got twenty-five years' work in them, and it would be as much as my place was worth to do so." Or a much younger man may be cited, aged only 38, who had lost his job in a shoe factory in Lancashire during the slump, had found his way to Leicester because he had heard things were fairly prosperous there, and had had in Leicester two weeks' work, replacing a sick man, since 1932. He was short and slight, with the appearance of an indoor worker, but it was evident that he was an excellent type of man, perfectly well fitted for a job in a shoe factory. Or lastly a young man of only 29, a boot and shoe operative, intelligent, fit and anxious to work, who is regularly told, like many others of his age, that he is too old. It is boys alone who are wanted. He had worked in a boot and shoe factory since leaving school, and was stopped five years ago owing to slackness of trade. When things got better, a lad was taken on in his place.

This last example brings out what we believe to be one of the serious features of the present situation. The factory nowadays claims a high proportion of lads when they leave school, and they are kept working there just so long as they can be sent home with a boy's wage. When that becomes impossible, considerable numbers of them are stopped. In Leicester, where the Boot and Shoe Operatives' Trade Union is strong, the proportion of juveniles to adults is governed by agreement between masters and men, but even in Leicester the practice has left perfectly clear traces on the register of long unemployed. They are to be seen not only among those registered as workers in the trade, but among those registered as "general labourers" also. A third of the general labourers long unemployed in Leicester, under 40, had begun their working lives in boot and shoe factories, and it was clear that several of the young men registered as boot and shoe operatives would in fact have to get labouring jobs if they were going to work again. Their state of mind is easily understood. In regular work perhaps till they are 18 or 21, they are turned out then, unskilled, with no experience of looking for casual jobs. Some of them join the army—and until the recent reforms become effective, that only postpones the problem, for we shall see elsewhere men who have come out of the army, unskilled, swelling the ranks of the long unemployed. Some of them go to Government training centres, and, if they are lucky, that fits them once again into the economic system and they do well. Others get engaged, and find it difficult to go away for training. They find that, married, they can get on the dole just enough to keep them going, and knowing others in the same position it seems the obvious thing to do. Perhaps the hardest hit of all are those who have transferred from the Special Areas, and whose labour has been snapped up eagerly by firms anxious for cheap workers. One observer of great experience in the Midlands said that she "shuddered to think what would happen in a few years' time to those thousands of young men from Wales or the North who are now in what seems to them good employment", but who when they come to the age for a full man's wage will, many of them, be turned off, without skill and without a permanent home, to take their chance in the queue. In prosperity such as there is at present this problem hardly begins to show itself, but if a slump should come and bring with it a crop of stoppages, the prospects would be gloomy. It is as well we should be aware of this before it begins.

An important element in the situation in prosperous manufacturing towns, then, is the labour that has been displaced owing to the renewal of machines and the simplification of manual processes which this effects. The men so displaced are residual unemployed only because as yet we have found no means of making use of their services. What is certain is that the majority of them are still potentially excellent workers, who need work and often want it passionately. Their situation gets concealed by the prevailing prosperity, which for them only makes things worse—for it cuts them off still more sharply from the wage earner bringing home good wages.

A few more strands in the Leicester situation may be disentangled before we turn to consider the position elsewhere. Here, as doubtless in every city, there is the technological problem of the man whose craft has become out of date, exemplified by a number of men who drove horses and have been left stranded by the development of motor transport. In Leicester there were two horse carters under 50 in the sample, each a fine type of man. In Deptford there were several carters, a stableman and a coachman over 50, though none younger. An unfortunate instance in Leicester, additional to the two mentioned above, was a young man of 32, of excellent physique, whom we considered a good type of man, not unintelligent. He had been originally an agricultural labourer, but had come to town because it was his "ambition to drive a horse van". Owing to the growth of motor transport he had not had his chance. He was registered simply as a "labourer" and, as he said, "the trouble with me is that I haven't got a trade". He would go back to farming but now he is married and his wife will not consider leaving Leicester. "I'd go mad if I lived in the country", she said, for she had lived in Leicester all her life and was used to the factory and the cinema. Clearly it was not too easy to fit in such a man, but, meeting as he does at the unemployed club scores of others his own age, it is scarcely surprising that he has become accustomed to doing very little else but play cricket for the club during the season. It is fantastic to regard such a man as unemployable, though unemployment is the line of least resistance for him. There are thousands of cases like his in England, waiting for someone to fit them in somewhere to work, but if it is not done soon, it never will be done.

Another type of case, which is residual, not because the quality of labour is poor, but for reasons entirely non-industrial in character, is that of the man with a large family. The birth-rate for Leicester is actually comparatively low, and yet of the men under 50 who were out of work no less than eleven of thirty-two had families of five or more children. The conclusion is irresistible: that men who get a large unemployment allowance (as all these men, of course, do) tend more than others to fall out of employment and "live on the dole". More will be said about this, for it is linked up with several of the problems later discussed. What is abundantly clear is that the industrial quality of the worker is in such cases not necessarily by any means residual. He may be thoroughly competent and yet be unable to get a wage which it is worth his while to accept.

Lastly there are in Leicester, as elsewhere, a small number of men of poor physique or low intelligence who are hardly employable. There was in Leicester a man of 24, registered as a general labourer. After leaving school he had worked till he was 18 in an engineering shop, after which he had worked in hotels. His clothes, which were a mixture of dinner jacket and lounge suit, summarized his industrial career. His only job since the slump was in 1934, when he had had some odd weeks' work washing wool. He was evidently very near being a mental defective, and his wife was epileptic. He was not unpleasant, and might have been able to do a low-grade job if once he settled into it, but he was evidently not what the Labour Exchanges call a strong placing proposition. The proportion of such cases to the register as a whole is small. Even in prosperous places they probably do not represent more than 5% of it.

What gives unemployment its special character in such a place as Leicester is the contrast between the general prosperity and the man, or the family, who is standing outside it but witnessing it all day and every day. He may react to this in different ways. Perhaps he tries to keep up the illusion that he is not one of the unemployed at all, and refuses to associate with others who are in the same state as himself. Several of the middle-aged or elderly men visited in Leicester evidently felt like this. Or he may throw in his lot whole-heartedly with them, in the unemployed club or the Unemployed Workers' Movement and fight for what he calls "his rights". The great majority of the younger men seen in Leicester were members of the unemployed club, and it is no accident that the National Unemployed Workers' Movement should have been mentioned more to us in Leicester than elsewhere. For the more the unemployed man feels that he is ignored the more resentful he becomes. In Leicester one of the most violent adherents of the National Unemployed Workers' Movement was a man who had for most of his life worked on his own in a very good position, and was obviously a thoroughgoing individualist. He would have been perfectly at home managing his own business, but now, thrown unluckily out of work, he had a grievance against society. It was as though he felt that there was a huge vested interest keeping him out of work; as though he felt that society knew he was a competent man but, to keep prosperity to itself, had closed its ranks against him. In prosperous towns such feelings as these are almost always, in some degree, present with a certain proportion of the unemployed. One of the greatest problems that the voluntary agencies working among them are set to do is to break down these feelings without breaking down a man's self-respect, and it is one that they find it very hard to solve.

(ii) DEPTFORD

In comparison with Leicester the Deptford situation does give us a much truer picture of a real residual problem. We have mentioned that the most important occupation, numerically, in Deptford is provided by the docks, the Royal Surrey Docks—just outside the Borough—,the Royal Victoria Victualling Yard, and the Grand Surrey Canal. One of the typical sights of Deptford is the handling of great stacks of timber "deals" on the wharves of this canal. Another large item in the list of occupations is "general labourers". Casual labour plays a very large part in the economy of Deptford (where indeed there is no problem of the semi-skilled worker long unemployed), and this is no doubt mainly responsible for the crowds of men who are always standing about at Deptford Broadway (near the Labour Exchange) or along Deptford High Street. But the reason why the long-unemployment register in Deptford is so different in character from that in Leicester is no doubt mainly the greater variety of opportunity that a London borough offers. Most London boroughs are to some extent dormitory, and men who live in one often work elsewhere. Thus the factory worker who falls out of employment in Deptford can travel to North or West London daily to work, whereas in Leicester there would be no such opportunities.

At the same time there is no particular reason for complacency over Deptford, and the places similar to it. We reckon that there are probably 15,000 families similarly situated to those of the long unemployed in Deptford in the south of England as a whole. Thus unemployment of this character is not a matter of negligible proportions.

The first feature that appears from a comparison between Deptford and Leicester is that the age structure of the long-unemployed group is decidedly different, there being a higher proportion in Deptford in the higher age groups. Of the sample in Deptford, 58% were between the ages of 55 and 64, 51% of the sample in Leicester. The figures suggest that, in Deptford, age begins to be a factor about the age of 48, but that it is not till the sixties that the stress of this factor is fully felt. There were nearly three times as many men between the ages of 60 and 64 as between the ages of 55 and 59 in Deptford, and a similar proportion appeared in the records of the P.A.C. cases of long unemployment in Deptford. These elderly men are the real core of the residual problem.

The second feature is that on the whole the quality of the men was poorer. The point can be illustrated by a comparison of the grading of physical health and intelligence in Deptford and Leicester. 40% were reckoned in Deptford as out of condition physically, 12% as unfit, and 19% were stated to have obvious physical defects. In Leicester the corresponding percentages were 29, 1 and 7. In Leicester 14% were classified as of superior intelligence as against 2% in Deptford; in Leicester 48% as of "good average" intelligence as against 45% in Deptford: and there are technical reasons for thinking that these figures may understate the comparative superiority of the Leicester unemployed. As we have seen, the Leicester unemployed were to a large extent semi-skilled men, while the Deptford long-unemployed men are the "odd jobbers", or men from the Docks and warehouses. They were classified simply as labourers or navvies or stevedores or porters, though there was a sprinkling of a different type, commercial travellers or shop assistants. The man who has been out of work for some time should be more likely to pick up an occasional odd job if he is looking for any kind of casual employment than if he is looking for something permanent. Thus, as far as the records could be traced, they showed that the Deptford men had been continuously unemployed for lesser periods than those in any other of the places visited, and the U.A.B. register in London as a whole evidently consists very largely of men who get a few days' work now and again at considerable intervals.

On the other hand, it is easy for the casual labourer to drift into prolonged unemployment, for he is used to losing jobs. Our records show that only eight of the forty-eight general labourers among the Deptford long unemployed had had good employment at some time during the last eight years, three having considerable periods of service with individual firms. But the great majority had drifted most of their lives. One example may be taken to show how an unemployed "general labourer" comes into being: a young man of 24. He worked in January 1932 for two weeks as a surveyor's assistant, and from March for four months as a restaurant porter. Then he was out till the summer of 1933, when for three weeks he minded a stall. He had a fortnight that Christmas in a shop during the rush, tried his luck for a day the following April (1934) as a newspaper canvasser, but gave it up as hopeless, worked for a week as a porter in a foundry in July, and for five days delivering bills in September. In 1935 he worked for a fortnight as a labourer laying cables, and for a fortnight at Christmas as temporary postman, while in 1936 he had an odd day or two unloading cargo. In five years he had had approximately thirty-two weeks' work, in ten different jobs, though in our judgment he was a man who looked for work. His record is quoted in detail as a good instance of that drift which eventually strands these young general labourers among the long unemployed. It is characteristic of the London situation in particular, though no doubt the same thing happens to some extent in all large towns.

The predominance of casual labourers among the Deptford long unemployed might suggest that the incidence of long unemployment in London in a time of prosperity is chiefly among the "social problem group" of the population, or what the New Survey of London Life and Labour calls "the lowest class of degraded or semi-criminal population". There is something in this, though not everything. The worker's grade, skilled, semi-skilled, or unskilled, does not necessarily correspond with any social grade, and the working-class family gets its standards from the housewife rather than from the breadwinner. Thus the general labourer, though he often lives at a lower level than the skilled man, does not necessarily do so. One of the most determined efforts that we saw in Deptford to maintain domestic standards, that were being gradually forced down by unemployment, was in the house of a general labourer. But the comparison between Leicester (where the problem was that of the semi-skilled man) and Deptford does suggest that broadly speaking there is a correspondence between work status and social status, and that the Deptford long-unemployed group, being mainly composed of general labourers, is on the whole not a cross-section of the working-class population but is drawn mainly from the lower social groups. We were able, in Deptford, to examine the records of the long unemployed who were receiving Public Assistance, and it was thus possible to compare the two groups, those receiving Unemployment Assistance and those receiving Public Assistance. The P.A.C. cases were living, on the whole, in a decidedly worse type of street (reckoned by the New London Survey standards); conditions in the houses were evidently on the whole decidedly dirtier among the P.A.C. cases, and a smaller proportion were classed as "respectable". This shows that, while the Deptford long unemployed may belong to a social group which is not representative of the working class as a whole, they do not belong to the lowest group, the P.A.C. cases being definitely inferior in type.[1]

[1] In several of these cases there was a record of the amount that had been received in relief over a period of years. In at least one this amount ran into four figures, and in a number it was £600 or £700.

We may take a general labourer, aged 48, living with a charwoman, aged 50, and also unemployed, to show the type of household at the lower end of the U.A.B. sample in Deptford. They were living in one room, mostly filled by the bed, in a street marked black on the housing conditions' map of the New London Survey; a street, that is, inhabited by the lowest class of degraded or semi-criminal population. An even greater drawback to the street is that it is permeated by the smell of the local bones and fat factory, the most noisome and most memorable of all smells, and a feature for which any new edition of the Survey might well devise some yet more sinister colour. In 1932 the man had worked on his own account street trading. He had done a fortnight's work in 1933 unloading timber, and five weeks in 1934, since when he had not worked at all. When one of us went in about midday he was in bed and in his clothes. There was a general atmosphere of squalor, set off by the dirty bedclothes, empty condensed milk tins, and scraps of food on the floor. Both man and woman were pleasant and ready to talk. He said that the main obstacle in the way of his employment was his address, which frightened off any prospective employers. The largest item in the family budget of 23*s.* 6*d.* was the butcher's bill at 5*s.* 6*d.* a week, equal to the rent. They spent 8*d.* a week on newspapers—the *Evening News* and *News of the World* ("You must know what's happening"). It is an interesting sight to see the newsboys walking down these streets with the "3.30 result" paper—a sight that indicates what are the hobbies of the neighbourhood; and this household was probably no exception. We got the impression that this man was a happy-go-lucky type, relatively content with low standards, and probably as ready to be out of work as to be in it. Most of the Deptford cases were less squalid than this, which was indeed more typical of the unemployed receiving Public Assistance rather than of those receiving Unemployment Assistance; but our view was that in a number of them a contributing factor to unemployment was this poor background, and we shall find that elsewhere, too, the residual unemployed consist in part of men living at a low level because they have never known anything better. This particular factor in unemployment can only be attacked as part of the general social problem of poverty—a larger task (and perhaps in its way even more urgent) than the attack on unemployment which is sometimes one of its many symptoms.

Within this group occurs that small number of fraud cases which create difficulties disproportionate to their numbers. There is unfortunately reason to believe that, in London as elsewhere, the number of fraud cases among younger men is larger than among the older. Among forty-two fraud cases in one of the South London offices of the U.A.B. the age distribution was as follows:

Age	Cases	Age	Cases
Below 21	2	41–45	2
21–25	5	46–50	2
26–30	10	51–55	3
31–35	7	56–60	2
36–40	7	61–65	2

The figures become even more significant when it is remembered that the numbers of older men on the register are higher than those of the younger. Here, as in much else, the difference between the pre-War and post-War generations is clearly marked. Deptford offers special opportunities for fraud in connexion with Unemployment Insurance or Assistance, as it is one of the parts of London where hawking thrives most. The young men hire barrows and take them up to the West End of London for the evening, stocked with fruit. Or they become attached to street traders in Deptford, where street trading is a prosperous industry. Some of them make substantial profits from these ventures, and add to them by claiming that they are unemployed and drawing Unemployment Assistance. This form of fraud is difficult to check. It appears, of course, among those who secure virtually no insurable employment whatever (except perhaps temporary work with the Post Office at the Christmas rush), and among the young men who fall into this category it accounts, in some prosperous places like London, for a considerable number. In one London office an intensive investigation into the circumstances of 118 young men (18–30) on the U.A.B. register led to 80 of them finding work, on their own, in order to avoid the trouble which the investigation was causing them—a very significant figure when we are trying to estimate the attitude of these young men to work. The Unemployment Assistance Board has succeeded in reducing this problem to manageable proportions. The chief harm done is the impression that there is something bogus about long unemployment in general, an idea that we hope this report may demonstrate to be utterly untrue—and in making necessary that close scrutiny of all cases which the more respectable families find so hard to bear.

There are in Deptford exceptional cases which fall into a quite different class from any of those discussed above. It is not easy for any elderly man, once he falls out of work, to get back again, whatever his occupation may be—a point that can be demonstrated from the unemployment figures for the country as a whole;[1] and a number of the older men among the Deptford long unemployed were of eminently respectable types. There was one, for instance, aged 61, who had been a ship's officer for twenty-five years, and then had got employment ashore as a commercial traveller. He had been for over ten years with the same firm, and had at times earned as much as £10 a week. He was a widower, living in good lodgings, and was obviously still competent to do responsible clerical work. Or there was a "holder up", aged 57, who had worked nineteen years with a firm of boilermakers and had been stopped early in 1932 owing to the firm changing hands, since when he had had only a series of odd jobs unloading barges. He was an excellent type of workman, and his household was well managed and the money evidently carefully spent. He had until very recently been an Oddfellow, and his son was an active Baptist worker. There was a small group of similar examples in Deptford, which can be taken to represent what is probably a much larger number of such cases in London as a whole than is generally realized. For a considerable proportion of the men of this type have small personal resources which make them independent of the "Means

[1] See above, p. 22.

Test", or refuse, until they are driven to it in desperation, to apply for assistance. Unemployment does not necessarily cease to be a problem in cases where the State does not maintain the unemployed man.

One other element in residual unemployment can be pointed out both in Deptford and in Leicester: the man who has a disability pension to help eke out unemployment assistance. This probably means that the recipient has serious physical disqualifications for work, and it also may mean that his pension plus unemployment assistance bring into the family exchequer a sum approximating to the wage he would earn if he were in normal work. Thus we saw a man of 35, who had lost a leg as a result of an accident while at work. He impressed us as one who, if he had had the advantage of a good education, might have made much with his life, for he was a man of real independence and intelligence. He was being paid 30*s.* in compensation for the accident and drew 17*s.* 6*d.* assistance in addition, having a wife and child of five. He hoped to get a sufficiently large "lump sum" in compensation to set up on his own with a business; but until that materialized he was content to live on as he was, unless a really good job should turn up. Or there was another case in Deptford, a man aged 43, with seven children, two of whom were already earning. He had lost a leg in the war, and his army pension of 16*s.*, plus unemployment assistance of 45*s.*, put the family well above the "poverty line" which we use in a later section. Evidently he had at one time looked eagerly for work, but he had "caved in" rather readily perhaps when he did not get it, and no doubt his pension was a factor. In all the places visited there was a certain proportion of cases like this. We shall see that in the Rhondda especially this element is important.

One aspect of long unemployment to which allusion has been made briefly above forces itself on the attention of anyone who makes the acquaintance of unemployed men in prosperous communities: the isolation of the unemployed man. In Deptford one-half of them, if we include those lodging in Carrington House, the big L.C.C. lodging-house, which because of its cheapness and cleanness attracts men from outside the borough also, were living on their own. Those living in Carrington House have indeed opportunities of meeting others similarly situated to themselves, but even in lodging-houses the unemployed man tends, as so many told us, to keep himself to himself. It is significant that one of the very few men interviewed in Deptford, who had while still unemployed a fairly full life as worker for a local church, was exceedingly suspicious at first of the one of us who saw him. He was positive that none of his friends or acquaintances knew that he was out of work, and suspected that some secret official investigation was taking place. Unemployment is, in prosperous places, something of which many men are bitterly ashamed, even when it is no fault of their own; and the man who succeeds in concealing from his friends for years the fact that he is out of work must be concerned pretty deeply to conceal it. With the younger men this feeling is evidently much less pronounced.

Residual unemployment may be analysed, then, into various groups. There are the old men—first, those in some way incapacitated through age, and secondly, those who, though they may be over 55, are perfectly fit. There are the unemployables, a small part only of the total; there are those whose social background makes it easy for them to accept idleness and the low standards that it brings; and there is a small group of the disabled, with pensions. But there are also, in places where unemployment ought to have been reduced to a bare residue, men who are out of work for technological or other reasons, and who fail to get work largely perhaps because they are confused with this residue. In many places which claim to be prosperous, there are hundreds of such men on the streets, and the only solution for them seems to be that steps should be taken by the authorities to fit them into permanent jobs. This will not be easy, but it is at present made harder by the fact that the Employment Exchanges have hitherto regarded the employer as having the foremost claim on them. While the system was being built up, this was certainly what they had to do, and they are no doubt right in considering that an employer will generally feel suspicious of a man submitted to fill a vacancy who has been out of work for twelve months or more. If our judgment is right, however, many of these men are potentially excellent material, and what keeps them out of work is their inability to force a way back for themselves. Here too, both in the restoring of self-confidence and also in the personal help needed to fit in such men, there are great opportunities for the social worker, and they are certainly in some districts being realized.

(iii) THE RHONDDA

The two places that have so far been considered are in the prosperous parts of the country, the Midlands and the South, and in neither was the proportion of long unemployment great. In the other four districts it is an utterly different picture. Though there is a residual element in each of them, it is almost entirely obscured by the vast overlay of industrial unemployment; the result of which is that in the Rhondda the degree of real unemployment is something like seventy times that of Deptford.[1] Thus in September 1936, just before the date of the sample, there were nearly 11,000 long-unemployed men in the Rhondda. The degree varies in the four towns, but in each of them there is a similar disproportion as compared with Deptford or Leicester. The reasons are generally similar, that considerable changes in the structure of industry have led to their economic decline. In the Rhondda it is partly due to the closing of overseas markets owing to the effects of the War and economic nationalism, partly to technical improvements which have made it possible to economize fuel or use low-grade coals where the high quality Welsh coals used to be needed, partly to the introduction of oil firing for shipping. We shall find that in addition to this decline in markets, there are in Wales certain other important elements in the situation due to technical changes within the industry itself, changes comparable to those of which the effects have been seen in Leicester. In Crook it is not so much loss of markets as the gradual exhaustion (or deterioration) of the coal resources of the region. In Blackburn

[1] See above, p. 14.

it is the rapid development of cotton manufacture in other parts of the world, and in Liverpool the relative decline in the importance of the Mersey as a port, resulting largely from the fact that the prosperity of the whole area that it serves has tended to decline, while the highly prosperous districts of the Midlands and the South are served by the ports of Southampton and London. Our task here again was as it were to analyse the human situation which these big structural changes have left.

Industrial unemployment of this kind obviously means that there will be large numbers of men out of work who are young, thoroughly employable and on any reasonable computation in a prosperous place would be working, and this was so in all four of these places. The facts are shown clearly in the following table giving the physical condition of the men interviewed.

TABLE XXVIII. PHYSICAL HEALTH (PERCENTAGES)

	Very good	Fit	Out of condition	Unfit	Obvious physical defects
Industrial unemployment:					
Rhondda	12	44	19	17	8
Crook	9	66	8	3	14
Blackburn	3	59	24	2	12
Liverpool	7	55	30	1	7
Residual unemployment:					
Deptford	3	26	40	12	19
Leicester	8	42	31	3	16

If columns 1 and 2 are taken as representing those in good physical condition, the condition of those in the areas of industrial unemployment is seen to be far better than that of the residually unemployed in Deptford and Leicester, the extreme comparison being between 75% in good condition in Crook, and only 29% in Deptford. Incidentally the table also shows that, of the areas in which there is this industrial unemployment, the Rhondda seems to be less well situated with regard to the physical condition of the unemployed than other places, a feature which will be considered later.

Though the physical condition of unemployed men in the Rhondda seems worse than in Crook, Liverpool or Blackburn, it is better than in a prosperous district, and there are thousands of fully employable men unemployed. An instance taken at random from this group in the Rhondda sample is a collier, aged 37, who served three years in the War and has now done no work whatever for five years. He is described as wiry and very fit, a "great walker, who always does his physical 'jerks'". But unemployed men are not simply units of employability who can, through the medium of the dole, be put into cold storage and taken out again immediately they are needed. While they are in cold storage, things are liable to happen to them. In the case of this man what had happened was that the "will to work" had been affected; he "seemed quite unconcerned about work". And the other thing which it seems from the records may have happened (though in such cases it is impossible to say for certain) is that the health of one of his children has been seriously impaired by the low level at which the family has had to live. His case is in fact an instant reminder that even with the most straightforward type of worker who can avoid acute mental depression and can maintain himself in health, long unemployment means something more than being out of work for so many months or so many years. Things happen, the results of which only become apparent, perhaps, when the possibility of work nearby, or in another area, presents itself. He is in danger of becoming indeed one of those men unemployed for personal reasons who have been said to be characteristic of residual unemployment, and it is this danger that lies at the heart of the Special Areas problem. The next instance that comes at random from the same group, a butcher's assistant, aged 29, recalls a point already made in an earlier part of this report, that unemployment in some basic industry leads to a considerable degree of secondary unemployment in the neighbourhood, in commerce, building, transport, and so forth. This man is described in our records as a "very good type, strong, independent, and good looking", and his employability is given as "excellent". He is capable and active, but would not consider any job other than that to which he is used. When in employment he worked himself up to being manager of a shop in the Valley where he earned £2. 15*s.* a week, with travel expenses and insurance in addition. He says he will not take any job at less than £2. 10*s.* a week though he could get work any time at 35*s.* Here, too, there is something more than a simple instance of a good man available with no work for him.

Before any further analysis of unemployment in the Rhondda is attempted, however, some of the factors underlying the situation there (and in most of the South Wales coalfield) must be noticed. One such factor, which according to some competent observers is tending to decline but which an outsider must still notice at once, is the antagonism against the management of the pits. Whether there is any justification for this we do not attempt to discuss, but it is certain that this antagonism does affect the whole situation, including the unemployment situation, in the Valley. South Wales is responsive to preaching of any kind, political preaching included, and here, if anywhere, a grievance becomes in a moment a battle-cry. Moreover, as the valleys are geographically bounded by the mountains, so those who live in them are bounded in outlook to their own concerns. They are not part of the world outside but belong to a world of their own, and a measure which has been taken for external reasons and which affects them adversely is in their thinking designed to crush them. They have the qualities of these defects, responsiveness to leadership, a strong community spirit, high standards—so that it would be almost truer to think of unemployment in Wales as a middle-class than as a slum problem—and evidently, once their loyalty is won, a great capacity for work. Many of those whom we saw described how they had lived for their work. "His life was his work", says the record of a visit to one of the old men, "and though he has given up all hope of working again no alternative will take its place." The sample brought us incidentally into contact with several men whose working life in the pits had been extended well beyond the pensionable age—

one for instance, the father of a sample case, who had actually seen sixty-five years' service underground, from the age of 7 to the age of 72.

Others of these elements may be illustrated from the sample. It was in South Wales that we heard most of unemployment that was due to "victimization". Thus two brothers, who seemed excellent workers but had "strong trade union views", as they said, had been stopped, one on the grounds that he broke tools belonging to the company, another because (so he said) he called the manager "Jones" instead of "Mr Jones", which led to him being permanently stopped when he had a short bout of sickness. In another case the record notes: "The only restricting circumstance is his preoccupation with politics, his views and the obtrusiveness with which he proclaims them. This might easily get him into trouble with an employer or foreman." "It's done quietly, but it's done all the same", said one man who alleged that in his district almost all the committee of the Miners' Federation Lodge had been stopped, one by one, while another gave what seemed a reasonable account of the process, when he said that there was little definite victimization for political opinions, yet "the foremen engage men they know of who will give no trouble." Over a period like the last few years where it has been possible to pick and choose among candidates for employment, this must have amounted to much the same thing. One of the young men interviewed, a general labourer aged 28, had left his last job because he was dissatisfied with his wages. He was at first suspicious, and said he spent all his time "lounging about", but afterwards his interest was roused and he explained that he was an active member of the Communist Party and spent much of his time working for it. Incidentally he was an example of the employment history to which allusion has already been made in the case of Leicester, the young man who is stopped at 21 because then he becomes eligible for a man's wage. Up to that age he had been employed underground in the Rhondda. This experience may well have contributed to his attitude. These are all extreme cases. Much more numerous were those who had a general reluctance to go back to work in the pits under modern conditions, who felt that the speeding up of all processes involved by mechanization was intolerable, and who said that it had altered entirely the relationship, once so friendly, between the worker at the coal face and the official.

To illustrate at all adequately the high social type which is characteristic of unemployment in the Rhondda or Crook or Blackburn (or even to some extent Leicester) in so far as it is in these places semi-skilled or skilled workers who have been thrown out of work, would need in itself an elaborate analysis. We give only one or two characteristic instances, one a man of 54, once a collier; a Quaker, with a great interest in all social problems, closely associated with the local Co-operative movement and evidently one who felt that he was helping to shape the social policy of the valleys. He spoke interestingly of transference, for instance, and described how he had once felt that the best thing was "to keep the young men in the Rhondda to preserve its character, but now there is no chance of a revival which goes much further, we feel we ought to encourage them to leave".[1] Another was a lad of 19, studying to pass the City and Guilds examination to qualify as a teacher in a technical school. He had been to London for nine months, working on a wage of 23*s.* a week. This he had found impossibly low, and he had anyhow been shocked to discover how ill-educated the Londoner was—many of those with whom he worked had never heard of a secondary school—so that he had returned to Wales. In a third instance, the case of an old collier of 60, one of us who visited him happened to remark on a magnificent old Welsh dresser and was told that it had been in the family for 200 years. We leave these few examples to suggest the quality of some of the homes affected by unemployment in South Wales, with the reminder

[1] The effects of the transference of young men in large numbers from South Wales on local social institutions were constantly mentioned to us by those identified with them. It is undoubtedly impoverishing the social and cultural life of many small communities, for naturally those who go are the most enterprising. For a discussion of these effects, see A. D. K. Owen in the *Sociological Review*, Vol. XXIX. No. 4, October 1937, and for an estimate of the numbers involved, see Dr H. W. Singer's Interim Report, no. III, mentioned in that article.

that in many of the areas where there is industrial unemployment, this is in some degree characteristic of the situation. Though such a factor must mean that the inevitable lowering of standards which accompanies unemployment is severely felt, it is in a sense full of hope for the future in its implication of what a period of relative prosperity such as the Rhondda enjoyed before the War may help to do for the worker.

All these, then, are factors, underlying and influencing profoundly the unemployment situation in the valley. When we find, for example, a number of long-unemployed men holding out for a high wage, though here (as elsewhere) this may be only a form of excuse for continuing to be unemployed, it may also be the genuine insistence that former standards must be recovered. Or when one—a colliery labourer of only 47—says: "Well, to speak candidly with you, I should find it very hard to work again. I found it difficult enough when I worked on the Council, I was that stiff. And what I say is, bread and cheese is a good meal for anyone when you get used to it, and those old farmers used to eat nothing but bread and cheese, though they had a good meal at nights when they came in"—it may be conjectured that here the contrast between conditions of work and the freedom of unemployment is affecting the man's attitude. The violent antipathy to mining which is to be found among many of the younger unemployed certainly derives partly from the feeling that in the past young labour has been exploited underground. There is, of course, the usual crop of residual cases who might be unemployed anywhere; a collier aged 28, living in neglected surroundings, very dull, with a stammer, described as "continually grinning and scratching his head". His sister was in a mental home, and we need have little hesitation in placing him in the residue, fed from the low-grade families of the virtually unemployable, and there are a number of others who may be grouped with him. But the existence of this section of slum population does not vitiate the general conclusion, that on the whole the social standing of the unemployed families in the Rhondda and Crook, and to some extent in Blackburn, is particularly high.

In addition to those who are unemployed for industrial reasons, other elements that are of importance can be observed. One feature brought out by the Rhondda sample was the high proportion, especially in the upper age groups, of physical disability, due in most instances to industrial disease. There was, for example, a much higher proportion of nystagmus and silicosis cases in the age group 45–54 than would occur in the working population as a whole. This high proportion of men who are not physically fit is another special feature of unemployment in the mining valleys of Wales. If the unemployment problem is one of getting men back to work, then for men in this category work of some special kind has to be found. This is not confined to the older men. It is frequently said that there is a shortage of colliers now in Wales. We visited in the course of the sample thirty-nine men between the ages of 35 and 54 who were still registered as colliers, and of these sixteen were found to be suffering from some form of physical disability, mainly nystagmus, silicosis, or dermatitis, contracted from their occupation. For these men it is not merely necessary to find work, but a particular kind of work. They can none of them work underground again, and do not form part of the "reserve" of colliers. Outside mining areas the proportion of men who are partially disabled is not nearly so large, but where it occurs on this scale, it gives a particular nature to the problem. For they form, as it were, a dead weight that the district has to carry, and until something is done to lighten this burden, recovery in the Special Areas is bound to be retarded. Yet it should not be an insoluble problem, for many of them are perfectly fit for work of an ordinary kind provided it is not underground.

This high proportion of disabled men, then, is one characteristic of long unemployment in South Wales. Another is the loss of qualifications which has resulted from rapidly changing technical processes. Mechanization has advanced rapidly during the past four years. If we take once more the unemployed colliers in the sample and examine the records of the remaining twenty-three between the ages of 35 and 54, it appears that only three of them are described as having experience of mechanization. The interviews showed that one of these three had a strong preference for getting work other than mining if possible. Another described work underground under new conditions as "not work, but murder", and is therefore not likely to be making great efforts to find work, and the third, aged 52, said that his health had broken down underground as a result of the strain of mechanized production. Otherwise it is stated in the men's records that they have "no experience of conveyors or cutters". Several of those in the late forties or fifties said that it was unthinkable for them to start working again under mechanized conditions, and one or two who had tried it had found it impossible to adapt themselves to it. And as a considerable number of men who were once colliers now appear in the sample simply as labourers (having had unskilled jobs since they lost their work in the pits), it is clear that this problem is one of considerable size. Below the age of 35 a man may reasonably be expected to adapt himself to the new methods. But life in the pits begins early. When he is 35 a man has been at work already for more than twenty years underground, and above that age, adjustment begins to get harder. Thus the paradox is true that there are still large numbers of colliers unemployed in South Wales, many of them comparatively young, and that at the same time a shortage of colliers is beginning to make itself felt. In Leicester clearer instances of this technological unemployment have been noticed, clearer because they are not complicated by the other problems of the Special Areas.

(iv) CROOK

There is another type of "Special Areas" problem, that of the district which has been dependent on an industry which is now doomed or dying. Coal-mining in South Wales is very far from doomed, and although the particular demand for Welsh coal (which is of specially high quality) is never likely to be what it once was, coal-mining in Wales will go on for generations employing tens of thousands of men. In certain parts of South

Wales, it is true, the industry is dying owing to the coal being worked out. An example is Rhymney, where the earliest mineral workings, now in ruins, are of the eighteenth century, and at the head of many other of the valleys (where the coal was first worked because it lies there nearest the surface) a similar situation is being reached. Crook, however, a town of about 12,000 inhabitants, is in the south-west Durham coalfield, an area which has been regarded as a whole as doomed, seeing that the most accessible seams are in many instances already exhausted. Coal-mining in Crook, which reached its greatest prosperity in the years 1851–71, was already depressed in the latter part of the nineteenth century, and though it later recovered to some extent, it enjoyed nothing like the boom conditions of South Wales in the decade before the War. The closing of White Lea drift colliery in 1904 threw over 300 men and boys out of employment, and another drift, at Stanley, was closed in 1911. After the War the decline was rapid. Cold Knott colliery was dismantled in 1924, throwing 540 men out of work, and Bowden Close, which employed 1,200, in 1931. In the intervening period more than half a dozen smaller pits near Crook had closed down and been dismantled.

Crook is the centre around which all these colliery villages lie. Some of them have become notorious. In one, most of the housing is of the worst "slum" character, the streets and alleys are unpaved and desolate, and the resulting low rents of the houses, which ought to have no commercial value whatever, are said to attract to them families which are contented to live on the dole. Crook itself, however, presents a completely different picture. It still has some collieries working near it. There has been a decided economic revival with the growing demand for coal during the last few months, and, what is more important, it has genuine vitality in its social life. In many respects we felt that the "atmosphere" in the homes visited in Crook was more satisfactory than anywhere else. There was little of the desperate poverty of Liverpool, there was more determination not to give way to unemployment and not to subsist on self-pity than there was in Wales. This is the more striking since on the whole unemployment has lasted longer here than in any other of the places visited. 71 % had had no work for five years or more as compared with 45 % in the Rhondda, 23 % in Liverpool, and only 3 % in Deptford. The Durham miner who has been out of work for five years has not a perpetual sense of grievance, but rather—though he is actually poorer on the whole than the unemployed man in South Wales[1]—a determination to make the best of things; to make his allotment or his poultry holding a life for himself, not as an alternative to employment, but rather to keep himself fit for employment, to help at the family budget, and to retain active interests. An old Irishman, working as foreman on one of the amenity schemes, expressed well the feeling of the place when he said: "I like to be tired. Before I had this, I used to go out and lie in the sun and come back again and do a thing or two and not know whether I was tired. Now I can come in and smoke my pipe and have my bit of grub and go to sleep."

The housing programme of Crook is typical of this sturdy refusal to give up. This programme, financed largely by the Commissioner for Special Areas, has provided for the clearance of some bad slum properties and the building of over 600 new houses during the past few years, a curious situation in a town which seems to have very poor economic prospects on any fairly long view. But even if it is unsound economic policy, it is characteristic of the mood of the place, which may yet succeed in overcoming its geographical disadvantages and attracting industry to itself.

The problem here, then, is that of a town in a district where what is virtually the only industry is, and has been for a long time, declining. It has been maintained[2] that the only real solution for such an area is liquidation, and that official policy should be directed towards securing this as easily as possible. We cannot consider in detail the merits or the disadvantages of this policy.

[1] See below, p. 108.

[2] This was stated most forcibly in the Report on South-west Durham, submitted to the Commissioner for the Special Areas by an independent firm of experts in 1936 (Sir Alexander Gibb and Sons).

In Crook itself there is a considerable body of resistance to it, and a committee has been formed which is trying energetically to attract new industries to Crook, on the grounds that the labour supply is of excellent quality, that modern methods of transport practically offset any geographical disadvantage, and that the "social capital" in Crook deserves not to be wasted. What we wish to do here is to examine the present situation in the light of the sample.

It illustrates fairly fully the methods by which movement out of Crook, and from the Special Areas in general, is encouraged. The young man who has been out of work for some time and is fit and intelligent is urged to attend one of the Ministry of Labour's six months' training schemes. One of these training centres is at Wallsend, near Newcastle, but the majority of men who accept training are sent from Crook to centres in the South of England where they will be nearer possible employment when the course is finished. The girls are given opportunities for going South into domestic service, and if a family man gets a chance of permanent work in a prosperous area, assistance is given to make it possible for him to move to it with the whole family.

The age structure of the sample suggests at once how effectively transference for the younger men is working:

TABLE XXIX. CROOK LONG UNEMPLOYED: AGE STRUCTURE OF SAMPLE

Age 20–29	30–39	40–49	50–59	60–64
15	34	25	31	13

There are less than half as many long unemployed in the age group 20–29 as in the ten-year age group above it. The smallness of the numbers in the lower age groups is shown even more clearly, if we compare the age group 19–27 with the corresponding age group (28–36) above it. In the former there were only nine men, in the latter thirty-two. And an examination of the nine cases of younger men shows that almost all of them are men who have actually been transferred from Crook, but for one reason or another the move has not been successful and they have found their way back. Seven of these nine were interviewed. All except one had worked out of Crook at some time, four in the south of England, one at Coventry, one at Scarborough. Three had been through Government Training Centres, and two had had three months' physical "reconditioning" courses at Government Instructional Centres.

Another point with regard to these younger men is important. Six of the young men under 35 were not, and had not been connected with the coal industry, but were instances of "secondary" unemployment. Of twenty-five others, fourteen had lost employment underground because the pit in which they were working had closed down, and not for any reason connected with their age, but 7 who had fallen out of work at the age of 21 had then been working in pits which were not closed down, and in 4 other instances this may have happened though the records were not explicit. In other words, of the young men under 35, the great majority of whom had entered the pits on leaving school, something over a third were now long unemployed because their services had been discarded simply on account of their age. Being no longer boys, the collieries concerned had no use for them. This particular abuse was for a time widespread in the coal-fields, but in Wales, at least, labour is likely to become scarce enough for it to be eliminated. From what we heard, however, it is not unlikely that a similar problem will recur in the case of the transferred factory workers, not only at 21 but at a later stage when they get married. For in many of the factories where they are working wages are not high enough to support a family. We met (outside the sample) one young man in Crook, of excellent industrial quality, who had had a steady job in a factory in the south and had left it owing to the low wages (35*s.*) he was receiving.

Sixteen of the families visited (17%) had sons or daughters living and working outside Crook. None of them complained, and several said how proud they were that the children should have found good employment and be earning good wages.

"One of the boys is earning £7 a week and the other is getting on to the top floor too." "They've all gone and are doing very well for themselves." "It's been a great success with the boy and girl, but I'll not go myself" (colliery horse-keeper, aged 57); "I know all the people in Crook, and if there was a job going here I might get it, in London I'd have no chance." "She's very happy in service. It's all right if you get with decent people. The trouble is girls want their evenings these days. When I was a young man I was told when to come in and I *was* in by then, I can tell you." All these were families of a decidedly good type, and it is plain that the better social types are also, on the whole, the most ready to move. In several instances the transferees had not yet got permanent work, but there was nevertheless in almost all of these families an atmosphere of hopefulness which was encouraging. It was in striking contrast to the atmosphere in Wales, where many complained that they had brought up their children with much trouble and expense and now, when they might reasonably expect some "benefit" from them, they were going away and benefitting their landlady rather than their parents.

A reference to Table XXIX showing the age distribution of the Crook sample shows that above the age of 30 transference has not been nearly so marked. Resistance to transference is to be explained in various ways. There were fifty-two cases in the age group 28–44 in Crook. Six of them (12%) were single, twenty-two (42%) were married couples living by themselves or with one child, twenty-four (46%) were married and living with two or more children. For these last two groups, and the last in particular, transference is obviously a problem, even when official help is forthcoming. A man with family responsibilities has to be sure of work before he moves his family. Two of those under 35, men of excellent type, were kept in Crook by strong institutional associations, which they were not prepared to break. They were leaders in the society in which they lived. "Durham can't afford to lose us all", one of them said. Two others under 35 were only kept from moving by the ill-health of their wives who could not be left. Six under the same age objected on various grounds; they had evidently settled down, and several of them gave accounts of the difficulties of conditions in London and the South: "The wife's brother removed to Dartford, earning £4 a week, but he says he's no better than he was in Crook what with the rent at 18*s*. a week and so on." One older man expressed it that "things are awful here, but they would be ten or eleven times more awful anywhere else" away from his few friends and his house. Among those under 35 who refused to consider transference were three of a definitely poor social type—such as one living on the outskirts of Crook in a caravan 16 by 8 ft. with his wife and five children.[1] These men might anywhere have been unemployed, residual cases.

The sample figures can be supplemented by official data for the Crook Exchange. Between October 1935 and December 1936 there were 45 assisted household removals from the Crook Exchange area and over 300 cases of assisted transference of individual adults, about a quarter of the latter being young women going into domestic service. During 1935 and 1936, 106 boys and 66 girls were also transferred through the agency of the local Juvenile Employment Bureau. A new development has been the scheme of transference for prospective employment, whereby suitable young men are allowed to visit prosperous industrial centres to look for work even when there has been no definite offer of employment. In the first five months of 1937 about 150 men availed themselves of this scheme, and only 12 returned having failed to obtain work.

These figures, taken in conjunction with the evidence of the sample, show how much is happening to resolve the problem of areas where industry is dying. But they suggest also that other problems are being created. We have seen that among the younger long unemployed in Crook the great majority were the failures of transference, the men who had not the enterprise or the resilience or vitality to carry it through. And the main

[1] Ownership of houses is not an important factor in Crook, in preventing transference. Only one man out of fifty-three between the ages of 28 and 45 owned his house.

effects of transference stop short about the age of 28 or 30.[1] Men over that age do leave Crook and get work, but not in numbers which are anything like comparable to the numbers of younger men. This means two things. It means first that the weight of unemployment in the Special Areas is in the upper age groups, where it is most intractable. Many observers both in Wales and in Durham told us that the essence of the Special Areas problem now was the problem of these older men living on in a community from which the vitality of youth had to a large extent been removed. Thus with the reduction in size of the Special Areas problem it has become to some extent more difficult, and the ordinary orthodox methods are not likely to solve it.

It means in the second place that there is a group of men left, neither young nor old—the family men which is (in Crook especially) disproportionately large, and consists of excellent material. Here are some of the recorded comments:

Miner, motor driver (*age* 36). He has kept his hands in condition by joinery, wireless repairing and manufacture, etc. Adaptable. Should make a very good semi-skilled workman with very little training. He worked 70 hours a week for 35*s*. in his last job (motor driver) just for the sake of working.

Miner (*age* 35). Cannot stand the heat of the pit, but is willing and able to take any other job. He is desperate and would take anything with both hands. There is no question here of the equality between wage and allowance having diminished willingness to work.

Joiner—but not a "tradesman" (*age* 28). Home exceptionally clean, an excellent man, very strong, the only bar the fact that he is not a qualified craftsman. Very anxious to get a job, and his wife is evidently very anxious also.

Miner (*age* 34). Very good home. Almost everything, clothes, etc. made by hand. Wife is determined to save enough to

[1] For further details on the age distribution of transferees from Co. Durham, see Dr Singer's Interim Report (III) issued in connexion with this Enquiry.

give son a good education, whatever happens. Difficult to imagine anyone more employable than applicant, who was apprenticed to a trade, but broke apprenticeship, when his father went to the War, to get better money coal-mining to "help his mother".

None of these men had had permanent steady work[1] within the last six years. All of them were anxious for work. One, the last, is now employed in Banbury. His wife told one of us how she was saving up to make it possible for him to go there and look for work. "Every week that there's an extra shilling I've bought a little extra cocoa or sugar or something to help me over the time he goes. My mother, who's got just a little of her own, will come here while he's away and that will help me on. But he's in a sweat about going, for he's heard that the people are not friendly. He likes to be able to talk to anyone he meets in the street."

The figures, too, are impressive, though figures in a matter of this kind must necessarily be put forward with reserve. 17 % of the men interviewed in Crook were classified as decidedly intelligent and 64 % as of good average intelligence—81 % in the two categories as compared with 54 % in Liverpool (11 and 43 %) or 47 % (2 and 45 %) in Deptford. Similarly their physical condition, if we group together those of "exceptional" and "good average" physique, was higher than elsewhere. 74 % in Crook fell into these two classes (12 and 62 %) as compared with 60 % (20 and 40 %) in Liverpool or 36 % (2 and 34 %) in Deptford. There can be little doubt of the quality of the material here available, nor that, as compared with the Rhondda for example, there is appreciably less of the physical disability (including industrial disease) that is characteristic of conditions there. With men like this fit and available for work it is impossible not to get an impression of waste. The new trading estates near Newcastle and at the southern end of the Rhondda Valley will do something to help, but even if factory sites are found near Crook itself it is probable that they will attract, to a large extent, industry needing women's labour. It is too early yet to say what

[1] One had had council relief work, one six months' motor driving.

effect the present local revival[1] in coal-mining will have in solving the men's problem, but what is now clear is that transference, as it has so far worked, will not completely solve it.

(v) BLACKBURN

In Blackburn the situation is made different from that in Crook or in the Rhondda by a number of factors. The predominant impression which Blackburn leaves is that of grimness, unmitigated by any natural pleasantness, for the city is too large for much sense of the surrounding country to penetrate it. Everywhere is a forest of tall brick chimneys, against a sky that seems always drab, everywhere cobbled streets, with the unrelieved black of the mill girls' overalls and the clatter of wooden clogs.[2] It was impossible not to be aware of a certain hardness in the people, a hardness which, because it implies independence and character, has much to be said for it, but which made the approach to an unemployed household far more difficult than it was elsewhere. "They like their diamonds rough", so we were told, and it became evident in the course of the sample visits that one or two of us did not entirely qualify on that score. Nevertheless, once the reserve was penetrated, there was a friendliness which was more real because it was not on the surface.

One thing which is no doubt largely responsible for this different atmosphere is the Blackburn tradition that the woman as well as the man shall work. Blackburn in the past has depended mainly on the cotton-weaving industry (though there are also a number of engineering works), and in that industry women work side by side with men. In at least one case that occurred in the sample, a man was unemployed because his wife could no longer work. He was not a skilled weaver, but so long as it had been possible for him to work side by side with

[1] For some details of the men who have got back to work in the Crook Exchange area since the revival, see below, p. 217.

[2] One detail will show how completely Blackburn is dominated by the textile industry. It was reckoned in 1910 that more than half of the children born in Blackburn spent more than half of their pre-natal existence in the mill.

her, he was able to manage. When his wife was stopped through sickness, however, he found, after a week or two, that he also had to stop. This practice of the women working gives them a kind of independence which was noticeable in Leicester also, where to a certain extent the situation is comparable (though in Leicester there is virtually no unemployment among the women). It shows itself in various ways. In one instance visited, where a young couple (aged 29) had both been unemployed for some years but had both recently returned to work, the husband, when asked whether his wife preferred being at work or not, replied: "Oh, she does not let on that sort of thing to me." Yet it was clear that relations between them were entirely satisfactory. It shows itself too in the value that many women in Blackburn evidently set on their financial independence. Unless they are "keeping themselves", they feel that there is something wrong, and several of those whom we interviewed, who had recently got back to work at a wage that left them no better off than they had been when drawing unemployment assistance, used expressions such as "but, of course, now my money is my own".

At the same time it was plain that, in a large number of instances, this feeling of the value of independence was breaking down as a result of long unemployment. Depression hit Blackburn earlier than it hit the country as a whole, and, after Crook, Blackburn showed the highest percentage of cases out of work for five years or more (51 % as compared with 71 % in Crook, 44 % in the Rhondda, and 31 % in Leicester). Unemployment has therefore had time to make its effects fully felt. Thus, while among the unemployed women in Blackburn there was a considerable number who clearly still regarded the mills as a second home, and could not be reconciled to unemployment for that reason, there was an almost equally large number who had evidently found that release from work meant the possibility of living a home life such as they had never lived before, and who would certainly avoid going back to work if it were possible to avoid it. In some cases, even though the unemployment allowances had been finally discontinued, they were not prepared to go back to work, though in others the threat of this had proved effective in inducing them to take fresh employment; for, shortly before the sample visits were made, a large factory for producing gas masks had been opened in Blackburn, and there were therefore fresh possibilities of work. Many of those women who excused themselves as being unable to work again, on account of their eyesight (though there must be something in the complaint that fine weaving of the kind now mainly required is trying to the eyes), were no doubt women who had discovered, through being unemployed, that they could lead a satisfying life at home. In so far as it may be socially more desirable for women to devote their main energies to their homes and families, this element in the women's unemployment problem will not be regarded as serious. Indeed, it will not be considered a problem of unemployment at all, but a matter of somehow making it possible for the change to be permanent. But such a view is against the modern tendency for the woman to enter industrial employment, and many would consider it out of date. It is often held that, by working outside the home as well as in it, a woman gains a new status which she may justly value, and that, with modern conditions, it is possible for her to do both. On this view high figures of women's unemployment are more serious.

The practice of women working in the mills makes a great difference to the way in which the family budget is constituted. When all members of the family, father, mother and children over school age, work in the mills, it means that even in a period of depression there may be one or two working. Thus in Blackburn the proportion of families (29 %), in which Unemployment Assistance was less than half the family's income, was higher than anywhere else, higher even than Leicester (26 %) or Deptford (23 %). There were one or two striking instances where the reluctance of women to return to work and the existence of such another source of income in the family occurred together. One household consisted of two middle-aged sisters and a brother. The sisters said they could never work again, but nevertheless they drew 15*s*. a week each in Unemployment Assistance, though the brother, a clerk, was earning 65*s*. a week. It is clearly a fiction to regard them as unemployed, and it is probable indeed that, under the revised regulations that came into force after the sample date, these allowances were substantially reduced.

What is of the greatest importance in this connexion is that, in spite of the fact that there was a substantial proportion of wage earners in the Blackburn families visited, the degree of poverty (measured by a weighted standard) in Blackburn was distinctly greater than it was in the Rhondda and comparable almost precisely to the general level in Crook.[1] There is here no question of this being due (as poverty in Liverpool is due) to the number of large families, for the proportion of those with three or more dependents was lower in Blackburn than anywhere else except Deptford (10% Blackburn, 5% Deptford, 25% Liverpool). That incomes should be on the whole low, in a place where Unemployment Assistance is supplemented to an exceptional degree by wages, is due to one thing only: the low wage level. This is in itself to be explained partly, of course, by the fact that wages have always been fixed in Blackburn on the assumption that several members of the family will be working. When we find a family of five: man and wife aged 33 and 34, with three children from 9 to 13, in which the man works three days a week on a motor lorry at a wage of 15*s.* 5*d.* (which is supplemented by Unemployment Insurance of 13*s.* for the other three days), it is clear that it was only possible for him to accept this wage because there were other resources—in this instance 17*s.* 6*d.* Unemployment Assistance drawn by the wife, a weaver. In such instances the U.A.B. is providing for a social rather than an economic problem. In a somewhat similar case the father of the family, aged 58, was earning 29*s.* a week as a weaver, and one daughter earning 21*s.* 9*d.* as a shop assistant. The mother and daughter helped to support the family by drawing Unemployment Assistance of 13*s.* and 15*s.* Here again the extraordinarily low wages earned are to be noticed.[2] In another case a labourer with a wife and small daughter was earning 33*s.* 3*d.* a week, and his wife drew 6*s.* 3*d.* Unemployment Assistance which made the

[1] For figures, see Table A 5 on p. 423 below.

[2] For some further instances of this, see footnote 2, p. 167.

wage a possible one. Our record notes that she has "no intention whatever of working". "She says that her hands are full with the family." It notes also that she "gave the impression of living a thoroughly happy life". The mill where she claimed to be seeking work was taking on hands at the time to do the type of work to which she was accustomed. Only an individual visit can show whether in any given case the woman wishes to work or not, for we had instances where Unemployment Assistance appeared, on the face of it, to be, as in those instances quoted, only a subsidy to wages, but where the visit showed that the woman was actually most anxious to work.

Here also there were examples of what happens in the Rhondda, where prolonged unemployment was having a marked effect on a man's anxiety for work. In Blackburn, too, there was a certain number of men who would not go back to work if they could avoid it. There was one, for example, aged only 21, who seemed fit and strong, but was neglected and rather shifty in appearance, of whom it is noted that "his ideal seems to be to send his wife out to work"; and another, in the thirties, fit and evidently decidedly clever, who steadily refused to learn fancy weaving because it would mean his getting work. His interest was in the construction of models, which he did skilfully, and the member of the family who alone took his situation seriously was his wife. Just before he was visited, he had had to agree to take part in a scheme recently devised for teaching fancy weaving, but it was evident that this was the result of pressure and that, left to his own devices, he would have done nothing of the kind and would have continued to live happily "on the dole". The proportion of such men who had come to acquiesce in unemployment and would find it difficult to take work again was exceptionally high (38%) in Blackburn—a fact which may be connected with the low wage figures we have noticed above.

But at the same time, as in the Rhondda and Crook, we were being constantly reminded that unemployment in Blackburn was fundamentally industrial in character. This means that here, as in Crook, or the Rhondda, or Liverpool, there is a large group of cases fully employable and anxious for employment. A good instance was a young man of 29, who had served his time as a weaver, but given it up to do general labouring because he felt that weaving was "finished"; "it's a woman's job now". With his wife and a daughter of six he was living well below the "poverty line". He had had three weeks' labouring work at 40*s.* a week, a little before the visit took place, after six years' unemployment. He described how his hands had swelled and blistered, his back and wrists were strained, and he got soaked through almost every day. "But", he said, "I took 3*d.* worth of Aspro to send me off to sleep at night, and I stuck it and loved it. I hoped then that I'd got back." The number of such cases, of all ages, left no doubt about the reality of this will to work, in many of them, if any work were there.

As in the Rhondda, in Blackburn also, continued unemployment was in certain instances due to technical changes to which the worker could not adapt himself. The difficulties of fancy weaving, which is in increasing demand, have been noticed above, and a certain number of men and women are out of work because they cannot, and others because they will not, adjust themselves to this requirement. One which is, from all accounts, less reasonable is the demand that a woman should manage six looms, instead of three or four. Several weavers told us that they could be in work immediately if they were prepared to manage six looms, but they said that the strain was too great. This objection was made in several cases where there was no doubt that the weaver concerned wanted work badly, if it could be managed.

Blackburn was the only place included in the sample where a substantial proportion of the cases selected had returned to work between November 1936 and the time of the visits. It was most noticeable that, though in many cases the remark was made that they were "really no better off working", yet the great majority said nevertheless that they were glad to be back at work. "Your money is your own, and that makes all the difference." It is hard to say whether this is mainly due to that Lancashire independence described above, or whether the same thing would happen in, e.g. the Rhondda, or elsewhere if the number of jobs available increased and a substantial number of long unemployed were reabsorbed.

(vi) LIVERPOOL

In many respects the unemployment situation in Liverpool, as shown in the sample, might be said to be intermediate between the Rhondda and Deptford. Liverpool is not too big and too diverse for local patriotism to be meaningless, but on the other hand it lacks the natural feeling of unity which is so sharply marked in the Rhondda, with its common cultural and social background. Its character is not that of Deptford, a specialized part of a larger whole, used by many of its population as a dormitory, and with many of its industries drawing their workers from outside; nor are its various districts self-contained, as are those of the Rhondda. Again, though there is not the wide range of occupations of all grades (apart from heavy industries) open to any Deptford man prepared to go outside the boundaries of the Borough, neither is there the predominance of one single industry as in the Rhondda Valley. It is true that Liverpool is nearly as dependent on its port as the Rhondda on its mines, but it is becoming less and less true, for the percentage of Merseyside workers attached to shipping, shipbuilding, transport and distribution fell from 50% in 1932 to 45% in 1936, and the Port requires a great variety of workers, of which scalers, carpenters, storekeepers, messengers, porters, dock labourers, stewards, seamen, warehousemen, riggers, firemen are but a few. Correspondingly, there is much scope for picking up jobs "off your track". One of the young long-unemployed men visited in Liverpool, aged 23, had been a bell-boy at sea for two years, a ship-painter's labourer for one year, a bell-boy again for three months, an assistant steward, and had finally taken to hawking—collecting scrap-metal near the harbour and selling it; while another of 20, who had been a baker's labourer, a porter, a general labourer, a worker in a pencil factory, then gone off to East London to try his luck, had succeeded finally in settling down as a scaler.

Thus of 247 Liverpool long-unemployed men whose employment record was obtained, only 23 % had failed to get a job worth mention during the past five years, which compares with 38 % in the sample as a whole, and is a smaller percentage than in the much more prosperous Leicester. It is remarkable, too, that the proportion of all unemployed who have been out of work for at least a year was not higher than in the country as a whole (about 1 in 5), although the general percentage of unemployment in Liverpool was nearly twice as high. This fact is in contradiction to the general tendency for the number of long unemployed to rise faster than the number of all unemployed as we move from prosperous to depressed districts.[1] Another sense in which Liverpool might be described in terms of transition from Deptford to Rhondda is that Liverpool is not scheduled as a depressed area, although unemployment is a serious problem there. At no moment, indeed, even during the crisis, was there a danger of Liverpool becoming a derelict community. The peak of unemployment, including seasonal factors, was 31 % of the insured population. On the other hand, unemployment has been higher here throughout than in the country as a whole; the recovery has been particularly tardy because of the structural decline of the relative importance of the Port of Liverpool compared with its chief southern competitors (a factor comparable to the structural decline of coal-mining), and at the depth of the crisis one of the most important industries, shipbuilding, was in a state of economic collapse similar to that of coal-mining.

Thus the Liverpool man who has been outside ordinary economic activity for a considerable time belongs to a small section of the industrial population, a section amounting to only 3 % (as compared with 0·4 % in Deptford, but 25 % in the Rhondda), and to a minority of the whole unemployed population, 23 % (as compared with 6 % in Deptford, but 63 % in the Rhondda). Yet the number of Liverpool long unemployed is nearly the same as in the Rhondda (10,318 as compared with 10,962), while there can be little doubt that among those who

[1] Cf. p. 14.

have been out of work for less than a year in Liverpool, there is a substantial number who are in fact long unemployed, and a figure of 20,000 might not be far short of the mark. Moreover, long unemployment in Liverpool is concentrated in the densely packed working-class districts of inner Liverpool, a much smaller area than even the narrow Rhondda valleys cover, and must, therefore, be considered as a mass (in a political, psychological, and economic sense), with mass phenomena and community values such as the unemployed community in the Rhondda has, whereas in Deptford the long unemployed are more truly regarded as 100 individuals than as a united whole.

It is not, however, only a transitional picture that the unemployed of Liverpool presented in the sample. There are many new factors which have a dominant bearing on the nature of the long-unemployment problem in Liverpool. Most important is the complete lack of an association of unemployment and age. A division of the unemployed men between 25 and 64 into the four decades shows that the oldest group between 55 and 64 is predominant in Leicester and Deptford, there being in both more men between those age limits than in all the other age groups together; the 45–54 years' group is the largest in the Rhondda, and the 35–44 years' group in Crook and Blackburn. In Liverpool, however, it is the first decade comprising men between 25 and 34 that is the largest. Out of every 100 long unemployed, 35 men were under 35 years of age, the figure elsewhere ranging from 28 in the Rhondda to 7 in Deptford. Among the 273 men who formed the sample in Liverpool, there were more men between 18 and 24 years than among the 665 men in the other five places. For this there are various reasons, ranging from a higher birth-rate in Liverpool to, e.g., the institution of the dockers' tally, which seems to keep the younger men out of such casual employment as is available. Here we are more concerned with the results than with the explanation. It means that in Liverpool there was a compact body of rather more than 3,500 young men under 35 who had not had a job worth mention for a year. And as it must be remembered that the sample excludes the cases taken over by the

Unemployment Assistance Board a few months after the enquiry started—a particularly heavy load in Liverpool—the actual number is perhaps not very far from 5,000.

The younger man is generally more sociable and more assertive, and it is not surprising therefore to find here unemployed public opinion largely dominated by the younger men's grievances and problems. The single man of 20 does not mix with the family man of 40 or the widower of 60, and the differences are indeed so obvious that they prevent the forming of a comprehensive unemployed community. Thus in places like the Rhondda, where there is a community of unemployed men, predominantly middle-aged, the young unemployed are comparatively isolated. In Liverpool, however, the existence of large gangs of young men, fairly stable in their membership (for a short casual job is not always a real interruption of long unemployment), together with the provision of special institutions for the young unemployed men,[1] make it easier for the young unemployed to evolve both an individual and communal pattern of life suited to his state of unemployment. About this we shall have more to say in other parts of the report.

The existence of these large numbers of unemployed young men means that there is not in Liverpool the contrast, such as exists to some extent in the Rhondda, for instance, between young lads in employment and the older men out of work and with virtually no hopes of returning to work. Nor was there, incidentally, the bitterness against former employment, such as was apparent in Wales. But the attitude of the older men in Liverpool suggested the discouragement which the sight of a large number of younger unemployed brings to the man who is getting on in years.

One fact of predominant importance was the heavy concentration of long unemployment in certain districts of Liverpool, and those by no means all the working-class districts of the City. In some parts sample visits (in Liverpool the sample being 1 in 35) took us to almost every street, terrace and court in the neighbourhood. In other parts, and particularly in the

[1] Cf. p. 342.

outlying estates, the homes of long-unemployed men, even if the density of the visits be multiplied by 35, are few and far between. A sustained effort of slum clearance and rehousing has been so successful that approximately one-third of Liverpool's people lived, at the time the sample was taken, in houses built after the War. Yet of the 273 visits or intended visits in Liverpool, only 25, that is to say not one in ten, took us into one of these new houses (18) or flats (7). The importance of this must be clear to anyone who knows the sordid but easygoing and sociable atmosphere of the old districts, which in Liverpool almost always means slum districts—where the unemployed man has his corner, his friends, his library, and his bookmaker, where he speaks freely when you call on him, where he calls his friends in to tell you all about it, where not much is spent on rent and next to nothing on upkeep. Such an atmosphere is utterly different from that in the housing estates, where the unemployed man takes an anxious look round when you mention unemployment to him and rapidly tells you to come in.[1] Not only is the unemployed man on new housing estates more isolated than in "his own parts", but as a consequence of the high rents paid, ranging in Liverpool up to 18*s.* 6*d.*, not less than 19 of the 25 unemployed in new houses or flats live below the "poverty line", and 11 of these 19 in "deep poverty".[2]

An example will illustrate these points, a married man, 37 years old, with a wife of 40 and a boy of 9 at school. This man became a clerk at 16, served in the War, and then set up in business, first with his brother, later on his own. He was at first very successful, and lived in a substantial house on the outskirts of Liverpool, but ultimately he failed and went bankrupt. He then became a storekeeper for a telephone company and held this responsible post for six years until he was dismissed in November 1932. For a week he tried to gain his living as a

[1] The small number of long unemployed we found in new municipal estates does not lend much weight to the often encountered reports about the clients of the U.A.B. being considered as "safe" tenants by Local Housing Committees, on the grounds that Unemployment Allowances include a sum for rent which is therefore certain to be paid.

[2] See below, p. 104, for the standard on which this statement is based.

salesman for a tailoring company, but gave up and he has done no work since November 1932. The U.A.B. pays him the comparatively high amount of 36*s*., but as he pays 18*s*. 6*d*. for his four-roomed house on one of the new estates, there remains only 17*s*. 6*d*. to feed, clothe, and warm three persons, 2*s*. 6*d*. a day all told. There was once another child. At the clinic they told his wife that the child was in need of extra nourishment, but—as he alleged—when the officer came round and saw a home of middle-class character, he said that no extra nourishment could be allowed. The child died. The home is still middle-class, as is the appearance and clothing of the household; but the furniture has gradually gone, a £85 piano fetching £35, a £30 bedroom suite £9, a £18 sewing-machine £3. There is nearly £4 owing on the rent; there are debts for groceries—although relations help. All insurances have been realized. This man applied to one of the voluntary societies for a loan, but was refused, "though in better times I often used to give them a guinea". He conceals the fact of being out of work from all his friends, if possible, and from his neighbours, and even the boy is not allowed to know the real position. He is dreaming of the day when he goes to College! Having been out of work for over four years, this man realizes that it will be almost impossible to get work, as he cannot produce any recent testimonials. He would take any job anywhere for £3. He has no institutional connexions of any kind. The idea of joining an unemployed club is absurd to him. If he had a little capital, they might start a business or boarding-house, but there is nothing save this last straw to which they cling, their respectability. The case is an exceptional one, but it illustrates, as only an extreme case can do, the struggle of that minority of the unemployed—a minority which is nevertheless a numerous body—who have slipped from a lower middle-class or skilled working-class background into the ranks of the long and perhaps permanently unemployed, and who are scattered and hiding in the newer and more respectable parts of Liverpool, and doubtless of other large cities.

Such cases, however, were a small minority, for 9,000 of the

10,000 long unemployed in Liverpool were living concentrated in the slums of inner Liverpool. Their problem is certainly not one of isolation, but a problem of environment and its formative influences. It is an environment which, as should not be forgotten, the permanently unemployed men share with a small number of permanently employed and a large number of men who are somewhere between steady employment and long unemployment. One thing which will remain in the memory of anyone going round among the Liverpool unemployed will be the appalling housing conditions and the low domestic standards, which are to a large extent a consequence of them. It is not always the same picture, but the same impression given through a variety of types. There is the common lodging-house, with a notice outside "Good beds for men", such as is the home of many an elderly single man, who divides his time between the sleeping room, which he shares with ten or twelve others, the common room,—where he keeps his bread and bacon wrapped in newspaper on the floor beneath his seat and takes it with him to the "Labour" because otherwise it will be gone when he comes back,—and the doorstep; for the most exciting incidents in his life, probably, are a band in the street or a street squabble, and perhaps his only interest is to remember the good time he had in the War, with decent food and hearty company. Or there is the solitary lodger, living apart from his family, perhaps, in a dark cold room, furnished with a table and two broken chairs, who is only at home when he has not been able to get a seat in the Public Library, and fall asleep in a warm place over the racing columns in the paper. Or there is the family—the Irish youth living with a blind father, a mother immensely fat, an asthmatic elder sister and a younger brother, all in a small overheated room, opening directly onto the street, a room so small that the table has to be moved when anyone else comes in, unless one of them goes up the narrow and steep staircase to the tiny bedroom above. Or there is the "general labourer" of 33 living with wife and four children (a daughter of 6 at school, another daughter crippled, a daughter of 2 and a son just born) in two rooms, small, dark, damp, with the plaster decayed, nowhere to wash, gas used all day at a cost of 2*s*. 6*d*. a week because there is no daylight—a necessity which substantially increases the gap between their net income of less than 34*s*. and the 38*s*. or so required by our "poverty line" standard. Is it too much to say that if a man living under these conditions is described as "a man of slovenly habits, dirty and unkempt in appearance", he may very well initially have been a different type, who has fallen into that hopeless vicious circle of unemployment—poverty, dirt, deterioration, dwindling chances of re-employment? Can we fail to connect his statement that he used to go to church, but that "a loaf of bread is my religion now" with the conditions under which he is forced to live?

There was an almost unending series of houses falling to pieces, long ago condemned as unfit for human habitation, and of families living under conditions such as to make any attempt at a respectable family life a heroic struggle. "The thing that keeps me away from home", as a middle-aged man, the father of two children and fond of them, said, "is the smell." So figures descriptive of home management, family relations, domestic standards, state of furniture among Liverpool unemployed, distinguish them clearly from the unemployed in the other five places. 41 % showed a low standard of furniture (20 % in the sample as a whole and 16 % in the Rhondda), 38 % a low level of family life (35 and 31 %), 14 % definite signs of mismanagement (12 and 6 %).

These figures should be read in the light of the environment of a Liverpool slum. In that respect the Liverpool unemployed has two disadvantages: he starts from a lower level when he falls out of work, and he lacks what is one of the main resistants to deterioration. And significantly enough, whereas the common fate of poverty, unemployment, and slum environment seemed to have wiped out the racial differences in the standard of living as between the English, the Irish, and other immigrant elements, it appeared to be the English worker whose domestic life gave way under the strain of this environment. Social workers and officials actually told us that they hesitated sometimes to put groups of unemployed men for a few weeks in decent surroundings, such as holiday camps or Government Instructional Centres or Wincham Hall,[1] because the effect of a return to the old conditions tended in some instances to make matters worse.

Housing conditions are the most obvious of these environmental influences which help to shape the life and mind of the unemployed man in Liverpool. But it became more and more plain, as the sample progressed, that there is a deeper and even more important sense in which the place of the unemployed man within the community is closely connected with the social and industrial setting of that community. In spite of all attempts at "decasualization", the labour required by the life of the Port is still largely intermittent, and this does not only apply to dockers. Down at the docks, there is no means of telling which of the men standing about are the "employed", waiting for their turn to be taken on and confident that they will be; which of them are those for whom jobs are far between; and which are the "long unemployed" who step forward, if a man is wanted, with the feeling that this is only another in an unbroken series of failures which they count by years. Often the appearance of their hands and faces is tell-tale, but the experience of being on the market to "wait for a job to turn up" is common to all of them, employed, under-employed, and unemployed alike. There is none of the experience felt so keenly by the unemployed weaver of Blackburn, when his "own" factory gates are closed and he must stand outside and watch the privileged go in. In Liverpool the queue is not a new or humiliating experience. The chances are that even during employment the worker has used the "continuity rules" to supplement his income by signing on.[2] To draw public money does not characterize a separate class of unemployed. The habit of lounging at street corners, or at a tea-room bar, or in front of the "pub" is not a painful new experience that is part of his adjustment to unemployment, but is long familiar to him and does not mark him as unemployed. His wife, too, has always been used to him coming home at noon and

[1] A working men's college in Cheshire for unemployed men; see below, p. 351.
[2] For an instance of this from Liverpool, see below, p. 224.

spending the rest of the day idle at home or in the neighbourhood.

Thus for the Liverpool employed man the unemployed are not beings of another world, struggling with problems alien to him, but they are in a state which he also knows to some degree. There are no dominating trade unions to be the special preserve of the employed men—for, in other places where such unions exist, the unemployed either tend to drop out to save the contributions, or, if they retain membership, do so under special schemes, and probably suffer a definite decline in their status of membership. It is, therefore, natural that in places like the Seamen's Institute, and above all in those more spontaneous growths like the "Cellar Clubs" or the "Irish Social and Body-Building Clubs" there is a fairly free mixing of employed and unemployed. Thus, although the long unemployed in Liverpool are a smaller portion of the community than in the Rhondda, they seem to fit much better into the communal life. In another part of this report we say something of the segregation of the unemployed. In Liverpool this problem has, paradoxically, only arisen in connexion with the work done by voluntary agencies there, partly as an inevitable outcome of the idea of provisions confined to the unemployed, and partly by the system of adoption of clubs by private firms and their personnel.

The figures which the sample has provided show in an arresting way that impressions of the poverty of Liverpool are not imaginary. Of the Liverpool unemployed men not less than 30% were living in "deep poverty" as compared with 17% in our total sample,[1] and altogether 48% were living below the poverty standard we have adopted, as compared with 30%. This degree of poverty is unparalleled in the other places of the sample. Its explanation reveals the major economic problems of the Liverpool unemployed. The most important factor is the large number of dependents of Liverpool unemployed. One hundred long-unemployed men in Liverpool represent, with their families, no less than 324 persons, as compared with 254 in

[1] For details of the standard used, see below, p. 104.

the Rhondda and only 184 in Deptford. 26% of all the unemployed in Liverpool have more than three dependents. In the Rhondda the figure is 17%, in Deptford 5%. One hundred long-unemployed families in Liverpool mean 64 children under 6 years and 80 school-children; 29 under school age and 51 at school in Rhondda, 10 and 28 in Deptford. Moreover, in Liverpool the proportion of men wholly dependent on the U.A.B. is higher than elsewhere, partly because there is so much unemployment among the younger and younger middle-age groups in Liverpool, but also because of the earlier marriage age and the tendency of families to break up much more easily[1] if the children become independent. The amount of any kind of earnings is proportionately much smaller than elsewhere,[2] owing to the low wage rates of earning juveniles. It would be unfair to emphasize the pauperization that exists in Liverpool without showing that it is at least partly explained by the disproportion between family budgets and family needs.

On the other hand, there are other factors, and this picture of the environment of the Liverpool unemployed would not be complete without the mention of one which seemed more conspicuous in Liverpool than anywhere else. It is the all-pervading atmosphere of football pools, greyhounds and horses. This has become such an important environmental factor that, for the individual unemployed, it is an effort to develop interests unconnected with them. The extent to which the interests and indeed the whole lives of so many of the Liverpool unemployed centre round the pools must be seen to be believed. The queues at Post Offices filling in coupons, the number of "guaranteed systems" for correct forecast on sale in Liverpool's poorest districts, the periodicals containing nothing but pool analyses, the dirty and torn sports columns of the papers in Public Libraries, with the rest of the paper untouched (apart from advertisements of vacant jobs), are some measure of the strength of this interest. It is not a direct interest in sport, but it derives

[1] Of the 27 young Liverpool men under 25, not less than 9 (33%) were married.

[2] Cf. Table XXX, p. 108.

from that and gives glamour to everything and everybody that has anything to do with sport. On a Saturday afternoon, when an important League match is on, the unemployed men in Liverpool turn out and gather along the streets where the crowds go up by foot, tram, bus or motor car to watch it. To watch a match is in itself a second-hand experience, and the unemployed man, not often able to afford a shilling for entrance, has to make do with this substitute for it. And he seems to derive excitement of a kind even from this. But there is a world of difference between this and the Tonypandy people turning out to the last man to welcome Tommy Farr with flags and posters and civic honours.

This passion for sport and betting influences the unemployed men in odd ways. The man who has been lucky enough to win money in the pool acquires thereby a definite social standing, and his views on very different matters are heard with respect. The unemployed man has more time to spend on these things than the employed man, and for him betting has a very definite function. For though it may be partly true to say that in Liverpool unemployment has in some cases replaced uncertainty and irregularity by security and regularity, yet there were few unemployed men (except for those with large families) who did not in some way seem to feel that they were gradually "going under", and led a "come day, go day" life, as one of them expressed it. To those who have ceased to believe that they will ever get the "green card" from the Labour Exchange, this is the field where "they stand as good a chance as anybody else", and where they feel they are fairly treated. In speaking to one of us, one of them actually drew a contrast between the fairness of the pools and the alleged favouritism of the Exchange.

Closely connected with this is the fact that betting offers to many unemployed men the only possibility of making a decision, of a choice between alternatives, in a life otherwise prescribed in every detail by poverty and necessity, and always the object of other people's decisions. This is precisely what the democratically run Service Club offers to its members, but the pool or the "bookie" offers it in a much easier way, which has a special appeal to the great mass of the unemployed.

Moreover, the pools give men something to hope for, that one day they may be able to get "out of the rut", and this is particularly important in the case of the unemployed man for whom the hope of betterment by promotion, efficiency, or a rise in wages, has ceased to be operative. But above all, betting is important as a means of contact. It provides the content of social intercourse, a partial solution of the "time to spare and nothing to do" problem, a way of spending one's time in the discussion, analysis and decision with a seeming sense of purpose and ultimate achievement. An attempt to see why the pool habit has such a grip on the Liverpool unemployed men in our sample seems, indeed, to reveal something of the most badly felt needs and desires of the unemployed man.

B. *THE LONG UNEMPLOYED*

I. PHYSICAL PROBLEMS

THE BACKGROUND OF POVERTY

(*a*) *Introduction*

By its terms of reference this enquiry was directed to consider the effects of unemployment on those most affected by it, and obviously there are economic and physical, as well as psychological and moral effects of unemployment. It was impossible for us to ignore these aspects. On the other hand, we had not the resources for a complete and detailed survey. In so far as it provides anything new, the following account is based on the impressions of the home circumstances as recorded by us immediately after the visits took place. We were also able to obtain particulars of the incomes of the families we visited (particulars which were invariably carefully checked, so that there is every reason for confidence in their accuracy) and to analyse them; and though this analysis has no claims to be based on newly discovered material, it may be of interest to those who do not know under what conditions the unemployed live. In few instances was it possible to collect family budgets, and we did not as a rule attempt this. If it had been possible, it would have modified the character of this section of our report. Any generalizations we make are naturally based on conditions as the sample showed them, and are not necessarily true, therefore, of places outside it.

It may be useful to anticipate here the general conclusions reached. Our impressions were that the economic level at which families were living in many homes visited was such as to cause nervous anxiety and in some instances physical deterioration. The sample provides little basis for comparison between unemployed and employed in this respect, but if, as we suggest later, there is reason to believe that many wage earners have an income not very different from that of some of the homes in the sample, this means that the level at which they are living is similar. Indeed it has been said that "unemployment is a great leveller"—that while it reduces severely the livelihood of those who are accustomed to some degree of comfort, and to the spending of money on other things as well as rent and food, yet there are others, whose value in the labour market is low, for whom unemployment assistance, by providing a steady income at a rate well above that of the lowest wages, definitely raises the standard. Certainly we were forced to the conclusion that if the rates of assistance were substantially raised, there would inevitably follow an increase in the numbers of those who were prepared to live "on the dole". But it does not make poverty any less unpleasant that the numbers are large, nor that one possible method of relieving it would create other perhaps worse evils. Not until something of what this poverty means is realized, something too about the kind of people it affects and the kind of lives they lead, will there be any prospect of effective changes being made.

(*b*) *The Cycle of Working-Class Economic Life*[1]

For the circumstances of these unemployed families to be understood, they must be seen against the cycle of working-class economic life. The manual worker, and especially the unskilled labourer, lives through a different cycle from that lived by the professional man. The latter can usually count on a salary rising steadily till towards the end of his period of service. The ordinary manual worker attains his maximum very early, and a pick and shovel labourer in the early twenties is as likely to be earning 1*s*. 2*d*. an hour as is the labourer twice his age. When he is young, therefore, he is comparatively rich. But when he marries and the family begins to appear, he gradually gets poorer until, if he has a large family of young children, he is probably living well below the poverty line. We may take a random example from the sample, a South Wales miner with a family of six, ranging from a baby to a daughter of 12 years old. The normal weekly wage of this particular man is given in the records as 48*s*. 6*d*., a wage which would leave the family considerably below standards regarded as minimum needs by most competent authorities. Scores of other instances from the sample could be given to illustrate this point, for unless a man is highly skilled or in some responsible position, it is the exception rather than the rule for his wage to reach such a minimum standard for a large family. He is earning the same as the unmarried man working in the same gang as himself, and, somehow, the wage has to be made to go round.

There comes a time, however, when the children begin to leave school, and to start earning; and then the family's position begins to improve. Boys' and girls' wages are not high, but they are enough to make a great difference to the family budget. Working men on the whole marry young, and the eldest child may be 14 when the father is 35, though it may be considerably later than this before the first child leaves school and begins to

[1] Mr Rowntree has recently treated this cycle in considerably greater detail than is possible for us here. Our account was produced independently of his.

earn. But when that happens a new era has begun, and it is one to which the father and mother are constantly looking forward. A woman of 45 in Crook with three unemployed sons, of whom the youngest, aged 20, had never worked and the other two, aged 22 and 24, were unemployed, said to one of us: "I can't forget how when my sons were young and my husband in good earning the old doctor told me: 'Mrs —, one day you'll be well off'—and now this." If her sons had been in reasonably good employment and her husband working, there might have been £8 or £10 or more a week coming into the household. For the few years when that is happening, the family is prosperous. One of the cases in Leicester, a man of 53, had a family of twelve children. The four who were over 14 were earning, one of them 11*s*. 9*d*., one 20*s*., one 26*s*. 4*d*., one 39*s*. 1*d*., and the woman told us that "the worst days were over now".

However, unless the family is long, the prosperous period is itself only too short. The sons and daughters go to homes of their own, and the couple is left alone again. Provided that the husband remains in employment all is well. They probably have enough for the two to live in reasonable comfort, at least until the old age pension is available at 65, though if the man has then to give up work and there are no savings or other income supplementary to the statutory pension, it means a serious drop in the standard and they may well have to resort to the Relieving Officer for help. In some instances the comfort of the elderly couple is assured by their living with married children in employment, or by one earning child staying at home to help them, or they may receive allowances from their more prosperous children.

Unemployment Assistance has an important difference from wages, in that its amount depends, among other things, on the number and age of a man's dependents. While, therefore, the young single man or married couple will probably be substantially poorer on Unemployment Assistance than they would be earning, as the family grows in size their allowance approaches nearer the amount of possible earnings. However badly off the unemployed man with several children may seem, his economic position is much nearer to that of the ordinary wage earner than that of others such as the single unemployed man or married couple, who often appear, by comparison with the minimum standard, to be better off.

(c) *The Income of the Long Unemployed Measured*

The variety of opinions existing about the standard of income below which no citizen should be expected to live is notorious, and until some standard is generally accepted, any standard of poverty expressed in income terms, is primarily a measure to decide whether one family is better off than another, the income being weighted according to the size of the family. It is inevitable, however, that when a measure is applied, the question should arise: Where on that measure comes the mark which divides those who are living in poverty from those who are not? The answer to this question is a matter of opinion. That which we have adopted is one formulated recently by Mr R. F. George, and when we talk of a family living "in poverty" or "above the poverty line" in this report, we mean that the family income, as measured by that standard, is below or above what Mr George reckons as the minimum necessary. The phrase "living in poverty" seems to imply something with regard to the conditions of the household. Actually it implies only something with regard to its income, namely that, if Mr George is right, the income is such that it will be almost impossible for the family to live at a reasonable level. The visits undertaken in the course of the sample strongly suggest the reasonableness of Mr George's standard. It leaves most married couples without children, who are living on Unemployment Assistance, a little above the "poverty line", and the general impression that visits to such households made was that, where the woman was a reasonably good manager and the household was prepared to curtail any form of outside interest involving a cost of more than a penny or two a week, sufficient food, clothing, light, and fuel could be provided. The real distress that existed in many such households seemed to be due to the maintenance of the same dead level (generally much below what it would be if the man was in employment), with no hope of an extra at any time, for Coronation payments are not items that are recurrent. On the other hand, where there were three or four children in the family the standard generally shows it (unless there are other resources, such as the earnings of a child or a disability pension) below the poverty line. In these families with children, our impression was that almost invariably there was definite want, either of food or clothing, or more probably of household equipment. The housewife's skill or lack of skill is of course a factor of enormous importance in each individual case. But the distinction we have drawn between families with several children and those without holds good as a general rule.

Mr George's standard[1] is based on the British Medical Association minimum standards for food requirements and on the standards used by various local social surveys in respect of clothing, cleaning materials, light and fuel. Mr George slightly increases, however, the British Medical Association standard in respect of milk, in order to bring its requirements into line with more recent recommendations.[2] In Appendix IV are given the weekly money requirements of the standard in terms of London prices ruling in July 1936.

The items reckoned in the household's needs are food, clothing, cleaning materials, light and fuel. We assume that each family is paying its rent and that is therefore deducted from the income before the amount available is calculated. For though families do fall into arrears with rent,[3] it is generally to meet exceptional needs, and the Board has power correspondingly to reduce the allowances, if rent is persistently unpaid. The standard makes no provision for items other than those stated above. Thus no provision is made for the replacement of household

[1] *Journal of the Royal Statistical Society*, 1937, Part I.

[2] Reports of the "Nutritive value of milk" (Ministry of Health Advisory Committee on Nutrition) and the "Physiological Bases of Nutrition", issued by the Technical Commission appointed by the Nutrition Committee of the League of Nations Health Organization.

[3] In a number of cases arrears of rent were being regularly reduced by small instalments, usually 1*d.*, 2*d.*, or 3*d.* a week. This expenditure has been considered as rent payment.

equipment, insurances (which we shall see later to be almost universal), doctor's fees, medicines, or any of the ordinary small luxuries such as tobacco, newspapers, and recreation. Some money in every household, and in many a fair amount of it, goes in such expenditure. If it was possible to deduct these items from the amount available, a general reduction in standard throughout the sample would be shown. On the other hand, London prices are dearer than prices in most of the districts visited, a factor which tends to work the other way.

We have had to modify the standard for our purposes only in one respect,[1] the fuel allowance. In the Rhondda some part of the fuel used is generally obtained directly or indirectly by coal picking on the tips, or by the co-operative working of the levels. It has been assumed, therefore, that the average weekly expenditure on fuel by Rhondda families is 11*d.* when there are less than five persons in the family and 1*s.* 6*d.* when there are five or more (as compared with 2*s.* 11*d.* and 3*s.* 6*d.* elsewhere except Crook). In Crook, where coal picking is less common, it has been assumed that the average weekly expenditure is 1*s.* 11*d.* and 2*s.* 6*d.*, according to the size of the family. In general we have made no allowance for light and fuel in the case of single men living in lodging-houses, and if they live in rooms only 1*s.* 3*d.* has been allowed for these items; for single men obviously economize in these by going to Public Libraries, etc.

The figures for family income relate throughout the whole sample to the week 20–26 November 1936. Since that time there has been a steady upward movement of prices, and the price level of food was approximately 7½% higher in November 1937 than it was in November 1936. The scales of assistance have not altered, but an announcement made by the Minister of Labour at the time the report was being drafted indicated that the powers which the Board has to deal with cases of need by increasing the allowances would be used to meet the difficulties caused by this rise in the price level, a rise which is naturally felt most acutely during the winter. There is reason to believe, therefore, that rising prices have been in part at least offset by

[1] Apart from a slight modification with regard to clothing; see Appendix IV.

increased allowances. There may well also be substantially more earning members in the households of the long unemployed in 1937 than in 1936. When families are living at the level to which most of these long-unemployed men's families approximate, they are particularly sensitive to any such variation in the cost of living. If the cost of bread goes up ½*d.* a loaf, it means a considerable difference to a large unemployed family. Figures given later[1] suggest that bread is a more important item in the unemployed family's budget than with most employed families, and a rise in price of this order may be the equivalent of a day's ration in the week. What actually happens, of course, is that the consumption of bread, which is "satisfying", is maintained or increased, and a reduction is made elsewhere. The sample visits took place at a time when prices were rising, and when the announcement of the steps to be taken to meet the rise had not yet been made. As a result, rising prices were mentioned frequently by those visited.

The income of an unemployed household may consist only of Unemployment Assistance, or it may be supplemented in various ways. In some families a little extra is earned now and then by the unemployed man doing odd jobs. Some families take in lodgers, and a few have property or small savings of their own. Many have children of working age, who bring in wages or unemployment benefit or allowances. Some have War pensions, Service pensions, Disability pensions, or Workmen's Compensation payments. Members of their families may have Widow's or Old Age pensions, or may be assisted by the Public Assistance Committees or be in receipt of National Health Insurance benefit. The Unemployment Assistance Board has to take some account of all this private and family income when it is assessing the needs of the applicant's household, though a very substantial proportion of it is generally disregarded.

In the sample, 55% were wholly dependent on Unemployment Allowances (or other forms of unemployment relief), 8% were almost wholly so dependent, 18% were mainly so dependent, but had other resources amounting to between a

[1] See p. 135.

quarter and a half of their total income, and 19% received less than half their total income from the Board. The distribution naturally varied between the six towns, and between the different age groups in each town. The position in the six towns was as follows:

TABLE XXX. SOURCES OF INCOME OF THOSE IN THE SAMPLE (MEN ONLY), BY TOWNS

Column I. Income only Unemployment Allowance (or other unemployment relief).

Column II. Unemployment Allowance (or other unemployment relief) more than three-quarters of the total income.

Column III. Unemployment Allowance (or other unemployment relief) between one-half and three-quarters of the total income.

Column IV. Unemployment Allowance (or other unemployment relief) less than one-half of total income.

	I	II	III	IV
Deptford	60 %	2 %	15 %	23 %
Leicester	45	9	20	26
Liverpool	67	5	15	13
Blackburn	36	11	24	29
Rhondda	61	8	15	16
Crook	51	16	23	9
Total	55	8	18	19

Where unemployment most affects families as a whole, in the Special Areas and in Liverpool, dependence on Unemployment Assistance is greatest. It is least in Blackburn, where the practice of both man and wife working often means that, when one is unemployed, the other is not, and in Leicester, where the general prosperity makes it relatively easy for younger members of the family to get work. This factor does not appear in Deptford because there is there a smaller proportion of families, and a larger proportion of the long-unemployed men living on their own, than in Leicester.

These proportions also vary between different ages. Many unemployed young men are living in their parents' homes, where there are others with incomes of their own of some kind, whereas between 25 and 44 the majority of unemployed men are married and have young children, and there are seldom any other sources of income. In the age group 45–54 there were a number of earning children in some of the families, with a corresponding decrease of dependence on Unemployment Assistance, which in the age group 55–64 (when the children have left home) rises again slightly. The figures are given in detail in an appendix.

The results obtained by applying Mr R. F. George's new "Poverty" standard (as modified for our purpose) to the cases in the sample may be summarized as follows:

TABLE XXXI. LONG UNEMPLOYMENT AND POVERTY

	No.	%
(i) Families in "deep poverty" (i.e. with incomes more than 10 % below Mr George's "poverty line")	159	17
(ii) Families in "moderate poverty" (i.e. with incomes less than 10 % below the "poverty line")	120	13
(iii) Families on "subsistence level" (i.e. with incomes less than 10 % above the "poverty line")	137	14
(iv) Families living "a little above the poverty line" (i.e. with incomes between 10 and 25 % above)	174	19
(v) Families living "well above the poverty line" (i.e. with incomes between 25 and 75 % above)	251	27
(vi) Families living in "moderate comfort" (i.e. with incomes more than 75 % above)	91	10
Total families in sample	932	100

Thus three out of every ten of these households of long-unemployed men were living below the George "poverty line" in November 1936. Over half of these were considerably below it. 44% of the families concerned were living at what Mr George would reckon to be bare subsistence level or below it.

A further analysis of the figures brings out several important facts. It shows the different relationships in which households stand in regard to our "poverty line", according to whether they depend wholly on the Unemployment Assistance Board for their income or have other resources. 80% of the cases living in poverty (i.e. in Groups (i) and (ii)) were cases wholly dependent on the Unemployment Assistance Board for their income. Of all those in the sample wholly dependent on the Board, two in five were living "in poverty" (see Table A 6, p. 424). The households of the "Means Test" cases, on the other hand (that is, those where there is income from earnings), were relatively speaking well situated. This point reminds us that the application of a poverty standard to the family income as a whole does not necessarily give a fair picture of the position of each of its members. The impression left by this particular type of case was that the parents were sometimes living at an exceptionally low standard (at least so far as the condition of clothes is a fair indication), the figures concealing two different levels in the household.

Analysis of the figures brings out also the local differences in respect of poverty between the various towns in the sample. Thus Table A 5 shows that the proportion of those below the "poverty line" in Liverpool is nearly a half, whereas in the other five places it was (except in Leicester, where the figure was 30%) under a quarter. And when we speak later of the high domestic standards in the Rhondda and Crook, we shall have to bear in mind that families there were on the whole considerably better off than in Liverpool. The reasons for these differences are complex. In the Rhondda and to some extent in Crook, real income was increased by the fact that fuel is obtainable cheap, while in Crook there were several "amenity" schemes working at the time of the sample which meant an increase in family income. In Blackburn there was a high proportion of earners in the households, and corresponding to this, a smaller proportion living actually "in poverty", though it is surprising how low, nevertheless, is the proportion living in the two relatively prosperous groups. In Liverpool, where there was much more poverty than elsewhere, a large number of factors have to be taken into account. Most important of them is the very high proportion of large families, and it is significant that Leicester, the other place where there was a fairly large proportion of such families, comes next to Liverpool in the proportion of those living "in poverty".[1]

One other thing which the figures bring out must be emphasized, that the incidence of poverty is progressively greater according to the number of children under working age in the family concerned. The age group where most large families are found is 35–44. Table B 4 shows that 50% of the cases in this age group were living below the George "poverty line", and these include the vast majority of men with families of two or more children. The high percentage "in poverty" in the 25–34 age group is, of course, also explained by the family men within it. This appears at first sight to be a peculiarly desperate situation, and it is indeed bad enough, but there are reasons for it. We have seen already that the unemployed man with a large family is living at something near the level at which the labourer in steady employment is living. The latter, as the former, may well be below our "poverty line". Poverty of this kind, then, is not particularly associated with unemployment, and to cure it will need something more than to get back the men concerned to work. And we shall see later that the approximation of wages to allowances is certainly and naturally a factor in a man's attitude to work. It is almost inevitable that if a man can get as much out of work as he can working, the desire for work should become less imperative. There is obviously here a dilemma which is not easily resolved. But if we take the Liverpool situation as an example, it becomes at once apparent how serious things are. Of the 97 families with two or more children under 14, 83 were living below the "poverty line". The progressive figures illustrate the facts even more vividly. Of the 38 families where there was only one child of school age, 20 were living below the poverty line; 21 of the 31 families where there were two children of school age; 24 of the 26 families where there

[1] For further reasons, see above, pp. 97-99.

were three children; all 13 families where there were four, and 25 of 27 families where there were five or more children below school age. And even in such a prosperous place as Leicester, offering many opportunities for the older children in large families to earn good wages, though 11 families with one or two children of school age or under were living above the "poverty line" as against 6 below, of the 15 families with three or more children of school age or under, 13 were living below the "poverty line".

The immediate effect on the children is not necessarily as serious as might appear, though we shall record below our impression that there is a greater degree of ill health in the large families which must come partly from the circumstances in which they are living. All of us were agreed that in most unemployed families the parents, and in particular the wives, bore the burden of want, and in many instances were literally starving themselves in order to feed and clothe the children reasonably well. But the indirect effects on the children are of course very great. They are inevitably growing up to accept low material standards, and growing up in an atmosphere of strain. Both these factors are going to play an important, though as yet not precisely calculable part in their lives. It will not be surprising if many of them feel that their future, to use the words spoken by one of the unemployed men in the sample to one of us, is to "stand behind their father in the queue". The families which are said to be living below the poverty line are not necessarily living just below it. In some cases the family income falls 20%, in some actually 30% or even more, short of what we have taken as a bare minimum standard; a standard that, in itself, leaves nothing for items on which almost all of them, as we have seen, do spend. Humanity is tough, and families may become accustomed to a low level of existence; but if they do, we can be certain that it will mean worse difficulties in the next generation.

The question, therefore, must be from what direction can the attack on this poverty best be made? Is the raising of allowances in itself a wholly satisfactory solution, and, if not, what are its limitations?

The facts we have given suggest that Unemployment Assistance, based on the scales in force at the sample date, was providing maintenance at a standard which, in view of the circumstances, was a reasonable one for many of those in receipt of it. Because all long-unemployed families are living on so narrow a margin, it is of primary importance that the scales should be sensitive to relatively small increases in the cost of living; and for calculating that cost, the peculiar features of the unemployed family's budget (e.g. the disproportionately large expenditure on bread) would provide a fairer guide than a general index of prices, if it were possible to make such a modification. The use of the Board's powers to meet exceptional needs in order to provide for rising prices may be the most satisfactory way of dealing with this situation.

There is another large group, however, approximately two in five of those dependent solely on Unemployment Assistance, for whom Unemployment Assistance provides maintenance at a level that cannot be defended except on grounds of maintaining the wage incentive. In the bulk of such cases this is, unfortunately, a valid reason against any general increase. We discuss this point later in a section dealing with the unemployed man's attitude to work. There is every reason to think that a general increase of allowances where it is most needed would enlarge the volume of unemployment. And because long unemployment is in itself a serious menace to the mind and physique of those who suffer it, such an increase must be avoided. The only safe way to attack this problem is to raise the wage level. It is essentially a problem of wages, not of allowance rates. This does not mean it can be shelved. If something is not done the consequences may be very serious indeed. In another chapter we discuss this problem further.

The case of the long-unemployed men over 50 or thereabouts is different. However much they want work, it is exceedingly difficult for them to get it. Though the figures show that these men are not living in such poverty as the younger men with large families, they deserve special consideration. We discuss later what is the best form that consideration should take.

(*d*) *Housekeeping, Good and Bad; Types of Household*

Though the amount of money available, measured by some needs standard, is obviously a matter of prime importance, it is equally plain that the good housekeeper has an enormous advantage over the bad, and that the answer to the question whether a family is actually living in poverty or not depends largely on the competence of the housewife. There was a great variety of conditions with regard to housekeeping and to expenditure on food. In some places such as Liverpool, even the exceptionally well-managed households never seemed to use fresh milk, while in others, Blackburn or Crook, fresh milk was the rule and tinned milk unusual. At one end of the scale were households where everything was clean, where the food was home-made and wholesome, and at the other those households where four or five people were living in one room, the floor littered with breadcrumbs and other scraps of food, empty tins on the table, filthy linen and an indescribably horrible smell. In all six towns visited, as might be expected from the description given above of the types of unemployment in each, there were some examples of these low-grade households representing in each the "residual problem", as there were also exceptionally good houses. Apart from these exceptions, however, there was no mistaking the characteristic differences; in Crook and in the Rhondda on the whole high standards of household management with a real feeling of traditional culture about the best of the homes; in Blackburn some households competently run, but fewer signs that a pleasant home had ever been appreciated for its own sake, and the sense that the mill had left little time for the home; in Leicester and the better type of Deptford household, rather ordinary equipment, more evidence of food being bought ready cooked or in tins, and of cheap clothing bought for the family from a multiple store, instead of made for them by the mother; in Liverpool these features greatly magnified, coupled with very bad housing conditions and dilapidation both of houses and equipment. Thus in a typical Welsh household of the best type when one of us called late in the afternoon, tea was on the table on a spotlessly clean white tablecloth. It consisted of tea and fresh milk, bread and butter and cheese, home-made cake and home-made jam. In a typical Liverpool family, where there were two children, aged 4 and 12, the family had nothing but bread, margarine and tea, with condensed milk, for breakfast and dinner, "but we always try to give them something hot for tea. We go to bed early so as not to feel hungry." Families in districts where there is a good tradition of household management, or where the housewife has been brought up in a good home, are obviously better able to resist the material effects of unemployment. In Crook and in the Rhondda, house after house was well kept and well managed, while in Liverpool house after house was dreary and ill-equipped.

Another general factor that affected the quality of household management was the age of the case and the type of household concerned. The young married couples, sometimes with one or two children, fall into two groups: first, those who are making an effort to form a home, and are concerned to keep the house clean and do what they can for the children; and secondly, those who care little about home-making and live in squalor. A typical instance of the former in Liverpool was a milk roundsman, aged 30, with a wife his age and a boy of 4. He drew 29*s.* unemployment assistance. Rent was 7*s.* 6*d.*, the rent of a tiny three-roomed house in one of the notorious old Liverpool "courts". They paid out 3*s.* 6*d.* a week for clothing clubs, 2*s.* 6*d.* a week for coal, and 10*d.* insurances, leaving 14*s.* 8*d.* a week for everything else for the three of them. The housewife was evidently competent (she had indeed managed the branch of the dairy where her husband had worked) so that the house was very clean and tidy and all the family were well clothed. It was interesting to note that even in a household of this quality in Liverpool, condensed milk was used. Plainly this household went short in various ways (they were below the "poverty line") and the housewife said that at the beginning of the week she sometimes had to go to the pawnshop, though she never had made a habit of it. As an example of the other group, we may take an apprentice printer in Liverpool, aged 19, who had broken his apprenticeship to marry a girl of 16. The baby was born before his wife was 17. He was rather surly in manner, and they were living in dirty surroundings. The clothes of wife and child were very bad. They were paying 3*s*. a week into a clothing club, and were buying some wretchedly poor furniture on hire purchase at 2*s*. 6*d*. a week, a sign incidentally that they had some rudimentary home-making instincts; all of which, with 7*s*. a week rent for two rooms, left 16*s*. 6*d*. for all other necessities. Among the young married couples the better type was in the majority.

The low material standard allowed for a large family by the present assistance rates means that in few families with four or more children is it possible to maintain the equipment of the household, renew shoes and clothes and also buy sufficient food. Naturally enough it is the food that is bought first, and the equipment either deteriorates steadily or is sold. But we have seen already that these families are living under conditions approximating to the normal for a working-class family of their type, a fact which is almost invariably noticeable in the whole demeanour of the men concerned. There was generally little in the way of furniture for these large families beyond the bare necessities, a table and a few chairs, often broken; but there was also, very often, a general happy-go-lucky air of contentment, due to this fact, that they are living at a "normal" level. A typical Liverpool family in this class, a few shillings better off than they might have been because the eldest son had just begun to earn, consisted of man and wife aged 36 and 35, and six children aged 2 to 14, the last a shop-boy earning 10*s*. a week. The Unemployment Allowance was 42*s*. 6*d*., and with rent at 12*s*. 6*d*., this left 40*s*. for the eight of them. The living-room, small for such a family, was in rather a muddle, and the furniture meagre; the family boots were not very good, and the small daughter's toes were showing through her shoes. A hen in the backyard spiritedly provided in good weeks an egg a day, earmarked at the time of the visit for the mother-in-law, ill down the road, but usually kept for the two small children. The day of the visit was "scrubbing-out day", which meant that after the family was in bed, father would scrub out the living-room and scullery. He said his time was fairly full with the family, and the domestic atmosphere was very pleasant. It was among such families that bad management and poor furniture were chiefly recorded. They did indeed vary to some extent, but almost all of them allowed equipment to deteriorate and had concentrated their efforts on food and necessary clothing.

In the normal working-class cycle, the couple in the late fifties and sixties live on their own and are comparatively "well off". The elderly couples on Unemployment Assistance whom we interviewed were for the most part living on 26*s.* a week, which places them, save in exceptional circumstances, above our "poverty line". Their houses were on the whole well managed, and in places where there is a domestic tradition, such as the Rhondda and Crook, or in the "skilled worker" type of home elsewhere, there are marks of taste in the homes of the older couples which make the hire-purchase furniture in those of the younger appear tawdry by comparison. But there is a hopelessness in such homes which is one of the most terrible features of the unemployment problem. It is virtually certain that they will go on at the present rate until the husband is 65 and ceases to be eligible for Unemployment Assistance. Then he will get the old age pension, 10*s.* a week, "and", as one of them said, "I suppose we'll have to go somewhere else for a little bit of extra", i.e. to the Relieving Officer. That will almost certainly mean a drop even as compared with the present level. Many of those whose husbands had been semi-skilled workers were wondering whether they would be able to keep the home together on the pension. A typical South Wales budget for an old couple shows them receiving 26*s.* a week and paying 6*s.* 3*d.* rent, leaving 19*s.* 9*d.* for all other expenses.

The single man is in a class by himself. The majority of those in the sample were receiving 17*s.*, unless they were living with relatives, though for those living in lodging-houses the allowance was sometimes less, and in exceptional cases it might be more. Sometimes the single man is able by living in a lodging-house and taking meals with his family to get the full allowance, though he is in fact living at home. Of those living on their own, the better type often pay 15*s.* for full board and lodging, keeping 2*s.* for their personal expenses. The majority generally pay 4*s.* or 5*s.* for a lodging-house bed and bring their own food in, cooking it on the stove in the common living-room. Sometimes they live alone in a single room, which tends to be at best a picture of desolation and at worst a filthy hovel, only surpassed by the conditions that two young single men, sharing a room between them, seem to be able to tolerate.

(*e*) *The Reduction of Income due to Unemployment; Economies and Debts*

The fact that households fall into the general types that have been discussed above at once raises a question that is central to this whole problem—the question of the relations between Unemployment Assistance and possible wages. How much of that poverty with which the sample brought us into contact is actually due to unemployment? Or to put it in another way, how does the income level in such families compare with that which would be available if they were earning? Unfortunately our material does not make such a comparison possible except with considerable reservations. By courtesy of the Unemployment Assistance Board we were able to obtain particulars in each case of the figure taken for official purposes to represent the wage that each man might reasonably be expected to earn. This figure cannot be considered as an entirely accurate estimate, and it probably overstates the wage in some instances. For the present, however, we take it as affording an approximate means of comparing income in and out of employment.

The proportion in the sample as a whole of cases receiving more than 70% of their wage as Unemployment Assistance is just over a fifth (21%). If we eliminate those cases in which Unemployment Assistance is supplementary to wages earned by other members of the family and does not form the main income, the proportion is substantially larger. We shall confine ourselves to this group, i.e. those cases in which Unemployment

Assistance forms the main income of the household. A comparison between the average wage and the average allowance in families in this group, classified according to the age of the applicant for assistance, yields the following results.

TABLE XXXII. INCOME IN AND OUT OF EMPLOYMENT. MEN ONLY

(Average wage for each age group compared with average allowance, in cases where Unemployment Assistance is main source of income. Cases where allowances are reduced on account of other sources of income excluded.)

Ages	(1) Average wage	(2) Average U.A.B. allowance	(3) (2) as % of (1)
	s. d.	*s. d.*	
18–24	33 7	22 4	66
25–34	45 0	29 3	65
35–44	50 1	32 5	65
45–54	51 0	26 8	52
55–64	49 9	22 6	45

Table XXXII has to be read, as we have said already, with reservations. In Blackburn for instance average wages were very low indeed, and if Blackburn were eliminated the results would be substantially different, figures in column (1) being correspondingly higher. Moreover, "average wage" covers a considerable range of wages, from 20*s.* to 70*s.* or 80*s.*, and, to get a fully adequate picture, column (1) ought to be split up into income groups, and there ought to be a further subdivision by family status. But as the number of skilled men in the sample was relatively small, the spread of wages is not so great as might be suspected.

There are, however, certain points that can be seen in these figures. They show how those families where there are several children (which occur mainly in the 25–44 age groups) are living nearest to the level at which they would live if the applicant were at work. Since this comparison is between Unemployment Assistance and gross wages (and eliminates, therefore, such items as wear and tear to clothes when a man is working, the need for extra pocket money, contributions, etc.) it substantially understates the closeness of the approximation, and if the figures were given by the size of families, the result would be far more striking. Moreover, the figures cannot bring out the importance of a steady income which Unemployment Assistance provides, a gain that may be, for the casual worker, considerable.

We give details in another section which suggest that for a semi-skilled worker in one district of Wales, for which a special analysis was carried out, the difference between Unemployment Assistance and possible wage is probably negligible if a man has more than three children. Of the 936 men in the sample as a whole, 158 had four or more dependents, and it is probable that for the great majority of these unemployment means little reduction in the standard of life. For most of those with six or more dependents, numbering 59, it may be an actual advantage in that the income it provides is more regular than what the casual worker would get. This will, of course, be specially true for those of them who from an employer's point of view are worth only a low wage, and if a man's market value in this way is low, it may pay him to become unemployed even if he has only one or two dependents. Many able-bodied men are drawing wages as low as 15*s*. a week with keep, or 20*s*. or 25*s*. a week and keeping themselves. If such men marry, Unemployment Assistance actually brings up the level at which they are living. Though an estimate is precarious, we may not be far wrong in supposing that about a fifth of those on Unemployment Assistance are as well off, or better off, than they would be working. Our observation which has already been recorded, that in the households with a number of children there was often a relatively carefree and happy-go-lucky atmosphere is no doubt primarily due to this fact, though we ought perhaps to remind ourselves again that the income of most such households is very low indeed when reckoned against a needs standard.

What is equally significant for our present purpose is the disparities that the table shows between the normal level and unemployment level for the great majority of unemployed households. This is particularly marked with the older men.

For them unemployment means a reduction to less than half the amount that would ordinarily be earned. Those who remember the effects on their own standards of reductions amounting to 5 or 10% made at the time of the slump are in a position to appreciate what the effects of a reduction, which cuts income by a half, will be. And even when the reduction is smaller, it is often sufficiently large for it to be almost insupportable for men who have been used to a regular wage, though in a place like Liverpool (where the great majority of those out of work have always been accustomed to spells of unemployment and reduced income) it is a different matter. The elderly miners in Crook or the Rhondda, the elderly factory workers in Leicester, and the elderly weavers in Blackburn have all been used to regular work, year after year, at a wage that is often understated rather than overstated by the figures from which the "average", given above, was obtained. This is what gives the sting of unemployment much of its virulence, the state, not of those who are living below the "poverty line" and might anyway be doing so, but of those who are living just above it, whereas, if they were in normal employment, they would be relatively comfortably situated.

Three cases may be quoted to illustrate this. All three families were living above the "poverty line" that we have used, and were cases where the management of the household was exceptionally good. The first is a young couple—for the same may apply to a young couple as well as an old where the man has been used to regular employment at a decent wage. Their ages were 26 and 23, and they were visited in Liverpool on a bitter February afternoon. It was snowing outside. The house could hardly have been better kept and both of them were neatly, though not at all flashily, dressed. Yet there was no fire, and so far that day (it was 3 o'clock) they had had nothing to eat, only cups of tea. They lit the fire when one of us came in, for the man said "his mother had just helped them out with a bit of coal", and so they could manage it. He said his wife "had something for the evening" and that "they weren't starved, though sometimes they had to go pretty short". The explanation of their position was partly that it was Thursday afternoon (the significance of which we shall see later), partly that this couple deliberately preferred living in an expensive house (the additional rent of which the Unemployment Assistance Board helped them largely, though not of course wholly, to meet), maintaining the house well, and spending rather more money than others on their clothes. There was no question of amusements that would have been extravagant for their circumstances; they had given up going to the cinema. The fact is that living on Unemployment Assistance does involve such a choice for a household that has high standards. The man's own statement that "they were not starved, though sometimes they had to go pretty short" applies to hundreds of other young couples living in such circumstances. If he had had good employment, their income would probably have been twice what it was.

The other two cases are also those of couples with no children, one in the Rhondda and one in Leicester. But they were both elderly, and we quote them to illustrate the point made above, that where a good wage has come regularly into the household, it is particularly difficult to become accustomed to the rates which Unemployment Assistance necessarily imposes. They were both indeed couples who in the interests and habits they had formed while the husband was in normal employment were almost middle class in character, and the Leicester home might from its equipment and decoration have been a middle-class home. They are a reminder that, especially in those districts where there is a considerable degree of industrial unemployment, thousands of families with standards and interests similar to those of the middle classes are living at the level we describe.

The South Wales example is that of a middle-aged collier, stopped through nystagmus. He had worked regularly all his life, never been much to clubs, never drank, and while he was a working collier any spare time he had was spent sleeping. "In the winter I never saw the sun except on Saturday and Sunday very often." His one recreation had been a motor bicycle, on which he used to go out with his wife at the week-ends, but unemployment meant giving that up, his one interest in life outside his work, just at the time he needed it most. No one could suggest that Unemployment Assistance should be raised to a level that would make it possible for this man to maintain a motor bicycle. Nor could they suggest a level which would have enabled the Leicester family to maintain its former habits: "If you want to know how it was with us when we were working, it was like this. Work, holidays, appearance, decent food. We never spent anything on the pictures or anything like that. Every Easter and Whitsun holiday we'd go somewhere interesting and go somewhere to stay in August. Well, now the work's gone, the holidays have had to go altogether, appearances have had to go partly, and the food too partly." The point is the contrast between the old level and the new, a contrast which is sharpened by the awareness (which both these men mentioned) that though they have many years of good work left in them, the prospects of their ever working again are on the present showing negligible. Long unemployment is not simply a problem of the "down and outs". It is also a problem of those who may perforce be gradually reduced to their condition, who are living on a sum that makes maintenance possible, but does not allow anything beyond it. There may perhaps be some way in which such families can be officially helped. Obviously, they set for the voluntary agencies a task that is *sui generis* and in a place like Leicester, for instance, where both types exist in considerable numbers among the elderly unemployed, quite different types of social organization might be contemplated for each of them.

These are the cases in which poverty, or at least hardship, is due directly to unemployment, and is not simply part of the general working-class background. Between such cases, where income has been approximately halved, and those who are living near the income they would often obtain from employment, there is a steady gradation of families. But the lowering of the income level caused by unemployment in something like 80% of unemployed families (if the estimate we have given above is correct) means that the outlines of poverty, which from all accounts are clearly marked throughout the working-class homes of Liverpool, are sharply emphasized among the long unemployed there, and that among the long unemployed everywhere they stand out distinctly, if not so obviously as in Liverpool. It is doubtless true that among the working classes and also among the middle classes a "weekly cycle" is often observed in the household, running from the day when the woman who keeps house is paid her money. In the unemployed home this cycle becomes painfully obvious, because the income level is lower, and because, at least for the long unemployed, there is no possibility of elasticity or credit. "The day you get your money and the day after", said an old man living half underground in a basement room in Liverpool, "are the only days that you get any relish; otherwise it is just bread and butter." No doubt the bread and butter is varied occasionally by a threepenny packet of fish and chips. But anyone who has visited many of these old men living on their own knows that there is something in what he says. They have little skill in managing their money, spend it largely on cooked foods, and as a result many of them certainly go short towards the end of their week. Remarks made by many housewives, both those who are competent and those who are not, emphasize the same point. One mark of this weekly cycle in pawnshop-ridden neighbourhoods such as parts of Liverpool, is that Sunday suits and any other likely articles go into the pawnshop at the beginning of the week, to be redeemed again, if they are lucky, on Saturday. In Liverpool two out of three unemployed families admit to having goods in pawn, and in some instances the whole economy of the home is so much dominated by the pawnshop that as soon as the clothes are bought through a clothing club, they go into the pawnshop and are never redeemed; and the clothing club thus becomes an even more uneconomical way of "saving". This process was described to us in Liverpool homes. In one, which was exceptionally well managed, the woman had had to pawn her engagement and wedding rings, and the watch given her on her twenty-first birthday by her husband, to meet the cost of an illness, and in others similar details were given. In no other place had pawning anything like such a hold as it evidently had in Liverpool.

On the other hand, elsewhere credit had taken other forms. When they are allowed to do so, families default on the rent to meet any sudden expense, and in the great coal lock-out of 1926 large arrears of rent accumulated in South Wales that have not yet been paid off. There were families in the sample in South Wales where arrears of rent amounted to £50 or £60. Rent arrears seemed to be spaced fairly evenly throughout the sample, with the younger families if anything more ready to run them up than the older. With other forms of debt there was a peak in that age group, 35–44, which contains the large families.

The majority of unemployed families buy clothing through a "club" into which they pay a shilling or two a week for the family—as also that impossibly recurrent item, children's shoes (if they get bought at all). These clubs are said to vary in character greatly from place to place. In Liverpool social workers seem to be in general agreement that it is a most uneconomic form of purchase and that the buyer drops something like one shilling in every three. It has been suggested that the Co-operative Societies could do a valuable service for the unemployed by providing clubs for those who want to buy clothing, and from what we heard of the clubs in Liverpool it seemed that, there at least, this would meet a pressing need. Many of the housewives there with whom we spoke complained of them, and some of the more ingenious had devised saving systems of their own. One, in a Corporation house in Liverpool, had asked to be allowed to pay the rent collector each week a little more than the rent. When the week came round that she had saved a week's rent in this way, the rent money was available for clothes.

All these factors—debts, pawning, and the difficulty of saving for major items of expenditure, are no doubt apparent in many working-class homes, but there is also no doubt that they appear far more clearly in those of the long unemployed. So, too, the necessity for economies becomes keener, and a great variety of forms of saving were described to us which, though many homes may have practised them before, were evidently associated, in the minds of those with whom we talked, with unemployment; walking farther to buy in a cheap market (an economy which is not easy to practise when there are small babies in the family), burning oil instead of gas, going to bed early so as to avoid using lights, or getting up late so as to do with only a cup of tea instead of breakfast. Picking coal from the tips is almost universal in South Wales, and (as most unemployed families everywhere evidently live to a remarkable extent on coal, as the warmth of the living room shows) it is a substantial saving. In reckoning the value of the allowances in South Wales we have felt it necessary, in order to get a reasonably fair comparative picture, to make certain adjustments on this account in the figures (see above, p. 106).

A feature that was noticeable in almost every household was the refusal to economize on the food or clothing for the children, though the parents would go short. Even in Liverpool this was the rule, and the cases where the children were in rags, while the parents were better dressed, were rare and almost always went with very low general standards. In several instances great efforts were being made to keep the children at school till 16, "even if we have to starve for it. Education is the only thing that matters now." It is common for the record to contain such notes as these: "Children very pleasant, rosy cheeks, clean white regular teeth; disproportionate amount spent on children who are neatly and sensibly clothed and appeared to be well fed and extremely healthy. Parents determined to do their best for them. Wife seems undernourished." "Children look in good health, wife is very thin." "Evidently this is a case where the wife goes short to give the children enough food and clothes." "They don't mind paying a few shillings extra in order to give their children better surroundings. They sacrifice in every way so that the children don't go short of anything; children had eggs, milk, cheese for the evening meal and certainly look healthy enough. The only luxury is once a month together to the cinema (adventure films)." The stress in cases like those just quoted comes because the mother is trying to keep up appearances as well as to buy a reasonable amount of food for the children. When they let things go and live anyhow among dilapidated surroundings, the strain is not so severe.

The facts are shown in the following analysis of all those families in Liverpool, where there were two or more children under 14, which were successfully visited. It is based of course only on impressions (though in many cases these impressions were the result of repeated visits) but as it is only the comparative figures that are important this does not make it any less valid. By confining ourselves to the larger families, we exclude a number of the more careful instances, where special thought is given to the child's welfare, and this makes the result even more significant.

TABLE XXXIII. LIVERPOOL: FAMILIES VISITED WITH TWO OR MORE CHILDREN UNDER 14. HEALTH AND CARE OF CHILDREN

(80 families; 10 above poverty line, 70 below. Effective visits only reckoned.)

Wife healthy	27
Children healthy	46
Wife unhealthy	26
Child or children unhealthy	19
Special efforts noted to care for children	14
Neglect of children noted	4

In approximately a third of the families visited, the wife was said to be unhealthy, anaemia or nervous debility being the two descriptions most often given. In rather less than a quarter of the families one or more of the children was in poor health. The number of instances where it was specified in our records that the parents were making special efforts for the care of their children was more than three times the number where the children were specifically described as neglected. Yet the great majority of these families—seven out of every eight—were living below the "poverty line" and many of them in "deep poverty". The analysis brings out clearly how the wives bear the brunt of unemployment in these large families. What it does not bring out is the only thing which makes it possible for them to bear such conditions—the fact that they are something like normal for those in as well as for those out of work in Liverpool.

(*f*) *Income Level and Environment—Poverty and Unemployability*

The general thesis that local and family traditions play a large part in determining the way in which the home is managed is irrefutable, and the description of Liverpool given in an earlier section provides a substantial part of the explanation why the Liverpool visits left such a deep impression of poverty. Households do not in fact spend their incomes as we suppose them theoretically to be spent. They follow the lead of those around them, or of their parents. There were, for instance, a number of cases of young single men in Liverpool who were nearly starving themselves because they must needs go to the cinema two or three days a week, and this because there was a number of them doing it and it began to seem the obvious thing to do.

Yet it is also certain and could hardly be otherwise, that the actual level of the family's income (measured on any standard that is varied according to its size) plays a considerable part in determining the kind of management that is possible. Thus the fact that the Rhondda houses were, on the whole, better managed than the Liverpool houses is almost certainly due in part to the higher net income which the Rhondda families can be shown to have had available (see above, p. 110) at the time the sample was taken, as also in part to the larger and more regular incomes they had had in the past. We find a similar close connexion if we split the figures up by age. The poorest of the ten-year age groups, as we shall see, is the group 35–44 where the large families occur. That is also where household management appeared to be the worst and where clothing seemed to be the worst. However good the management, one shilling cannot be made to do as much as two, and it might be questioned therefore how far our impressions of definitely bad management in these cases are to be trusted. Is not the truth of the matter rather that these housewives were faced with an impossibly hard task?

This is a question that is difficult to answer. The contrast in appearance between households in Liverpool and the Rhondda stands out sharply, and the figures show a similar contrast between incomes in both places, those in Liverpool being exceptionally low, those in the Rhondda exceptionally high (see Table A 10, p. 426). But the reason why the level in Liverpool was low makes it dangerous to assume too readily that there is a direct causal connexion between the two. It lies mainly in the disproportionate number of very large families there. These may be in themselves characteristic of the more happy-go-lucky type of household, which is that in which equipment and clothing and general domestic standards are allowed to deteriorate.

A comparison between the large families in Liverpool and those in Leicester does not yield any more definite result. The domestic standards of the Leicester families living on an income level comparable with those in Liverpool do seem to have been on the whole higher, but the numbers are not sufficiently large for any certain conclusions to be drawn. Here and there in the sample, however, there was a strong suggestion that the low level at which the large families were living had only been accepted after a period of struggle, and was not a "natural" level at all, but one imposed by the income available. A Welsh household comes to mind, in which there were seven children, the parents' ages being 36 and 32. The allowance was 43*s.* 6*d.*, and we reckoned the value of milk from the clinic and of free milk in school for two of the children at an extra 2*s.* With 8*s.* rent, this left 37*s.* 6*d.* available as against 52*s.* 1*d.* required by our "poverty" standard. The man was physically a very fine type, and was active-minded and intelligent. He had formerly been chairman of the local club, and was evidently a leader in the society in which he lived. Though the house was not particularly dirty, it was not clean, the furniture was meagre and in pieces, the clothes of all of them very ragged, and the general impression given was that any attempt to maintain standards in such matters had been abandoned as hopeless. Yet one of the daughters had recently gone to service in London, and her photograph showed a girl of neat pleasant appearance. It seemed that the family—which was not unduly large for South Wales—had not lost the consciousness of the standards that might be maintained, but that they had given up struggling to maintain them in the home. There is obviously a vicious circle, for when the task once gets beyond them, the effort to carry it through becomes progressively more ineffective. This is why in so many instances in Liverpool our record notes that the wife "looks years older than she is". While therefore the importance of the traditional factor has to be recognized, so should that of this other factor also. Yet, here again we must beware of asserting too roundly that unemployment is responsible. In the case just given, it can be stated categorically that it was not, for the man's normal wage was 45*s*. 6*d*., and if he had been earning it, his children would not have been eligible for the milk they were getting.

The point is one of the highest importance. Is unemployment causing a lowering of standards so marked that there is in districts where prolonged unemployment has been widespread, the danger of producing a pauper class? In our analysis of residual unemployment, as it is seen in prosperous places, we have noticed that the most intractable element is probably the low-grade social type, who live in bad conditions, who get enough to support them at their own low standards in those conditions, and whom it would be almost impossible to get back to work in any circumstances.[1] We saw that unemployment of this type occurs in the Special Areas, though it is not always so obvious there owing to the extent of the industrial unemployment that conceals it. If we take the effective visits in the Rhondda, about 17 out of 196 were living in really dirty and neglected surroundings. None of them had any of the initiative which, with things as they are in the Rhondda, is necessary to get a man back to work, and the majority evidently were content to go on as they were, living in squalor. They were spaced fairly evenly throughout the different age groups. But a significant fact is that most of them (unlike the P.A.C. cases of long un-

[1] This will be found strikingly illustrated in the figures on p. 438, showing the correlation between Attitude to Employment and Domestic Standards.

employment in Deptford, who were also of this rather low social type) had at some time in their lives had reasonably good employment. It is hard to believe that when they were in regular work, it had no effects on the standards at which they then lived—even if it meant only smarter clothing and more extravagant food. Nine of them, that is, something over 50%, were living below the poverty line.

Has unemployment reduced them to this condition or have they always belonged to it? In one or two instances we felt we could state fairly confidently that the family had been of that type even when the man was working; in one or two it was stated that deterioration might be due to unemployment. It is clearly a question which on appearances alone cannot easily be decided.

Yet there were some features of these Rhondda cases that were very significant. If we consider the families in this low-grade category which were living substantially above the "poverty line", for instance, we find that in two of them what brings them above it is the fact that there are earnings coming in from one or more of the younger members of the family. It is at least possible that in these cases the low standards that resulted from the father's prolonged unemployment before the children started to earn have not been improved even though there is now a possibility of improvement; and in one of them, significantly, besides the father, aged 57, there are two able-bodied younger men, aged 28 and 36, unemployed. The evidence may not be absolutely conclusive, but it certainly looks as if a deterioration in the social grade of the family was being produced. In another case (also well above the poverty line), the father, a man with a good working record, had been out of work since 1926. The two sons aged 22 and 24 are long unemployed, and have steadily refused to take any form of training. They had grown up in an atmosphere of unemployment, and it is hardly surprising. Another case is that of a man of 36, with a wife and five children. He used to be a collier, but has been permanently out of work since 1930. The eldest son, aged 15, has now started to work underground, and his 17*s*. a week brings the family above the poverty line; but their standards are still very low, and when the son of 15 is stopped (as he well may be like others in the industry) at 21, it will not be difficult for him to adjust his outlook to prolonged unemployment, for household standards are closely connected with attitude to work, and where they are low, attitude to work is indifferent or positively "work-shy". Another is a case where there is mental disease in the family, which explains well enough the general low standards, but it is hard to believe that when the man was in regular work, as he used to be, things were not better. In another case there are three young children now earning, and the family of eight has an income of over £6 a week, yet standards do not improve. Only one or two are cases where the man has never been a worker but always a "sponger", such as one of 46, with six children, who has done 32 weeks' work in the last fifteen years. Such cases strongly suggest that, sometimes at least, unemployment has led to a lowering of standards that has proved permanent, and that in one or two there is another unemployable family coming into being. Another case in the Rhondda may be quoted where deterioration had, as it were, gone half-way, to show how the thing happens. This was a middle-aged couple with three daughters (11, 15 and 17—the last being able to add a little, 4*s.* a week, to the family's income by doing some work as a shop assistant) and two sons, aged 20 and 21, who were at a local technical school. The man had been in skilled employment underground, earning a high wage, till thrown out of work by the 1926 lock-out. After that he had taken to business on his own account, and had failed. In consequence of this failure he was considered ineligible for a time for unemployment relief and was "on the parish", getting, as he and his wife said, a sum in comparison with which the 49*s.* they were now getting, though it left them below our poverty line, was wealth. But they were struggling to keep the boys at a Technical School, in the hope that they might become handicraft teachers, so that there was nothing over for extras, and evidently in the difficult period through which the family had passed the household equipment had gone to pieces and had never been renewed. The man was listless and apathetic, and it was evident that so far as he was concerned he hardly minded whether it was renewed or not. Yet he had been in a highly paid responsible position, and what was being done for the two boys showed that in some ways the old standards were still there.

Herein obviously lies one of the main dangers of prolonged unemployment. If we allow standards to be reduced, we are allowing a class to grow up that is unemployable. Poverty is not only a consequence of unemployment but a cause of it. It is this that makes the case (such as might be suggested by what we have to say about the connexion between low wages and unemployment) against a reduction of allowances unanswerable. Higher allowances alone will solve very few problems. But low allowances will certainly create them—and problems of the kind that we can least afford to create. No one denies that individual abilities count—that there are badly placed families who manage, and well placed families who do not. But there can be no reasonable doubt that prolonged unemployment does tend inevitably to lower the material standards of the families suffering from it, and that if this process goes too far that group of unemployables—unemployable not only for physical, but also for mental and moral reasons—which is the real "hard core" of unemployment will be enlarged.

(*g*) *Health*

In attempting to discuss the effects of unemployment on health we are again on difficult ground. None of us had the medical experience necessary for a thorough study, and such a study would have needed to include employed families as well as unemployed, for comparison. All we can do therefore is to state certain impressions, and see how far these can be confirmed by such objective material as is otherwise available.

With regard to the effects of unemployment on the health of the men concerned—as opposed to their families—it is difficult, here too, to distinguish the actual results of unemployment from conditions associated with it. The obvious example is the bad condition of teeth, both among unemployed men themselves and among their wives. This was noticeable almost everywhere, but most noticeable in Liverpool; which suggests that it is in fact associated with poverty in general rather than unemployment in particular, except perhaps as a cause of unemployment. The sample visits in Liverpool indicated that something over a quarter of the long-unemployed men in Liverpool, and a considerable number of their wives, either had no teeth at all or else had very bad teeth. This was not confined to the poorest types, one reason being that the need for teeth is one that can be met in Liverpool by the Public Assistance Committees, and as a medical need the U.A.B. has no power to do so. In several instances men had been told by the Board's officers to apply to the Public Assistance Committee for teeth, but refused to do so because of the stigma which still attaches in a few people's minds to the acceptance of poor relief. Where young lads were affected, their employability may be lowered, at least for some jobs in which appearance counts in getting work. A scientific examination of the eyes of these men might yield similar results, and it is difficult to believe that the spectacles bought from sixpenny stores, which were all that some of the men had got, do much to improve matters.

There is little doubt that many unemployed men are undernourished, and this is suggested emphatically by the results obtained at the Government Instructional Centres, or "Training Camps", as the men call them. These camps are generally situated in the country in healthy surroundings and those who attend them for reconditioning spend three months there. They start by doing only the lightest forms of work about the camp, but are gradually brought to do labouring work of the heaviest kind. Some of the Centre superintendents claim that men put on "an average of 7 lb." during their three months in camp, and one case that came within the sample, a Welsh miner of 36 (who was living with a large family on an income actually almost 40% below the poverty line), said that during ten weeks he had been in camp he had put on 18 lb. in weight.

An enquiry was carried out in Lincoln and the results published in 1936,[1] in the course of which the amount of food actually eaten by the men and women in six unemployed families was measured. For such an experiment families where standards of management were high had to be chosen, since it involved the weighing and recording of all food taken. The figures obtained may perhaps fairly be taken as some general indication of the way in which unemployed families of the better type live. In the case of the men the average intake of calories per day was 2,850 (as compared with requirements sometimes placed as low as 2,400 calories, more often 3,000 or even 3,400). It was 90% of the average intake of a much larger employed group. The most noteworthy feature of the diet was the high proportion of bread in it (117% of the average for the employed group). Incidentally, the sample fully confirmed this, that in the better type of unemployed home at least, bread tends to be the staple diet. So in a family of seven in Wales, in which the children were aged from 11 to 21, the record notes: "Saw five large loaves of bread; evidently it is the main diet." And in a Liverpool family consisting of man, wife and three small children, the wife said that a recent rise in the cost of bread of ½*d*. a loaf "meant 2*d*. a day to her, the children eat so much of it". Everything else was, according to the results of this experiment, considerably below the employed man's diet, and the "average" unemployed man took only 38% of the amount of milk taken by the "average" employed man, and 77% of the amount of meat.

These figures do not prove positive undernourishment, though the way in which the physique of the long-unemployed man responds to a change of air and to reasonably good food is suggestive of it. In many cases the wives of unemployed men said that when their husbands were out of work their appetite was poor and that they "did not seem to be able to enjoy their food, somehow". Thus poor physical condition would seem to be less due to the actual effects of poverty in reducing the diet than to a sort of nerviness or listlessness which is the accompaniment of long unemployment.

[1] Widdowson and McCance, *Journal of Hygiene*, vol. XXXVI, Nos. 3 and 6.

Here we are on somewhat surer ground. In the records of many visits it is stated that symptoms of what is called "nerves" were noticed—a twitching of the face or shakiness of the hand. This observation can be supported by the results of an investigation carried out by Dr J. L. Halliday in Glasgow, and published in the *British Medical Journal*.[1] He was examining a group of 1,000 sick insured people, to discover the reasons why they were incapacitated from work. He found that in approximately one-third of the cases examined the reason for incapacity was not "organic" but "psycho-neurotic", and an analysis of this latter section of the group made it possible for him to construct a table showing the progressive incidence of psychoneurosis according to the length of unemployment.

TABLE XXXIV

Duration of Unemployment	Months				Years		
	0	0–3	3–6	6–12	1–2	2–3	3
Psychoneurosis as % of all causes	32 %	27 %	37 %	42 %	41 %	37 %	33 %

The figures are of great interest, not only because they show an increased incidence of psychoneurosis among unemployed men varying according to the length of unemployment, but also because they may perhaps reasonably be taken to indicate the phases even of the normal man's attitude during unemployment—the man who does not become a pathological case but is nevertheless worried and distressed. Some of those examined by Dr Halliday had been in employment when they became ill. Among this section he found, as the figures show, that the incidence of psychoneurosis was actually greater than among those who had fallen ill within the first three months of becoming unemployed. As he says, commenting on these figures: "They suggest that after falling out of work there is a short period of a sense of release (a holiday freedom): gradually

[1] 9 and 16 March 1935.

anxiety and depression set in with loss of mental equilibrium; finally after several years, adaptation takes place to a new and debased level of life, lacking hope as well as fear of the future." In the next chapter of this report we shall have to trace in some detail how this process of adjustment is made. Here we note only that Dr Halliday's figures actually provide us with a "time-table" showing approximately when the various stages are most usually reached; and that they show conclusively how unemployment may be a factor in nervous illness.

Dr Halliday's view is confirmed by that expressed to us by the Medical Officer in one of the places visited. His opinion was that the principal effects of prolonged unemployment on the health of the unemployed men themselves were a subtle undermining of the constitution through lack of physical exertion, the absence of physical stimuli, insufficiently varied diet, and worry; and the emergence of abnormal psychological conditions characterized by disabling fears, anxieties, and sympathetic physical conditions, functional disorders and the like. He gave a number of striking examples of local men who had been apparently normal when in work, but who had "gone to pieces" after being unemployed for several years. The following cases are a few of the many which were quoted:

(i) Man, single, aged 40. In normal health until unemployed. After four years' unemployment complained of choking and pains in the head, but specialist reported no lesion. Later developed alleged throat trouble, but again specialist found no physical signs. Finally, had severe stomach pains for which there was no organic explanation. Only psychological explanation adequate.

(ii) Man, married (with family), aged 50. In normal health until unemployed. Developed constant aches and pains in head and became a chronic neurasthenic.

(iii) Man, single, aged 22. Normal health until unemployed. Began to suffer from "vague fears" after period of unemployment. Was admitted to hospital. Neurosis diagnosed.

(iv) Man, aged 39. Normal health until unemployed. Complained of severe abdominal pains for which X-ray examination revealed no cause. Later developed other signs of neurasthenia.

While it would be wrong to attribute the condition of these men directly to unemployment—the real cause of their trouble probably lies deeper—there is no doubt that the strain and anxiety of unemployment was the proximate cause.

Many of the difficulties which administrators have to face in dealing with long unemployment, and which are often obstacles also in the way of effective voluntary work, in clubs or societies, for individual unemployed men, are probably caused by this nervousness, which in such cases as those quoted has become exaggerated. The inability to settle down to any concentrated form of activity is no doubt due to this, as is the tenacity with which unemployed men cling to what little security they have, which is so potent a factor in the resistance to transference. In one official experiment recently made in Wales with the re-training of the unemployed, it was found that they could not be persuaded to take the double step of beginning to work and moving to a training centre some way away from their homes all at once, but that when it was made possible to divide the effort into two stages, by beginning the retraining in a local centre and moving some time later out of the neighbourhood, resistance to training in a new district was broken down. This was a remarkable instance of the association between that tenacity of "security", of which we have spoken, and unemployment. When employment began, the objection disappeared. In thousands of cases aberrations of this kind obviously occur as the result of unemployment, while in a few something more serious happens. Everyone who has had much contact with "normal" unemployed men knows how unaccountable and touchy they are, and this is no doubt a symptom of nervous strain. It is certainly not only those who are already psychological cases that are so affected.

What is probably much more serious, however, is the effect on the wives of unemployed men. This is brought out at once by visits to the homes, which alone can bring it out. Many of the men concerned do effect a sort of adjustment to unemployment and lead lives that are not unhappy. Their wives only very rarely are able to make such an adjustment—only perhaps in those cases where the allowance comes very close to usual wages. Dr R. D. Gillespie, who discussed this point in a paper read to the British Association in 1936, said: "My experience is that among the working classes unemployment is more apt to affect the nervous condition of the mother of the family than that of the breadwinner himself." It is certainly the mother who is most subject to the nervous anxiety which unemployment brings in its wake. The Medical Officer whose opinion has been quoted above was emphatic in stating that the most serious effects of unemployment were to be found in the wives of unemployed men. It was a matter of daily experience to observe the obvious signs of malnutrition in the appearance of the wives of unemployed men with families. They obviously did without things for the sake of their husbands and children, and it was by no means certain that they keep for their own use the "extra nourishment" provided expressly for them in a large number of cases by the Unemployment Assistance Board. Undernourishment, combined with the strain of "managing" on very limited resources and dealing with the domestic crises which almost inevitably crop up from time to time during a long spell of unemployment make heavy demands on the physical and psychic resources of mothers of families. In the majority of cases this does not result in specific forms of illness, but in a lowering of vitality, a diminished capacity for full living, and increased proneness to minor ailments. On the other hand, there are many cases where serious ill-health and major illnesses have arisen directly as a consequence of undernourishment and wrestling with the domestic problems of long unemployment. There has, it appears, been a marked increase in the number of women suffering from anaemia, neurasthenia, and other conditions arising directly as a consequence of malnutrition and nervous strain. There has also been a considerable increase in the occurrence of septic hands, boils and skin troubles, for the most part due to the same causes. The sample brought us into constant contact with anxiety of the kind that lies at the root of this lowered vitality.

The investigation into the diets of six unemployed families, mentioned above, contains indications of the way in which the unemployed man's wife suffers. It is generally reckoned that a man's wife needs approximately 83 % as much food as he needs. If we take the amount actually eaten by the unemployed man in the experiment as the standard (2,850 calories per day) that would mean the wives needed approximately 2,366 calories. Actually their average intake was 2,010, 70 % only of the husband's intake. What seems in fact to happen is that the wife's diet is reduced in approximately the same proportion as the husband's. But since he is not working he can stand the decreases, whereas she has, if anything, additional effort and strain imposed on her, which leads in many instances to real malnutrition, followed by debility and disease. This is one of the most serious features of unemployment.[1]

An Interim Paper by Dr Singer on Unemployment and Health, issued in October 1937,[2] pointed to similar conclusions. Dr Singer was using published figures which covered the period of the slump, to show the correlation between movement in public health statistics and in unemployment percentages. His method was to establish the different degrees of intensity with which additional unemployment during the slump affected the County Boroughs of England and Wales, and to compare with this certain movements in the vital statistics. He found that the effects of unemployment during that period were traceable, though only in a comparatively slight degree, in the figures of infantile mortality, diphtheria, and various other diseases, but that the connexion was clear in the case of maternal childbirth mortality. He reckoned that, in the county boroughs, there were approximately 850 additional deaths from this cause during the slump and that "if the figures for the county boroughs could be taken as representative for the country as a whole, the number of human victims of depression unemployment among mothers dying of puerperal disease may be estimated as 3,200". He goes

[1] The standard form of Maternity Clinic's certificate in certain parts of Liverpool for women needing extra nourishment during pregnancy, states that they require "an adequate amount of all ordinary foods for six weeks".

[2] Pilgrim Trust Unemployment Enquiry, Interim Paper, No. IV.

on to point out that this represents the effects not only of nervous strain and malnutrition, but of economies in the public medical services. What is important for our purpose, however, is the demonstration that the incidence of illness due to unemployment is clearer among the mothers than it is among families taken in general. Even in the worst households, the instinct to shield the children often remains. Thus there was one in South Wales, a collier aged 51, his wife aged 37, and a small boy of 3. The record notes that the house was "a picture of extreme neglect. Poor furniture; from what she tells me I believe that she makes some efforts to keep a decent home, but her husband and brother come in drunk, and she is ill and cannot stop them. She looks like death—a very poor physical and social type, only two teeth, yellowish face, rags of clothing. In contrast to her the child looks well and is neatly clothed." Throughout this section it must be remembered that the important thing is not those who are actual victims of disease or death, but the far greater number who, like this woman, are on the verge and do not cross it. The significance of all the figures quoted is thus not as showing the actual amount of death or disease that has happened but as suggesting the stress to which those who are sufficiently tough to pull through are continuously subjected.

With regard to children's health, the general conclusions to be drawn from reports by the Medical Officers of Health are on the whole reassuring, and indicate that among children there is an absence of disease due to malnutrition associated with unemployment. The Medical Officer quoted above confirmed this for his own district, and the figures support his view. This is confirmed also by our own impressions, that the children are almost invariably shielded at the parents' expense. The financial difficulties of large families on Unemployment Assistance mean that there is a greater proportion of ill-health than in the smaller families, due largely to overcrowding and dirt rather than to malnutrition, but this cannot fairly be attributed to unemployment since these families are living at something very close to the level of wage earners. One case may be quoted which will illustrate this, that of a labourer in Leicester, aged 37, married, with six children, the youngest a baby, the oldest aged 13. This man was gassed in the War, and at the time of the visit was a tuberculosis suspect. He had a disability pension on this account of 8*s.* His unemployment allowance was 41*s.* 6*d.* and there was a slight addition to the family income in the form of a free tin of food weekly, value 2*s.* 2*d.*, for the baby. Rent was 10*s.* and this, if we include in the income the two extras mentioned, meant that 41*s.* 8*d.* was available for all needs apart from rent. On our poverty standard the needs of this family were 51*s.* 6*d.* The wife was delicate, suffering from kidney trouble, and so was the last baby. At birth it had weighed only 3 lb., and extra nourishment was stated to be required for it. Nothing extra was allowed, however, for this man's ordinary wage was only 42*s.* to 45*s.* a week, and he was already getting almost as much from the Board. The administrative dilemma that such a case presents is not easy to resolve.

One unfortunate feature at present is that when a man has been out of work for long he often falls out of benefit with his approved Health Insurance society, while even if he remains in benefit, the rate which he draws bears no relation to his family needs. Thus a man with a small family, who normally draws 36*s.* Unemployment Assistance for it, may draw 15*s.* only in sick benefit. If he becomes ill, therefore, he still struggles to continue "signing on" at the Exchange to prove his fitness and eligibility for work, and real hardship is sometimes caused in this way. When he can stand it no longer and resigns himself to the temporary loss of assistance, additional anxiety is imposed on his wife at a time when she can least afford it. There was one instance in Blackburn of a young woman whose husband had died a few months back of tuberculosis. She pointed out that now he was dead there was actually more coming into the house (thanks to her widow's pension on his account) than there had been when he was dying.

The length at which we have treated these questions of poverty has its justification in the fact that this is the material background against which are set all the difficulties of the unemployed themselves, and of those who work among them; whether it be the officials, or those who are trying to provide, through the unemployed clubs and centres, opportunities for the use of enforced leisure. Those who actually visit the homes of the long unemployed, as we were able to do, cannot shut their eyes to it. To meet the men themselves is to be aware of depression, apathy, physical deterioration, and a score of other things, but it is only by contact with their houses that the poverty associated with unemployment is to be realized. To say this, is to multiply two or threefold the number of those who are directly affected by long unemployment, and this is the scale on which this problem has to be considered.

(ii) PSYCHOLOGICAL PROBLEMS

ATTITUDE TOWARDS UNEMPLOYMENT

1. *The Importance of the Subject*

One of the most frequently discussed of all the problems of unemployment is that of the willingness of the unemployed to work. The loss of the will to work may well be one of the disastrous effects of unemployment, and we were anxious to discover what the facts with regard to this might be. This involved an attempt to get behind the actual answers of those interviewed. We felt, and the opinion is confirmed by many who are in far closer permanent touch with the unemployed, that many of the answers given were "defensive" and do not represent a real attitude. If a man resents being asked about his anxiety to work, it is not necessarily an indication that he is trying to avoid it. It may show the sense of frustration that has come upon him from continuous refusals, or impatience at the inability of others to understand his difficulties. On the other hand, the evidence is incontestable that there are men who are "work-shy", and the experience of many Unemployment Assistance Board Officers, that an extensive investigation into certain sections of the register (especially among the young men under 25) may lead to a decline of numbers, cannot be ignored. If the threat of enquiries in itself proves enough to make men find work, it must mean that some men are avoiding it. We regarded it, therefore, as an important part of our work to try to throw some light on this question.

It is hazardous to attempt the simple classification of a complex thing such as a man's attitude to his work, and where figures are put forward in this section they must be treated with reserve. They may, however, serve as a general indication of the impression which we formed. There are, roughly speaking, three categories into which the sample can be divided in this respect, and throughout this section we shall be constantly referring to them. They are (i) those who think still only in terms of work; (ii) those who are beginning to accept unemployment as a normal state for themselves, though they still perhaps look for work, often as a matter of habit rather than with any conviction; (iii) those who have accepted unemployment as their normal state (sometimes because they have found satisfactory alternative activities) and for whom it would be hard to bring themselves to take work if it were available. We attempt to trace the process of "adjustment", to use Mr Bakke's term, by which the unemployed man gradually moves from one of these categories to another, and to give some estimate of their proportionate importance.

2. *Losing Work*

One of the main differences between the "working" classes and the "middle" classes is the difference of security. This is probably a more important distinction than income level. If working men and women seem to be unduly anxious to make their sons and daughters into clerks, the anxiety behind it is not for more money but for greater security. Rightly or wrongly, they feel that the black-coated worker has a more assured position.[1] The semi-skilled man is at the mercy of rationalisation.

[1] Figures published by Mr Colin Clark show that black-coated unemployment is not as extensive as is often maintained. See "The National Income", p. 46.

A week's notice may end half a lifetime's service, with no prospects, if he is elderly, but the dole, followed by a still further reduction in his means of livelihood when the old age pension comes. We take as an example a shoe laster from Leicester, who had worked thirty-seven years with one firm. "When I heard the new manager going through and saying: 'The whole of this side of this room, this room, and this room is to be stopped', I knew it would be uphill work to get something." He went on to describe to us how he had not been able to bring himself to tell his wife the bad news when he got home, how she had noticed that something was wrong, how confident she had been that he would get work elsewhere, but how he had known that the chances were heavily against him. For months and indeed often for years such men go on looking for work, and the same is true of many casual labourers. There were in the sample old men who have not a remote chance of working again but yet make it a practice to stand every morning at six o'clock at the works gates in the hope that perhaps they may catch the foreman's eye. There were young men who said that they could never settle to anything, but must be out all day, every day, looking for work. We had instances of men who had bicycled all over Lancashire and Yorkshire from Liverpool in the hopes of finding something. A young married man (aged 29) in Leicester, who was for some reason strongly criticized by the authorities for not looking for work, had tramped about for nearly a year in the hopes of getting some permanent, or at least temporary employment (his wife had gone back into service to make it possible for him to do so), but the only substantial work he had done during the whole period was pea picking. Another man, a shoehand, 38 years old, had come down on his own initiative from Lancashire, where the factory in which he worked had closed down, to Leicester. He was a neat, rather reserved type of man and had not perhaps the necessary push to squeeze himself into work, but he wanted it desperately. He tried to join the army and was refused for it, apparently on account of his age, and it was clear that as time went on he was getting a more and more defeatist attitude to work. He might go on trying, but his efforts were vitiated more and more by the knowledge that he was not going to succeed. The sample brought out scores of similar instances, but these two of comparatively young men in a city which by ordinary standards is exceedingly prosperous must stand for all of them. When a man is thrown out of employment the first thing that he wants is work, and very few of those who have a good employment history can settle down to accept the fact of unemployment till they have been out of work for months.

But when a man who has had perhaps ten years' steady employment is thrown on the streets, to look for work effectively is not always easy. A large number of the sample cases had lost good jobs at the time of the slump, when there was nothing else to be had. They had gone round from one works to another with hundreds of others all desperately anxious to secure employment, and failure after failure had gradually "got them down". The restlessness of which many wives spoke to us tells its own tale: "Now he's out of work he don't seem to be able to settle down to anything." When a man is out of work, anxiety is part of a vicious circle, and the more he worries, the more he unfits himself for work.

There were other symptoms of this nerviness. The high proportions of instances in which married men were living apart from their wives is certainly in some degree to be explained by it. Among many of the families visited, tension between man and wife was apparent. Thus we saw a man of 25 in Liverpool, who had had previously to 1935 a certain amount of work as a builder's labourer. At the time of the visit his wife was 19; they had been married when she was 16. The first child had died the day after it was born and the mother had suffered from anaemia and kidney trouble at the time. There was another baby a few months old, which was taken to hospital with pneumonia the night before the visit occurred. The man gave the impression of one who had been not unhappy for a time lounging, but was now getting to the end of his tether. Speaking of his wife, he said: "She's always crying. But crying don't make things no better": and the early marriage, poverty, illness, and finally the quarrel seemed to summarise in a single instance several of the worst features of the situation of the long unemployed. Friction may come out in other ways, also. The children may get on a man's nerves if he is at home all day. "When he was out of work we were always having rows over the children. He will never let them do anything. It's much better now he is at work." In several cases where the wife was earning but the husband unemployed, there was evidently unhappiness as a result. A striking example occurred among the Liverpool visits, the case of a printer, 42 years old, who had lost his chance of re-employment at his old trade, through a dispute with the union. A few weeks before our visit occurred, he had left Liverpool in the hopes of finding work in the Midlands, and the wife showed one of us a touching letter in which he told her that he had got work at 25*s*. a week and enclosed 10*s*. for her. While he was out of work she had been working regularly, with the result that he only drew 5*s*. Unemployment Assistance. She described how she used to lie awake at nights and hear him "tramping up and down the garden path, or up and down in the parlour, and it made her nearly mad; and it made her nearly mad to feel that she was keeping him by her earnings and they gaining nothing by her work". There was a somewhat similar case in Leicester, where the woman had left her work because she could not bear to be the breadwinner while her husband, young and fit, did nothing; another in Blackburn where a young married woman, working, with an unemployed husband, said that "it made him wild" to be about with no money in his pocket. It is in the light of such cases that we should read the figures showing the numbers of men in the sample who were living apart from their wives.

Similar questions are raised by the case of the man whose allowance takes into account the fact that his children are earning sums which permit of their contributing to his support and the general upkeep of the household. There were in the sample instances of men over 55 years of age who were either not in receipt of any income from the Unemployment Assistance Board, or in receipt of small amounts, 5*s*. or 7*s*. 6*d*., from the Board, because it was held that the household resources were otherwise sufficient. This view would be justified if the household were taken as a unit. The fact remains, however, that some men in this position feel the loss of an independent income, such as they enjoyed while on Unemployment Benefit, very acutely, and in many such cases the home appears to represent two standards, the earning children being often smartly dressed and happy, while the fathers were shabby and suffering from a sense of their dependence. Such men gave the impression that they purposely avoided making any effort to keep up appearances in case the children might think that they were drawing an undue share of the family income. While among the sample as a whole, bitterness against the Unemployment Assistance Board is the exception rather than the rule, in cases of this kind it was the rule rather than the exception. The question has two sides, and we came across several instances in which children were behaving most unreasonably in refusing to contribute towards the household expenses the sum, not large, which the regulations expect of them. Nevertheless, there may be a case, even here, for making some larger payment from State funds.[1]

The depression and apathy which finally settles down in many of the homes of these long-unemployed men lies at the root of most of the problems which are connected with unemployment. It is one of the reasons why they fail to get back to work. It is one of the reasons why the majority of them "have not the heart" for clubs or activities of other kinds, and it is one of the reasons why their homes seem so poverty-stricken. "I don't know how it is," said a young married woman in Blackburn, "but these last few years since I've been out of the mills I don't seem able

[1] If we do not add here those cases where unemployed sons have left home on account of the application of the Means Test, it is because the sample indicates that the distress caused by this is much less, and that the object of the regulations (which is presumably to suggest forcibly to young men the urgency of making further efforts to get work) is often achieved. The number of instances in which homes had been broken up was eighteen (this is, however, a minimum figure, representing only those cases where we could definitely trace the breaking up of the home to the Means Test). Generalisation from this figure would give a total number of about 7,500 cases. We came across several instances where leaving home was a "put up job".

to take trouble, somehow; I've got no spirit for anything. But I didn't use to be like that." One of us who saw her had little doubt "how it was". The woman looked thin and ill, and it was clear that what food there was was going to the children. Such a simultaneous onset of physical and psychological hardship can hardly help having serious results.

3. *What Work has Meant*

If we are to see how it gradually becomes possible for the worker to accept unemployment, it must be in the light of an understanding what work ordinarily means to him. The sample illustrated this, and showed how it differed as between individuals, as between places, or as between types of employment. Work provides for most people the pattern within which their lives are lived, and when this pattern is lost they have thrown on them a responsibility which, in the case of most unemployed men, their working lives have in no way qualified them to bear, the responsibility for organizing their own existence. They fall in ultimately with some new makeshift pattern.

"I was one of a gang", said a lad from Lancashire, "as we called it; there were twenty or more of us. We used to stay in bed late in the mornings so as not to need breakfast. I used to have a cup of tea, and then we would all go down to the library and read the papers. Then we went home for a bit of lunch, and then we met again at a billiard hall where you could watch the play for nothing. Then back for tea, and to watch the billiards again. In the evening we all used to go to the pictures. That was how we spent the dole money. In the end I thought I'd go mad if I went on like that. So I broke away from them and joined one of these P.T. classes. But I found it made me so hungry that I couldn't go on with it. If I hadn't had the chance of coming to this place" (Wincham Hall, a college in Cheshire where educational courses for unemployed men are run) "I don't know what would have happened to me then. I felt like going under, I can tell you."

Sometimes life is less elaborately organised and gives a yet stronger impression of pointlessness: "You see that corner?"

said a young man of 20 in the Rhondda, "Well, when I'm on my own, my time is spent between here and that corner." One feature almost always stands out clearly, the days on which a man has to visit the Exchange and sign on to qualify for Unemployment Assistance: and the queue "at the Labour" plays a big part in the life of most unemployed men. But the first and most difficult feature of unemployment is the very obvious one that it leaves the unemployed man with nothing to do, and that, until he loses his job, he does not realise how much it means to him in this way. "Time", one man said, "is my worst enemy now."

A job has meant other things also. The skilled and semi-skilled man almost invariably has great pride in his work. He will tell you that his was the "finest pit in the world" or show you the tools he once used, or tell you of the different countries and continents to which in the old days the products of the factory where he worked used to go. "When you're working you feel like a cog in a machine. When you're out, you feel that no one has any use for you, and to see your wife busy makes you feel ashamed." "When you've a job you feel you're doing your bit for the Empire." This latter argument may not be very clear, but the feeling it expresses is clear enough—the feeling of uselessness with which many of the unemployed are obsessed. Their remarks often show, too, the interest they have had in the management of the firms with whom they worked. "Of course the old gaffer used to run the business properly, and then the new one came along and was always doing something else and spent most of his time on the booze and we didn't keep up to date; and at last the place was closed down and all of us were turned on to the streets. Most of us had been in the firm all our lives." The sample left no doubt that the majority of skilled and semi-skilled workers were normally deeply absorbed in their work. Often their manner suggested that their lives had been wholly centred in their employment, and that the friendships made in the course of it and the association which it brought with fellow-workers was the most valuable thing they had. Thus in Blackburn the sample included a woman who after many years' work as a weaver had lost her job because she rashly complained, on behalf of a large number of those who worked with her, of a new supply of material that they considered defective and as increasing considerably the labour of weaving. She had later been forced out of the union, because she worked "blackleg" outside Blackburn during a strike in the hope of thus recovering permanent employment. "I loved the mills:" she said, "I loved the company and the people and everything about them. The mill was home to me. I'd do anything in the world if I could get back to them. I'd not mind working even if things were very much worse than they were before." Few men wear their hearts as openly as this on their sleeve: but the impression of isolation and loneliness which they give is, in its way, as vivid. What is sometimes the single link they have with their fellow-men has been severed.[1]

But while the work done by the skilled or semi-skilled man is normally interesting enough to occupy his mind or at least continuous enough to give him the habit of working, the unskilled man is in a different position. Only if he is lucky does he get work with one firm which is continuous and carries him through the best part of his working life. More probably he never gets more than a few months' continuous work, after which he has to look for something else, and in many cases, it is only a matter of a few odd days' work occasionally here and there. Experiments have recently been made with regard to decasualizing dock work, and to a large extent they have been successful, but the problem nevertheless remains considerable even in docking, and much more considerable in unregistered casual labour. The spells of casual work which a "general labourer" finds for himself are often not enough to give men the habit of working. A young docker met in one of the Liverpool clubs described how as he was tramping down to the docks in the morning he would find himself turning into the club to spend the day there. He knew that the chances were against his getting work, even if he went to look for it. The club was comfortable and there was plenty to do, so that gradually it became more and more difficult

[1] Cf. the table on p. 287.

for him to bring himself to take a job. He was an active and intelligent lad, and his case is illuminating. Work of the kind he does is clearly not going to provide that "pattern" of which we have spoken above. Though he may enjoy it while he is doing it, the chances are that it gives him no real interest and, as jobs get fewer and more far between, it does not worry him unduly, though his family feels the pinch soon enough. There are indeed casual labourers who are interested in their work; dockers with an extensive knowledge of the goods they handle, timber or whatever it may be—like one docker in the sample in Liverpool who had picked up a considerable knowledge of the fruit trade and was anxious to set up independently in it; and there are a few (like a splendid old workman whom one of us met in a common lodging-house in Leicester) whose interest in life has been to see the world and pick up jobs wherever they go to pay their way. But these are the exceptions. The ordinary unemployed "general labourer" in the sample evidently had very little interest in his work (though he often said he felt fitter while doing it) and this makes it much easier for him to acquiesce in unemployment.

Moreover, the general labourer on the dole has at least some form of security, and the frequency with which they find out that they are better off with regular money than many working, who get "rained off" for part of the week and draw only £1 or thereabouts in wages, shows clearly enough that they often appreciate this. Yet for these men, too, work means contacts with other men, and unemployment often turns them, especially the elderly, in upon themselves more and more. For many such men, shy, awkward and reserved, there is no other solution (if indeed they cannot be fitted back in work) than personal friendship, and even that will often fail to penetrate the isolation. It is not so difficult to help the elderly women, since their response is readier, and they will let themselves go whole-heartedly in any social activities provided for them. Outside the Special Areas the problem of this isolation is particularly acute, since the proportion of elderly unemployed men who are living alone is particularly high. Thus in Deptford, in the age group 55–64, there were 25 "single men" (if one includes widowers and those living apart from their wives in this category) as against 29 married, that is to say, 46 % were "single", while in Leicester there were 20 "single" and 26 married, the "single" men being 43 % of the total.[1] In Crook 10 were "single", 19 married (single 34 %), and in the Rhondda 17 "single", 37 married (single 31 %). Nothing is more urgent or more worth while than the attempt to do something for these older men, with whom may be reckoned for this purpose large numbers of old age pensioners above the age of 65. Things are being done, but not enough.

It remains to show in the figures this difference between skilled and unskilled. These are worked out, taking once more our three categories: those who refuse to accept unemployment, those who are on the way to accepting it, and those who have accepted it and would find it hard to bring themselves to take work, in Table C 1.[2] The facts could hardly be clearer than they are there brought out. Here and there, it is true, other influences distort the result slightly; and if the rise in percentage for the lower status in column III is not regular, it is because the sample of semi-skilled men is weighted by the figures for the Special Areas, where "adjustment" to unemployment is for various reasons easier. As a whole, however, the table leaves no doubt whatever that the status of the worker plays a significant part in his attitude once he gets out of work. To the skilled worker work has meant something of real importance and interest, and he finds it hard to reconcile himself to the loss of it. For the unskilled worker this is less difficult, and for the "submarginal" case, the man who has done such casual work as requires neither intelligence nor physique, it is easier still. At the same time, though the change is quite clear, it is not violent. Table C 1 shows that to a high proportion of unskilled men work has meant enough to make them refuse adjustment to unemployment, and

[1] The high proportion in Deptford is influenced by the fact that there is a large L.C.C. lodging-house there, where about 800 men are living. But the Leicester figures show that the generalisation is sound.

[2] See p. 436.

personal qualities are what obviously count most in causing the gradual drift into category III.

4. *The Effect of Bad Working Conditions*

So far those men have been considered for whom work was on the balance something which meant much to them and which it caused real distress to lose. But the effect of losing work may be different when unemployment, by breaking a connexion that has been accepted but never willed, gives men an idea of new possibilities, or at least a detestation of the work they used to do. This is common with those who have worked "underground", and occurs in some Lancashire towns among unemployed mill-workers, and it was noticeable too among the seamen of Liverpool. Conditions everywhere are changing, partly owing to the changing requirements of modern competition; and standards demanded by employees (e.g. by seamen, several of whom in the sample showed themselves well aware of the low wages and discomfort of this occupation) are changing too. This is most clearly apparent in the mining industry. Thirty years ago the miners were an aristocracy of labour. Wages were good, the collier was a craftsman, and he generally served a kind of "apprenticeship" with his father. The demand for coal was increasing steadily, and the seams worked were generally thick. Now, however, mechanization has speeded up production underground and the pace of the man working at the coal face is forced for him; he is no longer his own master. The noise makes it difficult for him to hear the sound of cracks on which he used to depend to foretell falls of roof. "There's someone watching the conveyor all the time. If they see less coming along they're down on you in a moment. They use plenty of this (pointing to the mouth): all they need is whips." "I've always been used to look up, not to look down." "This is not work, it is murder."

Moreover, the unemployed miner believes (and it is difficult to disbelieve it, in face of the cases that are quoted) that many men are working regularly in the pits for a wage below the legal minimum, knowing that, if they complain, they will be "handed their cards"—"There is plenty waiting to take their place at a lower wage"—and putting up with their position because they hope that in the ballot for better seams they may soon be luckier. Mining is anyhow a dangerous occupation. In the course of the sample a young man of 28 was visited in the Rhondda. He was slightly lame, and he had done no regular work for thirteen years. He described how when he was 15 he was working underground and he was pinned up to the neck, by a fall of roof, and was not rescued for three hours. His case brings out the dangers of mining, but they can be easily illustrated in figures.[1] The industry in South Wales leaves behind it a steady trail of human wreckage. The sample showed that almost exactly half of those miners over 45 who had been out of work for a considerable period in the Rhondda are in some way unfit.

It is, therefore, not surprising that many men should have had suggested to them by unemployment the possibility of giving up the industry entirely and adopting some different occupation, or should at least become more and more reluctant to return. It is no doubt possible to exaggerate this reluctance. As a collier of 52 told us, a man who by extraordinary persistence had succeeded at that age in fitting himself for a new trade, "If anyone were to ask for 4,000 men in Tonypandy, they would be forthcoming for the asking", and among them would be some who spoke of the dangers of mining as keeping them out of work, for the unemployed man is as human as anyone else and makes excuses on what might be called the "sour grapes" principle. But the sample leaves no doubt whatever that there is a substantial number who are reluctant to return to mining. As instances may be quoted a miner from the Rhondda who has made himself an expert gardener and talked lyrically of the discovery of the world above ground: "We people who work underground don't know anything about the things that make life worth living. Sometimes on the films I see one of those Californian giant Phloxes, and I think that is life": another, now working, who had made himself into a competent organist, and had evidently accepted only with great reluctance the offer of another mining job; a

[1] See Table A 7, p. 424.

man of 33 in Crook who, thanks largely to his social activities, had succeeded in becoming thoroughly competent to undertake a clerical post, and described how as years went by his liking for the pit had been turned into fear of having to return to underground work. And the number of older people who said that they would on no account allow their sons to go underground, in view of conditions in the mines to-day, was considerable, which is only another side of the same reluctance. No doubt the realization that the job no longer gives the security that it used to give also plays a part.

The effects of this particular "adjustment" can be seen plainly in the figures. They show that, if we take the age group 28–42 in the Rhondda, 46 men come in the category II of those who are "beginning to accept unemployment as the normal state for themselves", as against 10 in category I, those who refuse to accept unemployment as a normal state, and 9 in category III, those who have accepted unemployment as the normal state and would find it difficult to work again if work was offered them. The corresponding figures for Liverpool are: 40 in group II, 31 in category I and 25 in category III. The majority of the unemployed Rhondda miners in this age group are finding it comparatively easy to acquiesce in unemployment because their old job has lost its attractiveness for them, though the majority of them also would take eagerly enough fair work of some other kind in the valleys if they had the opportunity of it.

5. *Possibilities of Independence*

The insecurity of the ordinary working man's life seems often to be the reason for another idea which unemployment sometimes suggests, the idea that a family may be able to "set up on its own" in some simple independent enterprise. The ideal of many working men is a little business, a newsagent's or a fried fish shop. Thus—to take one of many examples—we interviewed a woman in Blackburn, aged 45, a baker. She had lost her work through illness, coming back to find her place filled by a girl she had trained. Her husband had originally worked in his father's confectioner's shop, then had been apprenticed to a wagon-builder, and had broken his apprenticeship to go to the War. Since the War he had picked up any odd jobs he could find, had "sold papers and anything to bring in a little"; but at the time of the visit he was recovering from a serious operation. "We've often talked about this (a little business)", said his wife, "and I've said to him 'If only we could get something to do on our own!' I've been turned away so often by other people that I feel I can't go round much more, and I want to be independent. I know we could make enough if we had a little business, for I know the working classes and we don't need very much, him and me." Some have tried running "books" of their own, a more risky undertaking than the taking of "betting slips" for established firms, by which means, to judge from the sample, a substantial number of men supplement their Unemployment Allowances. Others have tried to enter the commercial world by accepting one of the canvassing jobs which are described so rosily in the advertisements but are evidently in fact a social menace. We were told that the Labour Exchanges had warned a number of men of the dangers which these jobs entailed, and it was satisfactory to find that where the money realised had been meagre and the men concerned had given up the job on this account, their action had been upheld by the Courts of Referees.

There were also examples of men trying to make a living out of home industries such as painting of silk screens or the making of mats from scrap leather. A striking case of the latter was that of a clerk, close on 60, who had worked more than forty years with one firm and had lost his position owing to the firm going out of business, and had then, realising how strongly his age told against him, taken a clerkship at a much lower wage (which he lost after a few years owing to the bankruptcy of the new firm) and had finally spent a substantial sum of money on acquiring the tools for making a kind of wired leather mat in the hope of securing an honest living by it without having recourse to "the dole". Thus there was no question of his industry and persistence, but after a few weeks it became clear that it was impossible for him to make a sum anything like as large as the 17*s.* he would get from the Unemployment Assistance Board. He said indeed that to earn two or three shillings meant something like a full week's work. The sample visits gave other sidelights on the amounts that can be earned by these home industries. The wife of an unemployed man in Leicester, a woman of 70, spent all her spare time sewing up woollen gloves. She reckoned that something over two hours' work earned her about 2½*d*. But the two or three shillings a week earned in this way were a real help "with the gas bill and such likes". "I want to keep the roof over our heads, lodgings aren't the same thing." And she said that the Unemployment Assistance Board Investigating Officer had told her that they would have no reduction made in the allowance. From its nature, the sample only included the failures among those who had tried to set up independently, but those failures were sufficiently striking to suggest that the number of successes must be very small indeed.

6. *The Unemployed Community*

If a man has been out of work for more than a year, and he sees hundreds of others similarly situated, it is natural that he should think less of the work he may never suceed in getting and more of "how to make do" in the circumstances. We have seen something above of the evolving of some pattern for existence that this necessitates, and the majority of men who have been unemployed for long have formed this pattern for themselves and follow it regularly day after day. Very often this "pattern" includes meetings with other unemployed men outside the Exchange or in the Public Library or the Unemployed Club. Here is one example in the life of a dock porter (age 35) in Liverpool: "I go round and meet a few of my friends and have a chat; then down to the Labour or the Unemployment Assistance Board and have a talk or a lounge about for a bit. Then I come back and have dinner. If anyone'll take me to the pictures in the afternoon I go there, once a week or more; or sometimes I go to a billiard hall and sit there. I don't do much reading except in the newspapers. I do no boot repairing, and don't do much carpentry, for if I do it people can tell it's not a proper job. What I miss is having a few shillings extra to go across the water at week ends, or to the football match. I often travelled to Manchester and beyond to watch the team playing."

This man, we were informed, was regarded by the officials as a "respectable type, eager to obtain work". In our view, he would have taken work if he had been offered it, but he had ceased to be "eager" for it. And as his day is like the day of tens of thousands who have been out of work long, so his attitude too is characteristic. He is coming to accept unemployment as something which is natural and inevitable. It means that he has to make some changes; that he cannot take a trip across the Mersey or to the Isle of Man as he used to do, but he gets accustomed to the economies. His life is switched down to a lower economic plane and no doubt at first he finds it hard, but especially where, as in the instance quoted, he has always been familiar with spells of unemployment, he ultimately settles down to a new routine of existence. And one thing above all makes this comparatively easy for him, if he finds himself a member of an unemployed community.

How much easier it is for an unemployed man who is associated with others like himself to become used to unemployment can be shown by a comparison between the Rhondda and Leicester. If we compare the oldest age group, 55–64, in these two places, the difference in "ease of adjustment" is at once apparent.[1] The long-unemployed man in Leicester of that age is an isolated figure. In the Rhondda he is one of thousands. In the Rhondda it is easy for him to settle down, seeing how many others of his age are forced to do so, and something between a half and two-thirds of the men in this age group had so settled down. In Leicester that was true of about a quarter. In this town more than a fifth could not bring themselves to accept the fact that they would probably never work again, in the Rhondda less than a tenth.

In a prosperous area the unemployed community means not much more than the queue at the Labour Exchange, where the

[1] See below, p. 172, for figures.

unemployed man signs on and draws his allowances.[1] As each man is timed at the Exchange, the queues are largely voluntary, the men "hanging about" for a talk. Even in a prosperous area a man will see hundreds of others crowding in at the Exchange when he goes there, and often if he has not much enterprise and energy, he jumps to the conclusion that they are all in the same position as he is himself. "With so many young men out of a job, what's the use of a fellow like me going on looking?" The great majority of the young men are indeed only temporarily stopped, or, though out of work, will be fixed up with something in a week or two. The crowds round the Exchange are no indication of the extent of the real unemployment problem. But, if he can persuade himself that they are, this obviously makes it easier for him to accept his own position.

It is in the queue, at least in more prosperous places, that unemployed public opinion comes into being. Thus there are a number of standard complaints that one hears from one man after another, such as the complaint, made not only in Liverpool but in Leicester and London as well, that "everything is done here nowadays by this Irish labour". In most instances the complaint has little foundation, but it is passed on from one man to another because it is an excuse that each man can use readily for his own unemployment. When one of us was told in Liverpool by a coal-porter that "all the jobs nowadays are done by girls and machines", it was evident that this was an idea picked up in the queue, for even in these days there is not much displacement of coal-porters by female or mechanical labour. Another complaint for which there must be some foundation, but which is certainly exaggerated by unemployed public opinion, is that "work is only obtained through graft". Thus a Liverpool docker, to take one example of many, claimed that "most jobs go nowadays only to those who treat the bosses. The man upstairs is always at work like that. Any time in the pub you can see how it is done." Sometimes the complaint rang true enough, but in this instance, a rather disreputable young

[1] See below, p. 274, for figures, showing the lack of associations which is characteristic of the long unemployed in prosperous places.

man who told us that "he'd been pretty lucky in his day" betting, it suggested an excuse rather than a reason for being out of work. It occurred frequently enough to show that it is a commonplace of unemployed gossip. In one case where it was mentioned by a more respectable man, he said that though he had often heard of it, an instance had never occurred within his own experience.

Evidently the unemployed clubs are in many places the subject of unemployed gossip in the queue, and the frequency with which the laconic criticism "dope" is made against them, suggested that it was also an idea originating in this way. It looks also as if many of the unjustified views of the Unemployment Assistance Board regulations are derived from the same source. Many unemployed men, for instance, conceal small occasional earnings for which no deductions would be made from their allowances. The printed leaflet which they all receive explaining the regulations stands little chance against this strong public opinion. Similarly, one reason why it has been difficult to get men to attend Government Training Centres in the past has been this unemployed public opinion, formed in the queue; for necessarily the unemployed man meets there the failures, and not the successes, since the latter, after their period of training, have passed into employment, generally in a new district. Some of the more respectable men described how they had at first dreaded the queue, and how gradually they had got used to it, and "if you talk about the right kind of things in the queue, racing and football, it isn't so bad as it might be".

An unemployed man's friendships are largely formed in this way, and when he speaks of "going about with a few other fellows" that is how he has generally found them. A striking instance of this is one of the small number of men in the sample with prison records; a man who had served several short terms of imprisonment for house-breaking. He spoke after a time freely of the way in which this had happened. It was obvious that he was potentially a decent sort of man, and he had originally had good work which he left to emigrate. His passage to Canada had been guaranteed, but at the last moment, owing to the illness of his wife, he could not go, and it was impossible for him to get back to his old employment. "I'd never done anything of that sort when I was a child, but when I was out of work and we'd very little money I met one or two fellows down at the Labour who did that kind of thing and I thought I could do it too. It was exciting too, and once I got a bit of money that way it was very hard not to go on. But whenever I met a policeman it gave me the jumps, I never knew whether I'd come home again and I always knew they'd get me in the end. I never used to break into a house where there were people, but used to rob the coin meters in empty houses. Of course, I didn't want to take anything that belonged to anyone."

We have quoted him at length, for in so far as there is a connexion between unemployment and crimes against property,[1] his case shows how that connexion may arise. But for our present purpose we note only the way in which he met his associates, since it shows how many unemployed men's associations are formed.

There are more specific organizations which help in the formation of this unemployed public opinion and help to keep the unemployed community together. In several of the towns visited, the National Unemployed Workers' Movement had representatives, who stood outside the Labour Exchanges, on pay day, collecting the penny a week from the "dole" money. The sample cases seen were not asked whether they belonged to it for obvious reasons (as they were not asked anything about their politics), but in a number of instances they volunteered information. One or two had dropped out because they did not think it any use, and there were some criticisms of the local personnel of the Movement, but the majority of those who spoke about it evidently valued it. There can be no doubt, however, that

[1] See S. K. Ruck, "The Increase of Crime in England" in the *Political Quarterly*, vol. III (2), 1932. Mr Ruck gives a graph showing the connexion between the unemployment figures and crime, a connexion which may mean nothing more than that both are trade cycle phenomena. In our opinion, this particular instance was one of causal connexion, but in most of the instances in the sample the causal connexion was not so clear, and it was equally possible that the men concerned were unemployed because they had criminal tendencies.

especially in more prosperous places, the tendency of organizations of this kind, as sometimes (though not by any means always) of the unemployed clubs, is with younger men at least to encourage them not to get work.

In places which are less prosperous the unemployed community is less militantly defensive owing to its very size. It is accepted, whereas in prosperous areas the attempt is made to ignore it. In Liverpool there are various reductions in price made for the unemployed and notices appear in the shop-window to that effect. They can get their hair cut cheaper, for instance, and in many places they can get cheaper cinema tickets. On Tyneside some of the unemployed club members get free passes into the cinema as often as three times a week. Such advantages may be set off partly, though not wholly, by those which an unemployed man in a prosperous place gets from the greater efficiency of the social services. We are not arguing for a moment that these things ought to be curtailed, for conditions are bad enough even when these few small advantages have been reckoned in. The point about them is simply that the unemployed man notices them, and that they help to reconcile him to his position. And if, as often happens in depressed places, two or three adult members of the family are out of work, the sense of belonging to an unemployed community is natural, and it is much easier to settle down.[1] This was noticeable also in Liverpool, where we were sometimes told: "Why, there are only two families in this street where the man is working!"

7. *The Wage Factor*

All these factors tend to make it easier for a man to accept unemployment as his inevitable fate. There is, however, another which the sample has shown to be of first-rate importance, that

[1] In Deptford none, in Leicester 5 %, in Liverpool 8 %, [in Blackburn 27 %,] in Crook 12 %, in the Rhondda 15 %, of the men in the sample were living in such families. The percentage in Blackburn is not strictly comparable, owing to the practice of man and wife working there. It is noteworthy, however, that adjustment to unemployment had, on our figures, gone further in Blackburn than anywhere else.

of wages. The Unemployment Assistance Board scales of assistance are based on individual needs, whereas wages are not. As a result the man with a large family whose needs are considerable gets substantially more money than a man with no family, whereas if he were earning there would be no such increase made in respect of his family. If he is an unskilled man, the wage he would earn might not be more than 40*s*. or 35*s*. or even 25*s*. a week, while if he is drawing Unemployment Assistance he may have as much as 45*s*., 50*s*., or even (as in one case visited, where there were eight children, the eldest being an unemployed lad of 18 for whom the father was claiming) 57*s*. In such a situation, the "wage incentive" to work is non-existent, and the regulations naturally take this into account by having regard to the wage that the applicant would normally earn, and reckoning that the allowance should not come within 2*s*. of this figure. The trouble is that in practice this has to be disregarded. In many unregulated occupations wages are so low that they are not in any circumstances sufficient to support a married man. When a man marries, therefore, he leaves them and draws Unemployment Assistance instead, and he "cannot afford" to go back to work; and even with jobs at what is called a fair wage, a time may come if there are four or five children when the same is true.

The tendency towards this can be shown conclusively from the sample figures. If we take for example the men between the ages of 30 and 39, and compare the percentage who are in category III (i.e. those who have reached the stage when it would be difficult for them to take work) with that in the other two categories, it is at once clear that the size of the family has a great influence on these percentages.

TABLE XXXV. ATTITUDE TO EMPLOYMENT: MEN BETWEEN THE AGES OF 30 AND 39

Number of dependents	0	1	2	3	4	5	6 and more
Categories I and II	83 %	85 %	89 %	82 %	80 %	78 %	54 %
Category III	17	15	11	18	20	22	46

It is easier for the single man to acquiesce in unemployment than it is for the married man who has no children or only one, but in families where there is more than one child it becomes progressively more likely that the unemployed man who is head of the family will be able to reconcile himself to being out of work.

This problem is discussed from another point of view in a later section of our report. What we wish to do here is to give some indication of the attitude and difficulties of the men who fall into this group. But it must be emphasised here too that the problem is essentially one of low wages. To reduce the scales of the allowances is an impracticable, and indeed a very dangerous, though it might seem to be the obvious, solution, because the great majority of the families concerned are living well below the "poverty line". This particular problem is in fact associated closely with the poorest groups in the sample (see above p. 111), so that a reduction of allowances would cause suffering and distress among those families where suffering and distress are already very near.

The problem then is that many men with families find themselves as well off, or in some instances, better off, "on the dole" than they would be if they were working. The surprising thing is that, in spite of this, many of them should actually prefer to work. The sample, being drawn from the long unemployed, naturally tends to give a somewhat distorted view of the situation, for it does not take into account the large numbers of men who might be unemployed and lose nothing by it, but who are actually working; or rather, it throws light only incidentally on their position. Fortunately, there are enough of such incidental references to illustrate it. Let us take the case of two sisters, aged 60 and 61, living together in Leicester. Both had worked in shoe factories all their lives, one as a table hand, one as a lining machinist. The younger of the two was lame from birth, and it seemed astonishing that she should ever have worked at all, but until 1928 she had been in regular employment. Then she lost her job and had done virtually nothing since. She drew 15*s*. a week Unemployment Assistance. The elder sister was physically fit and was still in regular employment, earning for a full week's work 17*s*. 6*d*. Out of this came travelling expenses (tram fares to and from work) at 4*d*. a day, and 2*d*. a day in addition for "a cup of tea at dinner time". When these deductions from her wages are made, 14*s*. 10*d*. is left, out of which we have to reckon a few more coppers for insurance stamps. She was, therefore, getting actually less by working than her sister was getting by being out of work. And yet she told one of us: "Of course, I've always been the lucky one. I've always had regular work right up to now."

Or we take the instance of a labourer of 36 in Blackburn. When the family was visited it was found that he had got back to work. He had been drawing 41*s*. unemployment assistance, and his wife said that he used to go down and worry the Labour Exchange constantly to get him something to do. He told us that they had said to him at the Exchange: "When you're working you don't get extra wages for extra children", but he was determined to get something, and at last they had found him the job where he was now working. His wage was 41*s*., the same as his Unemployment Assistance had been, though his wife said that some weeks he could bring home a few shillings more by working overtime.

Another Blackburn labourer, aged 37, with three children (two of them aged 14 and 16 working), who was out of work at the sample date, was back at work when the visit took place. He was working as a weaver with four looms. He and his wife had between them drawn 18*s*. 6*d*. Unemployment Assistance when he was out of work. When he got back again, his wife was disallowed her Unemployment Assistance, and his earnings varied from 20*s*. to 22*s*. a week. He said that he was really only 2*s*. a week better off now he was working, but that all the same he was much more contented and anyhow he got his stamps. This last is characteristically important. For a man with earning children the opportunity for securing the requisite number of contributions to give him the right to draw statutory benefit if he falls out of work, is not to be neglected.[1] There was

[1] Because such a right is unaffected by the Means Test and he can draw benefit although his children are earning.

a substantial number of other similar instances in Blackburn, especially among the women who had got back to work. Most of them said that though they were working for very little money, yet they were happier.

These instances (taken with several others of men actually out of work who stated that they were willing to accept work even at a few shillings less than their allowance, and evidently meant it) leave no doubt that many workers, probably the great majority,[1] prefer to work even if the financial gain from it is slight. With the long unemployed, however, we are dealing among others with many difficult cases. We are dealing with some for whom the loss would be so substantial that they refuse to consider taking it, and also with those who are more ready to accept unemployment if it is an easy alternative. As an instance of the first can be cited another Liverpool seaman, a greaser, aged 33, with six children. He was drawing 47*s.* a week Unemployment Assistance, and his wife was horrified at the suggestion that he should go to sea again, for her allowance would then be only 35*s.* This man was certainly anxious to work. He was looking for jobs ashore and would have preferred himself to go to sea again, but he could not afford it. Such men know well, as their wives also know, that being in work in itself entails expenses. We were told in scores of instances that men needed more food if they were working; they need better clothes, often something for travelling and a shilling or two "pocket money" for an occasional half-pint. It is not surprising when all these are considered that men should be found, like a motor man in Liverpool with nine children, to describe themselves as: "A special kind of unemployed. I could get a job to-morrow if I could work for a single man's wage, 25*s.* or 30*s.*" Sometimes, as in the case of a labourer in Blackburn, married, with five children, they gave us the names of firms where they were offered from 27*s.* to 30*s.* a week; and this man said that his son, a lad of just 17, had worked for a time doing a "man's job" at 14*s.* 10*d.* a week.[2]

[1] For it must be remembered that the sample cases are those of *unemployed* workers, a very different matter from what a sample of employed as well as unemployed would show.

[2] We believe that the low rates of wages obtaining in many places are insufficiently recognized. Out of 108 instances of men's wages in the Blackburn

In attempting to estimate the size of this problem, we shall confine ourselves to a comparison between Liverpool and Leicester. The situation in Blackburn, owing to the fact that wages are particularly low (because in most families there is more than one member working) does not offer an altogether just comparison, while in Crook and the Rhondda, because industry for practical purposes means the coal industry, in which wages are regulated by agreement with the Trade Unions concerned, the problem is rather different in character. For the trouble comes largely from those innumerable jobs where wages are subject to no regulation, and where there is no organization of workers to maintain wage levels. And we shall confine ourselves also to the man under the age of 55, on the assumption that many of those over that age cannot be considered as still on the labour market. The figures are as follows:

TABLE XXXVI. ATTITUDE TOWARDS EMPLOYMENT OF MEN BETWEEN THE AGES OF 18 AND 55 IN LIVERPOOL AND LEICESTER

Category...	I	II	III
LEICESTER			
Cases where wage condition was not specifically mentioned	8	20	13
Cases where wage condition was specifically mentioned	1	8	6
LIVERPOOL			
Cases where wage condition was not specifically mentioned	51	60	26
Cases where wage condition was specifically mentioned	5	23	20

The figures show that in something not much under half of the cases of men in these two towns who were regarded by us

sample, no less than 9 are 30*s*. or less, and none are youths, all being over 30. The actual figures are 19*s*., 22*s*., 25*s*. (2), 28*s*. (2), 30*s*. (3). All these figures have been verified. None were part-time jobs.

is becoming used to unemployment or actually anxious to avoid work this factor was specifically mentioned. There is good reason to suppose that it was operative in a substantial number more than the figures show, for the topic is not one which will be discussed as readily as some others. And if we look into the Liverpool figures more closely, we find that though none of those in category I were actually recorded as having left jobs for "the dole", three of those in category II told us that they had left low-paid employment to be better off out of work, and five of those in category III said the same, or that they had recently refused work at low wages. Unfortunately jobs of this kind are not handled to any great extent by the Employment Exchange, or when they are, the prospective employer does not specify the wages he intends to pay, but leaves it to be fixed by agreement. If he did specify them it would be less difficult to secure the necessary figures for a statement of this issue. We should know how low are the wages for which many men are now working.[1]

Table XXXVI shows clearly what an important factor in adjustment to unemployment this question of possible wage proves to be. Here we have the other side of the insecurity problem. We have seen how this insecurity leads in many cases to nervousness and diffidence. In these instances precisely the opposite seems to have happened. The ill-paid unskilled worker or casual labourer who perhaps has never had a chance of earning regular money in his life finds when he is out of work that the rates of assistance, even if they are not generous, are at least secure. For once he knows where he is, and his wife knows it too. She works out her exact routine from one week to another: "Every week I take the pound note to the grocer's on Friday and change it there. I get there the groceries we shall need for the whole week." So they settle down, and another unemployed man is made.

There is another type of case which the sample has shown to be sufficiently important to deserve attention, that of the unemployed man's wife who might earn, but refuses to do so

[1] We have collected some evidence on this point in a later section (p. 201).

because they would be "no better off" if she did. In fact, of course, the Unemployment Assistance Board disregards a certain proportion of earnings of this kind. The family would be better off, and we have quoted above instances where wives went back to work when the husband fell out of it, to keep the home going. But we are here dealing with the attitude of those concerned, and the sample left no doubt that it was more usual for a wife to give up work when her husband came on the Means Test than it was for her to try to obtain work.

There are a certain number of men who reach the state of mind when they definitely prefer not working if they get as much or something near as much when they are out of work. We were told, about a young man, aged 32, in Leicester: "If anyone talks to him about getting a job, his remarks are: 'I don't want work while the dole is paying me £2. 1*s.* 6*d.* I can manage just nice with that and get plenty of beer'." Evidence like this from neighbours is certainly not to be accepted at its face value. But in this case the visit fully confirmed it. In another instance, a Welsh collier aged 36, with a family of five, our record states: "A case of a man having settled down as unemployed and clamouring for higher allowances rather than a wage." In another Welsh instance, a collier aged 28, also a rather inferior type, the man said that he would need £4. 10*s.* a week to move out of the valleys, and at least £3 to £3. 10*s.* if he was to work in the Rhondda. There was no prospect whatever of his getting work at this rate, and he knew it. Or less extreme instances can be taken. A Liverpool porter, aged 55, who explained that it did not pay him to get an occasional day's work. "In September I worked a day for 6*s.* They took off 1*s.* 7*d.* for the stamp and I'd have got 4*s.* 4*d.* dole anyhow, so I was working for a penny." This idea that a man is working only for the amount by which his wage exceeds his possible "dole" is natural enough. Similarly, another Liverpool casual worker, a dock labourer, said that if he could get a fixed job for six months or so he would take it, but occasional jobs were no use to him at all. "If your dole is 40*s.* and one week you earn £4, they dock you of two weeks' dole money, though you're out of work the second week."

These two instances are quoted to show the attitude of the men, not to illustrate the regulations, for in instances of this kind almost invariably the regulations are being misrepresented, and it is evident that the men are excusing their unwillingness to go back to work if it were available. What is true, however, in all these cases, is that the close relationship between Unemployment Assistance and possible wages has been the main factor in reconciling the men concerned to staying out of work. And we have seen already that to reduce assistance would be impossible because the great majority of these men are living at a very low level. Indeed, a further factor doubtless which makes it easier for them to adjust themselves to unemployment is that many of those who have large families can do a useful job if they stay at home and help to bring up the children. Thus one sample case in Liverpool was that of a general labourer aged 44, with eight children living at home, and one grandchild. He was drawing 54*s*. Unemployment Assistance. His chief interest was evidently his family, and he had not much use for any amusements and interests which he could not share with them. He found that looking after them was practically a whole time job for two people, himself and his wife, and though they have to go without food at times; "you can't complain. It's a lot of money to get for nothing. I wouldn't get much more in work than out of work."

8. *The "Work-Shy"*

So much has been said of the unwillingness of the unemployed to work that it is important to get some idea of the proportion which the various types discussed bear to the whole problem, and we attempt such an estimate later. We still have to consider, however, other types, and in particular the type where there is no such explanation as a low potential wage for the adjustment which has taken place; where (to adopt the phrase which is generally used) the man is "work-shy".

From this type we should exclude all the older men. One factor common to prosperous as well as to depressed towns is the difficulty of older men obtaining work, once they lose it.

Until measures are taken to create work for these older men, it is most desirable that they should be able to adjust themselves to the probability of not doing much work again for the rest of their lives, and it is cause for satisfaction rather than otherwise that some of them have found it possible to do so. Here the problem indeed is how to facilitate the adjustment where that has not occurred, for in a very large number of cases they refuse to make it. The older men were brought up with a different outlook and different standards from those which come to the younger generation, and many of them feel that they cannot be satisfied with the rest of their lives lived out "on the dole". Where, however, there is a large unemployed community such as in South Wales or Crook, the adjustment is more readily made, and a qualified observer who has known the Rhondda for fifty years said that in many ways the older men were probably now as happy as or happier than they had ever been. We are some way there towards the creation of a new "leisured" group of the old men who have been compulsorily retired from industry and yet are prepared to accept that as an opportunity to live as pleasant a life as their somewhat straitened resources will allow.

This adjustment has taken years to happen. The only question about it is how much harm is done by allowing such a group to exist among the nominally "unemployed". In the following table we compare the figures for the two places in the Special Areas with those for Leicester in order to show the extent to which such adjustment is taking place.

TABLE XXXVII. ATTITUDE: OLDER MEN 55–64

Category...	I	II	III
Rhondda	3 (7 %)	13 (31 %)	26 (62 %)
Crook	1 (4 %)	7 (31 %)	15 (65 %)
Leicester	10 (22 %)	22 (49 %)	13 (29 %)

The high percentages in category III in the two places within the Special Areas are most noticeable. The majority of the older men there know well enough that they will never work again, and they accept the fact. In Leicester, where there is great relative prosperity, adjustment is far more difficult.

That there is a certain number of "work-shy" men among the younger unemployed is of course not open to doubt, and the question is only what proportion they bear to the whole. In our view, the number is relatively speaking not large, and tends to be exaggerated by confusion with another group, which constitutes a much more troublesome problem, the men who have become diffident owing to continual unemployment, who find it more and more difficult to face repeated failures and who finally give up looking for work. Many such men have not in any way become used to unemployment; often there is no question of allowance approaching potential wages; nor is life made easy by associations, for many of them are living in isolation. It should be possible, if conditions of employment continue to be good, for the Exchanges to do much to help such men back to work. At present it is often assumed far too readily that because a man is young and has been out of work for some time, he is shy of work and therefore not the sort of man who can be sent for a job. Young men who are out of work in prosperous areas are not necessarily avoiding work, and if they sometimes answer shortly and "evasively", as we were told, to questions of the Board's Investigating Officers, it may be because looking for work has such humiliating associations for them that they hate the implied suggestion that they could get work if they tried.

The "work-shy" man is of a different type, though in a casual interview the two may not be easy to distinguish. The chances are that he is mixed up with some betting concern, or that he keeps greyhounds, or picks up something here and there in addition to his Unemployment Assistance by hawking or street singing. Often he does not even tell his wife whether he is working or not, and the share of the allowance which he keeps for himself is disproportionately large. He may be dressed rather flashily, and the chances are that he will complain of those men who won't work, contrasting them with the hard triers like himself. We may summarise the career of such a one, an extreme case, in a prosperous area: a married man aged 24.

After leaving school in 1927 he was for a few months an errand boy. He subsequently worked for nearly a year in a factory, then was six months with a firm of builders in 1931. That same year he had two days of bill distributing, and two months in another factory. In the summer of 1934 he pushed a barrow hawking fruit. Interspersed with these jobs he had done some professional boxing in several different towns, and being at one time (before he was married) disallowed unemployment insurance on the grounds that he had voluntarily left good employment, he went off elsewhere with the friend with whom he lived, and by begging and singing in the streets for about two hours a day they used to earn 8*s*. or so, "enough to keep the wolf from the door". When a lad of 15, he was first fined for stealing, and subsequently bound over for two years for the same offence. Incidentally he told us that he used to have an allotment, but "got fed up when vegetables got pinched". In 1932 he was imprisoned for thirteen days for assault, and at the end of 1934 he got six months hard labour for living on the immoral earnings of the girl he later married. His house was reasonably well furnished, and somehow he seemed to have acquired an excellent wireless set and apparently also a motor bicycle. One employer stated that it "appeared impossible for him to speak the truth, even when there was no reason for him to do otherwise". He had now evidently settled down on the allowance, eked out generously by less reputable sources of income, and expressed himself as quite contented. It would of course be easy to suggest many occupations in which such a man might do well. If, however, society can keep him quiet by paying him 33*s*. a week, it seems a not unreasonable bargain. But we have our doubts.

His is indeed an extreme case, though it must not be dismissed too readily for in each place visited there was, in category III, a sprinkling of men who had criminal records, or had been heavily fined for working with bookmakers. In Liverpool, for example, two or three of the men visited were of this type, like one with whom we had a useful interview in spite of a warning that he was a dangerous fellow who "throws culinary articles at his parents, habitually uses filthy language, frequents gambling clubs, and is a bookmaker's tout"; and that he "uses physical force where necessary". "A real clever boy", his mother (who saw the visitor first) described him. But the majority were less exciting, and much more depressing, as for instance a man of 25, living with his mother and sister. "When I called", our record notes, "at 12.15, he was still in bed. His mother opened the door. I heard her speak to him through the bedroom door. He said I should come again another time. When I asked him what time was suitable, he shouted it was no use, he would say nothing. His mother was very much afraid of him."

Almost always it is the same story: "Has not learned any trade." "Very little work since leaving school." "His mother says he would do better without the dole." "Gave the impression of not being over anxious to get another job." "Surly and reserved." "Said he wanted work, but I don't believe it." It would be mistaken, however, to assume that all these young men are necessarily inferior material. Anyone with experience of handling young men of 18 or 20 or so is aware of the odd aberrations for which allowances constantly have to be made, and obviously any aberration will be emphasized tenfold by the abnormality of prolonged unemployment. In one family visited in Liverpool though the lad who was the sample case was still unemployed, his brother aged 25 was also seen, and he was back in good employment after being out for two years. He appeared a fine normal type, yet he described how difficult he had found it to force himself back to work, and his mother said that while he had been out of work "he was terribly surly. He used to go upstairs to his room and refuse to eat." If he had been visited by one of us at that time, he might perhaps have been classified in the third of our categories, but the classification would evidently have been wrong.

Yet this problem of the young unemployed man remains serious, perhaps the most serious of all the problems of the long unemployed. It is especially aggravated by the conditions of Liverpool, the depression, the casual character of much employment, and the low standard, material and non-material, at which the Liverpool long unemployed are living

Here are the Liverpool figures for attitude to work split up into 15-year age groups.

TABLE XXXVIII. ATTITUDE TOWARDS EMPLOYMENT: LIVERPOOL

Category ...	I	II	III	Total
Age 20–34	20 (24 %)	39 (46 %)	25 (30 %)	84
Age 35–49	26 (33 %)	33 (42 %)	20 (25 %)	79
Age 50–64	27 (43 %)	24 (38 %)	12 (19 %)	63

It will be seen that eagerness for work declines steadily from the older men to the younger. We could wish that a larger proportion of the older men could accept the fact of unemployment, but they cannot, and we find that the proportion of them in category I is exceptionally high. Many of the middle-aged men with large families come into the group discussed above where the possible wages are so low that Unemployment Assistance is a satisfactory alternative, which explains the high proportion of middle-aged men in category II. What is most depressing, however, is to find from the figures of both category II and of category III that the young men are those who are most ready to accept long unemployment. It is hard to exaggerate the importance of this for the future. One other point must be mentioned here concerning the attitude of these young men. That association with an unemployed community which can be so powerful a factor in reconciling a man to unemployment is present probably more extensively here than in any other age group. Though they tend not to belong to specific organizations, the number who spend most of their time with other young men who are also out of work is large. In Liverpool these associations take chiefly the form of "cellar clubs". In Leicester it is the ordinary unemployed club which the young men patronize. But whatever the form, we find this feature regularly through the various areas into which the sample took us. It suggests at once one of the reasons for their continual unemployment, and also perhaps the possibility of a more effective institutional approach to them than has been made in the past.

9. *The Lower End of the Register*

Besides those who are "work-shy" though they ought to be working there is another group, those who virtually speaking cannot work owing to some physical or mental defect, or the association of both. Technically these men, if our judgment on them is right, ought not to be in receipt of Unemployment Assistance at all, but the Board has taken a generous view of their position, and on humanitarian grounds such a view is the right view. For especially in the case of those with physical defects due to age or accident, we are dealing with men who have in many instances served industry well, and whose claims to assistance on these grounds are very strong. We may take as a random example a man in Leicester, aged 60, a widower. He had spent all his working life in the shoe trade, and had been stopped owing to heart disease, developed after a bout of influenza. He was also having trouble with his feet, which were badly swollen, and this made it hard for him to get about, but he was a game little man struggling to make the best of things in spite of his disabilities. He had recently applied for a job as a schoolkeeper, and was greatly disappointed not to get it, for he thought such jobs ought "to be kept for the old 'uns". But to us it was perfectly plain he would never work again. In the same group, though different in type, are the cases with low mentality, employable only on compassionate grounds, and standing no chance in the ordinary labour market. This group is a relatively small part of the whole. Those who were physically unfit were less than one in thirteen of the sample as a whole, and those reckoned as absolutely unemployable were fewer than one in sixteen. We shall expect to find a high proportion of adjustment in such cases, and the figures given in detail in Table C 2[1] bear this out. The general tendency is unmistakable. Among those classified as unfit, approximately two-fifths were reconciled to the prospect of not working again, as compared with only a quarter of those in good physical condition. And we get a similar result if we look at the problem in terms of employability

[1] See p. 437.

(Table C 3[1]). Here, too, the result is so clear that it needs no comment. What is of course difficult is to decide how far in any given instance a "work-shy" attitude may have brought with it physical deterioration. In a certain number of instances this had clearly happened. But on the whole these figures are satisfactory, showing that the unemployables are at least better able than others to adjust themselves to the certainty of never working again.

10. *The Position as a Whole*

It remains for us to summarize in figures attitude towards employment as we found it in our six areas. What has already been said will show that there are two problems, distinct and indeed precisely opposite in character. With men who are still to be regarded as on the labour market, the problem is to maintain the work incentive. With men who must be considered as retired from industry, the problem is to reconcile them to unemployment. Accordingly we divide the figures into two groups, the first those under the age of 60, the second those between 60 and 64.

TABLE XXXIX. ATTITUDE TOWARDS EMPLOYMENT

Category ...	I	II	I, II	III
A. Under 60	198 (31 %)	284 (45 %)	482 (76 %)	151 (24 %)
B. 60 and over	23 (19 %)	40 (33 %)	63 (52 %)	60 (48 %)

In both groups it is the numbers in the third category, as compared with those in the first and second, that are important. We want, indeed, to know how many men of employable age form the intractable problem, intractable, that is, under present wage conditions, conditions of work, and so on. And we want to know how many men, above the age when they are likely on any reasonable computation to obtain ordinary economic employment again, are irreconcilable. Anyone who has visited a

[1] See p. 437.

number of these older men, and knows the hopelessness of men faced with an empty future—whom neither education nor work has ever given an opportunity to learn how to spend leisure—knows the urgency of their case. Five years in a man's life is a long time; and if at the end of five years' uncertainty there is only (as there is now) the certainty of a pension at a yet smaller rate, it is a fate that can scarcely be tolerated. The ordinary working man is not very easily moved, and the sight of some of these older men, broken down and unable to speak for the moment as they looked ahead into the future, is not one that will be soon forgotten.

The crux of the matter lies in two groups—those of employable age whose adjustment to unemployment is so complete that it would be hard to rouse them to work, and those above the age when there is any likelihood of their getting work, who yet refuse to accept their situation. We reckon[1] that there are some sixty thousand men in the first group, and eight thousand in the second. No revival in trade is likely to make a substantial impression on either of these figures unless some measures of a different character accompany it. And there is reason to think that both figures may grow proportionately; the first because it contains already more than its fair share of the young men and the second because as unemployment becomes less of a Special Areas problem, the numbers of older unemployed men in prosperous places will be a larger proportion of the whole.

[1] Magnifying the sample on the lines indicated above: see pp. 33 *seqq.*

III. MORAL PROBLEMS

THE SENSE OF INDEPENDENCE AND RESPECTABILITY

(*a*) *The Importance of this Question*

After the attempt has been made to analyse the effects of unemployment on a man's attitude towards employment and on the physical standards of himself and his family, a whole range of questions remains that comes rightly under neither of these headings, though they cannot be completely dissociated from either. These are questions concerning the effects of unemployment on men's sense of self-respect and their attitude towards society in general, questions which are partly psychological in character, partly moral. One of the adjectives which the English working man likes applying to himself is the word "respectable". It covers a multitude of virtues, and often a multitude of sins, for the man who says "I'm a respectable man" is often the old reprobate. One of us encountered a family in Wales, perhaps the worst case that the Rhondda sample brought out, which will be described in detail later. For our present purpose all that need be said is that the family were living under filthy conditions, in a room, half underground, which smelt intolerably, while it was clear that a substantial proportion of the allowance was spent on drink. Yet this man claimed that "of course" he was respectable. Similarly there was a man in Leicester—a skilled man at a certain type of light work, who, if he had wished to get back to it could no doubt have done so. At first he thought that the caller was on official business and protested hurriedly his anxiety for work. When he discovered it was not an official visit, he thought it must be the offer of a job, and protested equally vehemently that he was long past work—after which he launched out on a disquisition about workmen's clubs that started men on the downward path and with which he would therefore have nothing to do. Although his clothes and person were dirty, there was a certain shabby pretentiousness about them, and he too used the word "respectable" about himself. What is this quality to which the disreputable pretend, and which we felt instinctively in so many of the finer types of working man with whom the sample brought us into contact? Is it something that is different as between one generation and another? Is it something which is affected by unemployment? Is it anything that matters, or is there always something bogus about it—as in the two cases quoted—which means that we can see its passing (if indeed it is beginning to pass) without regret? These are some of the questions which the sample visits suggest.

Before an attempt to analyse the content of this term is made, something further should be said of its nature. What makes matters where respectability is involved different from matters of purely local custom, for example, is the way in which people feel about them. These feelings cannot be described except as moral. No doubt a large element of convention enters into ideas of respectability, as there is a substantial conventional element in all morals, but that does not alter the fact that the feelings attached to them are different in quality from the feelings attached to other customs and conventions and suggest a different series of problems. With all those ideas and conventions which are examined in this chapter, feelings of this kind appear to be associated.

No very simple answer to the questions we have asked can be expected. But of their importance there can be no doubt. In the first chapter of this report it was shown that long unemployment is, speaking generally, a new problem, dating from the slump and the years following. In that period, thousands have been added to the list of those receiving monetary assistance on account of long unemployment, and this fact is certainly not due simply to the absorption in the unemployment figures of those previously drawing poor relief.[1] And though there are a number

[1] In Liverpool the tendency between 1931 and 1935 was the other way. In that period the number receiving Outdoor Relief from the Public Assistance authorities rose steadily from 16,500 to 31,300, while the number of those receiving Unemployment Benefit or Assistance declined from 57,000 to 37,600. Circumstances in Liverpool are not of course representative for the country as a whole, though Glasgow is said to provide a parallel. But even in London there have been signs of a similar tendency.

of instances in Leicester for example of men who lost their work at the time of the slump, yet there were also many men in the sample who had had work since that time, but are now long unemployed.

Length of Unemployment

1–2 years	134
2–3 years	142
3–4 years	104
4–5 years	128
5 years and over ...	309

Even if all those who had been out for three years or more are eliminated, as having been thrown out of work by the slump, that leaves 276, roughly a third, who have been in work since the slump, and though a certain proportion of that number (especially in the Special Areas) are men who have actually been unemployed for five years or more but have had a spell of relief work, there is still a substantial group which must be regarded as having accumulated in the years since the slump. Though the figures for long unemployment, therefore, have been greatly reduced during the past few years, there has evidently been some movement into long unemployment as well as considerable movement out of it. Is the problem of long unemployment to some extent self-generating, as has been suggested? Is Unemployment Assistance a pied piper, and do people come forward to draw Unemployment Assistance because assistance is there for them to draw? This is evidently a question which is closely connected with those that have been suggested above.

(*b*) *Ideas of Respectability: Financial Independence*

An idea may first be taken, one side of which has recently received full and deserved attention, the idea lying behind insurance against death. To the maintenance of such insurance payments, which makes it possible to provide lavish funerals, this sense of respectability is certainly attached. Among the families visited insurances seem to be treated not so much as a means of saving, but with something akin to superstition. The sample showed that they are regarded even by families which are living in the worst conditions as something that must, at all cost, be preserved. Figures for the amount of such insurances were obtained only in a limited number of instances, and it is impossible to judge from them with any accuracy how often the practice has been given up. But where deaths had lately occurred in the families of the sample, it appeared that insurance money had been almost invariably drawn: and we shall probably not be far wrong in concluding that the great majority of unemployed families still maintain their insurance payments. In Deptford, figures for insurance payments are given in 39 of our records, payments averaging slightly over 1*s.* 6*d.* a family. It seemed usual to pay about 6*d.* a head, and in several of the large families as much as 4*s.* 6*d.* or 5*s.* a week of the family budget was spent in this way.[1] The only case specifically recorded as paying no insurances was a grizzled old man, living alone in a condemned house with the broken windows boarded up, in one of the worst streets in Deptford, a black street on the London Survey poverty map. It would have been hard to imagine a more neglected being, or one whose link with society had been more completely severed; and in the light of what we heard elsewhere, the absence of insurance in his case may be taken as a symbol of the last stage of hopeless apathy. For those who talked about insurance spoke of it with something like superstition. They keep up insurances so that (as a middle aged man living on his own in Liverpool said) "it'd be all right if anything should happen". A Liverpool family which had run up nearly £8 arrears of rent nevertheless kept up payments to the Burial Club. "The Means Test and the capitalists", said this man, "prevent me from having a decent life, but at least I will have a decent death". Several instances occurred in the sample of what this decent death meant. In one Liverpool case £24 was received in death benefit, and £18 spent on the funeral. There is something

[1] There is reason to think that these figures slightly overstate the "averages" for unemployed families as a whole, in which the amount is perhaps between 3*d.* and 4*d.* a head on an average.

peculiarly macabre in the sight of the plumed horses, the rows of black carriages or expensive cars, the family in deep mourning, and the flowers piled high on the coffin, as a funeral *cortège* moves from the door of a Liverpool hovel, where maybe there are two or three families living in five or six rooms. It is a triumphant but misguided assertion of the rights of man. If a man cannot live an independent life, at least his death shall be a charge on no one but his own family.

The contrast between this abhorrence of burial by the State, and the fact that burial by the State is, in another class, one of the highest honours that can be bestowed, almost inevitably suggests itself. The comparison is of course not altogether fair, but it does suggest a difference in attitude towards the State which is significant. To be buried by the State is something that the poor Englishman associates with the last degradation of the pauper. The State educates and cares for his children, builds his house perhaps, and provides him with a score of services—and yet it has not yet succeeded in persuading him that he is really a part of it, one who has something to give, as well as to take. It seems to do almost too much, and at the same time too little. He is prepared to take almost anything from it except that which will stamp him finally as dependent on it. Thus, though it takes many of his responsibilities out of his hands, it has as yet succeeded only partially in making him feel his citizenship.

This abhorrence of a "pauper's grave", then, seems to be at bottom an assertion of independence. If a man cannot be independent while he lives, he will at least be independent dying. This particular manifestation of the sense of respectability is apparently almost universal among the poorer classes and among the unemployed. There seems to be no good reason for thinking that unemployment has made a substantial difference to it.

When the argument is carried one stage further, however, and the question arises what is the attitude towards financial independence in everyday life, the answer is a very different one. Here again it cannot be given in simple terms. Some actual cases will illustrate this best. There were certainly a number of instances of families which felt deeply the loss of independence caused by having to draw Unemployment Assistance at all. "Is he glad to get back?" said one Blackburn woman whose husband had just got back to work at a wage that left them very little better off: "is he not! His money is his own, and that makes all the difference." It was in Blackburn, too, that the wife of an unemployed man, a woman of forty-one, said: "My father turned me out of the house because I was marrying a man that was out of work. It was just beginning then, all this unemployment. Lucky he is not alive now." There were plenty of other instances, for example a South Wales family of the old type, the father a collier of 50, an excellent man, married to a woman who was evidently a particularly careful housewife, with a son of 19. The boy was in old clothes, in itself a good sign, for the flashily dressed young men in South Wales (or indeed anywhere else) are not often the best. The family is described as: "Feeling very strongly the so-called stigma attaching to any form of charity. They regard even Unemployment Assistance as charity and feel a degradation about it. They resent the intrusion of the U.A.B. officer who is said to ask questions that do not concern him in the least. He may be suspicious because the house is so clean and the family so respectable."

Coupled with this desire for financial independence, as is seen in this last example, there is sometimes the insistent desire to keep the precise financial position secret. One old couple in Blackburn, both aged 61, evidently felt this desire strongly, for the man said that he hated the visits of the "Means Test men". "Every fresh investigation they ask to see the bank-book, though they know perfectly well what is in it." He did not object to their seeing it in the first instance, but felt certain that tales of his business must "get about", and evidently could not bear to think of this. And his wife said, "Sometimes I say to him, we'll have to keep enough to get a bit of a grave for ourselves, but they'll have to look after us" (i.e. at the old age pension age) "for all our money will be gone. Sometimes we think we'd better sell the house, but then you have your rent, which is worse."

Here then is a typical case, of the old idea of respectability, the desire for financial independence during the working career, after it, and above all, at death, and the anxiety that one's "business" shall not "get about". The Unemployment Assistance Board's officer has an almost impossible task in a house like that. Such a family cannot be reconciled to the principle of an investigation into their means. The impression formed by those who took part in the enquiry was that, on the whole, the Board's officers carry out their duty with tact and sympathy, but where there is a rooted objection to the principle it is impossible to avoid causing distress by it. "Everybody knows who the Means Test man is when he comes to call on you", as a man in Leicester said; and when another man in Leicester remarked that the Means Test was a constant worry to him: "not that I'm doing anything wrong but that I feel they're always spying", it was this cherished independence that was in the back of his mind.

On the other hand, such cases seemed to be the exception rather than the rule. Certainly those who feel that there is an element of disgrace in receiving Unemployment Assistance are unusual, and probably most of those who, like the clerk in Leicester, quoted above, at first struggle to make a trade pay on their own, get used to it. But something is lost in the process, the value of which, though it is hard to assess, is considerable.

There is some reason to think also that the distinction between Unemployment Assistance and Public Assistance is beginning, especially in places where unemployment is widespread, to become blurred in people's minds. One man was visited in a Rhondda village, and said: "I can remember the days when it was thought shame to accept poor relief. Now there's so many do it that there is nothing to it, and as far as I can hear, it all comes from the same place as the dole anyhow."

The position is certainly anomalous. One old unemployed miner in the Rhondda of respectable type said that he was still paying 2*s.* 10*d.* a month to his Friendly Society. He joined originally because he "did not like the thought of going on the parish if he was ill, and reckoned that by this and Health Insurance he would get 29*s.* a week if he was ill. Now his Health Insurance had run out and he would have to apply to the parish anyhow, so he does not see the point of keeping up his Friendly Society contributions". Men of this "respectable" type are conservative, and it is not surprising therefore that he was still paying those contributions, but his case suggests that the distinction between Public Assistance and Unemployment Assistance tends to get obliterated partly by the fact that many men of excellent type are forced to have recourse to Public Assistance when they become ill (for then, as they are not "fit and available", they do not qualify for Unemployment Assistance) and that Public Assistance is thus losing the stigma hitherto attached to it. An old labourer, living alone in a poverty-stricken room in a Liverpool slum, described how: "The man downstairs is as happy as he can be. He used to push a fish-barrow, then when the parish came along after the War, he gets 45*s.* a week and so he's never done any work since; he's as happy as a sand boy." It was plain that this old man was still rather shocked by his neighbour's willingness to depend on Public Assistance, but that the sight of the ungodly, flourishing like a green bay tree, was becoming somewhat trying to him and might end by breaking down his own resistance. On the other hand, a young couple in Crook (a quite exceptional household) still showed strongly the old feelings. They "started married life badly: after they'd been married six months came the Coal Strike, and their furniture money (savings) had to go to keep them. Their friends suggested that they should go to the P.A.C., but she's never done that so far, and intends never to do so. She feels she can't ask anyone else for anything." Incidentally there was here no feeling of disgrace whatever about the "Means Test". They grumbled about a particular regulation that had hit them rather hard, but the husband said he felt the Means Test man to be a real friend, and that he always knew he could talk over anything with him.[1]

The general conclusions to be drawn from the sample on this matter then are that unemployment does tend to affect the

[1] This personal element in the administration of the Board is one of the most valuable features of it. It is the provision of a service to deal with individuals and with homes rather than with forms and figures, and thereby some of the virtues may be discovered which have hitherto seemed inevitably lacking in administration.

attitude of men towards depending on their own financial resources. It could indeed hardly be otherwise. There is certainly a small section of men (who naturally did not come within the scope of the sample) who prefer to depend on their own slender resources so long as they last rather than apply for Unemployment Assistance, but the majority gradually become used to it. Such acquiescence is not by any means entirely unsatisfactory. But when it means, as it inevitably begins to mean in places where unemployment is widespread, that a whole village accepts permanent unemployment, and permanent Unemployment Assistance or Public Assistance, as the normal life for it, a serious situation arises. There is a danger that such a situation is, in some places, on the way to being created.

(*c*) *Ideas of Respectability: The Home*

Another point at which the sense of respectability in an unemployed man or woman is liable to attack lies in the home. Here too the feeling of independence enters in, though it may be entirely dissociated from financial independence. An example may be quoted from the small special sample of women visited in Liverpool, with the idea of discovering something about those who were unemployed but were not on the register of the U.A.B. at that time. This woman was aged 46, a café manageress, described in the case papers as "clean, capable, good type". She had had many years' experience of hotel and café work, and the last seasonal work she had taken was bringing her £2. 10*s*. a week and all found. She thus managed to save a little, and started a small business on her own, but it failed. She lived on the remainder of her savings till they were exhausted, then pawned her jewellery, and when that came to an end, she applied for Public Assistance. She lived with a friend, a seamstress, suffering from heart disease and drawing National Health Insurance money in respect of it. The joint income was 24*s*. They lived in one of the fine new tenements of Liverpool, and the room was very neat and pleasantly furnished, an object lesson in what could be done by a competent woman with such a small sum. Her manner was, according to the record of the visit, "decidedly snobbish, but this no doubt comes to some extent from knowledge of the people she is talking about, coupled with a desire to impress. She takes the worst view of the poorer Liverpool people, and says that in their block of flats (15) there are only 5 working and the rest do not want to work, but to live on Public Assistance. They twist the P.A.C. officers round their fingers, because if they are disallowed, they go to their local councillor, who gives them a note for the P.A.C." The interesting thing about her case was that she too was evidently quite content to live on Public Assistance, and was rather suspicious of the caller when he steered the conversation towards possibilities of work. What gave her the eminent feeling of respectability which she evidently possessed was the fact of living in a good, well-managed home which was her own.

The instance was particularly striking in the context of the other P.A.C. visits in Liverpool, which for the most part took us into somewhat nightmarish surroundings where there was no semblance of any kind of respectability preserved. But it illustrates a type which is fairly widespread. Sometimes when the possibilities of a move to another place to look for work were suggested, resistance based on this was apparent: "No, we've at least got a roof over our heads now, but if he moves elsewhere we'll end up in lodgings."

It occurred even in the case of single men, as with a Liverpool builder's labourer, aged 50, who "is afraid to leave his landlady because he has his few things there and he would be on the street". Many couples, young and old, had their interests almost entirely centred on the home, and though they did not always allude to it, it was plain that this was often an element of great importance to personality; older couples feeling for instance that it was of supreme importance to keep intact the "front room", hardly ever used, but conferring somehow through its shiny furniture a feeling of independence and status to them. How closely the home is associated with feelings of independence is shown by a remark made by one young Liverpool couple (aged 31 and 30, with three children): "We're very keen on the house, and hope to get a council house. But not a new tenement. Too many people know too much of your business."

A case has been quoted above where a respectable Leicester couple evidently felt bitterly that they had had to move from a house of their own into rooms.[1] So in the Rhondda a man of 43 whose wife died a few weeks before the visit took place, and who was left with his son of 10, in a house with five rooms, felt "indignant that the U.A.B. asked him to give up his home for which he has struggled so many years, and to move into lodgings". At the time of the visit the U.A.B. was making a special allowance for a housekeeper (9*s.* a week) to enable him to keep the house up, and the same is true of several similar instances elsewhere. And many people remarked on the great difference which the attitude of the U.A.B. official, as contrasted with that of the old Poor Law official, made. The U.A.B. official did not demand that pictures and equipment must be sold, whereas in many districts this demand used to be made as a condition of receiving relief.

So far as could be judged from the sample, it was generally possible for those whose feelings of independence were associated primarily with their homes to preserve them intact. Officials who come into constant contact with unemployed men and women told us that feelings of this particular kind were the greatest obstacle to transference, and that it is virtually impossible for example to persuade a woman who is living alone in a poor single room of her own to move because of the strength of the sentiment which, almost invariably, binds her to it. Cases occurred indeed, where under the stress of unemployment elderly couples had moved from their own houses into lodgings, and the resultant unhappiness was invariably great. But it was more common to find that the Board had made some special allowance in order that it should be possible for houses to be maintained.

One characteristic that seemed to be observable in a large number of instances in which outstanding efforts were being made to keep up a respectable home was a certain bitterness that

[1] See p. 51.

society had not recognized the value of these efforts, coupled as it seemed with a question in the mind, was the effort really worth it? Thus we found several who complained that the "professional cadger" got all the sympathy that was going, while the family which hid its troubles got no credit. And often, where this was not expressed, it seemed to be not very far below the surface. In Liverpool, for instance, the feeling of anxiety and nervousness did not appear to a comparable extent where respectability had been thrown to the winds, the house was dirty, and the children were in rags; but, where a real effort was being made, there seemed to be time after time the underlying doubt, who was gaining by it, and was it a real gain? The instance of a middle-class family which has already been discussed in our analysis of conditions in Liverpool may be cited.[1] It was evidently unthinkable still to this family that they should let go their standards; yet certainly the feeling was growing that if they had done so their material position might have been better. Or two other instances in Liverpool, in each of which the wife only was seen may be compared. One was the wife of a young factory worker. There was a certain reserve about her manner, and from what she said about her husband it was clear that he too did not mix readily with other people. The house was very clean with new furniture, beautifully kept, and she and her small daughter of six could scarcely have been more neatly dressed. It looked as though this was gained by her going short of food to keep the household well equipped, and the record notes: "A household where to keep up appearances, which are exceptionally good, sacrifices are made in other directions."

This woman gave the impression that she could hardly bear to keep up these standards any longer; and that she was beginning to wonder whether they were really genuine. The other was the wife of a general labourer, living (as were the family just mentioned) below our poverty line. The family, unlike the last, which had no debts whatever, owed between £6 and £7 rent. The record describes the household as a "reasonable working-class family with children fairly well

[1] See above, p. 93.

clothed and not too clean." She told us how they did not need to get coal, for there was a railway dump nearby, from which her husband was able to abstract enough for the family's needs. His hobby was ferreting, in which he indulged every Sunday "with a gentleman who has a ferret; of course, he gets nothing for it, but if he comes back again with a rabbit, so much the better." They were both members of the Methodist Church, but her husband was always complaining on that score because "Catholics can get work at the silk factory, Protestants cannot. We've only had one parcel from the church in seven years and my husband had to fight hard for that. In fact he said that if he didn't get it, he'd leave the church. He's a man that fights hard for his family, and what he can't get by fair means he'll get by foul. He mends the boots, too; I don't know what he couldn't do if he put his mind to it." In that family there was no nervousness, no tension. They fought for what they could get, and let go what they felt was not worth keeping. Respectability had gone and instead of it there was a free-and-easy contentment.

The impression left, therefore, is that there is, as it were, a line to be defended somewhere behind the front line of complete financial independence and the last line of independence at death, a line defended by those who keep up a good home at the expense of other things. But those who are doing this, like those who are clinging to complete financial independence, seem sometimes at least to feel that they are not being fairly treated by society. It is as though their lives had been based on assumptions which they now found were fast disappearing, leaving them with a sense of respectability which, whatever else there was to it, was now becoming out of date; as though they were relying on society to uphold them, but finding that it is not interested in doing so. If the unemployed man in the first of these two families gets back to work, the strain that has been undergone will be relaxed, and they may well feel that they have been justified at last, but meanwhile their anxiety is obviously acute.

If changes of this kind are taking place, that does not necessarily mean they are bad changes. In many ways it is unsatisfactory that a stigma should be attached to the receipt of Public Assistance. It will be in many ways satisfactory if the old idea of "keeping oneself to oneself", a phrase that was used scores of times to us with the suggestion that it was some kind of virtue, breaks down. But the point is that the old system did at least imply some sort of obligation, whereas the new may imply none. In the second instance quoted above, all awareness of obligations seemed completely to have gone. A gathering of unemployed men may be often heard speaking of the State's duty to maintain the unemployed. What is their duty in return? At present that question is unanswerable. But unless some sense of duties and obligations can be built up to replace the old that are disappearing, a very serious situation will be created. And it will be serious not only from a theoretical but from an administrative point of view.

(*d*) *Ideas of Respectability: The Fair Wage*

If all the examples of respectability that have been quoted in the last three sections could be gathered in one place, it would be obvious at once that on the whole they represented the older elements in the sample. That conception of respectability discussed in this section, however, is characteristic of the younger men. And a distinction must be drawn here between economic motives and moral feelings. In the last chapter, when the attitude of men towards employment was considered, something was said of the loss, occasioned by the proximity between wages and unemployment allowances, of the economic incentive to work. In this section we are not dealing with instances where there is this proximity, but rather with the situation where a man refuses work because he feels that the wage is beneath his dignity to accept, and that to accept it would be to lower his status and possibly threaten that of his fellow workers. On a cynical view it might be imagined that no such distinction exists. But we were convinced that, while there are many cases in which the economic motive is operative, there are some, too, in which it is this moral feeling that comes into play.

A Leicester instance will show what we have in mind. This

was a young married man, aged 33, living in an excellent house, comfortably furnished and very tidy. He was a hosiery knitter, and had been a foreman in a London firm, earning a very good wage, £6 or £7 a week, but the firm unfortunately changed hands and ultimately went out of business. Of this man the official view we were told was: "It is hard to understand why he does not get a job. My opinion is that he has not got enough 'kick' and fails to impress would-be employers." Our report on the other hand, says that he was "an exceptionally good type" who was "an expert on hosiery machinery and would be extremely happy in his work. He said he would be willing to start for £2 odd, but would rather go to the gutter than work for nothing." His unemployment assistance was 29*s.* In the case of another young Leicester married couple, there seemed to be the same bar. The man, who was a boot and shoe operative, drawing the same rate of allowance as in the previous instance, said that he could have had a job some time since but that he refused to work below Trade Union rates. He had made outstanding, if ill-advised, efforts to find work, and there was no reasonable doubt about his anxiety for it. But he was determined not to take it at a rate that would mean lowering himself; he was not willing to work (in the phrase current in Liverpool) "under the light". A young Liverpool seaman, a magnificent physical type, intelligent, and living in thoroughly respectable conditions, used the phrase, and said that he knew many who would take a job for 35*s.* but he would take nothing under 45*s.* or 50*s.*, for he believed he was worth that. And similar examples occurred in all the places visited.

It was distinctly noticeable that the older men set a lower value on their labour. There were some, like a skilled man in Liverpool, a steel roller shutter fitter, who had earned over £4 a week, who specifically said that they were willing to work for 30*s.* or even 20*s.* a week, and this was, as might be expected, most emphatically asserted in cases where the Means Test was operative.[1] With the older men the comparable form of respect-

[1] I.e. where the scale allowance was reduced on account of the fact that earnings or other resources were taken into consideration.

ability was the maintenance of trade union membership. It was most noticeable in Leicester, for example, that those who had maintained membership of the Boot and Shoe Operatives' Union in spite of being out of work for years, were the most respectable; not necessarily keeping up fancy domestic standards, but feeling, as it seemed, that solidarity with those with whom they had once worked gave them a sort of independent status in relation to the community as a whole.

When we encountered these qualities we could not help not merely being aware of them, but also being aware of the value of those in whom they were to be found, however difficult it might be to value the qualities themselves. The types of men in whom they occurred were those who were potentially excellent members of the community. Such men seemed to consider work as something that produces a wage—the wage being, as it were, a mark of the respect and esteem in which they are held. There is very much to be said for not undermining this sentiment. There is no doubt that some of the opposition which is made to amenity schemes, for instance, is not engineered for propagandist purposes (as has sometimes been said) but is perfectly genuine. Feelings of this kind are already too rare among the long unemployed, as the sample showed, and it is of the greatest importance that they should be preserved. There is a real danger, at the present time, that an unemployed class may be created. It is these feelings, which we have grouped together under the name "respectability", that can prevent it, and for that reason their preservation, if it is possible, is vital.

(*e*) *The Difference between Generations*

In this section we attempt to summarize briefly such evidence as there is that a change is taking place as between the older generation and the new—which means in practice the pre-War or the War generation and the post-War generation. We do not propose to quote in detail tables that we used elsewhere for other purposes, but simply to allude to them. The reader who considers this issue to be of importance can verify them for himself.

First, however, a possible misconception must be removed. It might be thought that in the younger generation we have a naturally lower type simply because employment does tend to skim off the cream from it, whereas where the factor of age enters in, the most admirable type of man may have the ill luck to fall out of work and suffer a long spell of unemployment. There is something in this but not everything, as the following table will show:

TABLE XL

	Intelligence (combined figures of "excellent" and "good average" intelligence)	Employability
Age 18–24	65 %	67 %
25–34	64	77
35–44	62	60
45–54	59	48
55–64	58	42

The differences in the "intelligence" column are not, indeed, of striking magnitude, but the tendency of the figures is steady and there is no reason to doubt the general accuracy of what they show—that the younger long-unemployed men are, on the whole, more intelligent, or at least, strike the ordinary observer as being more intelligent, than the older. And similarly, they are certainly more employable. If there are differences of standard in matters which affect respectability, therefore, there is no reason to think that they are due to the younger unemployed men being of an altogether lower type of intelligence.

Reference may now be made to figures quoted above. On page 61 are given figures of the fraud cases encountered in a London area office, set out by age, which at once suggest that here there is a most marked difference between generations, and that whether the young men are more intelligent or not, they are certainly readier to try to defraud the Unemployment Assistance Board, by working on the sly at low-grade occupations, pushing a barrow or collecting betting slips, and drawing assistance at the same time. Table XXXVIII on page 176 suggests that they are readier to acquiesce in unemployment, and, more than that, to reach the stage when they positively avoid such work as there is available.

The figures bearing on the state of the homes of those visited, according to age, are also illuminating:

TABLE XLI

Age	(Effective visits only included)		
	Dirty home	Bad management	Index of quality of family relations[1]
18–24	25 %	19 %	55
25–34	14	9	77
35–44	15	14	73
45–54	12	8	76
55–64	9	14	89

In reading these figures there are certain facts to be remembered, such as the high proportion of men with families in the 35–44 age group. If dirt in the home is more frequent in this age group than in the older, the reason is no doubt partly the number of large families, and the same is true of the drop in the index of family relations at this period. But the general conclusion to which the figures point seems to be inevitable, that in this sense of the value of a good home, which we have attempted to describe above, the younger generation has a different outlook from that of the older generation.

The same is true if we study the figures for Trade Union membership. But here something that has been said above may serve to correct any too rapid generalization. Because the younger men do not belong to Trade Unions, that does not necessarily mean that they have an attitude that is in no way comparable to that of the older men. It does mean, however, that at present at least, the right institutional forms for that attitude have not yet been found.

[1] Based on instances of separation, desertion or quarrel.

In some ways all this is explicable enough. We should probably not take too seriously the figures of fraud, for example. In other walks of life the state of mind they represent might be considered tiresome, but not much more. And an explanation of some of the figures at least is no doubt to be found in the statistics of those unemployed cases who are living in families where there are other unemployed members. The proportion, in the case of the youngest age group, 18–24, is decidedly higher than in the others (16 % as against 10 % in the age groups 35–44 or 55–64). The men with the lower standards, then, are those who live in families that are riddled with unemployment.

Another much more general factor that must be taken into account in these changing standards is the decline in the practice of apprenticeship. The older type of skilled man who is unemployed is insulted if a job of the kind that so many elderly unskilled men seek, e.g. night watchman, is mentioned to him. He is a tradesman, which means that by training he is far too good for such a job. But nowadays, even in the more respectable families, lads are very often not apprenticed, partly because the economic pressure to take jobs which (though "blind alley") are better paid is too strong, partly because working-class families are beginning to regard office work as the highest mark of respectability. "If I had a young lad", said a middle-aged man in Liverpool, "I'd not put him to a trade now. There's no chance of bettering himself in that way. He should go into a shop, into the office, where all the money is made." At present the state of affairs which exists in regard to training is only temporary. The control of the Trade Unions over apprenticeship is much less strong, and yet at present the "trainees" who are turned out by the Government Training Centres have no recognized status, and if they do make headway it is by a process which may be perhaps best described as "gate-crashing" into the Trade Unions. All this is having a profoundly unsettling effect on something which used to be the hall-mark of working-class respectability, the status of a tradesman who had "served his time".

But though these things may be a partial explanation of some of the tendencies described, they do not, of course, make them any more satisfactory. The picture we have given is not, indeed, a very rosy one. It must be remembered, however, that though the figures point to certain general tendencies, they do not show that there are vast numbers of disreputable young men, and they are not used for that purpose. They indicate only the changing proportions as between different ages. And it would be unwise to be too dogmatic. The qualities that are discussed in this chapter cannot be easily measured, and it may be that few of the figures given have a bearing on them. If we cannot answer definitely, then, the question whether there is a real difference of feeling in these matters of respectability as between generations, we can suggest that such evidence as there is available points to a difference. It indicates too that the attitude towards dependence on Unemployment Assistance or on Public Assistance is changing, and that the sense of social disgrace which once attached to the latter (in its earlier forms) is disappearing; and therein obviously lies one of the serious problems of the next few years. Lastly it shows that we cannot regard all young unemployed men as disreputable, and that there are among them some at least who are kept from working because they will not take an unfair wage. To guard one's rights is not a sign of pauperization (though "rights" are of course often used as an excuse for not working by the disreputable element among the unemployed), and if the Unemployment Assistance authorities have been caused more trouble in South Wales than in Liverpool, that is in some ways, at any rate, a symptom of higher standards in South Wales. For over a generation South Wales had enjoyed a higher wage level and a higher economic standard than Liverpool, and therefore resistance to the inevitable levelling caused by unemployment has been stronger.

The real trouble seems to lie in the fact that the principle of Unemployment Assistance is based on an assumption which is breaking down, partly owing to the widespread nature of unemployment itself during the last twenty years, partly owing to quite different factors. For three and a half centuries one of the assumptions underlying Western individualism has been that a man was responsible for the maintenance of himself and his family. For most of that time this has been a possible assumption, and only a very small fraction of society has refused to acknowledge it. But the scale of modern industrial enterprise means that in periods of depression thousands of men are thrown out of work by conditions outside their own control, and that it is virtually impossible for them to get alternative work of any kind, while changes in the structure of industry have brought even more permanent unemployment than that for which the trade cycle is responsible. When that happens, it is essential that the men affected should be maintained, as they are, by Unemployment Assistance, but it will obviously only be a satisfactory system so long as there is the recognition in the minds of those receiving it that the ultimate responsibility of maintaining themselves is still theirs. The widespread payment of assistance in itself tends to undermine this, while it is being undermined by many other forces as well. It looks as though some new principle will have to be put into operation, whereby a man is offered the chance to give as well as to receive. To-day it is virtually impossible to do so, and as a result he is losing his citizenship.

Part III

PARTICULAR ISSUES

I. THE WAGE PROBLEM

THE CASE FOR FAMILY ALLOWANCES FOR WAGE EARNERS

In previous sections of this report we have had occasion to mention the opinion, formed as the result of the sample visits, that there is a considerable number of men kept out of work by the fact that Unemployment Assistance is a reasonable alternative to low-paid employment. Two different types have been mentioned in this connexion; first the men with large families, whose unemployment allowances may approach the normal wage level for the unskilled or semi-skilled worker (see above, pp. 163 *seqq.*), and secondly, the "respectable" type of young man who, having once had employment at a good wage, refuses it at rates which seem to him to be unreasonable (see above, p. 194). These two problems are obviously distinct, for, with the second of the two categories, the question of proximity between unemployment allowances and wage rates does not necessarily arise. This is not the place in which to consider in detail possible solutions, but as the sample has shown these to be important as "personal" reasons for unemployment, we summarize in this section what seem to us to be the main facts.

The regulations of the Unemployment Assistance Board provide in effect that, except where there are special circumstances, an allowance shall be less than the amount which the applicant would earn if he were following his normal occupation. Cases have, however, come to our notice in which the Board's allowances exceed the amount which, so far as we ourselves can judge, the applicant is likely to earn.

We may take first certain cases in Liverpool where we were told what wages had been last earned. In the case of two men under 24 the details are as follows:

TABLE XLII

Age	Occupation	Allowance	Last wage earned
19	"Apprentice Printer"	29*s.*	15*s.*
23	Milk Roundsman	30*s.* 6*d.*	25*s.*

Two "family" cases show a similar state of affairs:

TABLE XLIII

Age	Occupation	Allowance	Last wage earned
28	Motor Driver	32*s.*	30*s.*
34	General Labourer	50*s.*	50*s.*

Next we can take two statements that work had been refused at a certain rate as giving some indication at least of the "market value" of the men concerned.

TABLE XLIV

Age	Occupation	Allowance	Job refused at
35	Docker	32*s.*	20*s.* and food (as restaurant porter)
47	Steam wagon driver (disabled, chest trouble, 28*s.* pension)	21*s.* 6*d.*	20*s.* (as night watchman)

And lastly there are instances mentioned in the course of the sample visits, but which were not actually sample cases, such as that of a Liverpool window cleaner, single, getting 24*s.* a week. When he married he gave up his job in order to get 26*s.* Unemployment Assistance.

There are, of course, reasons why the normal wage figure

taken for the purpose of limiting the amount of the allowance may exceed the wage last earned. We understand that it is the Board's practice to have regard to the amount which the applicant would probably earn in his normal occupation, rather than the amount which in fact he last earned. Further, as had already been mentioned, the limitation does not necessarily apply where there are special circumstances. In such cases, the Board's officer can exercise discretion. Nevertheless, it seems that there are many cases in which the applicant is given the benefit of the doubt and where, for the purposes of the assessment, the normal wages are over-estimated.

The following table is compiled from information very kindly supplied to us by the Board, showing in respect of the sample cases what normal or "stop" wage had in each case been taken as indicating the limit beyond which the allowance should not go unless there were special circumstances. The table indicates that, taken as a whole, the distance between allowances and possible wages is considerable. But there is a substantial proportion of men who are in fact in the "danger zone", and we believe that the extent of the "danger zone" may be greater than the table suggests.

TABLE XLV. CUMULATIVE PERCENTAGES OF MEN RECEIVING ALLOWANCES AMOUNTING TO MORE THAN CERTAIN PERCENTAGES OF "STOP" WAGE

Age	More than 70 %	More than 80 %	More than 90 %	More than 100 %
18–24	31	24	10	Nil
25–34	33	12	6	3 (5 cases)
35–44	38	22	7	2 (4 cases)
45–54	12	5	2	Nil
55–64	3	2	0·4	Nil
All	21·0	10·5	4·1	1·0

The problem is seen at once to be one of the younger men and family men. In the elderly age groups it is negligible in extent. If we remember that the wage assessment in some instances no doubt over-estimates regular earning capacity, and that, in any case, it naturally takes no account of the expenses incidental to work (travelling expenses, wear and tear of clothes and boots, extra food and pocket-money needed were all mentioned to us in this connexion), it can be seen that, below the age of 44, the proximity is considerably closer even than might appear from the preceding table. At times, the contrast between value in the Labour Market and Unemployment Allowance is fantastic. An instance was quoted to one of us by the Superintendent of a local training centre in the north of England. It was that of a young man, who had had one spell of work, as errand boy for a bicycle shop, and nothing more since he left school. He had married "on the dole", and at the age of 20 already had three children. He was worth, to an employer, perhaps 15*s.* to 20*s.* a week, but was drawing, in Unemployment Assistance, 35*s.*

A detailed analysis of 75 out of the 78 records obtained in Tonypandy, in the Rhondda valley, brings out the close approximation between allowances and the "stop" wages of the unemployed men with wives and dependent children in this area. In 16 of the 17 cases of men with wives and two or more children there was very little advantage in working rather than living on unemployment allowances, the difference being less than 15*s.* a week, without taking into account deductions from wages[1] and the additional expenses of working. In 10 out of 11 cases of men with three or four children there was probably no advantage at all in working—the gross difference in earnings and allowances being less than 10*s.* a week. In 6 cases out of 7 of men with more than four children there was probably a definite advantage, from the point of view of domestic economy, in not working, for the gross difference between "stop" wages and allowances in these cases was less than 5*s.* a week. There is every reason to believe that these results obtained from an

[1] State Insurances, Trade Union subscriptions, checkweighman's allowance, miners' welfare levy, hospital levy, and other small weekly contractual payments seldom account for less than 3*s.* a week and sometimes they account for much more.

examination of the Tonypandy records are typical of the Rhondda Valley and the other mining valleys of South Wales. It is possible, however, that the new wage agreement for the South Wales coalfield made early in 1937 may have had the effect of widening the gap between "stop" wage and allowances in some cases. On the other hand the payment of additional discretionary allowances to meet the increased cost of living will have the opposite effect.

In Crook, as in the Rhondda, wages of workers in the coal industry are fixed by agreement, and it is therefore possible to determine with a reasonable degree of accuracy the relation between Unemployment Assistance and potential wage. Unemployed miners in Crook with three or more children would probably find no great economic advantage in returning to work unless they were able to earn a good deal more than the fixed minimum. Ordinary shifters and labourers with three children might well find that they were at an economic disadvantage if they returned to work. Four or five children would probably make a return to employment an uneconomic proposition for every grade of work in the Durham mines, except in the infrequent cases of men who can earn considerably above the minimum wage for their grade even after being out of the mines for long periods. Very few other occupations are open to unemployed men in Crook, but in such as there are—general labouring, quarry work, brick works labouring and even retail trade—it is unusual for a man to earn much more than 45*s*. a week unless he has some special experience or skill. Local authorities work—such as County Council road work—is an exception to this rule, 56*s*. a week being a common figure, and this is the reason why this type of work was so often mentioned in the course of the sample visits as what men really wanted. The economic incentive, therefore, for a family man with three or more children cannot be very strong in this district. Most of them could and do willingly take Council work, but there is little else that would make their economic circumstances much better than the Unemployment Assistance Board has already done. Striking confirmation of our view that the economic position of many employed workers in the depressed area of County Durham is little better than that of the unemployed is provided by an analysis of the economic circumstances of the visitors to "The Fields", a rest house for the wives of both employed and unemployed men, at Etherley, near Bishop Auckland. The average family incomes of the two types of household in 1936 were as follows:

TABLE XLVI

Persons in family	Husband or other adult worker employed		No earners working members unemployed	
	Average income	No. of cases	Average income	No. of cases
2	32*s.* 11*d.*	7	26*s.* 3*d.*	32
3	39*s.* 10*d.*	8	30*s.* 9*d.*	15
4	35*s.* 7*d.*	10	32*s.* 6*d.*	18
5	42*s.* 1*d.*	5	34*s.* 2*d.*	12
6 and over	40*s.* 3*d.*	4	40*s.* 7*d.*	15

There is comparatively little difference between the economic position of the two types of families even among those with fewer than six members (normally including husband and wife). The average family income of unemployed households with six or more members was actually rather better than the average income of earning households of the same size.

The position in Liverpool is complicated by the vast range of different occupations, many of which are not regulated by collective wage agreements or subject to the Board of Trade regulation of wages. It was obviously not possible to undertake an adequate survey of this vast field and we have had to content ourselves with two very small samples which give certain general indications of the nature of the problem. The first sample consisted of a random selection of workers who are members of the households of Unemployment Assistance Board applicants at a representative Liverpool area office. The average earnings of these workers (men only) over the previous four weeks were as follows:

TABLE XLVII

	21–25	Over 25
Lower quartile	27*s.* 10*d.*	40*s.*
Median	29*s.* 8*d.*	49*s.*
Upper quartile	30*s.* 5*d.*	59*s.* 2*d.*

After the deduction of statutory contributions more than half the wages earned by the "21–25" group of workers would have been insufficient to induce a young married man to take up employment, even if he had no children. His unemployment allowance of 26*s.* would compare very favourably with the prospect of earning 30*s.*, less 1*s.* 7*d.* for insurance contributions, and the other expenses of employment. The average wages earned by half of the "over 25" group of workers might be sufficient to attract an unemployed man with not more than three children, but they would be accepted with hesitation if there were four or more dependent children—a not infrequent situation among the long-unemployed of Liverpool. A quarter of the "over 25" group were earning wages which would not make it worth while for a man with three dependent children to take employment on that account alone.

The second Liverpool sample was of jobs offered at the main Employment Exchange. These were the jobs for which an unemployed man in Liverpool might apply at the Exchange, and they have been analysed according to the remuneration offered in each case:

TABLE XLVIII

	Up to and including 30*s.* a week	Between 30*s.* and 40*s.*	Between 40*s.* and 50*s.*	Over 50*s.*	All
Restricted to men under 25	37	22	—	—	59
Unrestricted	14	1	30	27	72
Total	51	23	30	27	131

Most of the jobs restricted to men under the age of 25 were such as should have been attractive from an economic point of view to unmarried men living on their allowances or even to young married men without children if their wives were also earning a little. Similarly the majority of jobs in the 30*s*. to 40*s*. group should have been attractive on economic grounds to young married men with no children, but most of them would not have been very advantageous for a married man with one or more children. Married men with two or three children would have been confined to the selection of jobs offering more than 40*s*. whilst married men with four or more children would not have been tempted to take many of the jobs below the 50*s*. level. As most of these more highly paid jobs demanded considerable skill or special experience most of the long-unemployed men in Liverpool would have stood little chance of getting one of these.

These two small samples cannot be accepted as representative of wage conditions in Liverpool as a whole. Many employers do not engage their workers through the Exchanges and certain types of labour—for example, dock workers and seamen—are engaged through special Employment Exchanges. Nevertheless it is significant that so many jobs should be offered at wages which do not compare favourably with the unemployment allowances of married men with families. The cinema industry, retail distribution (especially small shops), window cleaning, hairdressing, and unskilled labouring of all kinds are examples of available occupations which offered little attraction for unemployed men with families. These occupations are for the most part unorganized and unprotected and there is little doubt that in many cases advantage has been taken of the depressed employment situation to offer very poor wages, sometimes for arduous work for long hours. But whilst average earnings in organized trades are appreciably higher than average earnings in unorganized trades there is no doubt that, even in the case of organized trades, average earnings are often not high enough to make it "worth while", on a strictly economic calculation, for unemployed men with large families to take employment.

There seems to be no doubt whatever, therefore, that the level of wages and earnings over a considerable section of industry is low enough for there to be little financial inducement for the man with a fair-sized family to work, if he is eligible for Unemployment Assistance. Yet the conclusion reached in an earlier part of this report was that among this same section of those in receipt of assistance, their economic situation, measured by a poverty standard, deteriorates progressively with increasing size of the family, and that where there are more than one or two children there is almost always evidence of hardship. These two facts, taken together, point irresistibly to the necessity for some system of family allowances to those who are working. If earning families are living at something like the same level as that of the unemployed families we visited, they will be suffering comparable hardships, and (if the problem is regarded from another point of view) there is no possibility of getting back into employment a substantial proportion of the long unemployed until some such a system is established. If it were established, it would certainly provide the additional monetary incentive needed for this particular group of men, and we have little doubt that, within a reasonable time, considerable numbers of them would return to work. On the other hand, unless something of the kind is done there is every reason to fear that the problem will grow in size rather than diminish.

It would be entirely out of place to make any detailed suggestions here for family allowances, but it may be as well to mention briefly systems which are already in operation. In Italy the head of a family was paid, up till the recent change which considerably extended the system, 4 lire a week (about 11d.) for each dependent child under 14 years of age. Contributions towards the fund that provides these allowances are made, as with the Unemployment Insurance Fund in this country, by the worker, the employer, and the State. The worker's contribution amounts to 1 % of his gross earnings, the employer's to 2½ %, and the State pays 0·50 lire to the authority administering the fund for each weekly allowance of 4 lire that is paid. The system now includes not only industrial, but agricultural workers, and certain modifications in the rate of allowances were made when this change was introduced. A system the effects of which are similar though the method is different, is in force in France.[1]

Mr Rowntree, in his book *The Human Needs of Labour*, has recently stated the case for some system of family allowance in this country from a different point of view. Mr Rowntree suggests that the allowance should be 5*s*. a head, and should be provided in respect of every child, after the third, between certain ages in the family of a working man. His case is based on the inadequacy of wage rates where there are more than three children. From both points of view therefore, both that of the needs of labour and the necessities of the unemployment problem, there is urgent reason for considering the family allowance. There might be a certain small number, under Mr Rowntree's system, of men with two or three children who were left with Unemployment Assistance approximating to their possible wage. But it would be enough, in a large number of instances where this approximation occurs, to provide the necessary incentive to work, for they are often those where there are more children than three.

The other aspect of the wages problem, where there is no very close approximation of assistance rates to possible wages, is a different matter, and there is no obvious solution to it. It is a commentary on the low rates of wages that prevail in many types of employment, and nothing but a rise in wages will cure it. The numbers involved are, comparatively speaking, small, but cases of this kind deserve very sympathetic consideration, for it is the better type of man who stands out in this way for a reasonable wage. The work-shy young man may use similar excuses, but there is no doubt that in many cases of the kind we have in mind, it is a reason rather than an excuse, and a reason which is fully justifiable. The root of the trouble seems to be that while State education is producing many lads of potentially excellent "social" type, some of them do not get the chance of an industrial or commercial training such as would put them beyond fear of prolonged unemployment. A young

[1] For the Italian system, see the *Ministry of Labour Gazette*, October 1937. For the French system, see D. V. Glass, *The Struggle for Population*.

man, like one interviewed in Leicester, who as foreman in a London hosiery factory had earned a very high wage, may have reached his position on personal rather than on technical qualifications, and if he loses his job for some reason—in this instance the failure of the firm—it may be exceedingly hard for him to get back at a wage rate such as he feels he deserves.

It would be easier to pass a judgment on the present position if adequate information were available with regard to wages. In one instance after another we formed the opinion that the low rate of wages that could be earned was the real reason why this man or that woman was not working. When we came across, for instance, a lad of 22 in a very good Liverpool household, who had worked on one of the "seasonal" jobs in a North Wales seaside resort, cycle repairing, and who left the job because conditions (he was living in) were so bad, and the hours were 12 or 13 a day, it hardly seemed surprising that he had thought the wage of 12*s*. a week inadequate; and his complaint was the more plausible when he said that the waiters in the same establishment had been even worse off than himself. Or when a Liverpool girl of 18 works as a factory hand for 10*s*. a week, or another some years older "leaves voluntarily" a Blackpool café where she is doing seasonal work owing to bad conditions ("working 9 a.m. till midnight, food insufficient and of poor quality") and has her objections sustained by the authorities, it is not difficult to believe that Unemployment Assistance is a tolerable alternative. What this means is that there is still a large number of occupations where conditions are bad and where wages are low, and that until improvements are made there will certainly be those who prefer, if there is the alternative of Unemployment Assistance, to take it. What is to be hoped is that the existence of this alternative may gradually force up the level of wages in these low-paid grades; but it is a bad way of raising the level, for it is through the unemployment of thousands of young men and women, and unemployment is, in itself, a serious evil.

Note. While the case for some sort of system providing for an addition to the real wages of the worker with a large family to provide for seemed to be unanswerable on our interviews and observations among this group, we are aware of the economic sacrifices which any such scheme would involve for workers, employers, and the taxpayer. In particular, in industries where unemployment is still high and the export situation as against foreign low-wage or subsidized competition is difficult, the additional burden may well create new problems and result in an increase in unemployment. Whether or not it is practicable to treat different industries differently, it is not for us to say. But we do believe that such a scheme need not result in a general discouragement of industry any more than the compulsory unemployment insurance scheme has done. In the long run the competitive power of this country depends on the quality of its labour, and this cannot go unimpaired, if a large proportion of the child population of the working class is growing up on an economic level injurious both to their bodies and minds.

II. THE OLDER MEN

During the last few months attention has been repeatedly drawn by the Minister of Labour, the Commissioner for the Special Areas, and many others, to the extent to which unemployment is an "old man's problem". In this section we attempt to state what in our view are the chief factors which have to be considered in any plan that is produced for the older unemployed man, and to make some tentative suggestions as to the lines that such a plan might follow.

Age begins to be a factor in unemployment long before the age of 55. Even in Leicester it was suggested to us by some of those well qualified to know that in a comparatively light industry like the boot and shoe trade, once a man over 50 is unemployed for more than a few weeks, he may find it exceedingly hard to get back, and their view was fully confirmed by the sample in Leicester. On the other hand, there is a marked increase in the incidence of long unemployment above the age of 60, and it seems that this, partly perhaps because the man over 60 gives up more readily, partly because he is refused more roundly by the employer who hears his age, is the most critical age. But if any measures are being undertaken for the elderly unemployed, there would be a strong case for making them applicable from the age of 50 upwards, especially if they represent an effort to draw back the elderly man into employment, temporary or permanent, and not only the provision of alternative interests for him.

The main questions to which the problem of the older man gives rise seem to be these. Is this, like many other of the difficulties connected with long unemployment, primarily a problem of the Special Areas? Is the elderly man out of work because he has become content to retire from industry on a small pension, or does he want work? Is he making use of the alternatives to work provided in some regions for him, and is he satisfied with them? And if he is not satisfied, is there reason to think that he could be brought back into industry or not, or what kinds of employment would it be possible to provide for him and for him to undertake?

To the first of these questions figures given in an earlier part provide some answer (see above, p. 20). There are depressed ages as well as depressed places, and the factor of age tends to cancel out that of place so far as the older men are concerned. The proportions of older workers unemployed in prosperous and in depressed places tend therefore to approximate more closely than do the proportions of younger workers unemployed in prosperous and depressed places, and almost a third of the long-unemployed men in this country over the age of 55 live in the prosperous areas of the South and Midlands. If anything can be done for the older unemployed men, these men in prosperous places will have a very strong claim for inclusion. On the other hand the problem is one that affects the Special Areas in a peculiar way. There as we have seen the situation is hardening. Unemployment is coming to be regarded as something normal, and there is the real danger that an unemployed class will be created. This situation will not be resolved unless and until something is done about the burden of unemployment, in the upper age groups, which the Special Areas are carrying. Prosperous areas can in one sense afford to carry it. It is borne comparatively lightly because it is distributed widely. It does not depress the whole life of the community, and even the older unemployed men are all hanging about the streets, it does not mean that at every corner there are the same groups of men standing inactive, week after week. The point can hardly be emphasized too strongly, that unless something is done to ease this and to re-employ those who are so often described, begging the question, as the unemployables, the morale of the Special Areas will not be substantially improved. More men may get back into employment, but there will remain something essentially abnormal and unhealthy about the situation. For it remains true that while in the Midlands and South about 3 % of all older unemployed workers are long unemployed, in Wales the proportion is nearly seven times as great (see above, p. 14). To that extent, therefore, this must be considered as a Special Areas problem, in that its solution is a *sine qua non* of relieving the situation in the Areas as a whole.

The second question is again one to which an answer has been attempted in an earlier section (see above, p. 178). If the evidence we were able to collect is a fair guide, it seems that in the Special Areas something between half and two-thirds of the older men have come to accept unemployment and might find it difficult to return to work if work were available, while in prosperous areas the proportion is very much smaller, probably something under one-third.

We need only add two things, one, that all of us recognized a particular difficulty in judging what the attitude of the older man was, for his natural reserve is not easily penetrated. It is at least possible that our figures overstate the degree of the "adjustment" which has taken place in this particular age group, but whether they do or not there remains a substantial proportion who, though they have been out of work for years, still refuse to face with acquiescence the certainty of continued unemployment. The other is that to a remarkable extent these figures showing the older man's attitude are a reflection of their fitness and employability. A special analysis of our records showed that three-quarters of those whose interest in work seems for all practical purposes to have been lost are those whose employability was classified as lowest. There are indeed a few exceptional cases where a man was regarded as having lost his active interest in work, though he was still fit for it, like a man of 56 who spent all his day on his allotment and poultry, of whom our record states that "he would be very upset if work was offered him"; or another, a foreman in an amenity scheme, who had happily given up all thoughts of regular employment, because the alternative of responsible work with shorter hours than normal was attractive to him, but who would have been lost if he had not had the possibility of such work. It seems, indeed, as if attitude, as far as these older men are concerned, reflects the objective situation to a very large extent.[1] If that were changed, the attitude would in many instances certainly change too.

We believe that the third question brings out one of the chief difficulties with which the voluntary movement has had to contend. It would be very satisfactory if fairly full alternative occupations could be provided for the older men. But the facts suggest that their provision is little real use. The older man will, and does, use the club for a smoke and a gossip, but it is exceptional for him to use it for anything more. The older man ought to be attracted by Subsistence Production, which we describe in a later section, since it was designed specially to help him. But in practice it is easier to get the middle-aged man to join the scheme than the older man. The older man ought to find in allotment-holding and other similar schemes a satisfactory alternative to regular employment. But here again, it is not he but the middle-aged man, or even the young family man, who does so, and thereby reconciles himself more easily to unemployment. We may give first the figures for Crook and the Rhondda, showing how allotments and other holdings are divided between men under and over 45 (see over, p. 216).

It seems likely that something over half the total number of holdings in the Special Areas, if conditions in Crook and the

[1] One indication of this in the figures is the high proportion among the older men in Liverpool who had failed to "make the adjustment" to unemployment. The reason for this is no doubt that there is some chance of picking up an odd day's work in Liverpool, owing to the variety of opportunities there as contrasted with the single industry of the Rhondda or Crook.

TABLE XLIX. ALLOTMENTS HELD BY MEN UNDER 45 AND BY MEN OVER 45

	Rhondda	Crook
Allotments held by men under 45	24	11*
Allotments held by men over 45	20	10†

* Including three five-acre plots.
† Including two five-acre plots and one poultry scheme holding.

Rhondda are representative, are occupied by men under 45. Next we can take the older age groups, 45–54 and 55–64, and compare the conditions in Crook and the Rhondda with those in Leicester—where alone of the other places the amount of allotment holding was substantial:

TABLE L. ALLOTMENTS HELD BY MEN IN AGE-GROUPS 45–54 AND 55–64

	Rhondda	Crook	Leicester
Group A (ages 45–54)	12	5*	3
Group B (ages 55–64)	8	5	7

* Including two five-acre plots and one poultry scheme holding.

The smaller number in the Rhondda upper age group is, to judge by statements made in the interviews, partly the result of geographical conditions. To reach the allotments often means a stiff climb, which many of the older men feel they cannot manage. As can be seen from the Leicester figures, allotments in the more prosperous areas tend to be regarded as an interesting hobby for old age, whereas in the Special Areas they are to a large extent providing a fairly full "alternative life" for younger men. Our impression was that though perhaps not quite all of those who would like allotments have got them, something near this is now true of the two Special Area districts visited. The number of those who said they would like to apply for small holdings was not, in these districts, very considerable. If the reason be asked why there is this failure to attract the older men, it is no doubt that unemployment has come upon them at an age when it is far more difficult to think in terms other than those of the ordinary work they are accustomed to do.

Are these men then fit for work, or is their labour (as has often been suggested) of such low potential value that they will never be able to work again under normal conditions? Fortunately we are in the position to give a fairly satisfactory answer to that question. Our own opinions as to the employability of older men might be put forward with certain general reservations; but we can instead quote here the actual facts relating to the re-employment of older men, during the last few months, in Crook. In the age group 55–64 there were, in the Crook sample, 29 men. Six of them got back to work during the year following the sample date, and in five of the six cases the return to work was permanent. One only had to give up after less than a month, a man who was described in our records as "absolutely unemployable owing to mental infirmity". The numbers are indeed small to form the basis of a generalization, and because they are so small we asked whether the total figures for the area could be obtained for us. By courtesy of the Ministry of Labour and the Colliery owners we are able to give them. During the period under consideration 103 men between the ages of 50 and 64 who had been out of work for a year or more were placed in the Crook collieries, as compared with 116 in the corresponding age group below (35–49) and 90 in the ages 21–34. In the older age group, 8·7 % of the placings were unsuccessful, as compared with 8·0 % in the ages 35–49 and 12·9 % in the ages 21–34. The older men held their own fully when re-employed under ordinary economic conditions.

It appears, then, that the idea that the older men are unemployable is at least greatly exaggerated. Appearances are deceptive. Many of them are as employable as, or more employable than younger men, though it is of course true that they are not so adjustable. Many of them want work, and more would do so (if we are right in the suggestion made above) should there be any possibility of work. They do not readily respond to the provision of alternatives.

In an earlier chapter we showed how unemployment affected their standard of living. If an elderly man is living alone or with his wife, he normally receives an allowance that puts him above the poverty line we have adopted. But he is living on an income that represents, in the majority of cases, less than half what his income would be if he were still in employment.[1] There can be very little over for amusements of any kind, and there is generally no hope whatever for him of anything that might vary for a week or two the dead level of existence at which he lives; only the certainty that when he reaches the age of 65, his income will be reduced by a further shilling or two, and that for part of it he will be dependent on Public Assistance. What can be done for him? The answer is, nothing, unless we are prepared to go further, which means to spend more money, than we have done in the past to help him. Many suggestions have been made with regard to some modification of the regulations which would convert Unemployment Assistance, under certain conditions, into a pension, so that a man would be able to earn freely a little extra here and there if he could. The sample has shown that, beyond doubt, many men receiving allowances do not yet know the regulations that make it possible for them to earn a little extra, and we believe that if such a change were possible it would do something to make things easier for them. But it would be no real solution, and, especially, in the Special Areas, it would leave the most serious elements in the situation untouched.

A more drastic solution must be considered. If work is to be created for these older men, it must be as cheap as possible to create, and must not therefore involve any heavy capital expenditure. There is work of this kind in abundance waiting to be done, in the Special Areas and elsewhere, clearance work which would be a national as well as a local asset. It might not be possible, at least in the first instance, to bear the expense of a full week's work for those who are thus employed. But the sample visits made it certain that the vast majority of those older men would take eagerly an opportunity for work which

[1] For the figures, see above, p. 119.

would bring in 32*s.* 6*d.* or 35*s.* a week. If they were employed on a thirty-hour week at a reasonable rate of wages—say, 1*s.* 2*d.* an hour—we have little doubt that the scheme would be very popular. But to be effective it must be properly organized work with hours strictly kept, and the conditions of normal employment observed. In some of the amenity schemes that we saw in the course of the sample, the atmosphere was casual, and nothing of that kind will change the situation in the Special Areas as it ought to be changed.

We do not suggest that it would be possible to employ all these older men all the time. What is needed is something that will make possible from time to time a change, even if it is only a temporary change, in the situation of the older unemployed man. It will be something for which he can hope, and that, we believe, is the talisman that might work the needed change in areas where unemployment has been prolonged and heavy. If these old men could expect six months' such work in every twenty-four, it would revitalize the life of the Special Areas and other districts of heavy unemployment. It would obviously be a matter for consideration whether such work made a man eligible to draw unemployment insurance benefit at the end of the six months. On present figures there would appear to be a case for suggesting this might be so. It would be for consideration, too, what authority ought to be responsible for such work, though obviously the State rather than the local authorities would have to bear the financial burden. The suggestion may be made that the Unemployment Assistance Board, as being in closest touch with the needs of the elderly unemployed, should be the authority through which such a scheme ought to be administered.

If this problem of long unemployment is to be attacked, it is going to cost money. The cost of the plan that we have outlined would amount, in wages, to £2,900,000 a year, supposing that a quarter of all the elderly men over 50 available (an outside limit) were absorbed into employment at 35*s.* a week for six months every two years. This compares with a bill for these same men for assistance (if they were not in employment) of approximately £2,000,000. The net cost of the wage bill would thus be £900,000 a year.[1] It is a large sum of money, and it would be increased by capital charges which we do not attempt to estimate. But the gain in human terms would be enormous; and the rot, which it would check, is already serious. What is certain, too, is that such a scheme would put an entirely different complexion on social service work among the older men, by ridding them of apathy and hopelessness. We believe that the work might in itself be of great value even if these much greater issues were not at stake.

The more that can be done to induce employers to take back these men into normal employment, the better. But there are two things that have to be considered, one a man's employability, the other his capacity for adjustment to new types of work. In many cases the former is unimpaired, but in most cases the capacity of the older man for adjustment is limited. If he can get back to work under the conditions he knew he can manage it. But changed conditions, faster pace, new machinery, make things very difficult for him. It seems that in Crook the chief reason why the re-employment of the older men has been so successful is that mechanization has not recently developed to any extent comparable with the Rhondda. But certainly in most areas of heavy unemployment, there is good reason to think that, apart from some plan of the kind we have outlined, nothing will make a substantial change in the situation.

III. THE YOUNGER MEN

The young man who has been unemployed for more than a year is plainly a person of whom something more ought to be known, and we regard it as the chief defect in the sample that it did not illustrate adequately this particular problem. In London and Leicester, though there are young men long unemployed, their

[1] This figure includes Scotland and is calculated on the basis of the number of elderly long-unemployed men, at the date of our sample, in November 1936. Obviously a wage of 35s. would not be attractive to men with a large number of dependents, but the proportion of men between the ages of 50 and 64 with large families living at home is small.

numbers are not very great if we use the sample definition; and, if it had been possible for us to carry out, as had been planned, a small further sample to throw light on unemployment among the younger men in London, we would have included in its scope any young men on the register of the Unemployment Assistance Board. If they are applicants of the Board, it means that their employment record is poor, and the real problem of the young unemployed in London consists evidently of those with a poor record of employment rather than with no record of employment. The sample at least showed this. The Board's latest report states that in the London area as a whole 9 % of the register consisted of young men under 25, whereas in the sample both in Deptford and Leicester it was only approximately 1 %. The mesh of the sample net was too coarse to catch the younger men in London, simply because they are not long unemployed under the terms of its definition.

It brought out, however, some significant facts. In the Liverpool sample alone was there a representative number of young men. Yet there were three other places, Crook, the Rhondda, and Blackburn, all areas of heavy "industrial" unemployment, where a similar high proportion of young men might have been expected. That there was not is of course due mainly to the effects of transference, unorganized and official, from these three places. There are still young men in the Special Areas, but an analysis made elsewhere[1] of the younger age group of the sample in Crook has shown that long unemployment among the young men in the Special Areas is now almost residual in character. This particular problem, then, cuts right across the classification we have adopted of residual and industrial unemployment. In the Special Areas, if we can argue from Crook and the Rhondda to the Areas as a whole, adequate steps have been taken to resolve industrial long unemployment among the young men. It remains a problem of very large dimensions in Liverpool, and seems, on the figures, to be considerable also in many places where the percentage of general unemployment is substantially higher than it is for the country as a whole, but

[1] See pp. 76–7.

which yet do not come within the scope of the Special Areas regulations.

To say that the long unemployment of young men in the Special Areas is residual in character does not mean that all the young men long unemployed are unemployables, but rather that it is possible to see in each individual instance some personal reason why unemployment has been prolonged. As an example may be cited a lad of 19 obviously intelligent and of good physique living in an outstandingly good home in the Rhondda, the parents' only child. He had been away to a Training Centre, but after a few days had become ill and gone home again. He had a slight stutter, which may have been a symptom of deeper nervousness, and it was almost certainly this that kept him from securing work, though he had travelled to more prosperous districts, and has done so again since, without success, to look for it. Or there are the "wage" cases, like a young general labourer in the Rhondda who left his last employment because he was dissatisfied with the wage, has active political interests to fill his mind and when he went to a Training Centre refused to take the training seriously because it "would not enable him to compete with fully trained men". Or the young married man, who feels he cannot leave his wife and children, or cannot afford to take work; or the single man whose brothers have all "gone to London", who has himself perhaps some slight disability, but does not move mainly because he feels he cannot leave his mother; or the young man who comes of poor social stock, is living in bad conditions, but is obviously contented with them. All these instances are from the Rhondda, and though no doubt in London, with its varied opportunities, most of these lads would get some employment, there is enough to explain why they have not taken a successful part in the general exodus of young men. We may conjecture that this kind of material, with no doubt a small sprinkling of young men with police records, would form the nucleus of the youngest section of the Unemployment Assistance Board register in London as a whole. Certainly those whom we met casually in the Unemployed Clubs of London suggested something of the kind.

In Liverpool it is a different matter. Here the remarkable feature of the sample was that it was, on the whole, young rather than old, and the 27 young men between the ages of 18 and 24, and the 70 between the ages of 25 and 34 in the Liverpool sample represent a total of over 3,000 men in Liverpool, in those age groups, who are long unemployed in the terms of the sample definition. If the fact of drawing Unemployment Assistance, instead of Insurance, is taken as the criterion of "long unemployment" rather than the sample definition, the full seriousness of the position can be better understood. In Liverpool, which includes Walton, Booth and Garston and the five clearing houses as well as the various offices directly under the main Liverpool exchange, there were unemployed between the ages of 25 and 34 alone on 1 November 1937, 17,091 men, of whom 9,847 were on Unemployment Assistance. The usual features of "industrial" unemployment appear, men who are in every way fit for work but yet do not get it. And there are some who evidently still try to find it and want it badly; but the very significant fact is the large number who have settled down relatively contentedly without it. This has been brought out in an earlier table,[1] but it is too important not to emphasize again. There is no doubt whatever that those feelings of independence which most of the elderly men of the Liverpool long unemployed still retain have ceased to be operative so far as a large number of younger men is concerned. This is a fact, which must be accepted as the condition of any solution. We have got to reckon, in future, on a progressive decay of such feelings, for circumstances have made them out of date. It is no good trying to restore them in the old form. Some new principle, which is consistent with the present situation, will have to be found.

There are, then, among the younger men the two types of problem with which we are familiar, the residual or personal problem of the man who does not get work because of some physical or psychological disability, and the industrial problem of the man who would get work if the work was there. But we must beware of the over-simplification of such a statement.

[1] See above, p. 176.

These men are at an age when many men are in some degree abnormal, acting on a violent impulse, subject to exaggerated excitement and exaggerated depression, trying to discover what their own position ought to be in the community in which they live and trying to get others to accept it. The sample visits left no doubt that it is those who are thus slightly abnormal who are most prone to long unemployment. Nor must it be forgotten that the young man needs much more food and perhaps may reasonably be said to need better clothes than the middle-aged or elderly man, though the unemployed single young man draws, probably, exactly the same sum in Unemployment Assistance as they. When prolonged unemployment comes at this age, and particularly if it follows on an unsatisfactory employment history, it is bound to have different effects from those of long unemployment on a more stable and mature nature, and this is the reason for the large numbers of young men to be found who "don't want work". They are not a real residue like the psychological oddities in the thirties and forties with whom the sample brought us into contact, and it is because of their age alone that unemployment has had such a serious effect.

What the ultimate results may be is shown by a Liverpool instance, a scaler, aged 24, small but strong and in our view absolutely employable. He was married, with one child, and drew an allowance of 31*s.* 6*d.* which included an extra 2*s.* 6*d.* on account of his wife's ill health. He said he wanted to go "on the roads" to do corporation work, which is highly paid. He described how he had been in the habit regularly of working as a docker three days and drawing insurance the other three; how when that became impossible he worked ten weeks to make himself eligible for a period of insurance, stopped work and drew insurance for as long as it lasted. Under the Transitional Payments regulations as a single man he had drawn only 5*s.* and so had begun to look for work again to get the necessary stamps, but now he was on Unemployment Assistance and married he was contented, and said that "he was not prepared to do an odd two days' work for 11*s.* 7*d.*, for they take off half of it". His case comes into line with several of which we heard in country districts, men who hinted that they were willing to be dismissed from their jobs since that would leave them eligible for Unemployment Assistance, but who were not willing to give notice, for in that case they would not be eligible for assistance. Any government will soon have to face this problem, for though the number of those who take this line may be, as is shown by the sample, small—at least in the towns—it is one which can hardly fail gradually to increase.

What are the conditions for a solution of these young men's difficulties? It may be pointed out first that one promising feature of the situation is the tendency for young men to combine in gangs. These are often exceedingly troublesome, but their existence shows that there is an inherent need for social organization and a capacity for group loyalty which offer big opportunities. A troublesome gang of young men in Lincoln was invited through the enterprise of social workers there to occupy and run for itself a workshop, and an objective was put before them, in the provision of equipment for playgrounds for the city, that was successfully carried out. The obvious weaknesses that had caused so much trouble at first—destructiveness and theft, offensive language and laziness—were to some extent eliminated, and when trade improved, all the members of the gang (fifteen or sixteen in number) not only got work but succeeded in keeping it, a most remarkable record. It is doubtful if this achievement could have been brought about by compulsion, but a skilful appeal to the loyalty of the gang and a skilful fitting of its existing social organization into the framework of another scheme was what brought about the result. Someone has said that the best nucleus of a boys' club is a few lads kicking a football in the street. A gang of young men who watch billiards in the afternoon and go to the cinema in the evening is similarly a chance for a good club; but on the whole the clubs have failed completely to take these chances. They do not see that what the young man desires is something that will make, not small, but great demands on him. The strictest rules in any club that we came across during the sample were those of an unofficial club run by a few young men in one of the Rhondda valleys.

It is partly the failure to capture their imagination that lies at the root of the trouble, and this can be seen in the young men's attitude towards training and transference. To travel from the North of England to the South ought to be an adventure. Instead it is something so easy that the gingerbread has no trace of gilt; it turns out to be nothing strenuous or new or exciting, only something that is slightly uncomfortable, with a prospect, very likely, of a wage that in the circumstances, with higher living costs, will represent very little improvement. The point can be illustrated by a letter which we print below, written by a "trainee" from a Government Training Centre in the South to one of his friends who happened to come within the sample. When the man was visited, the letter had just been received. It ran as follows:

You'll think I've been a long time writing but I've had a lot to write home. I hope you are keeping well and having a bit better luck. Don't think of coming down here, it's lousy. The bloke who came down with me has gone home, I am supposed to be learning sheet metal work, and I've been here 6 weeks and I can't make a blacking tin yet. You'd be surprised if you were down here. They say they can get a 3 quid a week job any time, but don't believe it, one chap went after a job to a brick ground and they offered him 30*s*. a week to work twelve hours a day. We get decent food at our digs but we haven't much room to eat it, there are 11 of us round a table made for 6. Well, Jim, I've been wondering how you are going on at..., have they won the cup. There are 800 men down here and I haven't seen one from...yet. I have been teetotal here, the beer's wicked we go to the pictures nearly every night. Well Jim don't advise anyone to come. When a chap has done his six months they find some of them jobs but there isn't one out of ten lasts a month and then they only get tenpence an hour. Well Jim, I can't find any more to say, so I will close wishing you the best of luck, and hoping you give Littlewoods a tanning.

Your old pal,

....

This letter is a most revealing document. If we wish to know why there is still a group of young men untouched by transference and training, this letter will provide as full an answer as is likely to be given. It could, of course, be countered with scores of letters of appreciation written by successful trainees to the superintendents of the Centres. Some of these letters we saw when visiting Centres, and those who take the opportunity of seeing the Centres can hardly doubt the excellence of the work they are doing. The point is to account for the failures as well as the successes, however, for it is the failures who turn up again in the ranks of the long unemployed.

Somehow, then, we have got to capture the imagination. And secondly, it must be realized that we are dealing with lads and young men whose psychological condition is a more important consideration even than it is with the middle-aged and elderly men. We must find a way of dealing sympathetically with them, simply because that is the only way to achieve a permanent solution. Many of those who run the Government Training Centres, and even the Instructional Centres, consider that the extension of compulsion would create considerable difficulties for them. We believe that, if it is applied individually and with some adequate provision for a reasonably permanent job at the end of it, there may be a case for compulsion, but if it is applied indiscriminately it may well have an exceedingly bad effect, because of the sensitiveness and instability of many who would be its objects. It is difficult to see what the alternatives are, and that something must be done to help men who are getting into a condition where they are wellnigh unable to help themselves, is certain. We feel that voluntary societies have not begun to exploit the possibilities which the situation offers. There is a great opportunity here for constructive action by them, and proposals that they bring forward which involve making real demands on the men concerned would deserve full consideration. There is reason to think, however, that the mere provision of comfortable clubs in itself may do more harm than good.[1]

There is another line of approach, equally important—prevention. One thing which is certainly responsible for the present situation is the treatment that some of these young men have

[1] Cf. below, p. 327.

had in the period immediately after leaving school up to the age of 21. Examples have been given already to show how the less competent or less fortunate of them are used as cheap labour up to the age of 18 or 21 and then turned off, without skill and without even the habit of looking for casual labour, into a world where there is already far too much casual labour and too little skill. What is being done to them is comparable to what was done, until the recent regulations were brought into force, by army service for men somewhat older than they. When we found in the Liverpool sample half a dozen or more men—each representing thirty-four others—who had been in the regular army, the effects of the old system were apparent, for though almost all of them were good types of men bearing still in their manner and physique some signs of their army service, their lack of skill had left them completely stranded. So with the younger men, their industrial history is often the explanation of their present position, and the old blind-alley occupation of the errand boy, who was "stopped" at 16, an age when apprenticeship in many trades was still open to him, was a less serious matter than the new blind-alley occupation from which a lad is discarded, without skill, at 18 or 21.

The Principal of one of the Colleges for Adult Education, chiefly for unemployed men, told us how he always asked the new arrivals at College to write some account of their life and educational development, and how in one instance after another it appeared that something formative had happened to them between the ages of 17 and 19. With the young unemployed man, it is precisely the wrong thing that has happened. He has perhaps been thrown out of what seemed a good job, introduced to the experience of living on insurance, and come into contact with other unemployed lads who have worked out a routine of unemployment. When that happens, its effects may well be almost ineradicable. It is vitally important not only to begin on this problem at what is unfortunately the wrong end, but also to prevent it being recreated endlessly. This is a question with which that of the school-leaving age is closely bound up. It is indeed decisive for the whole industrial future of this country, depending as it does on the maintenance of a high degree of skill.[1]

There is thus no short cut with the younger men's difficulties. We can try to prevent the same situation arising again, and we can realize that the present situation with all its unfortunate features at least presents a great opportunity. Somehow democracy in this country—not everywhere, for the youth organizations in Czecho-Slovakia were pioneers in a movement that has spread all over the Continent—has failed to catch the imagination. It is attacking social problems, but the attack has got to be psychological as well as material, and it is perhaps in this direction that the only real solution to this particular difficulty may lie.

[1] Cf. Jewkes and Winterbottom, *Juvenile Unemployment*, pp. 11–17.

Part IV

UNEMPLOYMENT AMONG WOMEN

I. GENERAL ISSUES

THE problems of women are in one important respect more complicated than those of men. A woman, whether employed or unemployed, has not one function in life, but several. Whereas a man devotes himself first and foremost to a career or to earning a living, the working woman has to be ready to have children and to bring them up, to support a home, cook, wash, clean and care for all in it, and she is at the same time often compelled to compete with men for work in the economic sphere, or, if unmarried or widowed, to be entirely self-supporting.

Tens of thousands of women in England to-day are trying to fulfil the three functions of mother, wife and breadwinner at one time, and that during the best years of their lives. Not a few seem to carry the load successfully, though with what effect on their own health and the health and well-being of their children it would be difficult to estimate. The fact that many women have to face the possibility, or rather probability of employment in all three spheres, though not necessarily in all three at the same time, has a fundamental bearing on many social questions, not least on that of women's unemployment. A woman ought, therefore, to consider the relation of one sphere to the others and the equipment required for each. And the nation which is responsible for the education of its children for life has in its own interest to decide for which of these functions girls must be fitted and how the training can be given.

In almost all working homes marriage is looked on as having a primary claim and other forms of employment are viewed in relation to it. The working girl who plans her future in terms of a possible independent career is an exception. The prospect of marriage thus conditions a girl's outlook on industry. It is the reason why all too few girls go into trades where training or apprenticeship is required. In some occupations there is a tradition for a woman to look upon her trade as a life-work, whether she marries or remains single, as for example in the cotton, weaving, hosiery, boot and shoe trades; but, except in cases of this kind, the girl of 14 tends to drift into the most remunerative employment immediately available, keeping the alternative of marriage always in view and hoping that she will sooner or later be freed from the fulfilment of a function in industry. The girl starts with a sense of responsibility for easing the position at home. Unless she is urgently needed to aid a sick mother or to replace her in the care of the family, her best contribution often appears to the family to be the earning of extra cash. Her future is not the important consideration of the moment, and she is readily enticed into any kind of factory or business that will take her, even when she knows the work offered will neither add to her skill nor, in many cases, ensure her steady employment. The immediate gain in money proves an irresistible attraction.

We may now distinguish the three types of problem as it affects women, encountered in the course of the sample. The first is that of women who do not normally engage in industry. This is the case, for example, in the Rhondda and in South-west Durham. Here there is no problem of the unemployment of women, but only of the effect on women of the unemployment of men.

Secondly we have, as in Blackburn and Leicester, the situation where it is normal for women to enter the factory at 14 expecting to remain in industry all their lives, carrying when married the double burden of industry and the home. The Blackburn and Leicester woman is a strong, independent, and often very capable type, but her interests are not primarily in the home. She is driven by the pressure of work. She has no leisure. She was fitted into an industrial mould at the age of 14. The burden of having children and looking after husband and home was added to this. Her social outlook is necessarily conditioned by the advantages and disadvantages of these experiences.

Our third type of problem is illustrated by Liverpool, where the girl of 14 tends to look upon industrial employment as what has been called a "meanwhile" occupation, marriage being the ultimate objective. This attitude to employment is apt to cause irresponsibility both in the girl herself and in some employers, who take advantage of this fact to exploit the woman worker, either by turning her out of employment at 16 or 18 years of age, or by the organization of more and more industries on a seasonal and part-time basis. The brunt of this unsatisfactory state of things is borne by the woman who does not marry young and may be left a spinster, or who has to be the main support of her family without the experience and discipline of a good occupation claiming her full interest. She may thus drift from one job to another when she is young, and so unlearn much that she learned at school. If so, she becomes poor material from an industrial point of view, and because she has not through these formative years between 14 and 21 learned to do something important well, she becomes worse equipped for the responsibilities of motherhood and of creating and directing a home for husband and children.

As a rule the working-class girl has to find time for some household responsibilities in addition to going out to work, and the married worker must always do so. The woman who is out of work, therefore, is not, on the whole, left stranded by unemployment as is the unemployed man; she has plenty to do, and looks perhaps as healthy or healthier, as happy as or happier than she did when she was working, so that the real problem is to increase the income brought in by her husband's wage sufficiently for it to be possible for her to reject definitely the alternative of going back to work, and settle down instead to make a home. The problem of the unemployed woman cannot be separated from the question of the function of the woman in national life, on which there are two tendencies of opinion. And though this opens up questions that lie beyond the scope of this report, the two conceptions must be stated briefly, since our attitude towards the problem of unemployment among women will be conditioned by the view taken. On the one hand where it is held that it is normal for the woman to work as well as her husband, there are certain definite advantages to be noted. There is the gain of independence to which we have already alluded, a gain which is perhaps not so great as is sometimes thought, if we compare with it the position of authority enjoyed by the Rhondda housewife. There is the advantage that where the husband is thrown out of work from time to time, his wife may continue in work and thereby a catastrophic drop in the family income may in part be prevented. This is one of the chief arguments in favour of the establishing of light industries on the new trading estates in the Special Areas, since these will employ mainly women.

On the other hand, the sample visits certainly suggested to those who took part in them that where a woman can devote her whole time to the maintenance of the home, a more genuinely civilized standard is kept up. It is significant that in Blackburn, where many of the housewives are also workers, the proportion of homes in which household management was recorded as indifferent or bad was decidedly high, an unexpected result in view of the Lancashire reputation for good management; while in the Rhondda and Crook we were impressed, not only by the excellent management of the homes, but by the high cultural level of the family. The woman held a significant place, not only in the family, but also in the political and social life of that community. She was making a contribution to the high standard of working-class civilization rightly valued in this country. The cause of this must lie partly in the fact that in the Rhondda or in South-west Durham the miner's wife does not ordinarily work in a factory, partly that the young girls after leaving school do not normally go out to work (except for domestic service, which is in itself a training for home-making), but stay in the family and by taking a considerable share in running the house get an experience that the girl who goes into a factory at 14 misses.

The view that is taken of women's unemployment must be largely influenced by the conception of one or other of these alternatives as the better. Do we consider that by making it possible for a woman to devote herself to her home society is securing for itself a paramount advantage in the maintenance of a high standard of home life? Or do we believe that this view is out of date; that the modern woman can both work and keep house, and that by doing so she gains a status of which her predecessors have always been unjustly deprived? If we take the second point of view, clearly our estimate of the importance of women's unemployment will be greater than if we take the first. The first view suggests that it is women's employment, rather than unemployment, that is the real social problem.

Of the six places visited Blackburn alone yielded adequate material for a study of women's unemployment through the original sample of long-unemployed men and women. It was therefore decided to take in Liverpool a further sample of 1 in 10 from the records of the long-unemployed women in Liverpool, whether receiving Unemployment Assistance, Public Assistance, or being non-claimants. It was not possible to visit the women in this additional sample, but the records it yielded gave us a much fuller picture than would have been otherwise obtained, and a few visits were made to selected cases drawing Public Assistance or non-claimants, in order to throw light on particular points. We were able in addition to make use of material from an enquiry conducted by interviewing one in three of all women on the Unemployment Assistance Board register in the autumn of 1937. In Leicester the problem on the women's side was so small as not to require a further sample. It was evidently a real "residual" problem, and the long-unemployed women there were either nearing the pension age, or were physically disabled or had some other obvious disqualification. In the three other localities, Crook, the Rhondda, and Deptford, the register of long-unemployed women is negligible though they all brought us face to face with the responsibilities of the wife of the unemployed man.

II. THE PROBLEMS OF LONG UNEMPLOYMENT OF WOMEN IN BLACKBURN

In Blackburn the tradition of men, women, and children working side by side in the mills is long established. The girl goes to the mill at 14—she used to go at 6 years of age—and stays in the mill for a lifetime. She has not been considered too old to work at 60 nor even sometimes at 70. She feels that she has a career and is proud of the skill she acquires. She may excel her husband as a spinner or weaver, and she is as much the breadwinner as he, for wages in most of the Lancashire cotton towns assume the double earnings of man and wife. The husband's wages alone would reduce many of the families to poverty, and it is consequently necessary for the wife to earn all the time.

The Blackburn woman is a sturdy independent type. She has to rise early and work late. Saturday and Sunday are not free days for her, for here too tradition requires of her standards of cleanliness and order in the home. Blackburn was one of the towns worst hit in the slump of 1931, and recovery has meant the introduction of new processes and industries. Many have had to learn a new technique, changing over from the simpler "plain" weaving to the more delicate and exacting "fancies", and others are faced with the demand that instead of minding three or four looms they should mind six. For generations they had concentrated on one particular process. They never dreamt of things being done differently, and they have not found it easy to adapt themselves to the new style. When unemployment came, they found it difficult either to turn to anything else or to seek fresh experience outside of Blackburn.

In Leicester, also, the girl of 14 who goes into the hosiery or boot and shoe trades, or weaving, looks upon her work as a lifelong career. There is not the same need for her to contribute towards the home when she is married, for men's wages are considerably higher. But the tradition is that the woman shall continue working and thereby raise the standard of living in the family. Moreover, the Leicester girl has the added inducement of a good wage and in most cases better conditions of work than are available to her sisters in Blackburn. The minimum wage for girls of 20 and over fixed by the Boot and Shoe Trade in Leicester is 37*s.* as contrasted with the average wage of 31*s.* 6*d.* for an adult woman in Blackburn.

At the date of our sample, 28 % of all insured women workers in Blackburn were unemployed, and of these 39 % had been out of work for more than a year. This is a big proportion of the total as compared with the figures in Leicester, where only 2 % of the unemployed women were long unemployed.

TABLE LI. LENGTH OF UNEMPLOYMENT AMONG WOMEN BETWEEN 16 AND 64

	Less than 3 months	3–12 months	Over 12 months	Total
Blackburn	2,517 (40 %)	1,354 (21 %)	2,412 (39 %)	6,283
Leicester	2,606 (86 %)	370 (12 %)	72 (2 %)	3,048

In Blackburn unemployment is concentrated to a great extent in one industry; in Leicester in two main industries. The following table shows the distribution of unemployment among the industries with more than fifty unemployed women:

TABLE LII

Industry	Blackburn	Leicester
General engineering	118 (2 %)	—
Hotel and restaurant service	153 (2 %)	50 (1 %)
Cotton	5647 (91 %)	—
Woollen and worsted	—	179 (5 %)
Textile bleaching	96 (1 %)	78 (2 %)
Distributive trades	205 (3 %)	109 (3 %)
Tobacco	—	86 (2 %)
Hosiery	—	1661 (46 %)
Boots	—	1112 (28 %)

Among the long-unemployed women in Blackburn, as illustrated by the sample, nearly half were married and no less than one-seventh widowed or living apart from their husbands.

It is evident from the age distribution of long unemployment that there is no serious unemployment among young girls in Blackburn, and of the younger women a considerable number had got back to work by the time the visits were made. At the time the sample was taken, long unemployment was spread almost equally over the other age groups above 24, and 47 % of the long unemployed were over 45 years old.

TABLE LIII. WOMEN IN BLACKBURN: LONG UNEMPLOYMENT BY AGE

Age 18–24	3	3 %
25–34	25	22
35–44	32	28
45–54	29	25
55–64	25	22
	114	100 %

In Leicester 13 % of the long-unemployed women were under 35 years of age[1] (compared with 25 % in Blackburn) and 43 % of all long unemployed were over 55. Long unemployment in Leicester is essentially the problem of the older woman, a feature which brings out its residual character which we have noted already.

In Blackburn long-unemployed women fall roughly into three categories. First, there are those for whom the market is restricted in the particular profession or industry for which they are trained, and those who find themselves handicapped by their age, younger girls being given first choice. Secondly, there are those on whom a claim is made by a family of small children, or a sick dependent who cannot be left—factors which may induce the woman to remain unemployed, under cover of the trade depression, for as long as she possibly can. Thirdly, there are those subject to

[1] The figures here were too small for the age distribution in Leicester to be taken as strictly accurate.

personal disabilities, such as sickness, eyesight, "nerves", general depression following prolonged unemployment, and, not least, lack of adaptability.

Table LIV shows the numbers in these categories in 71 cases where the reason was clearly given, and also indicates the proportion which had recently got back to work.[1]

TABLE LIV

Age	No individual disability (1)	Family and other claims (2)	Personal disabilities (3)	Back to work (4)	Total
18–34	1	3	1	11	16
35–44	2	4	4	7	17
45–64	17	3	13	5	38
	20 (28 %)	10 (14 %)	18 (25 %)	23 (33 %)	71

It will be seen that the age group 45–64 is pretty well divided between those who still consider themselves fit and able to return to work, and those who for a variety of reasons feel themselves to be handicapped by personal factors.

It is not possible to bring out the full significance of the determining factors in long unemployment under such general headings. There are young women with small children to care for who, nevertheless, are unwilling to make them their first charge. They miss the community life of the factory, and want at all costs to get back to it. Again there are some women of 40 who, once unemployed, are inclined to look upon themselves as in future deserving of such "pensions" as Unemployment Assistance might provide, and the more unemployment is prolonged, the harder it is for them to face the prospect of working again. Others, at 50 and 60 years of age, suffer real distress on account of the fact that not their capacity to work, but their age appears to be the cause of their further unemployment. Age is

[1] The high figure of those who got back to work within a few months of the date on which the sample was taken is primarily due to the establishment of a Government factory which offered both new work and the chance of testing the availability of some of the long unemployed.

evidently a bar where adaptability is a prime concern. In the 45–64 age group, represented by seventeen cases, the reason why most of the women could not get back to work was the introduction of new processes and lack of adaptability to changed conditions. But while some wanted to be retrained, others were not sufficiently alert to see the necessity for retraining, or had not the energy to take the initiative about it. With a little extra encouragement and, if they have been long unemployed, perhaps a "refresher" course, many of these older women would respond to any retraining or re-equipment necessary. They are by no means unemployable, yet many have become inhibited by the attitude adopted towards them by society and industry, and expressed nervousness and diffidence, that was obviously genuine, at the prospect of undertaking anything new to them.

Age 51. Believes she could do fancy weaving perfectly well, but is too nervous now. Says that if she could go to get into it for two weeks for nothing except Unemployment Assistance, she'd gladly do it. Clearly wants to get back more than anything else in the world.

Age 47. Though she does not say much, it is easy to see that being out of a job is a great blow to her, and that not entirely on financial grounds. She says she misses the company, and evidently she feels very keenly being told that she is too old for work.

That the prejudice against older women can be unjustified is shown by the records of a number of older women who had got back to work.

Age 56. Weaver. Back to work after 3 years' unemployment. Has learned fancy weaving and is doing very well even though it is hard work. She is obviously competent and steady.

The majority of cases in the second category are those of young women with small children to care for. It would not be correct to say that all such women prefer to stay at home though a number certainly do. There are housewives and mothers who prefer to retain their work in the factory.

Age 28. Weaver. 3 years unemployed. "I don't like housework and would much prefer to go to the factory but I am a widow and with three children between 1 and 4. I can't afford a nurse, even if I am in a job. What is needed is a crèche. I don't want the dole."

It would seem that for women like these, there is real need for a system of good crèches and nursery schools. There will always be women with children under school age who must go to work. If proper nursery schools were available for women so placed, some of the evils attendant on the neglect of these small citizens would be avoided, as they should be.[1]

There is, however, the other type of woman who does not want to do factory work while her children need her. She will draw Unemployment Assistance if she can to subsidize the family income, not because she likes being dependent on the State but because she feels she has no better choice. She holds that her years of work in the mills entitle her to this. "Her husband earns so little that there is no other way of obtaining adequate means to bring up the family properly." In typical cases from this group our records state:

She has a small child of two and nurses two other children but her husband earns only 35*s*. 3*d*. After the rent has been deducted the family of three would have to live on 25*s*. 4*d*. It seems only too natural that the wife should try to add to the family income what she can get from the U.A.B.

She evidently regards the additional help given by the Means Test as a sort of pension that is made necessary by the fact that "there is so little coming in". She does not consider herself as unemployed though she says she was very happy when working.

The existence of a group of women in Blackburn who, despite the tradition of continuous work in the mills and despite the low standards of wages earned by their husbands, yet feel the claims of the family to their whole attention is, we believe, an indication of social progress. It seems particularly unfortunate that as in one instance in the sample a young wife of 22 should have to go back to work while her husband remains unemployed: though she said she would much prefer to stay at home, if her husband were working, but with him out she has

[1] There was a good deal of evidence in our sample of women who had been in factories for years and, now that they had been at home for a while, wished to be able permanently to concentrate their main energies on their homes and their families.

no choice but to go back. Eighty years ago the women took their children into the mills, often when they were no more than able to toddle, and the children were encouraged to share in the work of adults. The passing of the Factory Acts forbidding the employment of young children brought about a salutary change. But to-day the situation, while different, is still an unsatisfactory one. The woman no longer takes her children to the mill but she herself goes back to the mill not infrequently one month after the birth of her child. From then on, till the child is able to go to school, it is placed by the mother in the care of whoever is available and will make a not unreasonable charge. Very often the child is "put out" into the care of an old woman who looks after a batch of children at a price which varies from 5*s*. to 10*s*. a week per child. There are in Blackburn, as we have said, no public crèches or nursery schools for the care of these small children. In Leicester there is said to be only one such crèche. The children inevitably suffer from the limited attention which they receive in these circumstances. Even when they are of an age to go to school, they return to an empty home or to one in which they are not given the individual care of the mother, and this is from the educational and psychological point of view highly undesirable. The same problem is found among the children of women employed in the factories in Leicester. The high rate of juvenile delinquency in Leicester may be due in some measure to this abnormal background.

We may group Blackburn women whose unemployment can be traced to personal disabilities under three categories:

(1) Those who are suffering from the effects of prolonged unemployment. The strain of being out of work for a long time has told upon them mentally and physically. They have lost confidence in themselves as workers. Lacking the discipline of the daily routine of the mill, and hearing of the difficulties of new processes, they have persuaded themselves that they could not stand the pace. They are convinced that their eyesight or their nerves would not be equal to it.

Age 43. "I would like to work but I can't. I am not strong enough. I am too tired."

Age 46. A weaver, too old and sick ever to work again. Eyesight alone would prevent it.

Age 58. "I am too old to go back to the mill, but I could look after children."

Age 59. "My eyesight is not good enough to do weaving any longer. What I should like would be cleaning."

Age 62. "I could do sewing, but I can't go back to the factory. The strain is too much for me."

Reconditioning might make many of these women fit again for some form of employment, especially those below the age of 60, and there is some reason to think that the complaint of bad eyesight is often due to nervousness rather than to physical causes.

(2) A second category consists of those who in addition to the difficulties just mentioned have all their lives been working under an undue strain. When unemployment came, the effect of the release from the overstrain was that of causing a breakdown.

Age 44. Husband (53) is a war wreck still suffering from wounds. There are two girls, 16 and 17, working but one has heart trouble. The woman is in a broken-down state of health. "Feels she is finished" and unsuitable for further work.

Age 45. She was stopped because she could not manage six looms. Further the noise and dust of the mill drives her crazy. What she would like would be to move into the country and get away from it all. Has never had a proper holiday in her life.

The largest section of this group was undoubtedly formed by the elderly women who are no longer fit for ordinary work and would be only too happy to have the chance of doing light work.

(3) The number of women in the third category, those who were simply poor material, was surprisingly small. One of these was a girl who was mentally deficient, physically ill developed and a sleepwalker. It was almost impossible for her to get a job as she was not strong enough for rough work and not intelligent enough for lighter work. Another case was a girl who came from

a home where the mother had seen better days and was always trying to "keep up appearances" which she could not afford. She instilled into the girl the idea that she was superior to her companions. The effect on the girl was disastrous. She was unable to hold any job, and was frequently dismissed. The third case was that of a rather neurotic girl. She was always at odds with her surroundings, had left her husband and her parents (though when interviewed she was living with them again), and was a definitely unsteady character. She had left jobs voluntarily and was disallowed benefit on one occasion for refusing suitable work. Her efforts to find employment were poor and ill directed.

The close study of these 114 cases in Blackburn led to the conclusion that unemployment among women in Blackburn has what we have called elsewhere an industrial character primarily. There are many who are fit for work, want it, and cannot get it. But this does not by any means account for all the long-unemployed women. It was clear that employment cloaks a number of problems which require at least as careful a consideration as the problems of unemployment. Since the date on which the enquiry was conducted in Blackburn there is a prospect of the re-employment of most of the younger women now on the register, through the demand created by new factories, which are expected to offer working conditions better than those in most of the mills to-day. In these circumstances many of the abler young women may be tempted to transfer from the mills to the new factories, and the retraining of the older women may become necessary to meet the demand for workers in the cotton mills.

III. LIVERPOOL UNEMPLOYED WOMEN— A PROBLEM OF EMPLOYABILITY

The problem of women's unemployment in Liverpool must be seen against the distinctive features of its industrial life considered in another part of this report; the organization of large sections of industry on the basis of casual labour, and the increasing number of new industries organized on the basis of seasonal, short-time and part-time work. These conditions have affected profoundly the working-class tradition there. Men and women have grown accustomed to a situation in which they do not know from day to day whether they will be working or not. They live in a state of uncertainty which is reflected in their whole outlook on life. Another important factor in all social problems in Liverpool is the deep religious and cultural difference caused by the influx of Irish families with a different standard of living, different capacities and different customs. This has not only caused a deep rift in the population but has also to some extent affected the attitude of the English section. The presence of a large unskilled population and the religious and cultural differences have hindered the growth of strong trade unions. There is consequently a complete lack of the solidarity which is born of a homogeneous cultural tradition.

Liverpool has suffered continuously and severely since the slump of 1931. It has a large surplus population for whom industry cannot provide. Hence to draw "the dole" and "to live on somebody else" is no longer regarded as a course to be followed only in the face of the direst need. Casual employment weakens resistance to reliance on "the dole". All these factors have contributed to the creation of the women's unemployment problem in Liverpool, which is predominantly one of poor material, of unskilled hands who have not had the advantages of a good home-life behind them. Until social conditions in Liverpool have been radically altered, this problem will not be really solved.

Tables LV–LVII show the distribution of unemployment among women in Liverpool compared with other towns of the sample, and the distribution between various occupations of women drawing Unemployment Assistance in Liverpool.

TABLE LV. LENGTH OF UNEMPLOYMENT AMONG WOMEN BETWEEN AGES 16–64. 21 SEPTEMBER 1936

	Less than 3 months	3–12 months	Over 12 months	Total
Blackburn	2,517	1,354	2,412	6,283
Liverpool	4,438	1,415	610	6,463
Leicester	2,606	370	72	3,048

TABLE LVI. LENGTH OF UNEMPLOYMENT AMONG WOMEN WORKERS BETWEEN AGES 16–17. JUNE 1936

	Less than 3 months	3–12 months	Over 12 months	Total
Blackburn	90	9	—	99
Liverpool	440	101	—	541
Leicester	38	1	—	39
Crook	2	—	—	2
Rhondda	20	3	—	23
Deptford	3	—	—	3

TABLE LVII. OCCUPATIONAL ANALYSIS OF WOMEN ON THE LIVE FILE OF THE UNEMPLOYMENT ASSISTANCE BOARD IN LIVERPOOL 1937

Factories	965	34 %
Residential and non-residential domestic work*	1,346	47
Shop assistants, clerks, commercial travellers, etc.	439	15
Tailoresses and waitresses	114	4
	2,864	100 %

* This figure needs to be qualified by certain observations made below; see p. 249.

These tables show that long unemployment, as understood by the sample definition, is proportionately a much smaller problem in Liverpool than it is in Blackburn. A very substantial section of the register in Liverpool (a section which, if the unemployed women who are in receipt of Public Assistance are added, amounts to nearly half the register) are evidently women with poor employment records, as the high figure of those receiving Unemployment Assistance shown in Table LVII clearly indicates. The problem among the Liverpool women, then, is largely that of those in occasional employment, mainly cleaners or seasonal domestic workers the demand for whom in the holiday resorts of North Wales and the Isle of Man is very great, though there is a substantial number of factory workers and a certain number of shop assistants and waitresses (mainly those who are reckoned as "too old") as well. In so far as there is a problem of long unemployment, it is the older women who are most affected. Of the women under 35 years of age 47% had had some work during the previous year and only 12% had been out of work over two years. But one-half of those 36–44 years of age and three-fourths of those over 45 years of age had done no work for more than two years.

An analysis of the material described above (p. 234) that was available for Liverpool, brought out the extent to which the register as a whole consists of young women. 18% of all unemployed women were under 21 years of age (as contrasted with only 1% in Blackburn, cf. p. 237). In Liverpool 74% of the women drawing Unemployment Assistance are evidently single women and almost two-thirds of these are under 35 years of age. 10% of the single women had illegitimate children. 26% of the sample were married women. Of these 9% were widows and 10% separated or deserted wives, and thus only 7% of the sample were unemployed married women living with their husbands. These facts suggest at once one of the most important elements of the problems in Liverpool, the relatively low social stratum largely affected by it; a point to which we shall recur later. It means that a larger proportion of unemployment among women in Liverpool than elsewhere is due to low employability, a factor which in Blackburn, as we saw, is very small.

In the autumn of 1937 the Unemployment Assistance Board was approached by both the Ministry of Labour and the Central Advisory Committee for Women's Work with a request for co-operation. The Ministry of Labour had not been wholly successful in enlisting women trainees for the Homecraft Training Centre and the Central Committee wanted some forty or fifty recruits for the two Reconditioning Courses. The U.A.B. undertook therefore a special enquiry with the following objectives in mind: (*a*) to ascertain the nature of the problems confronting the U.A.B. in the re-employment of unemployed women; (*b*) to study more closely the means of meeting them; (*c*) to find out how to improve or enhance the qualification of being "capable and available" which is a condition of eligibility for unemployment allowances; and (*d*) to stimulate individual effort in finding employment. Women who seemed likely to be suitable were invited to attend one of two Reconditioning Courses of approximately eight weeks outside Liverpool. They were interviewed personally, and 1,000 cases were investigated. The records of investigation in about half this number of cases were studied by us and Table LVIII is an analysis of them. The Reconditioning Course was planned to give those attending it a complete change of surroundings and of company, good food and the discipline of some simple domestic studies, with a view primarily to reconditioning them so that they could return to their own type of employment, and secondarily to fitting them for residential or non-residential domestic service.

Of the first 500 interviewed not more than 28 were found to be both willing and suitable for submission to a special panel appointed to consider the candidates for the Reconditioning Course. Of these only 10 were reckoned by this panel to be good enough material for this simple residential training and 5 of these 10 were eventually disqualified on medical examination. These figures again are a reminder of a point made already, the poor quality of labour represented by the unemployed women in Liverpool. The indirect value of the examination of these 500 cases was thus great, since it threw a searchlight on the quality of the material in this large sample and provided an opportunity of encouraging individuals in their efforts to find work.

Table LVIII illustrates attitude to possible employment.

TABLE LVIII

	% under 25	% 25–44	% over 45	Total	%
1. Want factory work only	3	3	3	12	3
2. Want "own job only"	8	10	13	51	11
3. Would take any available work	5	5	3	17	4
4. Not unwilling for residential domestic work	25	15	11	73	16
5. Not unwilling for non-residential domestic work	25	35	30	137	29
6. Expect to get work soon	14	10	8	51	11
7. Get seasonal work	5	5	5	25	5
8. Get casual work	2	3	1	10	2
9. No chance of getting work again	4	8	21	56	12
10. Want no work. Availability doubtful	11	6	5	37	8
	100 %	100 %	100 %	469	100 %

It will be seen that of the 469 cases by far the largest number, 210, stated that they were willing to do residential and non-residential "domestic work". We examine these cases later. 51 out of 469 wanted their own jobs only and of these 51 about 30% were factory workers, the rest were shop assistants, tailoresses, clerks at Littlewoods—a grade a little higher than the factory employee. The proportion of those shown as having no chance of getting work again is high in view of the fact that none were deemed unemployable if there was a hope of placing them in any of the other categories.

The number of those asking for factory work only would be

much higher, were it not that the factory hand who becomes unemployed for some time after she is 18 years old stands little chance of being re-employed in a factory. She may get employed as a café hand, a waitress or a seasonal worker in a jam factory, but for the vast majority of these girls there is no skilled or semi-skilled job open to them. Similarly the shop assistant, typist, tailoress and other semi-professional woman has no industry to which she can turn for re-employment if she loses and cannot recover a job in her own trade. This is the explanation of the size of the pool entitled "domestic work" in the occupational analysis, Table LVII, on p. 245, reflected also in the number of those stated to be not unwilling for domestic work in Table LVIII. It is in some ways almost comparable to the category of "Public Works Contracting" among the men, which we have seen above (see p. 17) to be something that exists largely on paper but not in fact. It consists partly at least of women who have no qualifications for anything that they have a chance of getting, and are reckoned as fit for domestic service because there is no other job which, without any qualifications whatever, they can be taken as fit to do. The term "domestic work" is in itself misleading, for it covers the roughest type of shop and office cleaning, done by what is often referred to locally as the "shawl type"; it is used in describing any kind of daily cleaner of public or private premises who would usually be described as a "char", and the category includes also some women, chiefly elderly, who have been domestic servants in cheap boarding houses, in private houses and then in public institutions, small commercial hotels, etc., women whose experience of residential domestic service has been galling and who have drifted from one mean place to another. They have never had an opportunity of the more highly skilled domestic jobs and no training for them, or they are women who have broken down in health and aged prematurely whatever their early industrial history.

The fact that as many as 73 out of 469 women interviewed were willing to consider some form of residential domestic work should not be taken as indicating that in all instances such work is their own first choice; nor indeed that all of these 73 women could be fitted into residential posts. By "residential domestic work" many of them meant work in institutions, hotels, hospitals, schools, etc., and for a good many of the better posts, even in institutions, many would not be fitted either by training or previous experience.

It is probable that more than half of these 73 women would not consider domestic work in private houses at all. This fact cannot be ignored and it is due partly to private domestic service having fallen into ill repute—it is classed, as we have seen, together with any form of char's job—and partly to the actual experience of women who have suffered bitterly in domestic service from the isolation, the long hours of work, the lack of freedom and privacy, and above all the lack of a "home of one's own".

Of the 137 women out of 469 willing for non-residential "domestic work" only a very small percentage had had any experience of daily domestic service other than office cleaning and charing. These women have mostly drifted into the group of domestic workers who would more properly be called "rough cleaners", from the pool of unused or discarded factory hands, thousands of whom, as we shall see later, have had poor chances in life. Most of them were born in slum areas or in homes with a low standard of culture.

A high proportion of the middle-aged and older women among them suffer from some form of physical disability which, while it need not necessarily prevent them permanently from going to work, does in fact handicap them in competing with younger women for unskilled jobs. The following cases illustrate this feature:

Cleaner, 58 years, single. Living alone. Last employment 1931 as hospital cleaner. Has very bad rheumatism. Left hand deformed as result of this, but states that she is fit for work. "She will never work again, though efforts are very good."

Chambermaid, 53 years. Suffering from bronchitis and should not be out of doors so far as I could see. Is very poorly clad and would not get post in these clothes. Pays 5*s*. for cellar, kitchen, and room and 1*s*. for electric light. A sad case of a woman who has almost sunk into unemployability. Will try to obtain better accommodation. Clothing should be looked to.

Cleaner, 55 years. Suffering from bad headache, probably due to very bad teeth. Most of them are out and the remainder are enough to poison her completely. Seeking work as a cleaner, not suitable for any other work. Last worked in May 1934, as public-house cleaner.

Then there is the tie of domestic possessions. The number of middle-aged women who have managed to scrape together a few bits of personal possessions, furniture, etc., and who are living alone unable to get work is high in Liverpool and also in some of the cotton towns. Very few of these women are willing to consider any form of domestic training,[1] nor are they willing to leave their homes. They hold on to these few possessions with grim determination. Even if all their belongings are only worth a few shillings, their present home is the only home they know. They realize that if they once sell up these possessions, take a job and fail to hold it, they will be even worse off than they are now. Their few pieces of property are of far greater value to them than an outsider can readily understand, and were they to go out into domestic service they would have nowhere where they could return if they failed.

These single women and elderly women in Liverpool have in many instances been harshly dealt with by life. The War took some of their husbands, or potential husbands, the trade depression threw them out of work, and younger women are preferred. They have had little education, little or no training for anything. Many of them have experienced their only happiness in making of their single rooms a "bit of a home". They have neither the strength nor the self-confidence to come out of the shell in which they have taken refuge. Something could probably be done personally and individually to equip some of them for further employment. We were impressed by what has been done for women of this type by holidays and refresher courses given to them at the Lancashire holiday house at

[1] They undoubtedly fear that the acceptance of domestic training would involve them in accepting residential domestic work, though this is not the case.

Grey Court. But openings must be found for them too, and primarily in better paid daily domestic work. The large pool of domestic workers is partly due to the inadequacy of the openings for women in Liverpool.

There is another group (not illustrated by the Domestic Training enquiry) among the middle-aged or elderly unemployed women, small but quite clearly defined—the very respectable woman who has had some professional job which she has lost on account of her age or some other factor outside her control. We have alluded in another chapter of this report to one such case,[1] a middle-aged woman, evidently very competent, who had been a café manageress and whose only disability was her age. A young appearance counts so heavily for many jobs of this kind that the woman who is no longer young, once she falls out of work, is at a serious disadvantage. Another instance was brought out by one of the original sample visits in Liverpool; a woman who was a musician, whose livelihood had been cut from her by the development of mechanical music in dance halls and cafés. Her situation is that of those unemployed for technological reasons whom we have discussed already. Certainly she was an excellent type of person, a woman who had once had a good position, married to a man who was comparatively well off and had his own hotel. She had left him, soon after the boy was born, because he would not give up drinking, and was struggling hard on Unemployment Assistance to keep up a respectable appearance and to give the boy a decent education. No doubt in all the big cities there are a few cases of this kind, and if some means could be devised of fitting them and testing their ability for responsible jobs the potential value of their work might be considerable.

If thousands of young Liverpool girls are not to pass into this large category of Domestic Worker as untrained unskilled women who can all too often be classified as of "poor employability", something more must be done to equip them for life when they are young and we consider later some of the institutions which are attempting to provide such equipment. The type of problem

[1] See above, p. 188.

presented to them by some of the girls and young women in Liverpool may be illustrated by a story of one young factory hand, visited by one of us as the result of a chance meeting in a club:

Rosy left school at 14. She was not a scholar but was not bad at school. Her spelling is good and her arithmetic average. Her father, who has been out of work for three years, is a bricklayer, aged about 52, with not much chance of getting back to work again. There is a sister of 21 working and a brother of 17 unemployed, but only temporarily. He will get back to work in the autumn. When Rosy left school there was no question of her not looking for work, for her wages were needed to keep the family going. She was at the time of the interview working in a tobacco factory, filling up tins and thinking that her wage of 15*s*. was very good. Some of her friends have only 11*s*. and one only 9*s*. The frocks in which Rosy goes to the factory are terrible. She either wears an old evening dress of her sister's, which is much too long and fits nowhere, or a very old second-hand frock, which is worse because there are holes in it. Her stockings are full of ladders. The visitor was rather surprised at this neglect of her personal appearance, for when first seen at the girls' club she was very nicely dressed and on another occasion at a dance she was really smart. When asked about this rather contradictory behaviour, she excused herself on the ground that in her factory there was no cloak-room[1] and as she could not change there, she said that she had to work in very shabby clothes. She added that of course when she stays at home in the evening it was not worth while changing; but for an occasion like a girls' club meeting or a dance she always tries to be as neat and smart as possible. Stockings present a problem: "I buy a pair for 6*d*. every ten days or so and throw the old ones away, but sometimes, you see, I don't manage on my pocket money and then I have to wear them longer and they get rather worn out."

The significant fact in this story is the girl's habit of dressing properly only for certain occasions and being neglectful at others. One can imagine that later, when she marries and has one or two children, there will not be many occasions when it seems necessary to dress properly, and very soon she will do so only rarely. It is doubtful whether a woman who has not learnt to

[1] This statement may be inaccurate. The Factory Act requires the provision of minimum cloak-room accommodation.

be herself clean and tidy will ever keep her home and children tidy and clean. Another aspect of the problem is illustrated by the story of Rosy. "She does not like her work", we are told. "She knows that she has to work but she wants to get through it as quickly as possible." This attitude was shared by many of the unemployed young girls interviewed in Liverpool.

With a view to obtaining information as to the ideas of girls about their own future a class of 64 young girls attending a Junior Instruction Centre were asked to state on a sheet of paper what they wanted to do with their lives. It may be assumed that the girls attending the centre had nearly all had some work and were there because they were out of employment and were doing their best to get back to work. The written statements were a striking revelation of their state of mind. Only two of the sixty-four spoke of the work which they had been doing as having any further interest for them, or as providing anything in the nature of a career, and these two were not factory girls. Nearly all the girls said that they wanted to get married. A proportion explained that they wanted to have a good time before they got married but the majority expressed the wish to marry someone rich so that they could either own a motor car or travel or enjoy other forms of luxurious living. The other phantasy running through the answers was the desire for escape from their present situation into some profession already outside their reach. One would have liked to be a kindergarten teacher or dancer, another a trained children's nurse, another a stewardess as a means of seeing the world.

The young unemployed woman has only one alternative to work and that is marriage. Her experience as a juvenile worker has not, as we have seen, in any sense helped her in her preparation for the career of wife and mother. She has never learnt to do anything worth doing really well and if in her married life she finds no escape from the sense of frustration which she experienced as a girl, she will be unlikely to settle down to the demands of married life. The proof of this lies in the high proportion of unhappy broken marriages. The lack of satisfaction which the work done by most of these girls offers, is one of the reasons for the high proportion of young women with illegitimate children.

There was plenty of evidence of the lack of skill in domestic matters. Twenty-five girls between the ages of 14 and 19 in a girls' club were questioned as to their ability to cook. Only five had any knowledge of cooking and had actually done cooking, and even these proved themselves to have very limited knowledge of the art. They had never had any help in learning to think of a well-balanced diet. The same group were asked if they could sew. Only two of them had ever made a frock for themselves. Only five could "alter little things". The Warden of this club told us that she did not think more than 4% of the girls who came to her sport and social classes could sew at all. This impression was confirmed on a visit to a Junior Instruction Centre. The number of girls who came to the classes who could hold a needle properly or do a simple seam when they joined the classes was very small.

Of the girls under 24 years of age interviewed in the enquiry, mentioned above, with a view to domestic training, 51% were classified as making poor efforts to get work. When one remembers that the mothers of many of these girls grew up in the same conditions it is not surprising to find the following description applied to a typical instance of one who was interviewed for further employment: "Very poor type. Clothes neglected, eyes swollen. Whole appearance so poor that it will be difficult for her to get any residential work unless it is in a poor type of home."

And again, we were told that thirty out of ninety young girls attending a special course during unemployment were to all intents unemployable either because of the low standard of their education (they had attended school irregularly) or because of their careless upbringing or because they had unpleasant personal habits. Here too we have a sidelight on the inferiority of the material of which the large number of unemployed women in Liverpool partly consists. It may be emphasized, however, that the poor quality of the labour available in Liverpool is largely caused by the poor quality of the jobs available. It is a vicious circle, which could be effectively broken, perhaps, if a number of firms with high standards were to open factories in Liverpool.

There are at least two types of institution in Liverpool through which girls in considerable numbers are given the chance of learning something new—the Junior Instruction Centres which all unemployed girls between the ages of 14 and 18 have to attend[1] and the excellent daily Domestic Training Centre.

The Junior Instruction Centre has the advantage that attendance during unemployment is compulsory, but it is handicapped by the fact that attendance of individual members may vary from a few days to several months, so that the girls rarely settle down to a responsible attitude towards the opportunities offered in the Centre. The patience and skill with which the teachers endeavour to persuade the girls to take this opportunity of training seriously must evoke admiration. A second difficulty under which the Training Centre labours is the shortness of the time at its disposal. The girls attend the Centre for only three hours a day, in order presumably that the rest of the time may be spent in looking for work. Three hours are too short a time for providing the education and steady discipline required. Moreover, girls who are working part-time, say, three days a week, form part of the classes and this is a further handicap to continuity and "team work". The material which the Junior Instruction Centres are trying to handle is on the whole poor material. Many of the girls are thoroughly out of hand, and neither their mothers nor anyone else seems able to help them.

The subjects taught in the Centre visited were English, Arithmetic, Geography, Drawing, Embroidery, Sewing, Cookery and Drill. The favourite subject is drill. This consists of gymnastic and dancing lessons, the object of which is definitely not to drill the girls, but to teach them to concentrate on a subject by free will and to develop their creative powers. The success of these classes is remarkable. One can notice the difference between fresh arrivals and those who have had the bad luck, or one might almost say the good luck, to be unemployed and

[1] All, except the very few who prefer continued attendance in school.

attend the training centres for some time past. It was a pleasure to see the grace with which some of these girls danced and moved about, and their faces showed how much they enjoyed the discovery of their new possibilities. We were struck by their ability to concentrate on learning a new step or a new movement. The mistress uses the drill class for another educational purpose. The girls have to change into drill costumes provided by the Centre. There are always difficulties about this changing. Some girls do not want to change because of their underwear, and this provides the mistress with an opportunity of teaching them some hygiene.

The sewing class also serves a valuable purpose. The girls learn to mend their own things and to cut out and sew children's frocks. Something more might be done, perhaps, to encourage them to do more to their own clothes. The opportunity might be more fully used to teach them to dress properly. If it is possible for advertisements to teach the girls to "perm" their hair and use make-up, it ought not to be difficult to create a desire to be properly dressed.

The geography class is popular because it satisfies to a certain extent the craving for adventure. English, arithmetic and drawing are definitely disliked, and there is not much enthusiasm for the cookery class. One reason for the lack of interest is that the cookery classes are too big and the hours too short. This seems a pity, for cheap and nourishing dishes need a long time to cook and it is specially necessary to teach the cooking of such dishes. The cookery classes are also unpopular because of the lack of facilities at home, inadequate housing, and the preference for a ready-cooked fish and chip meal, even when good food of another type is available. Further, the parents' method of shopping precludes their getting much variety, as they obtain goods at one shop on credit, and pay at the end of the week. Tinned and cooked meats therefore are largely used.

It seems a regrettable omission in the education of these young girls that no provision should be made for elementary lectures to prepare them for the care of home and children. The argument which was advanced against the teaching of these subjects in the Junior Instruction Centre was that young mothers have the opportunity of attending ante-natal and baby care clinics. This argument seems to us unconvincing in view of the fact that the proportion of young mothers in working-class homes who attend such clinics is small, and that when they do so it is often on too slender a basis of knowledge of the concerns of married life and the home to enable them to profit from the instruction. Some evidence of this was furnished by an enquiry in Liverpool regarding the extent to which mothers were using the clinics which showed that out of sixty families visited not more than twenty had ever been near a clinic and that of these only a small proportion had attended the clinic regularly.

Turning to the Domestic Training Centre, it is encouraging to see how much is being done for the girls who attend it. This is all the more impressive since recruitment for this centre is very difficult. The Centre tends to get girls from 18 onwards who can neither go back to a factory nor find any alternative occupation to that of rough cleaner. This Centre takes forty girls for a thirteen-weeks' period of training. The girls and women who attend it are given a standard allowance from the Unemployment Assistance Board, 15*s.* a week for women of 21 and over, 12*s.* a week for girls from 18–21. These allowances are, during training, paid irrespective of whether the amount is in excess of the household needs based on the family circumstances as a whole, though allowances may exceed this figure if necessary. Fares to and from the Centre and a good midday meal are provided. The girls arrive each morning at 9 a.m., and leave again at 4 p.m., from Monday to Friday. There are two girls in residence every night. They stay three nights and so learn the duties of a residential maid and at the same time acquire the experience of being away from home and seeing what residential service is like. Every girl who attends the Centre has to go through this experience. We were told that while they often begin by dreading it, they often end by actually enjoying it.

Those undergoing training are between the ages of 18 and 35. More than half are between the ages of 18 and 20, and the majority of the rest are under 26. The girls learn something of what every residential maid should know. Endless trouble is taken to awaken an interest in each part of their duties, whether in the cookery classes where they cook a whole dinner as it would be served to a family of six, or in the detailed care given to methods of washing, cleaning, learning to lay a table attractively, etc. When these girls have been through a full thirteen-weeks' training they have learnt the rudiments of skilled housework. If they can pass on to a mistress who is herself skilled and will continue their training they can become efficient and reliable domestic servants.

The girls come into the Centre frequently in a somewhat defiant and suspicious mood. They may have been unemployed for some time and many of them feel that they have come to the Centre under pressure of circumstances. Moreover, as a condition of receiving the training they have had to promise to try a residential post and of this prospect they are undoubtedly frightened. Many of the girls when they come to the Centre are of a rough type. They have had little or no discipline, and they have little idea of personal hygiene and sound habits. The lessons they need to learn have to be inculcated with understanding, tact, and consideration. We were deeply impressed by the skill of the Warden and her staff in the training of these girls, and by the combination of firmness with generosity and tact. The Centre supplies the girls with some necessary underwear. The Warden finds ways of providing more if necessary and sees that they have stockings which they must then keep clean and mended. They are supplied in addition with good uniforms on taking up their post, which become their own property if they continue their work for three months. The girls gradually begin to take a real pride in their appearance.

The atmosphere in the Centre was all that could be desired. Not only did the girls look nice and neat and happy as they went about their work but talks with them individually left the impression that they were being given a real chance in life, and that they knew this and responded to the opportunity. We were left in no doubt of the educational value of this Homecraft

Training Centre. Girls who attend it are better equipped to face life whatever their future. They had learned a good deal more than the rudiments of cooking, sewing and orderliness, all of which would help them in any vocation. Yet it is a pity that some of these girls do not have the chance of more expert knowledge, both as cooks and as housekeepers. There is a very considerable demand for the highly skilled home-maker which cannot be met among these short-course trainees.

The women trained in this Centre have undertaken to try a resident domestic post but nearly all of them really want work in institutions only. Unfortunately conditions of work obtaining in private domestic service, and especially in resident domestic service, are very rarely such as to make a girl happy and proud in that profession. The scarcity of maids is not primarily due to a dislike of housework among English working-class girls, but rather to a dislike of the circumstances of this work. This point of view was expressed in the following case:

A kitchen maid of 21 years of age and unmarried; she dressed well, had a pleasant appearance, and had just returned from a spell of seasonal work. She told the interviewer with great pride that her employer had been very satisfied with her and that he hoped to get her back next year. She liked kitchen work but she objected strongly to sleeping in. When pressed, she expressed herself cogently: "first of all, one is half a slave; the mistress thinks everything about one's life is her concern too, and because she is the mistress, one never has a chance to tell her she should mind her own business. And, what is worse, she very often has the power to disturb one's private life and interests. One is never free. Factory girls have certain working hours and then they are free. We have to work all day and there is never an end to it. On our free day the mistress tells us when we have to be back. One can never have fun or a long dancing night because usually 'it does not agree with the moral code of the mistress'. And, you know, in this way we are handicapped in our chances of marriage; we don't have so many chances of meeting men, and when we meet them, there is no way of getting to know them better, for you can't bring a friend in even for a cup of tea. Nobody knows why, for it seems quite natural to the mistress that her daughter should have her boy friends and invite them to her home, but of course we are only maids, and everybody immediately thinks that we and our friends have dishonest intentions. Do you think it is pleasant to spend one's whole life with people who make one feel inferior to them? The loneliness is another factor, for sometimes it is days before you can speak to somebody who understands you."

If girls are to prefer trained domestic service to the often less socially valuable expedient of the factory or seasonal and part-time employment, it must be given a new dignity. It must not be supposed to be work that anyone can do, or confused with every kind of service rendered in the home or office irrespective of its quality. It must be made clear that it is something requiring intelligence, alertness, and experience. The conditions of work must be consistent with the dignity of an independent and self-respecting woman. Fortunately the shortage of effective help in the homes of England is a problem which has forced itself upon the attention of the nation and there is a likelihood of experiments being made in different directions with a view to solving the problem. If all school children were given an elementary training in home crafts so that none go out into the world without some knowledge of how to look after themselves and how to keep a home, the problem would be substantially nearer solution.

If the whole status of service in the home can be raised to a higher level, on the one hand by regulating the conditions under which such service can be obtained (this might include both the extension of the full benefits of insurance to domestic service and the raising of wages),[1] and on the other, by helping a large number of young girls to get the training which will give them that status, something effective will have been done both to ease the difficulty caused by this problem, and also to absorb into employment a number of women who have natural gifts in this direction and are now unemployed. There is a great deal to be said for a move in the direction of making skilled domestic service non-residential. A beginning in this

[1] The wages recorded, for example, in the large number of instances where women had gone from Liverpool for seasonal domestic employment seemed exceedingly low. Similarly men's wages in Liverpool appeared very low, cf. above, pp. 206 *seqq*. Two-thirds of the long-unemployed women in the one in ten Liverpool sample referred to on p. 234 earned 25*s.* a week or less.

direction may ultimately make possible conditions under which residential domestic service can be satisfactorily organized.

If it is recalled that about 51 % of the girls under 24 years of age who were interviewed in a special enquiry were classified as making poor efforts to get work, it is unlikely that many of these young women could be considered suitable for transference to other parts of the country. In Liverpool, as elsewhere, many mothers are unwilling, and rightly so, to send away a child of 14 years for unskilled or semi-skilled work in more prosperous areas. The attitude of the mothers can be summarized in the following report of a discussion on the subject with a group of fifteen women: "We do not want our girls to lose all touch with home"; "Who will look after the girl? She is too young to plunge into new and untried surroundings away from home." "My girl was transferred to Stoke-on-Trent as shop assistant in a multiple store, but her lodgings were extremely bad and the money she had left was not enough to feed her properly. She had a very bad breakdown and I had to fetch her home. It took a very long time before I got her right again." "My girl was offered a post as canteen worker in London but I did not dare to let her go because a girl from the neighbouring house went there, was seduced, and is now home with the baby."

Another great difficulty from the mother's point of view is that of the loss of the girl's earnings: "My girl is 22. She used to earn 22*s.* and give me 16*s.* Now she is on the dole and gets 15*s.* and I get 13*s.* out of it. I couldn't let her go and have nothing, because if she goes I would have to give up my home here and where would I be? She does not eat 13*s.* worth of food."

The problem of long unemployment among women in Liverpool will only be solved when, on the one hand, the educational level of the girl before she enters industry has been raised and, on the other hand, industries have been brought to Liverpool which provide the women with better and more permanent conditions of work. More must be done to help the girl to equip herself for her full position in society. For this purpose different kinds of agencies might well co-operate. Films might be used, for instance, to show the various types of careers for which girls might reasonably hope to qualify and the value and significance of training in relation to the experience of a lifetime. A film for example which showed the skill attained by a girl in a needle trade, who, after marriage, falls on hard times and gets back to her old employment, would show the capital value of such training.

There is a trade school in Liverpool for girls between 14 and 16 years of age where, for a fee of £8 for two years, training is provided in a variety of professions and well-paid employment is guaranteed after the training is completed. The experience and importance of such a school is not sufficiently known either to the parents or to the children themselves.

IV. THE VOLUNTARY AGENCIES AND THE WOMEN'S PROBLEM

Unemployment is the focus of many social problems. Poverty is not confined to the unemployed, but unemployment makes it more acute. It is not only unemployed families who live in bad housing conditions; but unemployed families in a slum district seem to lose their morale far more easily than they do elsewhere. One of the things that unemployment has done is to bring into prominence the needs of the working women.

It is when a man or woman becomes unemployed that he or she realizes, perhaps for the first time, the importance of relationships, the dependence of persons upon one another, the need of adaptation to unaccustomed circumstances and the opportunity of learning in and through the new conditions.

A club for unemployed women is in one sense a contradiction in terms, for a woman's job does not end when the factory gates close against her. "Managing the house takes a lot of doing with what we get", said an unemployed woman in Blackburn when she was asked how she spent her time, and another said: "If there isn't work to do, I make it." But nevertheless the Lancashire mill-worker has discovered the need for clubs, and the wives of unemployed men in many different parts of the country have discovered the need for clubs; and out of these needs there is gradually coming into being something that may well be one of the most valuable permanent contributions of the social service movement.

In each of our visits we asked the woman we interviewed with what social institutions she was in touch. Did she belong to any club? Did she belong to a trade union, a church or a W.E.A. class? What did she most enjoy doing if, and when, she could choose what to do? The answers to our questions were extraordinarily interesting and they differed widely from place to place.

In the Rhondda and in Crook we talked with the wives of unemployed men. These women had never themselves been in industry. Not a few had before their marriage been in domestic service and seemed to look back on that period as having opened up to them new worlds of interest and provided training and experience which was of use to them in their present lives.

In the Rhondda, as in Crook, the work among women is closely connected in many instances with the men's clubs and is thus helping to give them the character of community centres. In the Rhondda clubs which are willing to lend premises, women's sections meet once a week in the club buildings for a lecture followed by dressmaking, singing, or fancy work; the membership being in a typical case about 90, rather more than half that of the local men's club, while there is also an "adult school" meeting for women attended by about 25 once a week. For the latter a small subscription (2d. a week) is charged. The total membership throughout the valleys is about 1,500, and it is believed that in the case of about 80% of the membership the husbands are unemployed. The work is organized through the Settlement, through which materials are bought wholesale for dressmaking and handicraft. Both the movement as a whole and also its connexion with the clubs is significant. They show the tendency for the clubs to become something more than unemployed clubs and for the Settlement to become a focus for social work of many different kinds.

It is characteristic that in Durham too, where, if Crook is to be taken as a fair example, the standard of household management is particularly high, the women's work has been exceptionally successful. It is reckoned by many to be as valuable as any of the work done by the Community Service Councils in this part of the country.

In Blackburn the mill has been the centre of the woman's social life. The friendliness of the mill has in the past filled a large place in her life, and when the association is broken by long unemployment, in many instances the loss is keenly felt. The aim of the clubs in Blackburn has consequently been in the first instance to build up new associations and friendships in place of those which unemployment has severed, and in this they have been remarkably successful.

We found in Blackburn three clubs for unemployed women packed to their full capacity. These clubs had a waiting list, for premises and organization did not permit the extension of the existing membership. Both single and married unemployed women were members of the club, and the membership included also a few wives of unemployed men who had never been employed women. About 17% of the women in our sample were members of these clubs. No one who saw these women in their homes and at work in the clubs could doubt the value of these institutions. In unemployment the centre of the woman's interest has changed to her home and through her home to the wider interests which she is learning to find in the clubs. Many were loyal members of their trade union but had little interest in politics. Those who were members of churches generally did not seem to take any active part in church life other than the attendance at church services, though there were exceptions.

In Liverpool an important factor is the social setting, which has already been described. Liverpool is a large city with a population scattered over a wide area. There are innumerable industries with a high percentage of unemployed. It is a town where wages for both men and women, but especially women, are low and where in consequence there is a distressing amount of poverty. Despite this fact the efforts of the Voluntary

Agencies are relatively small in comparison with the need. The reason for this is not so much lack of interest on the part of people in Liverpool as the fact that unlike most towns which have been hard hit by the depression, Liverpool is neither a Special Area (in which case it would draw on grants from the Special Commissioner) nor is it able to avail itself of the resources provided by the Ministry of Labour through the National Council of Social Service for voluntary occupational work in towns which have a population of under 200,000 and more than 20% of the insured workers unemployed. Voluntary work for unemployed people in Liverpool has thus to be provided by the citizens of Liverpool over and above what they do for the poor of the town as a whole. In no town that we know of have private citizens made more generous efforts to finance the voluntary work for their own unemployed. But the needs of unemployed men came first and it has been extremely difficult to find resources with which to relieve the needs of unemployed women.

The most significant piece of work is that done by the Personal Service Society through Economic Housekeeping Classes organized for the wives of unemployed men, but even this work, conceived and planned with every care, suffers from its dependence on the services of voluntary workers whose keenness to help, and skill in the teaching of a particular subject cannot take the place of the experience and understanding of the total situation possessed by full-time officers. These classes in housewifery are greatly needed and the efforts made deserve every praise and encouragement. The women attending the classes showed not only keenness to learn but a touching gratitude for the instruction and for the social opportunity.

There is only one club in Liverpool for unemployed women. This small club of 35 to 50 women is used exclusively by elderly women, single or widowed, and none of the women in our sample were members of it. Most of the unemployed women in Liverpool over 45 are of poor employability. In the 123 cases of the Public Assistance Committee's sample in this age group 45–64 80% were of low employability. It may be possible through the clubs to fit them into an occasional job; and where the authorities of the club can make extensive contacts so as to get into touch with possible light jobs of an occasional character, such as do not go through the Exchange, that is obviously a great advantage. But in the main the task of this Liverpool club is not so much to improve employability as to make life a little happier for these older women, and in this the club is successful. It is work that is abundantly worth doing.

The problems of unemployed women in Liverpool cannot be separated from the problems of the lower-paid women workers and of the wives of employed and unemployed men. No effort on a considerable scale has been made in Liverpool to meet these needs. Though there is large scope for such work in Liverpool little is being done along the lines adopted in some other places to provide some sort of social life for wives, whether the husbands are unemployed or not. That this problem has no essential connexion with unemployment is shown strikingly by the figures. During the past year, according to the Report of the National Council of Social Service, 1936–37, though there has been a decline in unemployment, women's clubs and groups increased in number from about 450 to over 550. The first thing which such associations can provide is relief from the strain of continuous work at home, and this, with the forming of new friendships and the developing of new interests shared with others, is undoubtedly the most valuable work which such groups are doing. The women are also in the "Keep Fit" movement, which has spread with great rapidity, helping to battle against that physical deterioration to which the unemployed man's wife is particularly liable. The clubs are making a real, if indirect, contribution towards lightening the burden of poverty by educational work of a kind that can definitely help to raise the standard of living, through needlework, dressmaking, cookery and thrift craftwork of different kinds. The effects of this must be gradual, but there is no doubt whatever that it offers a promising approach, perhaps the most promising yet open, to that very difficult task of making it possible for all housewives to use what money there is available to the best supervision. The number of members and the distances separating the units mean that to each member most of the others are not known personally, and with the expansion of the scheme this mutual trust is based more and more on the effect of co-ordination by the organizers and the General Committee than on personal confidence in the other members. In this way co-operation within the scheme is becoming more and more similar to the general "unseen" co-operation within industrial society; and this is, as we have seen in a previous section,[1] an indispensable source of personal content, independence, and social prestige to the English worker. Where it succeeds in reviving this, the scheme gets deeper in its treatment of unemployed men than an unemployed club can hope to do. "There are 1,500 people depending on me", said one of the members proudly.

The tendencies are to develop this working community into a living community, but not much progress has been made in that direction. Family parties on the lawn were, naturally, a great success, but evening classes are only just about to be started in co-operation with the Workers' Educational Association and their success is still uncertain. A Sports Club has just been founded, and the charge of 1*d.* a week for the Sports Club is a "statutory" deduction for each member. These "statutory deductions" (there is also 1*d.* a week for the Hospital) are another way in which industrial traditions are preserved by Subsistence Production. But the organization of leisure and of a community life apart from work is a task which has not yet been tackled, and is so far considered as side-tracking the main preoccupations of the scheme, which are practical and quasi-industrial. But in restoring to the unemployed members of the scheme much of what they had lost when they lost their job, in material and spiritual values, and giving them in addition some things which they have never had before, the scheme is an indication of what voluntary agencies can do for unemployed men.

The scheme is backed by a small band of men who believe in the future of the principles on which their work is based, and for

[1] Cf. p. 150.

necessary purposes. They recoil from the thought of spending time in the company of other women in a strange building where they may have to learn and think about things which are new to them. Some women will only be won by individual interest and persuasion, but once this initial shyness is overcome they become keen club members.

There is no doubt at all that where the clubs have been successful they have won their way largely through the personalities of their leaders, most of whom are local people. In many cases the leadership has come from unemployed women themselves. In Blackburn the clubs owe much to the inspiration of the women who created them. These leaders have made a friend of every member. Each comes for advice and help in time of difficulty and the clubs give the impression of being far more of a family than an institution.

Many of the women in our sample testified to the benefits of the work done on their behalf. It would be difficult to convey the pride and gratitude which these women expressed when they showed us things they had made and when they spoke of the way in which the club had taught them to sew, to make warm and useful things out of scraps bought in rummage sales—things which they could not have possessed if they had not been members of the clubs. But even greater than their appreciation of the material advantages is their sense of what they gain from the experience of friendship and understanding. A load of loneliness and weariness is lifted from their shoulders. They find themselves introduced into a world of new interests and new experiences, which enrich not only their own lives but also their homes and surroundings. Among the women we met we found a growing interest in problems of many kinds and an increasing desire for education. There were requests for more talks in the clubs, especially on such subjects as child welfare, local government or some aspect of personal hygiene, and there is little doubt that, with understanding and the right kind of help, more women might be helped into Workers' Educational Association classes.

From the foregoing description it is apparent that the Women's

Club Movement, having its origin in places where clubs for unemployed men had already been established, has reached out into wider fields and is becoming a national movement for community education and recreation. Its aims are, first, to provide social amenities for women of the working class; secondly, to help them to improve their standards of living; and, thirdly, to further adult education in a form adapted to their needs. The clubs are intended to provide opportunities for their members to help themselves and to help one another. A condition of membership is the payment of a regular subscription, and all forms of help which undermine self-respect are rigorously excluded.

The women's club movement owes its vitality both to the imagination of individuals who have experimented on the basis of local needs and to a small number of full-time officers of the National Council of Social Service who have helped each local unit to pool its experience with other local units and to draw on the resources of the all too small but very efficient staff of instructors for the clubs whose services are lent to different districts. Without such help the movement could not possibly have reached its present degree of efficiency.

The national movement has its central power-house at the Beeches, near Birmingham, which is used primarily as a centre for training in club activities and management, but also as a means of giving club members a refresher course and a holiday. The women come for a fortnight's work and are given an opportunity of learning in a great variety of ways how to make their clubs more effective. In this centre, which is delightfully furnished and has accommodation for thirty-one women—a warden and a staff of three, one of whom is a craft instructor—,each fortnightly group of women settles down to intensive work.

The mornings are generally given to craft work, the early afternoon to rest and recreation and the late afternoon and evenings to talks on educational subjects and on the problems of the movement. Most of the women who attend the centre are wives of unemployed men. We were much struck, not only by the happy and effective atmosphere of the place, but also by the delight of the women in escaping for a whole fortnight from the burden of anxiety which they carry at home to what for them, despite the hours of work, seemed to be a glorious holiday. This fortnight not only gives the women new ideas and a new outlook, but sends them back to their homes determined to make the women's clubs as worth while as they can possibly make them.

The movement has three other centres, one at Grey Court, near Lancaster, another at The Fields, near Etherley, County Durham, and one at Ormsby on Teeside. They fulfil somewhat the same function as the Beeches, but in a local rather than a national setting.

We saw no piece of voluntary work in the country more worth while than these centres which provide for the women who attend them training, refreshment and new stimulus.

If the women's club movement is to be developed from this encouraging beginning into a nation-wide movement of the kind that is desirable, something more must be done to help the women's clubs to obtain better equipment and, above all, better premises. Given such aid, we are convinced that the movement is potentially one of great importance to the country. It may contribute powerfully to the strengthening of real community life. It may do much to foster what is best in English working-class life and to conserve and develop the instinctive disposition of the members of the working class to help one another. It can assist the women to become competent in their own homes. It can awaken and foster a desire to participate in the life of the neighbourhood and to enrich it in a variety of ways. It can create in women a sense of responsibility for their homes and through this a feeling of responsibility for the community and thereby aid in the formation of a new cultural tradition and a new integration of the social life. The movement will take its place alongside other national women's movements working for social progress in a world where there is much need of co-operative effort to this end.

Part V

THE SOCIAL SERVICE MOVEMENT

I. GENERAL PROBLEMS OF THE CLUBS

(*a*) PAUPERIZATION AND THE SENSE OF INDEPENDENCE

In considering the unemployed man's problems, we have seen that they fall into two broad divisions, according to whether the area is one of industrial or residual unemployment. In areas of industrial unemployment, the unemployed are a cross-section of the working-class community, with the best material, as well as that which is poorer, among them. In such places the unemployed clubs might be representative of the working class as a whole. Where unemployment is residual, the material for unemployed clubs will be the "down-and-outs", men of low employment value, the psychological misfits who cannot force themselves back to work, and the older men.

We have discussed their various difficulties, the difficulties of poverty which they share with many who are working; a changing attitude to work with a gradual tendency to find unemployment an easy way out; and a lowering of the sense of independence which makes it yet easier. How far are the clubs meeting these difficulties? Are they helping those who might get work to do so, or are they making the process of adjustment to unemployment easier? Are the voluntary societies making a useful contribution towards the solution of the problems of poverty? Is any of the work that is being done of such a kind that it is helping to undermine independence? And what of the man for whom "time was his worst enemy"? Are they helping him to fight that enemy in the best ways they might do? What of the man who has lost, with his job, his one active contact with the world outside? Are they finding him and helping him to make another? These are the questions that must be implicit in any study of the movement.

Before we discuss the clubs in the light of the sample, there are certain general principles that must be considered, and these form the subject of the next three sections. One that is, from the point of view of the voluntary movement, central is that of the preservation of independence. The threat to this is one which has been realized throughout, but it is difficult to avoid, and the resistance to it varies enormously from one district to another. In the Rhondda, for example, there are relatively few traces of pauperization, while in some areas it has gone very far. The difference is not only that in a prosperous area the contrast between those who have money and those who have not is apparent, whereas in a depressed area poverty is almost universal. It is a matter of independence and self-reliance or self-respect, and it is closely connected, too, with a man's social life. Those who have strong associations with the community in which they live seem to be, on the whole, much less subject to pauperization. The more civilized they are, the more successfully they avoid it.

Both in Crook and in the Rhondda there are many factors which make for such social solidarity. Where one industry predominates, society has a homogeneous economic basis. In the Rhondda geographical conditions also contribute. A hundred and thirty thousand people live in the two narrow valleys, isolated by the mountains, to a quite extraordinary degree, from the world outside, and this concentration helps to make that exceptional vitality and intensity which the institutional and social life of the valleys has apparently always had. The Rhondda is indeed a hotbed of institutions. Not only is there a great variety of them, but they are warmly supported. Unemployed men in the Rhondda sample belonged to institutions ranging from Conservative Clubs and the Communist Party, through churches and chapels of many denominations, to a Dancing Club and a Brass Band. And the support given to institutions may be fairly regarded as one index of civilization.

The point is important enough to be illustrated in figures for the sample as a whole:

TABLE LIX. UNEMPLOYED MEMBERSHIP OF INSTITUTIONS AND ASSOCIATIONS IN THE SAMPLE TOWNS

	No. of visits effective for this purpose	Not connected with any institution	Members of Church or Chapel	Trade Union	Workmen's Club or Institute	Unemployed Clubs	British Legion or Old Contemptibles	Cellar Clubs, billiard halls, pubs, etc.	Others*	Membership for effective visit
Areas of industrial unemployment										
Rhondda	187	37	70	72	35	35	5	9	35	1·46
Crook	90	12	25	28	16	48	4	—	—	1·49
Blackburn	89	29	27	23	4	14	5	3	3	0·888
Liverpool	226	109	57	12	6	5	3	21	29	0·509
Areas of residual unemployment										
Leicester	84	40	12	10	5	15	—	1	5	0·571
Deptford	70	44	13	5	1	0	0	6	5	0·428

* Includes regular attendance at lecture halls, membership of unofficial gangs, football clubs, etc.

We have not included in these figures membership of Co-operative Societies, because the records make it clear that such membership means something different in one neighbourhood from what it means in another. In the Rhondda they tend to be real social institutions, and men described themselves as "staunch co-operators, and their parents before them", whereas in Liverpool and Deptford the Co-operative Society seemed to be almost entirely an economic institution joined for saving purposes. If these figures were included, the Rhondda would have shown a still further increase on the other towns, for it is only less important there than the Church and Trade Union. We have included membership of various unofficial associations, which, though they have no definite organization, often evidently play a large part in the lives of those who belong to them.

Table LIX is significant in several ways. It is natural to think of the great cities as possessing a wide variety of social institutions, and the smaller places as having fewer opportunities.

The table shows that this is at best only a half-truth. The figures in the right-hand column fall exactly as the size of the urban unit rises. Small villages may not have the buildings to house community life and activities, but it exists in them in a more real sense than in the big city, and the larger the unit the less easy it is either to give a sense of community life to the whole or to organize smaller institutions within it that are active and alive.[1] This is partly due to the competition of cinemas and greyhound racing tracks, but there is obviously much more to it than that. In the case of unemployed men, for example, the sample visits suggest strongly that it is not because they spend time going to the cinema or taking part in other commercialized pleasures that in large towns it is so difficult to run effective clubs for them; but rather that in the large towns they live very much emptier lives and that they probably go less often, not more often, to the cinema. There are of course exceptions, but broadly speaking, the real obstacle in the way of building up a good club in a large city is not the competition of commercialized amusements but the lack of any social foundations on which to begin. In the descriptions which follow of some clubs visited, there are one or two which show how this can be overcome, but it is significant that one of the most successful in this way, the Lincoln Club, originated in what was already an active social institution, an enthusiastic Workers' Educational Association class.

The table shows that the number of the isolated unemployed in the Rhondda is small. One of us noted about an unemployed miner in the Rhondda: "He has lived for 40 years in the same place, in which he knows every corner. He likes to plunge back into the past, and tells how hard work was when he was young... when agriculture was still carried on on the hills, and the rent of his double house was only 15*s.* a month. He knows everybody in the neighbourhood, and what he likes to do is to stand at his door."

[1] Institutional membership is also an indication of the degree of residual unemployment. The more residual its character, the smaller the institutional membership. The figures for Liverpool, however, show that it is chiefly the size of the urban unit that counts.

Anyone who knows the Rhondda will recognize the picture, but it is of something alien to most of the big cities. It is this social spirit that makes possible good clubs, or indeed good social institutions of any kind.

Men who know each other well make much better enemies, as they also make better friends; and so there is something very much alive in the factions which rend most of these social institutions from time to time. It is doubtless largely the geography of the Rhondda Valley which makes the underlying unity that is, fundamentally, of much greater importance than all these apparent differences. Characteristic of this unity is the traditional neighbourliness, which the unemployed Welshman who moves to England misses so much.[1] The Rhondda family does not consider that "keeping itself to itself" is a canon of respectability. Everyone knows its affairs, and if anything goes wrong, there is sympathy and help readily forthcoming from the house next door.

The table given above shows how outstanding is the position of the Rhondda and Crook in regard to social institutions generally, and we may profitably consider in rather more detail what are the reasons for this. The Rhondda, of the two communities, is that which picks itself to be treated in detail, because, as the table shows, in Crook the very high figure for institutional membership is due to the success of the unemployed clubs, rather than to previously existing institutions. At the basis of the varied community life of the Rhondda seems to lie the cultural tradition which no one who spends much time there can fail to notice. It was in the Rhondda that one of those visited confessed to reading Balzac in his spare time. His only serious competitor in the sample was a self-made scholar in Blackburn. A casual conversation among unemployed South Wales miners may be on a point of politics or theology or logic—often indeed very imperfectly understood—where in the Midlands or London it would be a series of monosyllables answered

[1] One wrote to his family (visited during the course of the sample) from London: "I am sitting in Hyde Park. There are thousands of people all round me and not a single one has spoken to me."

with a series of grunts. Other expressions of traditional values are a sensitiveness to the beauty of the mountains and moors—a number of those interviewed said that they often spent days out walking on the mountains—and appreciativeness of a pleasant home. The best of the houses are furnished in an exceptionally charming way, with an oak dresser hung with old lustre as the central feature of the parlour. And another, as everyone knows, is the music which, though by English standards it is sentimental, is in execution superior to anything that is to be found among comparable communities in the South of England.

Such a community has its defects as well as its qualities. Though the impression we formed was that on the whole there were fewer poverty-stricken households among the unemployed in the Rhondda than in some places,[1] and that many[2] had settled down fairly happily to an existence which was, if not comfortable, not intolerable, yet there is more self-pity among the unemployed in South Wales than anywhere else. The phrases which are sometimes used in public about it suggest a state of mind which is almost pathological—as did, for instance, an otherwise very reasonable memorandum on the working of the Means Test published in the Rhondda in October 1936, which spoke of it as "an attempt to inflict a barren and hopeless misery on people already poverty-stricken", and as a "process of scraping bare the sore of poverty day after day by a well-organized government machine". There is a danger that self-respect may be undermined by this self-pity, and if that should happen, it would be disastrous to the civilization of the Rhondda.

The civilization of the Durham villages (if Crook may be taken as an example) is different in character. The Durham miner has a less erratic temperament than the Welshman. Though the quality of family life was noteworthy in the Rhondda, in Crook it seemed even higher. Thus while unemployment almost everywhere was accompanied with a marked deterioration of family relations, one sign of which was the number of unemployed men living apart from their wives, in the Crook sample,

[1] This point has been considered in detail in an earlier chapter; see above p. 110.
[2] See Table A 11.

as in the Rhondda, only one instance of this occurred, while family solidarity on the whole seemed even surer in Crook than in the Rhondda. We give later some figures which illustrate this (p. 312). And though a rather higher percentage of households in Crook were living in slum conditions, there was a higher proportion of well-managed households in Crook than anywhere else, and the proportion of those who had taken part in some form of adult education was also high, though not so high as in Wales.

TABLE LX. FAMILY STANDARDS. UNEMPLOYED FAMILIES IN CROOK, THE RHONDDA, AND LIVERPOOL

		Household conditions			Family relations	
	Effective statements	Exceptionally good or good conditions and management	Indifferent conditions and management	Bad conditions and bad management	Effective statements	% of worse than normal relations
Crook	78	52	12	14	94	29·8 %
Rhondda	165	98	46	21	193	31·2
Liverpool	189	86	79	24	194	38·1

On the whole, Crook may be fairly taken perhaps as an excellent example of English working-class civilization of the older type, based on the characteristic working-class institutions, the Trade Unions and Co-operative Society. It was noticeable that unemployed men in Crook seemed more determined to make what they could of the situation, rather than give way in the face of it to self-pity.

A disquieting fact brought out by the sample was that even in the Rhondda and Crook these institutions, which have proved in the past such a valuable feature of working-class civilization, have not the hold on the younger generation which they still keep on the older. It was perhaps to be expected that the same would be true of organized religion. This means that the young men even in Crook and the Rhondda who are growing up amidst unemployment will not have that same traditional backing as their parents had. "I do not believe", said the wife of an unemployed Rhondda miner to one of us, "that we should be able to bear this as we do bear it, unless we had been well brought up, and had good food, too, when we were young." The speaker was a woman of 53. Her words remind us that both in Crook and the Rhondda a long period of relative prosperity and high wages was a condition for the formation of the traditional background we have been discussing. This condition no longer exists, and it would not be safe to trust that the young men unemployed in South Wales or Durham for year after year will be able to stand up to unemployment as their parents have done without serious deterioration. One of the big tasks ahead of the voluntary movement is to find some institutional expression which will win the loyalty of the younger men.

There is another fact which is significant in this context. Too much must not be made of it, for information on such a point is hard to obtain and the value of it is difficult to assess. The most striking evidence comes from one of the most isolated of the Rhondda villages, a village which used to be famous for its working-class solidarity. One of the men interviewed was discussing the possibility of earning a little extra to supplement "the dole". "The neighbours are on to you at once," he said, "if they hear of you earning. No one wants to see a shilling or two more going into other people's houses than goes into their own." He was thinking of the anonymous "informers" through which the Unemployment Assistance Board sometimes may get information of illicit earnings, and he maintained that such things would have been unthinkable a generation ago. There was at least one instance in the sample where a man had given up a perfectly legitimate spare-time occupation owing to a neighbour's threat to make trouble for him with the Board, and others where such trouble was mentioned. If practices of this kind became widespread the effect on the morale of the community would be deplorable. On the whole it seems unlikely that this particular trouble has gone very far.

If the work done by the voluntary agencies has been more successful, then, in the Rhondda and in Crook than in some others of the places visited, it is partly because there is, in these two communities, enough social cohesion to make the task of avoiding pauperization much easier. We shall see that the Rhondda clubs, to an increasing degree, are becoming real working-class institutions, growing out of the society which they serve, not superimposed upon it and stifling it, as clubs in some places are liable to do. At present, however, it is only the more general point that needs emphasis, that, disastrous as the social effects of unemployment may be in the Rhondda, the personal effects of it are not so disastrous there as elsewhere, because the individual has some sense of support from the community to which he belongs. The fact that a large proportion of that community has been directly affected by unemployment has to some extent made this easier, for though it is certain that in some parts of South Wales a social cleavage between employed and unemployed is beginning to take place, there was no case in the Rhondda sample where this cleavage was underlined, and several where men specifically said that their friends were among employed and unemployed alike. When severe unemployment attacks a community which has no such background, its personal effects are much more deeply felt.

Both the voluntary agencies themselves and also the State administration are closely concerned with this problem of pauperization. It has been generally recognized for a long time that indiscriminate charity is likely to lead to pauperization, and is in a democratic society a dangerous thing. But it is a very different thing to avoid it. The "scrounger" type occurs everywhere, though in a place like Liverpool, where traditions in this matter of pauperization are bad, the numbers are disproportionately large. It is unfortunate that in several of the places visited, the type seemed to be associated, in the minds of many of those interviewed, with the clubs. There are cases in which gifts of clothing and money may be invaluable, and it is inevitable that in such cases some should have gifts made to them which do more harm than good. But even the provision, through charity, of a comfortable club room is not necessarily in the best interests of those who use it.

The organizations which have grown out of the working-class movement in the country, Trade Unionism and the Co-operative Movement, seem to have latterly become narrower in their scope as the economic issues which they are facing become clearer, and to have lost something of the general cultural quality which they once had. Nothing is more desirable than that the support of these movements should be recaptured for social work, and that they should help in shaping its future. There has been local co-operation between Trade Unions and social workers, but on the whole more suspicion than co-operation. Some of the men visited in the course of the sample objected to the clubs on "Trade Union" grounds, i.e. they said there was a danger of men "working" in the clubs, at boot repairing, painting, and even building, "for nothing" and thus "doing down the tradesmen". For these reasons it has not been easy to get men who know the working class from the inside associated with the control of the voluntary movement. Social work among the unemployed is constantly described by those responsible for it as "educational in the widest sense", and this means that it must, if it is to succeed, be something not alien to the society for which it is planned, and sensitive to the needs which unemployment creates. The teacher of art must be aware, not only of the badness of the trash which the hire-purchase system is foisting on us, but also of the particular charm which a working-class home at its best can have. Some practical examples of this which came within our knowledge may be cited; that of a woman teacher, for instance, who was instructing a class of the poorest Liverpool women in bread-making, but said nothing of the value of wholemeal flour, and assumed that the women all had gas ovens available. Similarly one of us met, in a Lancashire town, an unemployed metal worker, exceptionally intelligent, married, with children. His life had been transformed by a class he attended, from which he had learnt unfortunately among other things that it was better not to work, and that he could manage on much less than he was getting if he could only persuade his wife to confine the family diet to milk and fresh vegetables. In much of this there was an element of truth but when the wife's story was heard, it was evident how remote it all was from the man's real needs. "He is never at home now, and he never helps. It makes me so unhappy that he will not work. You should have known what a marvellous worker he was, and so nice and intelligent, everybody liked him; but now he is out of work he does nothing, but has funny and stupid ideas in his head. It's all the tutor's fault; he says he should not work. Oh, how I hate that man! But don't dare say nothing about him or my husband goes furious." And because with the working class local values are specially important, the teacher has to be aware of these also. One brilliantly successful (and yet wholly improbable) experiment in this direction may be quoted, the translation of an act of Shakespeare into "Tyneside", an experiment which played a considerable part in the extraordinary progress of dramatic activities among the unemployed clubs there.

The practice of adoption, which is fairly widespread in the financing of the unemployed clubs, has done, and is still doing admirable work, but carries with it dangers of paternalism, if it is not carefully controlled. Adopting bodies usually raise their funds on the strength of a compassionate appeal. It is natural, therefore, for them to wish to spend at least some part of their funds in an obviously compassionate way. Christmas treats, children's outings and presents, gifts of equipment and clothing, free timber for woodwork or free leather for boot repairing, are the sort of objects of expenditure which make a ready appeal to members of adopting committees. Expenditure of this kind carries certain dangers of pauperization of the beneficiaries by undermining their initiative and independence. There have been examples where groups of unemployed men who have raised money themselves in various ways to provide club equipment, gardening tools, club wireless, concerts, children's parties and outings, have lost all will to continue these things since they have learned that a request to the adopting body would "do the trick" without further effort on their part. Club committees, which had previously devoted themselves to careful planning of projects involving the raising of funds by their own efforts, have in some cases lost all interest in anything except devising projects and thinking of club necessities for which the adopting body can be induced to pay. In several places visited by one of us in Durham, it was not difficult to detect an attitude of getting what could be got from the adopting body, and associated with it, a readiness to bluff about the real character of much that was going on, which would have been unpleasant had it not been so naïve. In one case at least an election to a club committee had been fought (by private canvass) on the basis of "getting more for you out of the adopting body". In several clubs which were visited distributions of clothes sent by adopting bodies had been the occasion of very unpleasant recriminations.

It may be stated here most emphatically that we do not wish to be interpreted as condemning the system of adoption, which has certain notable advantages. There is something very valuable in bringing a prosperous area or a prosperous society into direct contact with one less prosperous. We came across numerous instances where such contact had evidently been to the great advantage of both sides. Adoption has played a big part in the finance of the voluntary movement, and it is greatly to be hoped that that part will continue to be extended. On the other hand, the contact must be close enough for the real needs of the less prosperous society to be understood. Everything depends upon the wisdom of the adopting committee and their willingness to take the advice of experienced officials on the staff of local or regional community service organizations as to the best way to spend their money. There was plenty of evidence in many places that these dangers of pauperization had been recognized and were being guarded against in a large number of clubs. Several wardens held what can only be described as violent views on the subject and they were perhaps over anxiously vigilant against any unwise manifestation of tenderheartedness on the part of the adopting body.

A further danger is that adoption may undermine the democratic character of unemployment welfare organization. Interference in the actual running of unemployed clubs by adopting bodies is comparatively rare where the distance between adopters and adopted is considerable. On the other hand, in places such as Liverpool where the adopting bodies are local, there is a tendency for adopted clubs to accept a certain amount of benevolent dictation. But local adoption also can be beneficial, and there is at least one Liverpool club where the warden has succeeded in "mixing" members of the adopting body with the club life as a whole, for which there is obviously everything to be said. Yet the part played by the adopting bodies in Liverpool does certainly contribute to the general spirit of patronage, as distinct from that of democracy, which characterizes the Liverpool voluntary movement as a whole.

One powerful safeguard that the clubs can provide against pauperization is the opportunity for giving a sense of achievement to the men who use them, and in Liverpool it was in so far as they succeeded in doing this that the best work of the clubs was effected. It may come in different ways, with the effort of constructing or reconstructing the club buildings, through the craft work or dramatic or re-educational activities, or through the effective management of the clubs by the men themselves. There are clubs in which premises are fully provided by external "charity", and in which there is very little democratic management by the men themselves, perhaps because they are not the type to be interested in that particular aspect; and in which, nevertheless, the members, often through the personal success of some brilliant craft instructor, have their confidence and self-respect restored through this sense of achievement. This is a factor which some of those inside the movement itself tend to underrate. A good example of such a club was visited by one of us in East London. What made it was the man who ran it, who spent his day working side by side with the unemployed men who were members of it. The fellowship of work, as everyone knows, is much more real than the fellowship of casual contacts. It is significant that this club had an exceptional record in "refitting" men for work. A club of this kind may conceivably be the only possible club for an area where there is no democratic tradition and no interest in politics, while in another, just because it was not democratically run, it would fail.

The State administration is concerned equally closely with this problem of pauperization, and the vast numbers which it has to handle, and the necessity of dealing with those who want work and those who do not through the same organizations, make the problem particularly difficult. Anyone who has seen the work of the Unemployment Assistance Board in different areas will agree that on the whole its success in this respect has been remarkable. What is essential (as is indeed generally recognized) with both the Board and also the Employment Exchange, is that they should be services for the unemployed as well as for the employer and for industry; that the man who is concerned with them should not feel he is being treated as though "anything was good enough for him". For him the State is represented by the Employment Exchange and the Unemployment Assistance Board, and while very few would deny there are times when he has to be treated summarily by them, that ought to be the exception rather than the rule. We found a few instances in which there was resentment against clerks in the Employment Exchange who were apparently using their position unfairly, and a few instances of similar resentment against Unemployment Assistance Board investigators. One example may be quoted, not because it is typical, but because it shows the sort of dangers which are to be avoided. It is a remark made by a man of over 60: "Do you see this bench?" he said. "When the Means Test man saw it, he asked me if I ever made anything on it for other people, and then he said, 'you needn't answer, for we'll get to know almost before you do it. Someone will write and tell us.'" If this attitude were allowed to spread, any effort to help the unemployed man to keep his independence would be doomed to failure. The authorities of the Board are certainly fully alive to this, and it has been said already that this instance is by no means typical.

If by pauperization is meant the profession of poverty, not only as a way of making a living, but also as one of the main interests in life, the proportion of such cases in the sample is very small. But there is an intermediate stage in which a man gradually begins to value his independence less and less, and to rely more and more on provision being made for him without his having to take any steps about it himself. He is gradually ceasing to be a responsible member of society. This is a more subtle danger than pauperization by misjudged charity, and whereas in the Rhondda there is little risk of the latter, many who know South Wales well would say that the more subtle harm had now penetrated much deeper. Many social workers believe that application of compulsion in any form to the unemployed would be a serious threat to their independence. While we do not believe, as stated in a previous chapter, that this is necessarily true, the view is held sufficiently widely to deserve great respect, and we are convinced that the preservation of this sense of independence is the most important objective of the voluntary social work among unemployed men and women.

(*b*) THE ISOLATION OF THE UNEMPLOYED MAN

In earlier chapters of this report something has been said about the isolation that is caused by unemployment. We have seen that one thing for which work is valued is the contact with others which it brings.[1] Loss of work means the loss of this association, and not till then is the great part this has played realized. The result of unemployment may thus be a gradual turning in of the individual upon himself. Thus, when one man was asked what were his interests: "To tell you the truth," he said, "it's keeping out of the light as much as possible. I've always been used to having decent clothes, and I don't like to be seen about like this." The suspicion arises that, when the answer comes (as it comes time and time again to the question why a man does not join an unemployed club) "I keep myself to myself", there is more to it than might at first sight appear. Is the fact simply that very large numbers of the human race are what might be called "unclubbable"? No doubt many of them are; but the probability is that unemployment has made many others un-

[1] See above, pp. 150, 151.

sociable by accentuating any tendency to shyness or diffidence that may have been there already. We found that isolation was much less characteristic of the two Special Area samples than of the man in more prosperous districts, no doubt largely because in the Special Areas unemployment, being far more general, carries no social stigma with it; though it may also be partly due to differences in the normal social habits of different places.

This problem of isolation is seen in its most acute form in the case of the older man who is a bachelor or a widower, living without dependents. (Table LXI.)

TABLE LXI. ASSOCIATIONS OF MEN OVER 55 (EFFECTIVE VISITS ONLY INCLUDED)

	Living with dependents	Living without dependents	Number of those living without dependents with		
			(*a*) active associations	(*b*) occasional associations	(*c*) no associations whatever
Deptford	26	15	1	2	12
Leicester	30	16	6	2	8
Rhondda	38	8	5	2	1
Crook	20	3	1	—	2
Liverpool	35	5	—	3	2
Blackburn	22	4	2	—	2

The figures show that it is a problem much more marked in the prosperous places. Conditions in Liverpool in this respect approximate to those in the Special Areas. The table seems almost to suggest that isolation, in prosperous places, is not only an effect, but a cause of unemployment; as though the man with no social "backing" loses heart more easily and drops out of the race sooner than the man who has the support of family life or other associations behind him.[1] We were often told how casual employment was to be picked up in the public-house by "treating" foremen, or how so-and-so had been "fitted in" by a friend. No doubt the numbers of men without associations

[1] Cf. p. 398.

who do not get work, is to be explained partly in this way. The Deptford figures may be exaggerated, owing to the chance that there is in Deptford a large lodging-house for single men, but the similarity of the Leicester situation shows conclusively that this is a real tendency. The table must be read in the light of the fact that we are here dealing with numbers of men who will probably never work again, and that we can add to them the far greater numbers of men over 65, who are similarly retired but did not come within the view of our sample.

All this is at once a difficulty and a challenge. It means that there is a need to be met and a peculiar difficulty in meeting it, a difficulty which, incidentally, is not so great with women as it is with men. Most of the clubs for older women, that is, for elderly unemployed spinsters, or for the wives of unemployed men, are an unqualified success, and the women take to them with the greatest enthusiasm, whereas men do not associate nearly so readily and are evidently afraid of "giving themselves away". This suggests that it is to a certain extent the loss of status and of occupation which are at the root of the difficulty, since there is always an occupation for the woman in her home, which in itself gives her a status. The older men need friendship and sympathy just as acutely; but it has to be offered to most of them, in the early stages at least, individually. Individual friendship brings with it a warm response. There were many who seemed to welcome even the casual chance which our visits gave, to speak their minds and feel better for it, and it was not unusual for them to say that "they'd never had an opportunity for speaking to anyone in that way before". It was the most diffident who seemed to feel this most strongly, and our experience suggested the need for the addition of more and more "pastoral work" to the labours of those, many of them indeed already heavily overworked, who are concerned with the club movement. This is, of course, no new discovery. The social workers attached to many of the South Wales Settlements have been doing something of the kind for a long time, but in the majority of districts it has not yet become part of the ordinary club organization. And in particular it is needed in prosperous districts, where the breakdown of isolation may be the most important step in getting a man back to work.

The sample brought out a significant fact in this connexion, that in one place at least, Blackburn (the situation in the clubs of which is described later), what might be called in some places the isolation of the unemployed man is in reality a matter of class distinction. These class distinctions are not easily observed by the outsider, but there is no doubt that they are important, and that (in prosperous places, for example) one reason why the unemployed man does not associate with employed men is that on the whole he belongs to a lower social stratum. But this is not the whole explanation, for isolation occurs among the upper strata of the unemployed as among the lower. It means, however, that the local situation has to be carefully studied before effective "community" work of any kind can be done, and that the first necessity may well be the breaking down of those subtle distinctions between one social stratum of the working class and another.

One group of people in the sample whom isolation did not affect, were those who had retained active membership of some social institution to which they had previously belonged. Comparatively few of those who had played a full part in the life of churches or trade unions had dropped out of them as a result of unemployment. A Methodist minister in Cumberland, replying to an enquiry as to the effects of unemployment in his area, said that it affected "adherents" of the church much more seriously than "members", and "rank outsiders" more seriously still, while another in Durham described how "those on the fringe of the church drop off and join the army of the aimless"—answers which illustrate the point precisely. Thus the best remedy for this particular need is not the formation of special *ad hoc* social institutions, but the support of already existing institutions and the strengthening of the ties which their members have with them during employment, in order that when the lean years come there will be something which still keeps those who are thrown out of work active members of society. Membership of the unemployed club does not necessarily cure that dissociation from the community as a whole to which unemployment may lead, for the unemployed community so often is something apart from the employed community, carrying a social stamp of its own. As one man in Leicester, a lorry driver aged 47, said: "I'd never hear the last of it from my father if I went to an unemployed club." This unwillingness to take on oneself the character of unemployment, thought to be given by joining an unemployed club, was often expressed in several of the districts visited. To rely on existing institutions however may be, in some circumstances, to underrate the effect which unemployment has of itself in isolating men and keeping them away from their fellows.

In some trades, association with the Trade Union automatically lasts so long as a man remains on benefit. In Leicester most of the jobs available in the boot and shoe trade are filled through the Trade Union, which acts as a sort of employment exchange for this particular type of work; and unemployment insurance, so long as that lasts, is paid through it. This is from the point of view of the problem we are now considering an admirable arrangement, in that it keeps a man in close association with his trade during the first months that he is out of work. But when he runs out of benefit and is turned over to Unemployment Assistance, it is drawn no longer through the Trade Union but through the Labour Exchange, so that at the moment when it is specially important for a man's connexions to be maintained, one important connexion is severed. Many of the older men in Leicester do retain membership of the Union in spite of this, and they undoubtedly get something very valuable out of it, though precisely what it is cannot be easily expressed in words. The wife of an unemployed shoe-laster said: "I've always made him keep it up, because it means that if anything happens you've got the trade behind you." In many places, such as the coal-mining districts, the unions allow unemployed men to retain Union membership on special terms, carrying sometimes a different status. We feel that anything that can be done to make it easier for membership of the Trade Union to be retained during unemployment would be a great gain, and that if it were possible for those who draw unemployment insurance through their Unions also to draw assistance through them when they run out of benefit, it would be a real contribution to this particular difficulty. So far as existing social institutions can shoulder the responsibility for unemployment, they are the right institutions to do it. An *ad hoc* club is almost inevitably a second best.

In the Special Areas this problem has a different aspect. On the one hand a man is not so likely to feel himself cut off from the rest of the world, but on the other, the existing social institutions have been hit so hard by the effects of unemployment that it has been difficult for them to carry on. An instance can bring this out clearly. In 1935 an analysis was carried out of the position of the churches in mid-Rhondda (an area about a quarter that of the district as a whole) with a view to comparing their present position with the position in 1928 and again in 1921. As between 1928 and 1935 the adult membership of forty churches and chapels in the district was reckoned to have fallen from 6,980 to 5,070, chiefly owing to migration. The debts of many of the chapels had greatly increased during the same period, though some had actually managed to reduce debts. No exact figures can be given for the reduction in membership since 1921, but in some instances it was reckoned at over 70%. Almost all were badly in need of money for redecoration and repair. Average collections remained quite reasonably high, in some instances as high as £2. 15*s*. per member per year, and this was regarded as an achievement by the churches and chapels in other parts of South Wales, in many of which a considerable decline has taken place. The pastors themselves spoke particularly of the loss of leadership among the younger people as being the most disastrous feature. In a reply to an enquiry as to the effects of unemployment on the Methodist churches of South Wales, it was said that "...any impartial observer would say that the influence of the churches in the life of the community is less to-day than it was before the depression set in. I think that this is due to the fact that the burden of finance has loomed so large before both ministers and people in the district that they have been able to see very little else and that there is a tendency to feel content if one can get the balance sheet of the church somewhere near balancing." The answers to this enquiry from South Wales, Cumberland, and Durham almost all tell the same tale of heavy debts incurred since the slump, though many describe too the gallant efforts made to meet them: "Since we started our effort to deal with the debts in the Rhondda-Ely Valley Circuit, I have received from the Mardy Women's Meeting over £20, and there was no one in that meeting at the time whose husband was in work." Here, surely, there is a clear duty, where those social institutions are connected with larger organizations outside the Special Areas, that those outside should help them to solve at least their financial problems. Indeed, the adoption of some social institution by one of similar character outside the Special Areas would seem to be one of the most valuable forms that adoption could take.

Many of those inside the social service movement, emphasizing the harm which can come from the formation of separate clubs specifically "for the unemployed", are trying to change the character of the clubs into something more general, an institution which is available for those who wish to use it whether they are unemployed or not. The sample has shown emphatically that harm can actually be done by the provision of the wrong kind of clubs for the unemployed, and that there is, in fact, much less likelihood of this happening where the club has a more general character and is not confined to unemployed men alone. The instance which at once comes to mind is that of the young man in the prosperous area. It is certain that the provision of a comfortable club, so far from helping him to solve his problems, may make the solution harder. The unwise provision of facilities of this kind—of a club, that is, which has little more to it than comfort—is, in some instances, making it harder for them to make the effort to get back. They need help perhaps more than anyone. But the wrong kind of help can certainly do more harm than good.

(c) LEISURE AND THE UNEMPLOYED

Purposelessness, which is only too often a feature of the unemployed man's life, seems to underlie all the psychological difficulties of unemployment. The workless, or at least those who have been workless for long, are not the social asset which they ought to be. Why is it that the unemployed man's life is so often not a life of leisure, but of apathy?

In answering this question there are several points to be borne in mind. The first is a qualification. There are unemployed men who not only enjoy their leisure, but have found in unemployment the opportunity to develop aspects of their personalities which during employment have never had a chance. A young man in South Wales, now in employment, who spent several years out of work, told one of us that those years had been the best he ever spent. New doors had been opened in his mind and through the Settlement he had met men of intellectual distinction such as he would never have met if he had remained steadily at work. And the remark made by a young man in Liverpool to one of us is a good indication of what may happen: "Isn't it marvellous", he said, "to think of all those rich old men sweating their eyes out in offices so that the likes of me can have a really good time?" His case is something of a warning; for though he was evidently in a sense happy, it was equally clear that he was getting into the habit of being out of work, and that in the long run this was going to do nothing but harm.

The second is that the problem is bound up with a larger social issue, that of the general decay of cultural standards. When we come to discuss in detail the work done in the clubs, we shall see how much more effective this can be in places where the decay has not yet gone so far as it has done in others. If in the Rhondda, for example, we find that the educational work done in the clubs is of a higher quality than that which is done in many other places, that is mainly because the march of progress has not yet had time to crush out of existence the traditional standards of culture in the valleys. Many of the present generation of unemployed men in the Rhondda were affected by the great religious revival which took place there in the pre-War years. They were brought up on those stirring Nonconformist sermons which, by all accounts, have played such a part in the development of modern Welsh culture. One man brought up in the Rhondda described how the chapels there "used to be the educational settlements". On Monday evening there was a prayer meeting, on Tuesday a literary meeting for younger people, on Wednesday the children's meeting, on Thursday the meeting for testimony, on Friday the general literary meeting. Sunday school was attended by young and old alike, and the discussions that took place in it brought sharpening of wits and a training in serious thought. In England, an increasing degree of literacy has not, unfortunately, brought everywhere with it an increase in cultural standards, and those who were brought up in the country on the Bible and *Pilgrim's Progress* and spent their lives on traditional occupations had, many of them, far more genuine standards than their modern counterparts.

We do not propose to dwell unduly on this point, though it is serious, nor to deny that modern facilities are capable of being used to cultural advantage. And if modern social activities do not take the old forms, that does not imply that they are culturally useless, though it makes them harder for those who are only familiar with older forms to understand. But anyone who has spent much time among unemployed men in the big cities (the fact does not apply, for reasons which we have already touched upon, in the two places in the Special Areas which the sample included), must be struck forcibly by a contrast—the contrast between the general good sense on the one hand, and the facility and the shoddiness of cultural values on the other. To meet, as one often does, an unemployed man who is interested in the breeding of dogs or the rearing of pigeons is to realize that, potentially, thousands of these men are connoisseurs. The fact is that things which are unreal appeal to them simply because they are unreal. They escape into an imaginary world by buying, as a Deptford newsagent said, "magazines to forget their troubles". The fault is partly in the conditions in which they live, but only partly in this. It is partly because an appetite for the unreal and the shoddy can be commercially exploited while genuine sensibility cannot. Anyone who has any illusions on the matter should examine carefully a selection of the reading matter which is on sale in the newsagents' shops in the poorer parts of London.[1] He will find that men are buying eagerly twopenny magazines with stories, bad of their kind, of schoolboy adventures, pirates, buffalo ranches, and highwaymen, and that the columns which are labelled "sport" are actually simply lists of forecasts for those who wish to bet on match results. He will find that the one absorbing interest of many unemployed men is betting on football or horses. In the sample there occurred not one only, but several, examples of men who had been fined up to £20 for taking betting slips in the streets. The amounts show that large profits are being made out of this "industry" and that it is therefore widespread. He may feel that the film magazines read by the young women, well produced at their price and obviously valued largely for the help they give in cultivating a smart appearance (in itself something not to be despised) suggest a line along which this problem may be most profitably attacked, through the cultural standards of the women. This is a point on which the organizers of the clubs have seized during the last few years with excellent results.

It is primarily owing to this decay of cultural values that the difficulties of making the clubs into something more than shelters where men can sit, smoke, and play cards are very great. But unemployment touches the problem of leisure still more closely, because it seems to bring with it so often a restlessness and hopelessness which makes any kind of leisure, whatever a man's background may be, impossible. There are thousands of men who spend much of their lives on the street corners, and sometimes it is because they are too uneasy to settle down to any occupation. The point was well shown by an analysis of the

[1] The point is not that these magazines are read by unemployed men, but that where *employed* men read this kind of stuff, they are unlikely to be able to make constructive use of their leisure, in this particular direction, when they fall out of work.

borrowings made from the Public Libraries in Deptford at the time of the slump. The Librarian publishes these figures year by year according to the wards in which the borrowers live. An examination showed that in the poorer wards, without exception, there was a downward tendency during the slump, while in the middle-class wards (where no doubt people were economizing by giving up subscriptions to private libraries, and by borrowing instead of buying books) the tendency was, without exception, upwards. It seems that in general a period of unemployment, unless it is known to be temporary, is too unsettling to be used constructively. The same conclusion is borne out again and again by sample visits. The wife of a young unemployed man in Liverpool told one of the investigators that "he had not got any heart to do anything; he must always be up and out looking for a job".

And there is another important factor working against the success of the movement, the character of the jobs which these young men, who are the new material for the clubs, have done since they left school. Hitherto, till the passing of the Factory Act in 1937 made it impossible, many of them have left school to work anything from forty-four to sixty hours a week in factories, or a twelve-hour day as van boys,[1] or to work as cable messengers or press boys late into the night. In poor homes they have to go for the good wages, which unfortunately seems to mean that they go for the bad jobs. It is not surprising then, that only something like an eighth of them in one of the London boroughs were associated with evening institutes, and that of the remainder only a quarter had any regular connexion with clubs. The first few years after leaving school are a danger-point concerning which it is vital that some further action should be taken, if we are not to be faced with an even more serious unemployment problem in the future. In considering this question of leisure, also, we are forced back to that crucial point in the worker's life. His capacity for using his leisure well

[1] In fifty-seven examples of van work investigated by the Bethnal Green After Care Committee recently, ten boys were working a twelve-hour day or over. (See their *After Care Experiment, Final Report*, 1936.)

throughout his life depends partly on his experience at that time.

As the sample study was confined to those who had been out of work for a long period, it is not possible to give any detailed estimate of what is being done, and what might be done, for the leisure of those whose spells of unemployment are short. But from the talks we have had with workers and with unemployed men, it is clear that the ordinary worker is too much tired out with his job to devote much time normally to leisure activities that make any positive demands on him. The real opportunity comes when he is "temporarily stopped". In a few days he will be back in work again, and so he has no sense of insecurity, but has a few days he can call his own. So far as we have been able to see, this, which is the right opportunity for constructive work, has been relatively little used by the newer organizations that have sprung up to work among the unemployed, which have concentrated largely on the long unemployed.[1] To use it will obviously present difficulties of organization, for in some industries it may be hard to forecast when the periods of slackness are likely to arise, and very often it is not a case of a period at all, but an occasional few days here and there. But the experience of some colliers, working short time on a seam that is good enough even in such conditions to produce a reasonable wage for them, shows what an opportunity this is, and suggests what might be done if and when industry is organized in such a way as to provide similar opportunities for most of those engaged in it.

[1] There is no doubt that some of the Workers' Educational Association's most effective work has been done where these conditions existed. Many collieries have a slack period regularly, almost every summer, when hundreds of men are temporarily stopped or are working short time, and a period of this kind provides an invaluable opportunity. The same is true in other industries also.

II. THE CLUBS AND THEIR MEMBERS IN THE SIX TOWNS: THE RESIDENTIAL CENTRES

(a) THE RHONDDA

The sample method adopted for discovering the effects of unemployment had some advantages and some disadvantages from the point of view of the study of the clubs. Because club membership in some places is only a small fraction of the long unemployed, as in Liverpool, the picture it gave was sometimes inadequate, and had to be supplemented by information otherwise obtained. On the other hand, it made possible a comparison between the clubs and other social institutions, and an external view of them, which must be a condition of any judgment of their value as social institutions. In the following part of this Report we maintain the general distinction drawn in earlier parts of this Report by treating first those clubs which are in areas of industrial unemployment; and secondly those that are in areas of residual unemployment, with the "Lincoln" experiment which is meeting this particular problem of residual unemployment, attempting to compare them, on the basis of the sample, with other social institutions in the areas concerned. We discuss the Liverpool clubs separately, as they do not fall naturally into either group, and we also treat separately the "Upholland Scheme", which is not dealing with the same problem as the clubs in the areas of industrial unemployment where its two branches are situated, but is an attack on the problem of poverty.

To form an external view of the club movement, clearly a study of those who were not members is as important as the study of those who were, and we can best begin a description of the movement in the Rhondda with a description of those in the sample who remain outside it. They fall, so far as concerns their social relations and their individual interests, into several clearly defined groups. There were first those who, though not members of the clubs, were active members of other social institutions. We are at the moment referring not to Trade Unions (except where the man visited was an official, or took some active part in the organization of the Union), nor Co-operative Societies, nor Friendly Societies, nor to any other bodies existing primarily for protection or insurance purposes, but to churches and chapels, in so far as membership of these was active and not merely nominal, and to choirs, bands, football clubs, workmen's institutes and so forth. This group itself falls into two divisions, those whose membership is maintained for social purposes only, who spend much of their day sitting in a club room and smoking, with an occasional game of dominoes or billiards, and those whose membership means that it makes greater demands on their mind and personality. In the former of these two divisions there was a preponderance of older men, while the figures of the latter showed that in the Rhondda it is the middle-aged man who throws himself most readily into the life of social institutions in general. The figures are as follows:

TABLE LXII. RHONDDA SAMPLE: MEMBERS OF SOCIAL INSTITUTIONS NOT INCLUDING THE UNEMPLOYED CLUBS

A. *Active members* (men taking a full part in the lives of chapels or churches, members of choirs, bands, etc., active members of other organizations).

B. *Members for social purposes only* (including membership of Workmen's Institutes, British Legion, Social Club, etc.).

Age	A	B	Totals
18–24	1	—	1
25–34	6	4	10
35–44	9	5	14
45–54	15	7	22
55–64	5	8	13
Total	36	24	60

A detailed examination of these records shows that those in group A belong to a section of the community with exceptionally high domestic standards. The great majority of them were recorded as having homes that were outstandingly clean and bright, and in this respect there was a marked difference between the two groups. A sixth of those who were in group B were living in dirty surroundings, and the general average was decidedly lower. Group A is, indeed, part of the cream of the Rhondda's long-unemployed population.

Another group, much smaller, but equally clearly defined, consists of those who depend on their family associations for their main social life. Those in this group may be members of churches or chapels, but evidently what dominates their lives is their interest in home and children, or an intimate circle of acquaintances. This group again falls into two clear divisions; first the young married men, and secondly older men approaching pension age. Ten cases in all (8% of the non-members) were reckoned in this group, half young men, half old men, none in the intermediate ages. The group as a whole represents only a fraction of those whose general home relationships appeared good, and consists only of those cases where these seemed in some measure to exclude, or form a substitute for, other social activity. One reason why most of these remain outside the clubs is no doubt that the clubs have not yet found a way of catering for the interests shared by man and wife. But they probably need outside contacts less than any others.

Then there were those who were preoccupied by some hobby which left little time for anything else. These, numbering eighteen (14% of the non-members) in the sample, were evenly distributed through the various ages. The majority were men with gardens or allotments, though only those cases were reckoned where the men showed a special interest in them. A sprinkling were those who spent their time reading and studying on their own—useful material, these, for the educational activities in the clubs if they could be attracted to join them. One or two had sub-occupations (such as working on farms), while one was the odd case of two brothers, bachelors, who lived alone in their old home and evidently spent all their time and interest on the house.

There is also a small group (fifteen, i.e. 12%) of those who seem to have depended exclusively on employment for their institutional and social connexions and who are correspondingly lost when they are thrown out of work. A characteristic of these men is their intense desire to get back to work and their refusal to adjust their attitude to the new conditions under which they are living. They think only in terms of getting back to work, and no alternative is much use to them. Among them, however, were some who, without being associated with clubs, spent much of their time working in levels. We describe these levels later; they are, in fact, miniature mines where the collier finds the kind of work to which he is accustomed, and this is no doubt the reason why they have an appeal for this particular type of man.

Lastly, there is the much larger group of those who have no effective social connexions, and no great interest in hobbies or in getting back to work. This group is much less definitely marked than the others. At one end it approaches our first group, in that it contains some who have some associations, which do not, however, appear to be very close, with institutions of various kinds, and at the other it seems to contain the sediment of the unemployed; those who never knew how to make any effort to "keep things going", or, if they did, have long since given it up in despair. The group as a whole in the Rhondda sample numbered forty-two (33 %). Rather less than half were living under reasonable standards of cleanliness. About a quarter were probably unemployable on any just assessment, and had settled down to existence "on the dole", in dirt and untidiness—their only contact with the outside world being in the shops, or with the rent collector and the "Means Test man".

This type is one of the great problems of the voluntary movement as of the statutory authorities. Some of them, no doubt, are possible material for reclamation, but most are probably of the type that would be harmed rather than benefitted by contact with the club movement, at least in the forms which it takes in the Rhondda. In the families of this kind of man there is often intense misery which seems to cry out for help, and yet help is worse than useless. A case which occurred in the sample may be quoted; that of a young man, physically a splendid type, with a wife and two children, who was shown to have gone round to voluntary organizations to get clothing which he pawned, spending the money, as he spent most of his allowance, on his greyhound. Much of the interview was spent in complaints that the Coronation gifts to the unemployed were so totally inadequate. This young man, aged 25, had done no recorded work, except for a spell in prison. It is possible that some form of discipline might make him into a useful member of society, but it is almost certain that any contact he had with the clubs would only do mutual harm.

We are now in a position to examine the Rhondda club membership in its context. There were, in the sample, thirty-two members of unemployed clubs, and one whose name was on the waiting list for membership. In addition, there were twelve who had at some time been members, but had now for various reasons ceased to belong. The club members can be classified in two groups, corresponding roughly to those in which the members of other social institutions were classified, viz. those interested in some activity and those who used the club mainly for social purposes. The figures are as follows:

TABLE LXIII. RHONDDA SAMPLE: MEMBERSHIP OF CLUBS BY AGE, ETC.

Age	Present club members			Total	Former members
	A Active members	B Social purposes only	C Inadequate information		
18–24	3	1	–	4	–
25–34	5	2	–	7	3
35–44	3	2	(1)*	6	5
45–54	3	3	–	6	3
55–64	4	2	4	10	1
Total	18	10	5	33	12

* On waiting list.

This suggests that here too there are two social groups represented, one with decidedly high domestic standards, the other with standards that are not so high. The sample showed that this was, in fact, so. Four cases among the club members were recorded as living at an average domestic standard, two as living in dirt and squalor. All six of these cases belong to the group who use the club for social purposes only. Domestic standards are not everything. But it does seem to be, broadly speaking, true that the good social type is also a good domestic type. It would appear then that the clubs are beginning to be able to challenge serious comparison with the other social institutions in the valleys—the churches, chapels and workmen's institutes; and there are some signs that they are becoming more, rather than less, serious institutions. Several of those who were recorded as having once been members of clubs, but had subsequently left them, had done so because they found there were other less exacting social institutions for the man who wanted to sit about for an hour or two over a game of draughts. Only one, a member of the Salvation Army, said he had left because the club did not give him time for more serious things. One or two, however, had left because they found that with the advent of some measure of recovery the clubs were losing their best men, and because they did not care to continue membership when their friends had left. This is an indication of the serious trouble which the clubs, in common with all other institutions in the valleys, are having to face in the loss of adequate leadership. Transference takes a natural toll of the most vigorous and enterprising men.

The sample suggests that, among the Rhondda unemployed at least, there is not very much likely material for expanding the membership of the clubs. It is possible that the movement might attract a certain number from the last social group discussed, that with no particular interests and no active social connexions; and it certainly appears that recruitment has come mainly from those who, while they were in work, belonged to this category rather than from those who have always taken active part in the work of the churches and chapels. It is more likely, however, that those clubs which have a prominent future before them, whatever economic development takes place, as some of the clubs certainly have, will expand their membership among the employed rather than among the unemployed, though the degree to which this is as yet happening is limited.

The club organization in the Rhondda differs from that in the other places visited mainly in its connexion with the "Settlement", Maes-yr-haf, at Trealaw.

The educational settlements which have recently developed in South Wales and of which this is one, are a new form of social institution. Maes-yr-haf was the first in the South Wales coal-field and, like the others, it owes its origin to unemployment. Relief work was started by the Society of Friends during the Coal Lock-out of 1926, and in the early months of 1927 Maes-yr-haf was purchased by an *ad hoc* committee under the chairmanship of the Master of Balliol. But it is now something very much more than a centre for relief work. It has been described as a "spiritual power-house" for the valleys. It has its own buildings and permanent staff of lecturers, physical training instructors, handicraftsmen, musicians and social workers. Some years ago it secured an old Malt House near the Glamorgan coast which is used as a holiday camp, and thousands of unemployed men and hundreds of their wives have enjoyed holidays there. The growth of the club movement (there are now between thirty and forty clubs) has largely been stimulated by the settlement. In the early days it was able to give extensive financial help out of its own funds towards the cost of adapting old buildings or constructing new ones for club premises, for though the necessary work has been carried out by the unemployed members themselves, old buildings or sites have had to be bought, and materials had to be found, the cost of this sometimes amounting to several hundreds of pounds. This help has now been extended further through the settlement acting as intermediary between the National Council of Social Service and the clubs; and the growth of the settlement staff has made it possible to develop educational facilities for the clubs, including not only purely academic classes, but general discussion groups, the production of plays, operas or choral works, physical training, and handicrafts of many different kinds. Both in the Rhondda and elsewhere in Wales the existence of such settlements has made it possible for voluntary effort to be kept in the closest touch with the needs of the district, and the development of allotments (to take one example) was first planned for the Rhondda and then extended to the rest of the country.[1]

Much of the work which the settlements do is as difficult to describe in definite terms as it is impressive. They are doing much of that intangible work which in the past has been done, where it has been done at all, by the churches. They are places where those who use them can find the friendship and wisdom which are beyond price—more especially in a community marked by the effects of unemployment unprecedented in scale, and prolonged now in some instances for half a generation, for some of those now out of work in the Rhondda Valley have actually been out of work since 1921. Men and women come to the settlements with their personal and with their family problems. They seek the settlement's help to get into touch with long-lost sons and daughters, or to resist pressure brought to bear on them by rapacious landlords, or to buy the instruments for a brass band, or to persuade the Commissioner for the Special Areas to make a grant towards the cost of levelling the site for a playing field. They know that the Settlement is in touch with the official world, and they know too (what is equally important), that its independence is always preserved. They find that it can often help them directly and that, even more often, it can put them into touch with the right person to help.

To win such a position must be a matter of time and personality. Bricks and mortar do not make a settlement, and to get the right man is more important for a beginning than to get the right building. The warden has got to feel his way into the life of the society in which he is living. His job is not to attract every activity under his wing, but to make the active and independent organizations which he sees to be doing social work of value feel that in the settlement they have backing of a new quality. The settlement has no essential connexion with unemployment,

[1] It was financed here, as in many other places, by the Society of Friends. The Quarter Acre Schemes, on the other hand, were financed and planned by the Land Settlement Association.

except in so far as it is specially aware of human problems and can treat them with a less mechanical and more personal touch than an official organization. For this reason one of the effects of unemployment throughout the South Wales coalfield has been to stimulate the growth of these settlements, and they seem to provide the most successful response to the unemployment problem which the community has yet found.[1] This is partly because unemployment is to some extent an opportunity for educational work, but even more because their approach has been a human approach, and because where personality is as much affected as it is by unemployment, an institution which can treat the problem as personal is bound to play an outstanding part.

If social service of this order is to be done, it must be done by exceptional people. They must have a wide familiarity with regulations and facts and figures, and they must also have rarer personal qualities. The settlement must be in itself a real community, and there must be something more even behind its work than a deep concern for the welfare of the neighbourhood. The settlements have not all been equally successful. But that they are playing an increasingly important part in the life of South Wales is certain.

If such an institution is to succeed, it must be free from undue paternalism. This is difficult to secure, and the history of the Rhondda clubs shows the price that has to be paid for it, as well as the advantages it brings. The independence of the clubs is guarded as jealously by the settlement as it is by the clubs themselves. Each is run by a democratically elected committee, and ten years or so of committee experience has produced a remarkable group of leaders. The education in democracy which the clubs have provided is, probably, the most valuable educational work they can do. But this organization means that the clubs have often been split by factions, and that powerful demagogues appear who at one moment turn the club into a

[1] It was not unfortunately possible for long visits to be paid to any of the settlements except Maes-yr-haf and Bargoed. Generalizations made in this section, therefore, are mainly based on these two.

dramatic centre for the neighbourhood, roping in the whole membership to paint scenery or to work spotlights or to act, and at the next hurl the dramatic group into outer darkness and establish a billiard table among the ruins. No one attempts to manage their affairs from outside, the two principles of the settlement being that if a split takes place, the group that can show the largest body of support controls the club, and that no money is paid over to the club until it has shown the determination and capacity to help itself. As a result the movement has real vitality. It is not, and was never expected to be, a solution of the unemployment problem. The club leaders are often absorbed heart and soul in their work for a few years, and then begin to feel that they must find something more satisfying; and some of them have gone on to very good jobs outside the valley.

Thus for many men the clubs have provided something permanent in an experience of democratic organization. The work is generally done by a few members, and out of a membership running into three figures, often only twenty or thirty have actually taken a share in the building of the club or its decoration. But the lay members are nevertheless alive to what is happening, as anyone who has sat through the stormy general meetings of the clubs can witness; and we have seen that those who take part in some form of activity are in a definite majority in the clubs.

The social institutions which existed in the valleys before the depression have been unable to carry the weight which it thrust on them. The Miners' Federation has been concerned, and rightly, with the threat to the workers' standard of living which the vast body of unemployment constituted, and in trying to cope with this threat it has lost sight of the unemployed man's problems. A fair proportion of the unemployed retain their membership, and some of them value highly the advice which in many districts the Federation makes available in dealings with the Unemployment Assistance Board and Courts of Referees, but this leaves many more needs unsatisfied. The Miners' Institutes, the excellent buildings of which were financed, some by the Miners' Welfare Fund, others by the collieries before the Welfare Fund existed, have similarly not yet succeeded in adjusting themselves to the new situation created by extensive unemployment. Very few have been willing to make special provision for unemployed members. When men are idle all day, special provision must be made, and there has been some friction between the unemployed clubs and the institutes, the latter complaining that the clubs are attracting away their membership, to which the clubs retort that their needs have been inadequately recognized by the institutes. Even the churches have not succeeded in modifying the tradition of Sabbath smartness which is such a marked feature of the Welsh Sunday, with the result that unemployed members have sometimes been shy of attending, though they retain membership of the "Brotherhoods" and "Sisterhoods" since these meet on week-day evenings, when they are not expected to be so smartly dressed. And all the older social institutions have found that economic difficulties are sometimes inexorable; "They've paid my fares for these concerts", as the wife of a collier said, "but you cannot expect them to go on paying as things get worse, and I lie awake thinking how far off is the 3*s*. or 4*s*. I need for the Eisteddfod." Thus the work of the settlements has been made possible by the financial support which they have had from outside the district.

As the variety of clubs in the Rhondda is considerable, none can be selected as typical. The club which we describe lies towards the head of the main valley, and is one of the most successful by a test of membership, for it has a waiting list and no fluctuations of membership such as most clubs. But we have purposely not chosen one of the clubs that are specially remarkable, such as that which has recently undertaken and carried out with great success the conversion of a large commercial building into club premises; or one which has built itself a particularly good building, has worked up a fine library and is locally described as insufferably high-minded; or one of the poorer clubs which approximate to the "shelter" type. It is characteristic of South Wales that the most popular of the Rhondda clubs should show a peculiarly active membership. Shelter clubs never win anything like the loyalty that clubs which are active achieve.

The club we describe is housed in a modern building put up by the men themselves on the same plan as that followed in most of the new club buildings in South Wales (a plan drawn up for the South Wales Council of Social Service by their architect), and is exceptional only in having a well-kept garden round it. Both the approach to the club and the atmosphere in the room itself give the same impression—an impression of conscious direction; so that though the main room, with its tables and chairs spread about and the large billiard table at one end, may generally be filled with men, perhaps forty or fifty of them, smoking, talking, reading or playing games, the casual visitor gets at once the feeling that the club is well run and that there is a real consciousness and pride about it. The membership remains throughout the year round about 200. Because of its waiting list, members who get back to work are not encouraged to retain membership. When the considerable extensions projected have been carried out, conditions in this respect may change.

The immediate purpose of the extension is to provide more room for occupational activities. Boot repairing at present is carried out in a small hut in the garden; here, as always, done by members for members at cost price, the greatest care being taken, in order to avoid competition with the trade, that nothing of the kind should be done for non-members. Woodwork, which is popular, is also inadequately housed in a small extension of the main hut. It is superintended by an unemployed man, a collier aged 35, who for this full-time job gets no payment. He has made himself into a skilled craftsman, but what the members would like is "someone to teach us about the theory of it all". This would mean either a lecturer from outside, or sending their instructor to Coleg Harlech (an institution of which we have more to say), but he finds that the Unemployment Assistance Board regulations, though they go a long way to make it possible for him to do this, do not in his view go far enough. He considers his small family would be "worse off" and accordingly will not go.

The club has various other forms of activity. It has a strong choir of about sixty members, and its drama group has only just ceased its activities owing to its leader getting back into employment. Through the winter classes are run, with an average attendance of twenty-five or so, in economics and history—a very typical South Wales "bill". One significant aspect of the club's work is that it has formed a committee to protect the members' interests in respect of their unemployment allowances. This committee is an able group of men. Its relations with the Unemployment Assistance Board are friendly, for the good reason that those who take part in the work are thoroughly familiar with the regulations of the Board, and refuse to handle a case unless it is a good one. Their reputation depends on success. This is a good example of successful democratic organization. That the club is rooted in the society it serves is shown, too, by the strict Trade Union principles which are maintained in the craft work. This club does not, as do some others, make its building available for women, boys and girls at certain times of the week.

Other Rhondda clubs are of quite different character. Some are becoming clubs for the elderly; in one, for instance, 74% of the members are over the age of 45, and about 50% over the age of 55. Some are almost purely recreational in character, though almost all have some popular lectures, the most popular being on such a subject as the legends and folk lore of Wales. One or two classes have been unsuccessful, in one club a class on ambulance work and another in shorthand. Elsewhere we were constantly reminded that "the clubs did not help you to get back to work". That such a vocational class as shorthand should fail is characteristic of the valleys in which abstract speculation has so ready an appeal. Some of the clubs allow those who get back to work to continue membership on certain conditions and there are in some clubs up to about a fifth working, but control tends to be kept in the hands of the unemployed section.

There are three coal levels in the Rhondda. Throughout the South Wales coalfield seams of coal outcrop here and there and these have often been worked by the men, in periods of strike or depression, to obtain coal for their homes. Seen from below the line of the seams can often be traced along the hillside by the holes made to win the coal, like a string of large rabbit burrows. The work was often done carelessly and there used to be serious accidents. As worked by the clubs, however, the levels are always in charge of someone with the necessary qualifications under the Coal Mines Regulation Act, a fireman's certificate. One may meet in them the old type of Welsh collier who has at last found something like satisfaction in getting back to his real job. Something like £150 worth of capital in the form of timber, rails, tools, etc., provided by the National Council of Social Service, has generally been put into their equipment. Some levels operate on a considerable scale, and the number of tons produced in several cases has reached well into five figures. Membership varies from thirty or so to two hundred or more. The members pay a subscription, about 3*d.* a week, for the running expenses, in addition to the ordinary club subscription, normally 2*d.*, and work on one or two days a week, according to the difficulty of the level, for two bags of coal. The richer levels are able to supply coal for old age pensioners and widows, a valuable form of social service. For a certain type of man, this undoubtedly brings him nearer contentment than anything else could do.

This account of the South Wales clubs began with an attempt to assess the place of the unemployed clubs in the society of the Rhondda. It must end with the estimate of one of their members, who was visited in the course of the sample: "For an outsider", he writes, "who views the situation from the angle of people in the abyss, or the slum worker out of work, the idea he gets of the depressed areas or Special Areas may be totally wrong. They are in a category of their own....I want to suggest that our people are fully conscious of the economic principles which have brought the change to the valleys. The question is, to migrate or remain. I have chosen to remain. There must then be an alternative life. There are about 30,000 in that particular group who have no industrial future, and have twenty or more years of life to face in some new way. So I remain in the club to continue my social contact with my unfortunate workmates, to prepare for the new community that will necessarily arise, and to keep myself fit I work in the level."

(*b*) CROOK

The sample visits in Crook showed similarities with the Rhondda in some ways and strong contrasts in others. Like the Rhondda, Crook has a flourishing club movement. But unlike the Rhondda, in Crook there was little organized cultural activity previous to the beginning of the unemployed clubs. There was no library except the travelling county library; no reading room; very little adult education and no W.E.A. class. The working-class movement, represented by the Co-operative Society and the Durham Miners' Union, has evidently always been strong, and it looks as though the creative period in the life of Crook, when these working-class institutions were formed, was the 'sixties and 'seventies of the last century. Since then the place has lived on its tradition (a very good one) without adding significantly to its social equipment, except through the County Education Authority. As in the Rhondda, churches and chapels, which date from the "creative" period, are active institutions, but whereas in the Rhondda men had associations representing musical or intellectual interests, not many traces could be seen in Crook of any such organized cultural societies. The high figure for institutional membership in Crook (Table LIX, p. 274) is explained by the large numbers in unemployed clubs, and in purely social institutions such as in the Temperance Club there. Thus the foundation of that culture which was apparent in the homes of Crook seemed to be family rather than institutional life. It was noticeable that in an exceptionally high proportion of cases in Crook elderly couples[1] had one child living at home with them. It looks as though this was considered a family duty, and this may be taken as a sign of the strength of family life there.

Forty-eight of those visited in Crook were members of the unemployed clubs (i.e. 49 %), a proportion far exceeding the figure anywhere else. A further thirteen had at some time been

[1] Of the men between 55 and 64 in the sample in Crook, 43 % were living with wife and one child at home. The proportion in Leicester was 16 %, in the Rhondda 19 %.

members of the clubs so that, if the sample visits in Crook are a fair indication, over half the long-unemployed men there are or have been at some time members. The clubs were indeed, at the time of the sample, obviously the most important social institution in the neighbourhood. There were a number of active churchgoers of many denominations (25, i.e. 26%): and there were members of Workmen's Institutes and local Temperance Clubs (16, i.e. 16%) who correspond to those members of institutions "for social purposes only" who have been noticed in the account of the Rhondda. These with the young men who were Territorials—an activity which is popular—complete the institutional membership of the sample, for we do not include in this category the Trade Union or Co-operative movements, neither being a social institution of the sort here considered.

It looks then as though, in Crook if anywhere, unemployed clubs have met a need. "His wife is enthusiastic about the difference the centre has made to the village. She has lived here all her life and this has made all the difference, what with the dancing, craft activities, etc." Several of the records contain similar statements about the part which the clubs play in the life of the district. The unemployed clubs are the first centres of general social and cultural activity that some places like Crook have had.

This is not to say that the unemployed clubs have always settled down easily into the life of the community there. The visits brought out a large crop of stories of quarrels in the clubs. The number who had left the clubs was large, and from them we had laconic comments such as "used to be a member of the Centre but left after a row; says they are always quarrelling"; or "left owing to disagreement with secretary over policy". In one or two of the clubs (which differ greatly in character), families had left because the club was getting into what they considered to be bad hands. "We used to be members of the club, and wanted it to be a centre for everyone to enjoy with plays and that sort of thing; but now it's simply got into the hands of those who want to get what they can get out of it, and all the respectable people have left."

Again we have the two types of club, the active club, and that which is only a shelter where games are played and newspapers are read, and quarrels in the clubs are largely due to the conflict of these two principles. It may be significant that the majority of those who had left the clubs were of a respectable type, though it would be dangerous to make too much of this. But certainly with regard to at least one of the centres included in the sample area in Crook, there was a strong and convincing body of criticism among men in the sample who had been, or were still, members, and said that the club was falling into the hands of those who wanted "something for nothing".

A point made clear by visits is that some men use some of the clubs only as organizations for saving. They pay their weekly subscription because it entitles their children to an annual outing or themselves to the Christmas dinner, but do not use the club premises at all. There were over 400 subscribing members to the Market Place centre, for instance, in March 1937, but it was estimated locally that not more than 50 of them used the centre at all regularly. The children's outing which is the attraction is partly subsidized by the proceeds of a carnival, and the value of such savings is thereby increased. Incidentally, the readiness of men to contribute in this way, and the need for good "savings clubs"—to buy clothing or whatever it may be—suggest that this is a direction in which voluntary agencies might well go further than they appear so far to have gone.

There is also a substantial proportion of active members in the clubs. The sample suggested that the proportion of active members, who use the clubs for their educational facilities, physical training, or craft work as compared with those interested purely in the social side, is about two in five. One of the most remarkable achievements of the movement in Crook has been the success of a W.E.A. class, something new to the district, in one of the clubs. Throughout three six-lecture courses, an average attendance of something over sixty was maintained for eighteen weeks, a fine record for a first attempt. We should probably not be far wrong in saying that in many of the towns and villages of Durham, as in Crook, the opening of clubs has meant the beginning of a "movement" which may bring great things with it, provided it is not allowed to die out, should a return to comparative prosperity take place.

The history of the movement in Crook is a good example of the rapid expansion from small beginnings that has happened in areas of industrial unemployment. The first moves to provide for the social welfare of the unemployed in Crook appear to have been made in 1930. There had already been a modest amount of charitable provision: gifts of clothes, food and money had been distributed by the local clergy and ministers, and through the Miners' Lodges, at the time of the long coal dispute in 1926, and this practice was continued in a fitful way during the years which followed. But there was no provision for the recreation and leisure of the unemployed as such until 1930 when the old Council Offices in the Market Place, a small old-fashioned stone building recently vacated by the Town Council, was made available for the unemployed to play games, read newspapers and sit round a warm stove. Cards, dominoes, darts and other games were played and newspapers were provided. But the centre's premises were dark and unattractive, and it was in no way equipped to meet the needs of those who required facilities for new activities.

At Helmington Row, a hamlet about a mile and a half out of Crook, the provision of a recreation centre for unemployed men arose partly out of a search for premises for a young men's club, started by the present Warden of the Crook clubs. The principal colliery in the neighbourhood closed down in 1930, and the local Workmen's Club was another victim of the depression. When a club for young unemployed men was founded, it had at first no premises but met in the open air for football, boxing and "physical jerks". Eventually it obtained the use of a barn for meetings. The young men paid 3*d*. a week and subscribed for 30*s*. worth of sports and gymnastic gear in the first three months. For a time the club continued to meet in the barn, but early in 1932 a new development enabled the young men to use the old Workmen's Club premises.

Early in 1932 a meeting of the Crook Unemployed Service

Committee had been held at which it was suggested that the unemployed men at Helmington Row should use the Recreational Centre in the Crook Market Place. Objections were raised to this on the grounds that it was overcrowded and unsuitable, and eventually a suggestion was adopted that the old Workmen's Club should become the Helmington Row Recreational Centre for the Unemployed, and the Young Men's Club was allowed to use the premises three nights a week. The young men spent three weeks in cleaning and painting the premises. A wireless set was bought. Daily papers were ordered. Cards were introduced and a small billiard table was presented to the members. But it was found that the centre attracted a rather poor type of man, gambling became the chief activity of some of the members, and there was a good deal of criticism. This came specially from the wives of unemployed men who were coming home with short money after drawing the "dole". The Helmington Row Committee decided therefore to organize an outing for members and their families—a shrewd move to conciliate the women—and to re-equip and decorate the club. £5 was raised for re-equipping and decorating the centre, and £8 was raised later on for the purchase of leather for boot repairing and for a new wireless set, while a garden was laid out round the building. Thus interest was maintained and some of the abuses which threatened the club's usefulness at an earlier stage were avoided.

The next step was the result of an appeal to the Tyneside Council of Social Service. Towards the end of 1934 a meeting, attended by representatives of the National Council, the Bishop Auckland Labour Exchange, and of the Ministry of Health Staff Social Service Association[1] was held in Crook, which led ultimately to the Ministry of Health Staff Social Service Association offering to become the "Adopting Body" of the Crook "movement" and to provide financial assistance for certain types of activity in the centres, an offer which was soon accepted.

[1] This Association was founded on 9 June 1934 at a meeting of the Ministry of Health Departmental Whitley Council.

The first appeal of the Ministry of Health Staff Social Service Association yielded £1,348, subscribed by about 1,550 members of the staff (including the official side). It was decided to use this money to finance Occupational Centres at Crook, Helmington Row, Stanley, and (later) Sunniside, and to provide for certain pressing needs in Crook and district. Thus sums were granted to cover the cost of materials for draining the Crook Poultry and Allotments scheme, for the cost of materials for building a storage hut for poultry food, and for expenses of decorating the Helmington Row Centre, the actual work being done by the men themselves. A supply of boots was purchased for distribution to needy children and a regular supply of gifts of clothing, boots, blankets and household linen from members of the Ministry of Health Staff was organized.

It was decided also to open a new centre for occupational work in Crook. A disused fruit warehouse capable of adaptation as a centre was leased for five years and an enthusiastic team of unemployed men re-equipped the place, put in a floor, built a stage, and decorated it throughout. The National Council of Social Service made a grant towards the expenses of adaptation, and towards the cost of a new wooden hut for occupational work at Helmington Row. Local committees of unemployed men were formed at Stanley and Sunniside in October, again with the help of National Council building grants.

In June 1935 the Ministry of Health Social Service Association appointed a local organizer and leader and assistant. In March 1936 this assistant was appointed Warden of the Crook centres, with a part-time "Assistant Secretary" to help him. The salaries in both cases are paid by the Ministry of Health Association. Each centre has its elected centre committee and these are more or less effective organs of self-government. But their horizons are naturally limited and they tend to overlook the interests of the Crook movement as a whole. The result, therefore, has been that the Warden has had no adequate backing from the men themselves where wider issues were concerned. A District Executive Committee, however, has been formed and may be important in bringing the townsfolk of Crook into much closer touch with the Social Service Centres as well as in giving the Warden some sense of backing other than that of the Ministry Association in London. The existence of a district organization makes possible inter-centre games, social evenings and so forth, and it has also been responsible for two exhibitions held in a public hall in Crook which have successfully drawn attention to the work of the movement. All these things are obvious gains from centralization.

The Crook clubs are affiliated to the Durham Community Service Council and draw on the advice and help of the organizers and instructors who work from Durham. The Durham Community Service Council makes no direct grants to the Crook centres but has played a great part in shaping their development. It provided expert advice and assistance when the huts were being erected. It has suggested and encouraged new lines of activity; supplied equipment; provided speakers, instructors and educational tutors. It has also provided the means whereby unemployed men in Social Service Centres in different parts of the county can share their experience and engage in inter-centre activities over a wide area. Without the stimulus, expert advice and guidance of the staff of the Durham Community Service Council, the Crook centres would not have developed in the way they have during the last two years, and its specialized services have meant that the life and activities of the Crook centres have been varied and enriched; Durham Community Service instructors for these activities, and for physical training, visit Crook weekly.

The four occupational centres mentioned above, with the Market Place Recreational Centre (and another new centre outside the area of the Crook Social Service Association, but within the area of the sample) were the clubs whose membership was represented in the Crook sample. The Recreational Club, as we have seen, differs considerably in character from the rest, and a number of those who are members of it are also members of the occupational centre where they can find more active interests. The age of membership in the centres depends largely on the employment situation in the individual locality. Thus, at

Helmington Row at the time of our visit (where there was no work to be had) membership was predominantly young, 78% of the members (who numbered 188) being under the age of 40 and actually 17% between the ages of 18 and 21. In Stanley the membership was decidedly older, and of 154 members 64% were over the age of 40; while the other clubs were somewhere between the two. The sample showed the following age distribution for membership of clubs in Crook as a whole:

Under 25	1
25–34	12
35–44	14
45–54	10
55 and over ...	11

The distribution is roughly proportionate to that of the numbers of long unemployed in Crook, this being the cause of the rather large numbers in the young middle-age group.

The activities of one Crook centre may be described. The chief educational activity is the W.E.A. six-lecture course on current problems and events, but there are also occasional single lectures, a wireless discussion group, and a small library. There is a flourishing dramatic instruction class. Craft work includes woodwork, French polishing and boot repairing. There are also occasional classes in upholstery, weaving and silver paper work (for women). Classes average from fifteen to twenty. The centre has a separate women's section (two evenings a week with an attendance of between forty and fifty), the principal activities being weaving, quilting, rug-making, knitting, dress-making, and plain sewing. There are also occasional lectures and a "keep fit" class for women.

One other feature of the activities of this particular club calls for mention; the poultry scheme organized early in 1935. There are twenty holdings, and, in 1937, men working on this scheme were prize winners at the County Show. It provides a whole-time activity which, even though the monetary reward for it is inconsiderable, yet brings men back to some extent into the ordinary economic life of the society in which they live.

(c) BLACKBURN CLUBS AND THEIR MEMBERSHIP: CLASS DISTINCTIONS

The Blackburn men's clubs are shown by the sample to have an important difference from those in the Rhondda and Crook. Though Blackburn is not in a Special Area the unemployment situation there at the date of the sample was serious enough to mean that men of excellent personal and industrial qualities were out of work. But whereas in the Rhondda and Crook the unemployed clubs represented the working class as a whole, in Blackburn this is not so. The type of man who uses the Blackburn clubs is not representative of the sample there as a whole, and, on the whole, he does not use the club in the same way as the Rhondda or Crook clubs are used, but rather as a purely social institution or shelter club. We shall have to qualify this generalization later, but as a generalization it appears from the sample to be valid. In Blackburn the sample brought out a strong volume of criticism against the clubs, based on reasons which are discussed below.

A word should first be said of the general character of institutional membership in Blackburn, as it could be judged from the sample records. Table LIX (p. 274) shows that there is a substantial proportion of the long-unemployed in Blackburn, about a third, who are members of no institution whatever, as compared with less than a fifth in the Rhondda. And whereas a fair number of those in this minority in Wales were of a not very high social type, in Blackburn there are some who seem to keep themselves apart from any social institution rather because the tradition of independence which they have inherited causes them to do so—from feelings of "respectability" or whatever we choose to call it. And whereas in the Rhondda men who belonged to churches or chapels often spoke of them as though this interest filled their lives, in Blackburn several times we had the answer: "Oh yes, I never miss a Sunday"—as though the important thing was (once again as a sort of hallmark of respectability) not to miss it, rather than as though it were an association which affected them in many different ways, socially, culturally and spiritually.

With this in mind we may examine more fully the club membership in Blackburn. There were among those men effectively visited in the Blackburn sample, two men graded as "minor commercial", four as skilled, forty-eight as semi-skilled, and thirty-three as unskilled, that is to say, considerably more than half were graded as semi-skilled. Yet the figures that were kindly supplied to us by the authorities of Community House, one of the two unemployed clubs in Blackburn, show that three-quarters of the membership of that club, which is the larger of the two, is unskilled, and the sample suggests (though the figures are too small to speak with certainty from them, if there were not this additional evidence) that the club membership in Blackburn taken as a whole consists more of unskilled than of skilled men (eight unskilled, six semi-skilled). This may be contrasted with the figures of the church membership, where of the twenty-nine who said they were regular church-goers, eighteen were semi-skilled, and eleven unskilled. The sense of "respectability" mentioned above is stronger among the semi-skilled than among the unskilled in Blackburn, and this is keeping them, to some extent, from associating with the clubs. There are weavers who belong to them, but their membership consists to a much greater extent of the labouring type of workman.

The criticisms that came up during the course of the sample show conclusively that there is this idea of club membership being something not very respectable. Thus one man said that the "something for nothing" type were those who went to the clubs, where they got food, light and warmth for very little or nothing. Another described club members as going "for what they can get out of it" in the way of clothes and cups of tea. Another said that his son would not join an unemployed club because it seemed to him like begging. These criticisms are quoted, not necessarily because they are true but because they certainly represent a significant section of opinion about the clubs among the unemployed men in Blackburn.

The records of those fourteen men who were members of clubs in the Blackburn sample make it plain that, as elsewhere, they fall into two groups, those who use the clubs for some activity, and those who use them for social purposes only. Five of the fourteen were active members, several being keenly interested in woodwork, one a member of the choir, one a self-made scholar, one an elderly man who "goes to lectures and thinks it is very exciting listening to discussions though he cannot speak himself"—a good instance that the clubs are doing much more for some of these elderly men than may appear.

The activities available at Community House are similar to those available in the other clubs we have been discussing, though there are some interesting differences. The club has its own baths and a hair-cutting, as well as a clothes-cleaning and pressing section. At Community House, as in so many other places, much of the original work needed to make the building habitable was done by the men themselves, and this has created strong ties with the club so that it is becoming increasingly common for those who get work to retain membership. Of the twenty-nine who obtained work during the year 1936–37, twenty-three kept up membership. Almost all the remainder had moved out of Blackburn.

Though there were a number, then, who evidently valued the opportunity for activities offered by Community House, others specifically said that they only went for recreation. What is at least clear is that the clubs do not represent "the community" as do those of the Rhondda and Crook. They are on the way towards those clubs in prosperous areas which have to be considered later, the membership of which consists of the residually unemployed. Another clear indication of this is the high proportion of single men who go to Community House in Blackburn (107 single, 114 married). In the Rhondda clubs, on the sample figure, less than a fifth were single, and most of those were young men living with their families. It may be no coincidence that in the Rhondda among those who had belonged to clubs but had dropped out there was a predominance of elderly single men. It looks as though the "normal" institution is one to which family men belong as freely as single men, in about their relative proportions. The club with a disproportionately large membership of single men is not representative of the community, and will never become a community centre. It is doing the different task of providing social amenities and opportunities for friendship to those who might otherwise live lives of isolation.

Some of these points are brought out in the difficulties which the other Blackburn club—the Gamecock Club—has encountered. This is held in the Y.M.C.A. in Blackburn. It is found that the members of the Gamecock Club do not mix readily with the ordinary Y.M.C.A. members who are in employment, a fact which was, we were told, "partly due to the deplorable appearance" of the unemployed members of the Gamecock Club. Those who are accepted readily in the building are "the older men who keep to their own reading-room, and do not take part in the ordinary Y.M.C.A. activities". Difficulties such as this remind us that one great advantage possessed by the "club movement" in the Rhondda and Crook is in the fact that there is apparently only one class in society there. In Blackburn there is more than one—at least, if we can take as an indication of class the consciousness of differences (whether real or not) between social groups, which the account just given of the Blackburn situation suggests. What seems to be the difficulty here, then, is not a distinction between employed and unemployed, but a class distinction. No doubt both elements enter into the situation, but to describe it only in terms of the "inevitable segregation of unemployed from employed" would be wrong.

If our view of this situation is right, the conclusion is important for an understanding of the relation between the community centre and unemployment work. It has sometimes been suggested that, where there is a community centre, there will be no need of an unemployed club. It seems truer to say that, where an unemployed club exists in an area which has only one "class" in it, an unemployed club may merge into a community centre, but that where there is a strong consciousness of differences between social classes this has to be broken down first. Unless that is done, the community centre will become the preserve of one group only and will be avoided by others; and the split will be not only along the line that divides employed and unemployed, but along other lines which are far less apparent to the outside observer, but which to those who live in the society concerned are all-important.

(*d*) AREAS OF RESIDUAL UNEMPLOYMENT: LEICESTER AND DEPTFORD

One of the disquieting facts brought out by the sample was that the residual problem included a substantial number of men who could not be regarded as unemployable on any just assessment, though the general quality of person in a district of residual unemployment was relatively low. In Leicester and Deptford unemployment represents a series of personal problems. Any account of unemployed clubs in these districts must give rise to the question what are they doing to help solve such personal difficulties? Are they bringing the unemployed man back into the community where—unless he is elderly—there are jobs waiting for him; or are they allowing him to settle down to unemployment and apathy as his normal régime? And to what extent are other institutions, apart from the clubs, offering a helping hand?

Institutional membership as illustrated by the sample in Leicester had its own distinctive features. In Leicester it was even more true than in Blackburn that the retention of membership of the Trade Union, during a period of long unemployment, was a mark of special "respectability". It is more expensive than unemployed membership of Unions in Wales or Durham, so that only those who have a real interest in it keep it up. The younger men in the Leicester sample had, without exception, dropped membership after being out of work some time, but some of the older men retained it, and the way in which both they and their wives spoke of it proved that they attached an almost ethical importance to it—save for one, who gave his reasons with surprising frankness. "I've had a good deal more out of the Union than ever I paid into it." A certain number were members of churches or chapels, and here again it was the steadier type, the sprinkling of men with dark clothes and stiff collars. The other important social institution in Leicester has been the workmen's clubs. A number of those in the sample had belonged to such clubs, and a few retained membership, but they were evidently purely social institutions, and as such here, like everywhere else, the long-unemployed man tends to give them up. It is the institutions that have some meaning, beyond social contacts alone, which tend to keep their hold even during unemployment.

There are in Leicester clubs of various types. Perhaps the most interesting of them is one which does not directly concern the men included in the sample—the Government Training Centre Club, which has been recently established. It is designed to meet the social needs of the great numbers of "trainees" at the large Government Training Centre, men between the ages of 18 and 35 drawn from different parts of the country, who attend the centre for six months to learn a trade, and who at the end of that time are for the most part placed in employment in Leicester or elsewhere. It was opened in September 1937. It is recreational and social, but that does not exclude some activities such as drama and music. So far as could be judged soon after its opening, it was likely to be very popular among the young men whose needs it is planned to fill. In this club the members are men fully employed, under conditions of normal employment, at the Training Centre, throughout the day.

The other two clubs are specifically unemployed clubs, one a recreational club where older men can meet, rest or read. The other is the occupational centre, with a full-time Warden, who thus has an opportunity of getting to know personally and studying the individual problems of those in the club. It has about 130 members, about 30 of whom are under the age of 35, 65 between the ages of 35 and 50, and the remainder over 50. Thus it is predominantly a middle-aged club with a fair sprinkling of younger and older men. Approximately 280 to 300 members have passed through the club, and the Warden says that, apart from the older men, the membership is constantly changing. He considers that the policy of the club should be to help men who are "in and out" of work, and to provide a place where young men can come during periods of unemployment; but he stressed the fact that they are not encouraged to remain members of the club for more than brief spells. The Warden emphasized too that the club regarded it as part of its task to deal with some of the "difficult cases", who form, in a prosperous place like Leicester, an important proportion of the residual problem as we have attempted above to analyse it. The possibilities for personal work in such a club are great. So on the record of one of the younger men visited, the note appears: "Many use the club simply for repairing boots, but he obviously gets far more out of it than this, not least being friendship with the organizer."

If we compare the age distribution of this club with the age distribution of the club membership as reflected in the sample, some interesting features are apparent:

TABLE LXIV

Total membership (approximate)		Club membership in sample	
Under 20	1	Under 25	1
20–35	30	25–34	7
35–50	65	35–44	3
Over 50	35	45–54	3
		55 and over	4

What stands out in the sample figures is the large proportion of younger men, eight below the age of 35 compared with ten above that age. This suggests at once that the majority of young men who are long unemployed (under our definition) in Leicester are members of the club. Eight out of nine in the sample under the age of 36 were members. But the total membership column shows that the club as a whole is predominantly middle-aged. This means that while the great majority of the young unemployed belong to it, a far smaller proportion of the long-unemployed men over that age are members, and above that age, therefore, the membership must consist to a large extent of the "ins and outs"; men who get enough casual employment to take them out of the scope of the sample.

The question which at once arises is whether clubs of this kind in prosperous areas make it easier for young men to acquiesce in long unemployment? Certain points that come out of the sample show that this may be so. One man described how he had heard other young men there complaining at being offered employment, and said that the club was more comfortable for many of the members than their own homes. Another lad described how he often went to the club for "cards and society", and how there were numbers of other lads of his own age in the club. The interviews made it plain that these activities were in themselves harmless, the only question being how far they made unemployment attractive in a city where employment ought not to be hard to pick up. Others of the young men said that they went for billiards or to read the newspapers, two that they were interested in the occupational work, but the general impression left by these eight visits certainly was that club membership was making the process of "adjustment" considerably easier for the younger men, and (for what this is worth) several of the middle-aged and older men who were members made this same criticism. The only young man in the Leicester sample who was not a member of the clubs was one of outstanding quality. His case has been described above in the chapter on "respectability" to illustrate our view that a certain number of younger men are keeping out of employment from the genuine determination to get a wage that represents their worth. There would be little objection to all this if the members of the club were unemployable. One or two of these younger men may be reckoned as that—one with something of a criminal record who has so far failed to stay long in any job he has found, and another of decidedly low mentality who draws 29*s.* Unemployment Assistance and would probably not be worth as much to an employer. His wage is indeed given at only 30*s.* It is disquieting to find, however, that the others are relatively good material on the whole, men whose unemployment is a real puzzle. We are faced with the awkward fact of eight young men, six of them fit and active and apparently fully employable, securing between them, in a place where there is real prosperity, fourteen days' work from November 1935 to November 1936. The total numbers affected are not indeed large, for the sample included one in five of the long unemployed in Leicester. But it is not a problem that can be lightly dismissed, and in prosperous places throughout the country more serious consideration must be given to the question: "What is the best thing, in the way of voluntary help, to be provided for these young men?" The figures suggest that the problem is not anything like comparable (in Leicester at any rate) for the middle-aged men who are fit and might easily pick up some work. Whatever is keeping them from doing so, it is not (at least in the case of the long unemployed) membership of the club.

And indeed among the middle-aged and elderly men there is every indication that those who are attracted to the occupational centre find its facilities of great value. A man of 59 may be cited as an instance, an excellent type of man whose home was exceptionally well kept, and who would have been regarded as outstanding in any of the places we visited. He appreciated greatly the occupational centre where he was able to give help as an informal instructor in his trade; and he described how good those who ran the club were at "provoking discussions". The sample showed that there were several men who were great readers and were promising material for some kind of educational work, who had not come into contact with any organization which made this possible. Leicester has exceptional facilities for them, and this shows what has been stressed in another context, the necessity for "pastoral" work among these long-unemployed men to put them into touch with the organizations that can help them.

An examination of the figures given above relating to institutional membership by places (p. 274) shows what a meagre share the Deptford unemployed man has in the organized life of the community. We cannot take the figures of that table as giving a fair indication of institutional activity in Deptford as compared for instance with the Rhondda as a whole, for we saw that even in the Rhondda the "residual" element among the unemployed tended to have less active connexion with social institutions than the rest, and as this element is a so much larger proportion of the long unemployed in Deptford it might be expected that institutional membership would be proportionately diminished.

This deeply affects the unemployed clubs in Deptford. Only two regular members of unemployed clubs in Deptford occurred in the sample, both elderly single men, and we have therefore little information from the sample about them beyond criticism; several men in the sample complained that they were for men much younger than themselves, others that they were for older men, and so on. What is behind these criticisms it is hard to say. Evidently they are given partly to excuse non-attendance at the clubs, and they may partly represent gossip in the queue among the contemporaries of the men concerned. In the Deptford High Street Club about 40 of the regular members (of whom there are 100 or thereabouts) are over the age of 55, while there is also a fair number of younger men, "about thirty" so we were told soon after the sample date. Four men in the sample had once been to this club, but none retained regular membership, and they represent that fluctuating section of the membership which was mentioned to us by the organizers.

It would be of the greatest interest to know whether in this club the same problem arises as we have just been considering in Leicester, that of the young man whose adjustment to unemployment is made much easier by the comforts which the unemployed club provides. The sample gives no evidence of this, but to get a more certain answer it would be necessary to come into contact with some of the young men in Deptford, who have been out of employment for some time but for less than a year, for there were, in Deptford, hardly any young men long unemployed in the terms of our definition. If the three with whom one of us talked on his visit to the club are a fair "sample" of the rest, there is no reason to think that club membership in Deptford has the effects we have traced in Leicester. One was a skilled tradesman, thrown out of work soon after the time that he became eligible "for his money" like so many other young men even in prosperous places. He had never been happy at his trade, and unemployment had decided him to give it up and find, if possible, some sort of clerical work. He had had a certain number of odd jobs, but in spite of the great efforts of the club organizers, who believed that he would be an excellent worker and had tried to get him various positions, he had so far not secured anything permanent. Like others whose problems we have discussed, he was holding out for what he considered a reasonable wage. The opportunities which the club offered had greatly improved his qualifications for the work for which he was looking. Another, a meat porter, who was helping him in work connected with the running of the club, was in casual employment, with odd days' earnings supplemented by Unemployment Insurance for the rest of the week. Another was one of those young men "invalided out" of a heavy job by an illness that unfitted him permanently for the heavy work to which he had always been accustomed. Such men often find it hard to get themselves work of an entirely different character, for if they have originally chosen labouring the chances are that they are not of an enterprising type.

Occupational classes for unemployed in Deptford are run in the Deptford High Street Unemployed Men's Club and in other centres. In the High Street Club they consist of cobbling, leatherwork, metalwork and carpentry. Married men are entitled to have one pair of boots repaired free every month, single men one every three months; otherwise 6*d.* is charged for boots repaired, or 1*s.* to those men "in employment" (mostly of a casual character) who use the club. Men are expected to repair at least three pairs of boots as "class work" for every one they have free, this class work consisting chiefly of old pairs of boots and shoes that have been given to the club and are repaired before they are distributed.

The organization of these classes is an important feature of this work in many parts of London. Since 1933–34 the L.C.C. has voted every year £5,000 for the provision of day classes for unemployed men and women. Classes are run in connexion with the L.C.C. Men's Institutes, though they are for the most part held in the centres which came into existence during the slump at the instance of churches, chapels, and local committees. They are generally not confined exclusively to unemployed men, and where possible shift workers and others who are free at the times the classes take place are encouraged to use them. The arrangement has the great advantage that it brings unemployed men into touch indirectly with the men's institutes, which are one of the most remarkable products of educational enterprise during the last fifteen years. A good instance of the way in which this has worked is provided by the history of a tailoring class run in the Deptford Men's Institute. This class originated in the days when some form of "test work" was a condition of the receipt of outdoor relief, and thus it drew mainly a section of the unemployed with an even poorer industrial record than that we have examined in the sample. When test work was abolished, those who formed the class pressed for its continuance, and it was incorporated into the programme of the Deptford Men's Institute. There is even a story of the band of a National Unemployed Workers' Movement branch becoming the Theory of Music Class in a Men's Institute, thanks to some lively banter between the head of the Institute and the adherents of the Movement at a public meeting.

In considering the place of institutions in the life of the districts visited, we have been constantly impressed by the fact that the man who has a strong contact with any active institution generally maintains that contact during unemployment. Naturally there are exceptions, but for the sample at least this seems to be the rule. The problem of the unemployed man's leisure is not nearly so acute, therefore, if he has formed ties of this kind during the time he is normally in work. But we found in examining club membership in South Wales, for instance, that it consisted mainly of men who had formerly had no such ties, but had depended on their work for social contacts and on casual reading or whatever it might be to occupy their leisure. For such men the Unemployed Club in the Special Areas has proved a godsend.

What is happening in London is that a serious attempt is being made to form these associations and to build up friendships, based on active interests, while a man is in employment. If this succeeds, the next spell of unemployment, if it is not too long drawn out—and if poverty and insecurity do not make peace of mind impossible, a very important condition—may be a gain on the balance instead of a loss. The parallel between the work of the institutes and the unemployed clubs in certain areas is indeed a close one, and their success in certain directions is very suggestive of what can be done. One of us heard an interesting discussion, following an informal travel talk given by a local professional man in the Greenwich centre. This was organized through the Deptford Men's Institute as part of a weekly series, and it proved conclusively, if proof were needed, that the elderly working man has a fund of experience which he greatly enjoys talking about if only the initial reserve can be broken down. It is perhaps only that initial reserve which gave the impression of dullness among the elderly men that is implied in Table XL above, and if anyone more skilled and experienced with this particular type of man had taken part in the interviewing, the result might well have been different. In Deptford the view is taken that most of these old men are "good at lectures and doing odd jobs, though they have not much use for the occupational classes; and a few of them are only interested in counting the dots on the dominoes". For them, in that they may be considered to have retired, the provision made at Deptford is at least a partial solution. What is more difficult is to know whether the problem of "fitting in the misfits" is being seriously tackled, and the numbers of younger men on the Unemployment Assistance Board register in London as a whole strongly suggest that there is here a very big job remaining to be done.

(*e*) THE SOCIAL SERVICE MOVEMENT IN LIVERPOOL

The history of the Social Service Centres in Liverpool starts in 1931 with the individual action of a lady who induced unemployed men in January 1932 to convert stables into a club in the south end of Liverpool, with accommodation for 100 men. At first only games and the like were provided, but there was soon a general demand for occupational work as well, and provision was early made for woodwork and boot repairing. Organized action followed a few weeks later when the Liverpool Council of Voluntary Aid, the forerunner of what was in the following year to become the Liverpool Council of Social Service, started organizing centres with a general appeal for money and, above all, an appeal to local bodies and firms to take over the financial responsibility, either alone or jointly with other bodies, for individual centres. Thus the system of adoption has been connected with the movement in Liverpool from its beginning. It is almost true to say that, apart from the first experimental centre started by private initiative, there were patrons and adopters of clubs before there were any clubs at all. It is also important to keep in mind that the movement has arisen in an organized way and not spontaneously, from above and not from below. It was brought to life in a meeting consisting predominantly of business men who considered what could be done to "help the unemployed to help themselves". Evidently the dangers of excessive paternalism had not escaped attention, but the history of the movement suggests strongly that the stress was on the "help the unemployed" rather than the "help themselves". The account given of Liverpool in an earlier section will readily indicate how difficult it would have been there to put the emphasis the other way.

Another feature which was characteristic of the movement from the start was the superiority in financial resources as compared, for example, with the clubs in the Rhondda. The fact that Liverpool has a broad and socially disposed middle class, is the headquarters of many wealthy firms, some of them with a world reputation, an old-established commercial centre, and the home of a charitable tradition, could not fail to tell. The original appeal immediately brought in over £3,000; the sum raised by the system of adoptions, subscriptions, and donations for the Unemployed Centres Fund with the Liverpool Council of Social Service (as it was by then) amounted to over £4,600 for the first full financial year April 1933 to March 1934. Accordingly there was available, apart from any outside resources, contributions from central funds and members' subscriptions, a sum of not less than £900 for each of the nine centres that had been opened by the spring of 1934—a figure beyond the wildest dreams of any promoter of the same cause in either the Rhondda or Crook or elsewhere.

Within five months of the organization of the clubs by the Council of Voluntary Aid, eight centres had been opened in addition to the pioneer centre. Only two of these centres proved to be capable of life. One centre was transferred to other premises, and later on, in 1937, when membership was severely affected by demolition of property in the new neighbourhood, it was temporarily closed, and is now running on an entirely different basis as a special club for young lads. Three were very short-lived; all three of them were located in difficult neighbourhoods, particularly in need of social service work. Whether or not a more careful preparation of the ground would have led to the successful establishment of permanent centres is a matter which it is not possible to decide now. Quite rightly, at that date when there were some 90,000 unemployed men in Merseyside, the important thing seemed to be to do something quickly here and there. But acting quickly meant also that the housing of these six centres (opened in the first half of 1933) had to be in ready-made buildings, so that much, though not the whole, of the important first stage of "building it up" had to be missed by the members, though there remained much adaptation and equipment work to be done.

In the second half of 1932, two more centres were opened, one of them being built by the members themselves on a new housing estate. In the spring of 1933 another centre was opened (later transferred to a different neighbourhood) and, in addition, a section at the Seamen's Centre was opened. In the summer of that year two more centres built by the members themselves were started. All the existing Liverpool centres were opened within eighteen months, at the height of unemployment, and they owe their existence to one single organizational effort. No new centres have been opened during the past four years, and although there has been some modest expansion of the existing centres, there has been on balance contraction rather than expansion since, owing to the closing of three centres.

There has been contraction of membership as well as of accommodation. By the end of 1933, it is stated, there was an average weekly attendance at the fourteen centres then existing of "some two to three thousand men". During 1936, average membership at the ten men's centres was not much over one thousand—1,129—and if average attendance is measured by the number of subscriptions paid, it was considerably less than one thousand, i.e. 777. Unemployment, even in Liverpool, has gone down from the high level reached in 1933, from 85,000 to some 65,000, which partly explains the decline. But the fraction of the unemployed men coming within the orbit of the movement was, even in 1933, so small that the decline is suggestive of a real failure of the movement to "catch on" as extensively as it has done elsewhere. It does not show the gradual and organic growth natural in a young movement, whose symbol is the young cockerel "scratching the surface" of a vast problem, but the picture is rather that of a rapid rise and a long-drawn-out subsequent decline, so that the atmosphere of pioneer enthusiasm which is so infectious in the clubs of some places is here almost inevitably lacking. On the other hand, the period of contracting membership has been one of completely reorganized administration with vast improvements in efficiency and the quality of the work done in the clubs.

The administration is no longer in the hands of a sub-committee of the Liverpool Council of Social Service, but of a special body (the Liverpool Voluntary Occupational Centres Association) with a separate organization and a full-time staff of eleven persons; the General Secretary, the Educational Organizer, the Recreational Organizer, and eight Instructors, two each for Woodwork and Physical Training and one each for Upholstery —the most recent addition to the organized classes in the centres—Boot-repairing, Metalwork, and Tailoring. For reasons which can be understood in the light of the above historical sketch, the Central Body is, as a whole, in a weak position relative to the clubs, although some of the clubs are more dependent on it than others; some rely on the Association for little more than the provision of instructors for their classes. The Association is not the "spiritual focus" of the clubs, as is the Settlement in the Rhondda Valley. The clubs have one representative each on the Council of the Central Body, but on the Executive the club representatives are in a minority of six in twenty-two. The deciding factor, however, which makes the Central Body in its relations to the clubs an external body is of a financial nature.

Five of the clubs are adopted, four of them by private firms. In at least three of these five, the Warden has been appointed without the consent of the Central Body; one of them was a retired employee of the adopting body. In two instances the sequel has been wholesale rebellions among the members and a wholesale "purge"; and details given later that refer to one such club show some of the tension that lies at the back of such occurrences. Apart from influencing decisively the selection of the Warden and paying his salary, the adopting bodies exercise a dominating influence on the Management Committees of the centres. These Committees, of between four and sixteen members, are a unique feature, unknown in the other towns of the enquiry, and unthinkable in the Rhondda or Crook. They exercise the real control. The House Committees (the members' representation) have no control over the resident Warden, which is indeed almost inevitable, but they have no control either over club expenditure, or matters of club policy. In four clubs there is no representative of the men on the Management Committee, in one club the Chairman of the House Committee is on the Management Committee; but in this respect the five adopted clubs are not different from the five non-adopted clubs. In one of the adopted clubs, the House Committee itself is actually selected by the Warden and the Deputy-Warden. In two of these clubs, the Warden acts as the secretary of the Management Committee. For the financial year 1936, the income of the five clubs from adoptions, donations and subscriptions, apart from the members' own subscriptions, amounted to £2,122, whereas grants made by the Central Body amounted to only £200. Grants from the Central Body were thus less than 10% of the independent income through adoptions, etc., which covered over 60% of the total expenditure. Three of the clubs did not have any grant at all from the Central Body. The income from adoptions and donations varied between £200 and £600 per club, total expenditure between £500 and £900. The club with both the lowest income from adoption and the lowest expenditure is at the same time the largest Liverpool club, so that expenditure per member is particularly low in this club. Incidentally it is decidedly the best, not only of the five adopted clubs, but, by general consent, of all the Liverpool clubs, and is a fine example of what can be done in the peculiarly difficult conditions of Liverpool. Here there is an obvious sense of fellowship as between the Warden and the men and it is clear that the activities of the club are leading to a growing independence and (interestingly enough) to the awakening of some intellectual interests also among the men, with discussions and wireless listening groups. This is a strange contrast with those Liverpool clubs where we were told any sort of discussion was discouraged as likely to be subversive. But it shows what can be done.

For the five non-adopted centres, the situation is different. Each indeed has its own group of principal subscribers, whose attitude and sphere of influence is not essentially different from those of adopters. Two of the clubs are specially linked up in this way with two subscribing corporations, one each; three with a joint group of collaborating subscribers (private firms and corporations mixed). None of the five Wardens however has been appointed in opposition to the Central Body. The House Committee is in all cases elected, and the Warden has no direct influence on the election. But in only one centre is there any provision for a representation of the members on the Management Committee, and another unsatisfactory feature is that two of the Wardens are paid less than £3. 10s. a week which is the standard rate for the adopted clubs. For the financial year 1936, the income of the five clubs from donations and subscriptions, apart from the members' own subscriptions, amounted to £1,162, as compared with £2,122 for the five adopted clubs. In all five centres this income, which covered 45 % of total expenditure (60 % in the adopted clubs) had to be supplemented by grants from the Central Body, totalling £430 or just under 40 % of the private outside income of the club (less than 10 % in the adopted clubs). For these clubs, the grant from the Central Body thus begins to be an important item (18 % of total expenditure as against 6 % for the adopted clubs), but even here the independent outside income remains the *pièce de résistance* of the budget. Total expenditure per club ranged from £280 to £830 (£500 and £900 for the adopted clubs). Members' subscriptions cover 8 % of total expenditure of non-adopted clubs, but only 5 % in the adopted clubs. It appears from a comparison of the average roll of membership with the subscriptions paid during the year 1936 that in the non-adopted clubs subscriptions were paid by 72 % of the men on the roll, but by 67 % only in the adopted clubs, with the result that the average member on the roll paid about 8*s*. 3*d*. a year in the non-adopted clubs, but only 5*s*. 1*d*. in the adopted clubs. The inference, that in the adopted clubs which are financially better off, members' contributions are not coming in with the same regularity, does not seem wholly unjustified, and it is an important addition to what has been said in earlier sections of this part of the Report about adoption.[1] The alternative explanation, that the average membership on the rolls of the centres was more "effective" in the non-adopted centres is not less interesting than that advanced just now.

In addition to more strictly exacted, or more willingly offered, members' subscriptions, there is one further difference between non-adopted and adopted clubs, which increases the pecuniary advantages of the adopted clubs to the members. A scrutiny of

[1] See above, pp. 282 *seqq.*

the Annual Accounts for 1936 shows that the five non-adopted clubs had a deficit on the "Activities" account of £40, that is to say, the value of the club amenities and facilities[1] not covered by payments from members was about 2*s.* 1d. a year for each member on the roll. In the adopted clubs, however, there was a total deficit of £187, and the value of club facilities received free by the average member was 5*s.* a year. Membership in a non-adopted club, apart from the services of the instructors, entailed thus a net annual contribution from each member of 6*s.* 2*d.* (a payment of 8*s.* 3*d.* set off to the extent of 2*s.* 1*d.* by free club provisions, mainly of work materials), whereas the net contribution from a member in an adopted centre amounted on the same basis to the nominal amount of a penny a year. The club activities would seem to be more self-supporting in the non-adopted clubs where independent outside income flows less freely.

To sum up some of the facts arising from this short survey of finance and organization, bricks and mortar mean much more in Liverpool where the self-built hut is unknown. In view of what has been said above[2] about housing conditions in Liverpool, there is deeper meaning behind this difference than just differences in financial situation and the necessities of an urban area. One of the functions of the Liverpool centres is the provision of better accommodation, offering for some members an escape from intolerable housing conditions. The sample did not yield a large enough number of interviews with members of the centres to determine the importance of this. But talks to men in the centres and particularly at Wincham Hall left no doubt about its existence.

The second thing is that financially the centres in Liverpool are an enterprise with a not inconsiderable monetary turnover, particularly the adopted clubs, whereas the Rhondda and Crook Centres are much more on a "barter and service" basis. A scrutiny of the financial structure of the individual centres leads

[1] These advantages accrue in part to members' friends or other outside persons, e.g. at house parties, concerts, etc., but we may neglect this point here.

[2] See Part II, p. 95.

to some differences indicative of the dangers inherent in the financial advantages bestowed on the centres by the system of adoption and subscription. The individual financial independence of the clubs is also largely behind one other important difference. In the Rhondda the movement is influenced, if not controlled, by the interplay between the clubs and the Settlement, but in Liverpool it is the interplay between the Warden and his "Management Committee", the men and the Central Body being reduced to an inferior position. The link of the men with either of the two real powers is slender. For the Management Committee, it has already been said that the men are as a rule not represented on it, and in the few centres where they are represented, they are in a small minority. As to the link between the men and the Warden, this varies from club to club. In two centres the men have thrown up their own leader for the post of Warden, but some of the Wardens follow a deliberately anti-democratic policy in that they think it is for the benefit of the club to keep the men away from any interest in control. The influence on the running of the centre which the Warden concedes to the men seems invariably bound up with his behaviour in the club; which determines to a large extent its "atmosphere". The two extremes are the Warden who by mixing freely with the members and by discussing with them questions of policy makes his club into a place where men can find real friendship and a restoration of self-respect, and the Warden who considers his office as his castle, from which he rules over the club like the mysterious never visible Tashi Lama; and who insists, like him, jealously on the signs of reverence due to his high station, "having his tea brought into the Office for him like a lord", as it was put by a disgruntled ex-member of the second type of club who happened to come within the net of the sample. On the merits of the policy of making decisions rather than discussing things with the men, one should be careful not to condemn rashly. Where the Warden who believes in a firm rule happens to be a personality and really interested in his job, the club may be smoothly run and work done may be highly efficient, with the members proud of it even though it is not "their own show". For it must not be forgotten that many excellent unemployed men have no definite opinions on the way in which the club should be run and no desire to have a say in it, and are not less suitable club members on that account, while the comparative lack of any traditions of democracy and independence in Liverpool would mean that a club run on Welsh lines for instance was doomed at the outset to turn into a "cellar" club. They are more interested in "doing things for themselves" or "keeping their hands in", and do not mind being told how to set about this and what to do as long as they feel the "boss" knows his job and is a person with a sense of responsibility for the welfare of the members. The worst of both worlds is, however, where an unsuitable Warden follows the principles of autocracy, and we had some opportunity of gaining an insight from the members' point of view into the disastrous effects of this combination.

As for the Central Body, it has also only weak links with either of the two dominant powers, the Warden and his Management Committee. The Central Body is represented by its secretary on the Management Committee of three only of the centres, to which might perhaps be added a fourth seat held by the Secretary of the Council of Social Service. The twenty-three members of the Council of the Central Body not nominated by the centres themselves, hold between them only two seats on the Management Committees of two centres (both non-adopted). On the other hand, all the club representatives on the Council of the Central Body have been taken from the Management Committees, six of the ten being chairmen of these committees. The hold of the Central Body over the Wardens has already been described as weakened by the dependence of the Wardens on their adopters and principal subscribers to whom they owe in some cases their appointment. The instructors, though appointed centrally, are purely technical advisers whose influence on the club is restricted to the technical arrangements of their class; their relations with the club Wardens are rather vague. They depend on the Wardens for bringing the classes to the notice of the members, arranging suitable hours and accommodation for their classes, and maintaining the men's interest in the intervals between classes.

Turning from questions of organization and administration to the club membership, we find that in Liverpool it is drawn from the ranks of the younger unemployed rather than the older. An age analysis is available for a date in June 1937, a slack season for the centres. Of 871 members in the ten centres, 575 or 66% were under 35 years of age. This is higher than either the percentage of men under 35 among all the Liverpool unemployed (49%) or among all the Liverpool long unemployed (36%) according to the enquiry's sample.[1] The incidence of club membership is therefore twice as high among the younger unemployed under 35 than among the rest, if we consider total unemployment, and not less than three and a half times as high if we consider long unemployment. Although no precise records have been kept, it can be judged from pictures taken in the clubs in the early years of the movement that young men predominated from the beginning. This explains the vitality and popularity of the sport side of the Liverpool movement, which includes not only a keenly contested football "knock out" competition with no less than twenty-five entries from Occupational Centres in Merseyside, but also a Football League, a Baseball League (very popular), and a Cricket League (not so popular). The high reputation of the football team of one of the centres is the most powerful advertisement, and this club is now by far the largest of the centres both in total membership and in membership of young men under 35,[2] and the sample yielded at least one example of a man who had left one of the other clubs on account of the inefficient organization of the football team and its constant defeats. There have, however, been signs during the last few months of a changing age distribution among the club members, chiefly owing to increasing re-absorption of the younger members

[1] The percentage of young men among the U.A.B. clients, on which no precise figures are available, is somewhere between these figures, c. 42%.

[2] It is not suggested that this is the only or the most important reason for the rise in membership. The club is for instance situated in a neighbourhood with fewer rival attractions such as cinemas or "cellar" clubs than is the case for any other of the centres.

into industry. This is reflected in a definite falling off of attendance figures at Physical Training Classes. It has been suggested that the increase in the cost of living may have something to do with this too. That "physical jerks make you feel more hungry" and "physical jerks on an empty stomach are no use, anyway", are statements from young men which became familiar to us.

It has already been mentioned that one of the clubs has just been restarted on an entirely different basis, as a special club for lads under 25. It has been the general experience in the centres that the various age groups do not mix. The proportion of 2–1 for men under 35 and over that age in the Liverpool clubs is fairly uniform for all the clubs except one which has tended to become the *dominium* of young men of the Roman Catholic faith. In this club over 90% of the members are under 35. The other exception is the largest centre, of which mention has already been made; it is situated in a new housing estate, built by the members themselves, and is being run on a more democratic basis than the other centres. Here there is an equal proportion of elder and young members, and there are more than 100 of both categories. Here the number of members under 35 is not higher than was to be expected, considering the number of young unemployed men in Liverpool. Between these two clubs there are very significant differences in the degree of fluctuation in their membership. If we measure stability of membership for the year 1936 by the percentage of all men who have been members for at least four weeks, paying their weekly subscription in an average week of the year, we find that the percentage is 53 in the club with a fair number of middle-aged men (higher than in any other centre), 41 in all centres taken together, but only 30 in the young men's centre. This indicates some of the problems created for the centres by a young membership, for it means that any long-term policy is difficult owing to the rapid turn-over in personnel, due mainly to seasonal and casual employment in the summer months. In the centre which has been practically monopolized by the young men, out of a monthly average membership of 107 on the club roll, no less than 33 got back, at least seasonally, into some kind of steady employment for the summer, and most of the members found at least casual work. The seasonally employed do not, as a rule, retain their membership, and club activity is therefore at a very low ebb in summer.

Among the club members there is, of course, a high proportion of long-unemployed men. An analysis of the membership of four Liverpool clubs, kindly undertaken by the Liverpool Occupational Centres Association for our purposes, for a recent date in October 1937, after the "Second Appointed Day", showed that of the 404 members of the four clubs there were:

In regular employment	13	= 3%
In casual employment (Unemployment Insurance or no extra)...	39	=36%
In very casual employment (U.A.B.) ...	105	
On insurance (short unemployed)	37	= 9%
On U.A.B. (long unemployed—over 6 months)	188	=47%
On Public Assistance	20	= 5%
Non-claimants	2	
	404	

There are, however, very considerable differences among the various centres. In the centre where 90% of the members are young men and which is near the Docks, where a man may very conveniently drop in for the afternoon when he has not found work in the morning, or where he may even spend a rainy day instead of looking for work, the bulk of the members (76 out of 101 or 75%) fell within the category of "very casually employed", and alternating between their occasional earnings and Unemployment Assistance. In the centre with a fair proportion of middle-aged and elderly men, in a new housing estate far from the Docks, the bulk of the members (77 out of 113 or 68%) were wholly unemployed men on the U.A.B. register, that is to say, the group from which the sample has been drawn.

The incidence of membership among the long unemployed is thus considerably higher than among the other section, as the following approximate figures for the clubs as a whole show:

TABLE LXV. LIVERPOOL MEN, SUMMER 1937

	Total number	Club members	%
Employed	c. 150,000	35	0·02 = 1 in 4,250
Short unemployed	c. 27,500	c. 390	1·4 = 1 in 70
Long unemployed	c. 9,000	c. 325	3·6 = 1 in 28

But it is obvious that even among the section on which the effort of the movement has been most concentrated the impact is very small, over 96 % of the long unemployed not being active members. It is also clear now that our sample of 273 Liverpool men (with about 250 effective visits) could not be expected to give any representative indication of the work of the clubs, as not more than half a dozen active members could be expected among them.[1] The sample could only be representative of the 96 % outside the clubs, the vast potential field of the movement.

As has been mentioned before, the turn-over of membership is fairly high, and even in the one single year 1936 and with the very casual members eliminated, about three times the number of men who are active subscribers have been on the roll of a club for some time. The sample therefore yielded certain information on the reasons why men do not keep up their club membership. It yielded, also, one "full hit" in the person of the former Vice-Chairman of the Men's Committee of one of the adopted and autocratically run clubs, who had been in the club from its very beginnings, and helped to build it, but had left disgruntled. Two of us spent an afternoon with him, and without necessarily taking all his vivid descriptions at their face value, they came back with a deep impression of the conflict likely to arise between the control vested in the Warden and his Committee and the democratic ideas of some of the better types of young unemployed men, who are jealously proud of independence and what has, in a previous section of this Report, been called "respectability". This young man came from a very respectable home; his mother, a native of North Wales, preserved what are

[1] The actual figure was five.

in Liverpool uncommonly high standards of domestic decency and efficiency. He had been heart and soul in the movement and it made all the difference to his life. He spent most of the day in the club, and the furniture made by himself was an obvious source of pride for him and did much to re-establish his status in the eyes of his mother, who showed that piece of furniture to our enquirer before the son came in. "That's the sort of chap he is," she said.[1] From what he said and even more from the way he said it, it was clear that to him the club, in spite of all the good points which he readily acknowledged, had become a definite threat to his sense of independence. The most intolerable incidents were visits to the club by the workers of the adopting firm, when the employed men came in and benevolently "inspected" the work and activities of the unemployed; a social function with the girls of the adopting firm present at the club, when the Warden in front of the girls made a speech which, to the mind of at least one of his hearers, amounted to an exhortation to the members to be thankful to these girls who by their weekly contributions "kept" the club. It was when he thus realized that by continuing in the club he was going down the slippery road to pauperization that he decided to break a cherished connexion.

This is an exceptional case. There may not be many men of this type, and the fact that he came of Welsh stock may have something to do with his attitude. Few of the members who sever their connexions with the movement, apart from re-employment, are likely to have motives similar to these. Actually the probable motive was, in several cases which we came across, the exact opposite of this one, namely, that the man had become so used to taking advantage of the preferential treatment accorded to the unemployed in Liverpool by the innumerable charitable

[1] His case illustrates both the possibilities and also the dangers of the club movement in Liverpool. Clearly a man who has his interests developed in this way is gaining something of permanent value for himself; and in a place like Liverpool where there is traditionally so little encouragement for a man to do something for himself, such provision is particularly well worth making. But unfortunately what he found was that the way it was made rendered its acceptance intolerable.

organizations and the preferential treatment of unemployed men in the way of cheaper cinema tickets, etc., that he no longer experienced the sentiment of pride in improving his situation by his own exertions.

In most cases the stronger appeal of the "cellar" clubs in their various forms where a man can do as he pleases and where there is also a freer mixing of the employed, semi-employed and unemployed, seems to be due partly to the general restiveness and inability to "hold on to a thing" which is again in its turn partly common to many younger men in Liverpool who have no steadying social or working background, and partly a particular result of the aimlessness of an unemployed man's life. In that light too we have to see the inability of the clubs to make permanent adherents of the men that join them. Their failures are not only the steady respectable type. Figures that show this fluctuating membership can be given, thanks to the analysis kindly carried out for this enquiry by the Liverpool Voluntary Occupational Centres Association. In the four Liverpool clubs for which figures were obtained it appeared that of 623 members on the roll at a date in November 1934, only 117 or less than one-fifth were still members two and a half years later in the summer of 1937,[1] and they represented just over one-quarter of the membership at the later date. Of the 815 members on the roll in November 1935 only 194, less than one-quarter, were left on the roll eighteen months after. Even of the 603 members on the roll in November 1936 only 238, less than two-fifths, were left in July 1937, eight months later, the majority having dropped out.

[1] It must again be understood that the summer is a slack season for the club and that some of the Old Guard, though temporarily off the roll in summer, may return in winter. But there can be no doubt of the fact that the vast majority of the club members drop out again after a fairly short time.

(*f*) THE RESIDENTIAL CENTRES ASSOCIATED WITH UNEMPLOYED CLUBS

The growth of the Colleges for Adult Education in connexion with the voluntary work among the unemployed has been one of its most noteworthy successes. It has been possible for one or more of us to visit King's Standing (a centre directly under the control of the National Council for Social Service), Coleg Harlech, at which men from the Rhondda and many other parts of Wales, England, and even from the Continent take educational courses, Wincham Hall, which serves Liverpool and the surrounding area, and Hardwick Hall, which is the "regional house" for Durham. The last three were closely connected with the areas included in the sample, and all four of the colleges were represented in the sample by at least one man who had been to them. While we do not attempt to give any detailed survey of their work, therefore, it is possible to state what part they play in the general scheme of this work among the unemployed, as it has been considered in the last few sections.

These four institutions differ in many ways, as do all institutions that are genuinely educational. The differences are partly due not merely to individuality, but to the fact that the colleges have differing origins. Coleg Harlech was founded before the slump, and it was not connected originally, therefore, with the idea that enforced unemployment should be used constructively for some broadly educational purpose. It is an Adult Education College, planned as a place to which the worker who is lucky enough to secure the opportunity (through a scholarship or through the far-sightedness of his employer) can go for a year's further education, and return to employment at the end of it; or perhaps find new employment as a result of the new outlook and new knowledge that he has acquired. On to this stock has been grafted, very skilfully, another branch, courses for unemployed men, and this has been done without the character of the institution being at all changed. King's Standing, on the other hand, was planned as a national institution for the purpose of training club leaders. It thus had from the start a direct connexion with the unemployed club movement, and this has naturally conditioned very largely its development. It is bound to be concerned primarily with those activities that are general in the clubs rather than with the more individual task which an academic bias makes almost inevitable. Hardwick Hall is comparable with King's Standing, in that it has a close connexion with the club movement and originated in it, but its associations are with one region, the north-east, and it has always been linked with the Durham Community Council. Wincham Hall is different again because, though it started in connexion with the unemployed movement, it has always been concerned primarily with the possibilities of individual education, and essentially therefore it is more similar in aim to Coleg Harlech than to Hardwick Hall or King's Standing.

There are also general similarities between them. They are all residential, and in all of them there are short and long courses, the former of about three to six weeks (as at King's Standing, for instance), the latter six months or sometimes, as at Coleg Harlech, a year. The difficulty of the club movement has always been to secure good leadership, and it is becoming more acute as changing conditions re-absorb into employment some of the most enterprising men. These short courses are designed, primarily, to encourage club leaders. It was thought that if a man had a short residential course, he could go back to his club with new ideas and with his skill in some craft considerably increased; and that the results would be as valuable to the club as to himself. But though the emphasis was originally on the advantages that the clubs would secure, the claims of individual education are becoming more and more important. The longer courses, indeed, have generally been recognized as a possible gateway through which the exceptional man, whose abilities had been discovered through his work in the clubs, might pass on to a wider experience. Thus men went on during the year 1935–36 from Wincham Hall to Fircroft residential college for a year's course and to Avoncroft Agricultural College, and others have gone on to Oxford. Several of the Settlements have men on their staffs who were originally members of the clubs, and were first brought by them into contact with some form of further education.

Coleg Harlech obviously has a great advantage over the others as far as the more academic kinds of work are concerned, and the academic work there reaches an exceptionally high standard. For those who are tolerably familiar with the conditions of school life but have seen very little of resident adult education, the atmosphere of Coleg Harlech is something new, a reminder that schools were once places in which men as well as boys spent their leisure. And because the Welshman has not only the gift of what might vulgarly be called "the gab" but also the gift of a decidedly active mind behind it, Coleg Harlech has particularly promising material. Moreover, it is situated in the very heart of Wales, so that it can exploit fully the cultural traditions of Wales, in a Welsh-speaking area of Wales, and its buildings are admirably equipped. None of the other colleges have libraries which can compare with that at Coleg Harlech, certainly none which will compare with the projected library there when that has been built, and it has a good hall with a very fine organ. It represents an educational experiment of first class importance. It is something far more than an institution for the unemployed and for producing club leaders, and its connexion with unemployment is only by chance. Indeed, when any college can get hold of unemployed men for six months or so, feed them well and start awakening their interests in all sorts of new directions, things begin to happen which have little or nothing to do with club life, as much of it is at present organized, and at Coleg Harlech, though recruitment is arranged partly through the settlements (and thus indirectly through the clubs, as it is also at Wincham Hall), there is no other essential link. They are educational institutions planned to give men who would not otherwise have it the chance of further education. The fact that many of those at Coleg Harlech are not really unemployed means that unemployment is not in the air there; for, as far as we could judge, even those taking the short course lost the immediate sense of being unemployed.

This is a serious consideration, and it is partly this that marks off Coleg Harlech as exceptional. Wincham Hall is attempting, with much smaller resources, to do the same kind of thing, but one handicap which it suffers is the fact that its connexion with unemployment is more obvious than that of Coleg Harlech. Here too the connexion, as is pointed out in the last annual report, is accidental rather than essential, but it certainly makes a great difference to the atmosphere of the place, and if firms in Liverpool and the neighbourhood would endow places for a few of their workers at Wincham Hall, it would be a real contribution towards the well-being of the college as well as a great opportunity for the men themselves.

The association of Wincham Hall with the Liverpool clubs is much less close than that for instance of Hardwick Hall with the Durham clubs. The "old Winchamite" sometimes finds that the Liverpool clubs do not afford him the chances of developing the interests which Wincham Hall has begun in him. This is simply a reflexion of the principle that has been stated above—that in fact the best work many of the colleges are doing is personal in character.

> The value of a period at a residential centre is that it enables a man to escape for a time from his limiting conditions. He can sit back and, looking at the limitations objectively, reshape his values, rediscover himself. As some men have put it, they did not realize there were so many things a man could do with his life.[1]

In the process it is scarcely surprising that he should find it difficult to return to the same life as he led before. And it is certain that as a result of the widening of his interests he becomes a better citizen. What is unfortunate is that this should take place within a community which is inevitably deeply affected by the fact that almost all its members are unemployed. Not quite all—for at Wincham Hall (as perhaps nowhere else to a like degree) the wardens and staff have found the secret of becoming equal members of the same community as the students; a fine achievement, and one that is no doubt responsible for the extraordinary friendliness of the atmosphere there,

[1] Wincham Hall Annual Report, 1935–6.

and the close bond that unites "old Winchamites" long after their course is over.

This point, that the work of some of the colleges is essentially individual, is of practical importance. All the colleges recruit a certain proportion of their membership directly or indirectly through the clubs, and there is a tendency sometimes for club Wardens simply to consider the point of view of the clubs when the choice is made. It is also made sometimes on compassionate grounds, and though this can be understood, if too many men are selected for this reason it may easily tend to lower the standard of work. For refitting of this kind the summer camps run by most of the settlements and by the National Council are probably the right instrument, though obviously a week in camp is not the same thing as six weeks or more with good food and healthy surroundings at a residential college.

The "main course" for the unemployed men is generally some form of practical work, woodwork or gardening or upholstery or whatever it may be, though this is regarded as affording a useful approach to more academic work, while at Coleg Harlech the men taking longer courses are almost always concerned with some academic line of study. King's Standing has always specialized in craft-work, however, and the records which were obtained for us of those men from Crook who had been at Hardwick Hall during the year 1936 suggested that it was as a regional centre for craft-work instruction that Hardwick Hall was most valuable. Of the thirty-eight men who went to Hardwick Hall from Crook during that time eighteen had taken the woodwork course, six physical training, six upholstery and the others horticulture, boot-repairing, weaving, and music and drama. The records showed that a high proportion were considered to have increased their usefulness as club members thanks to the visit, and only four men of the thirty-eight were said to have lost interest in the centres since returning from Hardwick. Hardwick Hall has also run a number of special courses in drama which have contributed to the conspicuous success of the dramatic work in the clubs of North-east England. The close connexion of this college with the club movement is shown by its sensitiveness to the recent changes in the unemployment situation in Durham. As prosperity shows signs of returning, the younger men, and the more enterprising, get back to work, and the authorities of Hardwick told us that the effects of this were noticeable already in the age and type of man who came to the college. If we are right in assuming that the work these institutions can do is to provide opportunities for men who have not had them and yet deserve them, it is obviously unfortunate that those who would derive most benefit from a course at college are not always those who take it. If the position in the areas served by them improves still further, and if some of them remain colleges for unemployed, it may well mean that the personal results will not justify the efforts spent.

The progress of these colleges has taken them a long way from the original concern of some of them—unemployment and the fostering of leadership for the clubs. Some of them have always envisaged a wider mission, but it is virtually certain that all those which we have seen will come ultimately to do so. They are gradually becoming an integral part of the educational system, offering the opportunity of further education to some of those thousands of men who, in spite of their ability and enterprise, for one reason or another have had no organized secondary education. Many of these men realize what they have missed, and when they get the chance of it, it seems often to be conspicuously successful, partly because there is some basis of experience in the learner on which the teacher can build. Discussion seems to come more readily, and is certainly more real than it often is when those who are learning are younger. It has been abundantly shown that even with apparently unpromising material remarkable things can be achieved at these residential colleges, and it would be a disaster if any of them were allowed to disappear because unemployment is not as bad as it was. But what can be said definitely is that any too explicit connexion with long unemployment is a hindrance to their work, and though unemployment obviously offers chances for extended educational work, it may also destroy the level-headedness that educational work requires, if it is allowed to create the atmosphere of the place. An unemployed view of society is necessarily distorted, and a philosophy based on the acceptance of long unemployment would obviously be a very harmful acquisition.

III. SPECIAL SCHEMES

(a) THE VOLUNTARY MOVEMENT AND POVERTY: THE WIGAN SUBSISTENCE PRODUCTION SOCIETY

The club movement is dealing primarily with the unemployed man's leisure. It is attempting to help him to use this enforced leisure profitably by enriching his education if the word is taken in a very wide sense; and to offer him something that will counteract the loss he suffers through the severance of relations with his fellow-workers which unemployment implies. The Wigan Scheme, formerly known as the Upholland Experiment, in Lancashire now has a counterpart in Monmouthshire. It represents the most important of the efforts made by voluntary societies to do something about the poverty which unemployment brings with it. To say this is not to belittle the work of those women's clubs which, by helping the wife of the unemployed man to raise the household standards, are making a most significant contribution, even if it is indirect, towards this problem. For the idea of the Wigan Scheme is to make a frontal attack on poverty, and at the same time to provide, in a greater degree than is possible in most unemployed clubs, a restoration of the fellowship of work. That this was a part of the original idea is shown by the Subsistence Production Societies' expressed aims, which include that of "checking the process of social disintegration, and releasing a community life that is new, vital and integral".

The conception behind the experiment is that of the creation of a separate economic community, as self-contained as possible, to help to provide for the needs of the members. At present there is no possibility, and there seems to be none in the immediate future, of making them independent of the "dole", and the ordinary member of the scheme still depends on that for his livelihood. But by pooling effort on a large scale with a complex organization behind it, the scheme makes Unemployment Assistance go much further. Thus some parts of the scheme are devoted to agriculture and dairy produce, some to manufacture and so on, and each man is entitled to a share in the goods so produced.[1]

The ideal unit which the organizers have in mind is a mixed agricultural industrial unit, an area of manageable size, where "more than 500" members are producing a wide range of commodities (including clothes, coal and houses for the members), which shall be in regular exchange of specialities with similar units, and is a living community not only of work but also partly of leisure. The organizers of the scheme would be the first to agree that the Wigan Subsistence Production Society is far from this ideal, but in view of the short time and the many difficulties they have had, the distance that has been covered towards that aim deserves respect and admiration. Subsistence Production gives the impression that it is now entering a critical phase of its development, but that it has "caught on" there is no doubt.

The Lancashire Scheme in its present form is not a compact unit but comprises four isolated sub-units, each of them several miles north, south, or west of Wigan; the dairy farm and pig-breeding centre with 55 members, a small isolated agricultural outpost with 40 members, and another less distant with 50 members, which supply potatoes, pigs, eggs, tomatoes, vegetables, and woodwork; and one central unit with 130 members, producing the full agricultural range of pigs, eggs, potatoes, tomatoes, and vegetables, and including also the administrative department, the transport section, and the industrial centre with wholesale stores, tailoring shop, bakery, butchery, jam factory, and hardware stores. The four units are thus widely dispersed so that the daily milk round actually extends over twenty miles, and this lack of concentration adds considerably to costs and difficulties of administration. On the other hand, the membership of the three smaller units is to a considerable degree re-

[1] For further details of the scheme see the two annual reports so far issued by the "Order of Friends".

cruited on a neighbourhood basis, and this and the smaller number of members means that the sense of unity is more real.

Whether it would have been an advantage for the scheme or not, after the first experimental year in Upholland, to start on a grand scale in a fully equipped building with agricultural sections attached to it, and to rely on the effect of a ready-made unit for the immediate attraction of a membership large enough to work it, is a matter which only the men who started this scheme and work in it can decide. They think that it was better to go the arduous way, and the pride of having "built it up" is certainly there among the organizers, the staff and the older members of the Subsistence Production Society. The material benefits to the members of the scheme once it is completed (or of a scheme which started ready made) could no doubt be higher than at present.

The underlying assumption of Subsistence Production is that "idle hands can be trained to produce goods", but it is obvious that its aim is not to compete with Government Training Centres in giving men skill in new occupations. Indeed, one of the most impressive and valuable sides of the scheme seemed to us to be the evolution of new methods of technical instruction calculated to make it possible for the unskilled man to understand and perform processes which are ordinarily done by skilled workers. A member of the staff of the scheme has taken particular pride in this work, and the results in this direction are remarkable—for instance, in the woodwork section. The members of this section take great pride in turning out work which is much beyond what an unskilled man can do as a hobby. Of the 261 members in September 1937, 113 were miners, and 68 general labourers, and even of the remaining 80 only a small number are doing work connected with their previous occupation. Not in all directions has the education of unskilled men in skilled processes been equally successful. In the work of the tailoring section, for instance, the work of unskilled men nullified one of the aims of the scheme to turn out goods not inferior to those that can be bought, for good workmanship has a high educational value, and the feeling that "the worst is good enough for the unemployed" or "a bad suit is better than no suit" would be fatal for the success of Subsistence Production. This line of work was, therefore, temporarily abandoned, until some of the members should acquire skill in tailoring and cutting by attendance at Evening Classes at the Technical College. But on the whole, the scheme shows that unskilled men can go a long way with proper help and consideration, even though it may not pay to employ them in this way at an industrial wage.

That it is not intended to train men for specific functions and in that way reach a maximum of efficiency for the scheme is also shown by the ease with which the members switch over from one section of the scheme to another. Whenever possible, arrangements are made to grant any applications that are made for transfer. This is an important feature of the scheme, for from what we heard about these transfers, it seemed that they are an expression of the restlessness of the long unemployed, to which allusion has been made above. In ordinary industrial life, this restlessness and failure would probably lead to new unemployment and hopelessness, and perhaps to trouble with the official agencies by which the men are maintained. Subsistence Production can make allowances for this restlessness, and several of the members with whom one of us talked had obviously been enabled in this way gradually to find a new balance of mind.

Yet if Subsistence Production does not aim at training unemployed men, this is sometimes the effect. The man in charge of the shoe stores had, in a comparatively short time, as he said, seen all the "secrets of the trade". He took evening classes in book-keeping and accounting, and feels now quite capable of setting up on his own if he could get the capital. The transport section does all the repairs to the buses, vans, and cars such as are done at an ordinary garage.

A conflict between efficiency and principle is apparent in the question of paid men outside the managerial staff. The necessity of having some men on whom it is possible to rely, whenever and wherever they are wanted, is obvious in a scheme of this scope.

On the other hand, the aim is universality of the barter principle within the scheme. The presence of paid men among the members, who may have the latent suspicion, constantly encouraged by outsiders, that they are being used to "work for nowt" is the source of possible friction and difficulty, as the organizers well know. At present four paid men are employed at the scheme. Everything depends on how these paid men "hit it off" with the unpaid members of their section. Signs are not lacking of a resentment among the members against the paid men—very different from the attitude towards the members of the staff. "They are doing jobs which we cannot do." It is also tempting to leave the hard jobs to the men who are getting paid to do them. But there are also signs of that most desirable solution of the scheme—the members throwing up their own leaders who carry on without the need for a paid organizer.

The organizers believe that the scheme, as it stands at present, is still in process of expansion, and that the optimum size for one unit should be about twice the present size of 260 members. The expansion of the scheme, has, however, recently been slow, and it will be difficult under present conditions to attain this. From a membership of 140, attracted when the scheme was first properly launched by Lord Nuffield's gift, there had been a slow rise to the figure of 280 in the summer of 1937, but in the autumn the number had declined slightly to 260. The net expansion during the past year has been only 40 members. It would be wrong to conclude from this comparatively slow development that the bulk of the present membership consists of the faithful old guard with a few recent additions. The total number of men who have been members of the scheme for some time was considerably higher than 260, namely about 620. The great majority of the men who had a try at "working for nothing" left the scheme again for some reason or other. A certain number joined only to get "something for nothing", and so they did; for they left the scheme after two or three weeks, but not before some had run up a high bill at the Subsistence Production Society store, and perhaps helped themselves to as much as they could.[1] Things like this are inevitable in any attempt of this kind, and it would be wrong to magnify their importance. Others started with good intentions, but left disappointed. It was impossible to ascertain how many got back into employment, but the number was considerable. One young member of the transport section had just been placed as Corporation bus-driver at the good wage of £3. 5*s*. And the general complaint that the best and most promising men are leaving because they find work applies to the Wigan scheme no less than to any other work done by the voluntary agencies. Much of the employment offered is, however, temporary, and we met several members who had got back into temporary work and rejoined the scheme on falling out again.[2] The slow growth of the scheme has been accompanied with a constant influx of new members and a nearly equal number of old members leaving. Thus of the 261 members working in the scheme in September 1937, only 59 had been in the scheme at the end of 1935, the first year of its full working, 98 had joined in the course of the year 1936 (about 70 of the 230 members at the end of 1936 must have left during the first nine months of 1937), and 104 had joined up during the first months of 1937. Nearly one-third of the present members had less than half a year's standing. For a just valuation of the impact of the scheme, we must keep in mind this picture of a large fluctuating membership. The permanent nucleus, 59 men, is relatively small.

This fluctuation is certainly to a large extent the expression of the mental and social strain which "working for nothing", contrary to deeply ingrained working-class habits of money-paid work and all that it means, imposes. We have been struck by the signs of this strain among many of the members who found

[1] The rules are now that a new member, during the first week, has a right to a pair of overalls free, but not to any other goods; after the first week to the full range of ordinary goods but to no credit goods; after five weeks' work to working boots on credit, and only after ten weeks will he enjoy the full rights of membership.

[2] This does not, however, explain a part of the high turn-over in membership, because a member who rejoins the scheme is not counted twice.

themselves "working for nowt" and bringing home a bag of meat, eggs, vegetables and bread from the day's work (seven hours)—goods paid for with money collected at the Exchange at nine in the morning before catching the special bus at the market square. For the bulk of the members the feeling of being the forerunners of a new order of society was entirely absent. This is not surprising, for such a thing as the ultimate aim of the scheme can only grow slowly and in a natural way with a small number of members. The organizers of the scheme certainly do nothing to force artificially the growth of a new attitude and pride in work independent of a money wage, a feature which, though it is a matter of principle, is perhaps open to criticism. The difficulty of detaching the industrial worker, even if he has been out of work for a considerable time, from the conception of ordinary working life, is shown by the fact that to many members the organizers of the scheme are still "the bosses" and the "boss" is compared, favourably, it is true, but on the same level, with the old boss. The members watch carefully to see that the ordinary rules of working life are observed in the scheme, e.g. a new and more efficient system of potato-picking which the organizers suggest introducing at the agricultural outpost is closely examined and discussed by the members there to decide how far it conforms to Union rules. The members working in the bakery are insistent on the ordinary local privilege of a loaf of bread per shift in addition to "wage" (right to buy goods at the store). Those who, whether from an official or commercial standpoint, view the scheme with apprehension, lest the members should be permanently alienated from the industrial community, seem to underestimate the strong forces in the make-up of the unemployed preventing this. They may rest assured that this will not happen. It is an entirely different matter, and one which has nothing to do with Subsistence Production, that most of the members who have been coalminers before prefer their present state—the "dole" plus work under better conditions plus the supplementing of the "dole" by Subsistence Production to their former work underground. Some of them most emphatically do. But that this attitude is not confined to the scheme, the interviews in the Rhondda and Crook show.[1]

An even more important obstacle to permanent membership in the scheme is the social strain to which the members are exposed. The scheme is looked upon with suspicion by the majority of the Wigan workers, both employed and unemployed; less so by their Trade Unions than by public opinion. The privileges which the scheme enjoys with the Unemployment Assistance Board and the Employment Exchange (above all the suspension of the application of the Means Test as far as the results of the Societies' work are concerned, and of the "available" regulations for the members, the privilege of signing on at special hours convenient to the scheme, and in at least one case of which we heard, successful intervention by the organizers in favour of one of their members, which resulted in a temporary increase in his allowance) contribute to this suspicion. A member who sticks to the scheme does so in the face of social disapproval, "nagging" by friends and neighbours, and perhaps of more serious difficulties. There is, of course, some opposition on the part of the local shopkeepers. Although only 3 % of the Wigan unemployed are at present working in the scheme (and even they remain dependent on shops for some of the staple commodities, such as margarine and sugar), while the orders placed for the equipment and running of the scheme in the Wigan shops are, so far, considerably in excess of the losses suffered, the shopkeepers who lose are not the same ones as those who gain. We were told of a case in which a member of the scheme was ejected from his house, which belonged to a shopkeeper. The alternative of leaving either the house or the scheme was bluntly put to him and he chose to leave the house. Pressure from a shopkeeper with whom a bill has been run up is not by any means a rare reason for lapse of membership.

Nagging of the "blacklegs" or boyish obstruction of the Society's milk-van does probably not amount to more than harmless teasing and is settled in good temper. But the unemployed man in a depressed district, who shares a collective fate

[1] Compare above, pp. 154 *seqq.*

and whose rhythm of life is shaped by collective force, is sensitive to the temper of his surroundings and loath to increase his difficulties. In the case of many members, it is apparently the wife whose influence keeps them in the scheme. It is she who sees the rise in quality and quantity of the family diet, the better health of children and husband, his better temper; and there is a great difference in her attitude to this scheme and to the Government Instruction Centres. It does not take the husband, and part of his money, away from home.

One of the most important things in overcoming these difficulties and creating an atmosphere conducive to success is the restriction of illicit resale to outsiders to the unavoidable minimum, particularly in order to preserve the standing of the scheme with shopkeepers and Trade Unions; while resale obviously conflicts with the principles of Subsistence Production. Precise accounts are kept of each individual's purchases and wherever these seem in excess of the member's own requirements, the matter is carefully considered, and, if there is any reason to suspect resale, referred to the committee of the member's unit. Whatever resale does take place can only be on a very petty scale. During the first nine months of 1937, the committees had to deal with about ten such cases of suspected petty resale.

In general, Subsistence Production is not a self-sufficient system which could work regardless of the outside world, and even less one which could afford to antagonize it. Not only is the whole scheme dependent on the suspension of the Unemployment Assistance Board regulations regarding extra earnings, but also on outside contributions for capital expenses, management and expansion. The running cash costs of producing, distributing, and supervising must amount to not less than £250 a week, even at the present scale. Prices are fixed with an eye to the shop prices, for if the margin falls below a certain amount, members might prefer to buy elsewhere an inferior quality of the same goods. Egg prices, for example, are fixed by wholesale prices on the Preston market. If Preston prices are 10*d.* or 11*d.*, Subsistence Production price is 7*d.*; if Preston prices are 1*s.* or 1*s.* 1*d.*,

Subsistence Production price is 8*d.*; and so on. The average member spends about 11*s.* or 12*s.* in the scheme, so that even excluding his rent he will still spend more in the outside world. It has just been explained that the members still think in industrial terms, and thus the scheme is an isolated economic unit to a lesser degree than the description of it would suggest.

The visitor to the scheme, who has heard that this is a scheme for elderly men, whose hope of return to employment is remote, who must be considered as a permanent industrial surplus, and in whose case Unemployment Assistance may reasonably be considered a pension, will be astonished at the comparatively large number of younger men he will see. Less than one-third of the members are over 50. Their age distribution is as follows (September 1937):

Age	Number	
Under 25 ...	1	Average age: 44
25–30	19	
30–35	34	
35–40	52	
40–50	71	
50–60	53	
60 and over ...	31	
	261	

Actually there are more men between 30 and 40 in the scheme than either between 40 and 50, or even between 50 and 64. It should not be concluded, however, that the younger men who should be looking round for work drift into it and settle down on the "dole" plus subsistence. The twenty young men under 30 are mainly employed in the Transport Department, where membership, in many cases, is frankly temporary. They acquire mechanical knowledge and experience in garage conditions, they get a driving licence (paid sometimes by the scheme), they pass the driving test (fee sometimes paid by the scheme), and then later they may leave again, to go into employment or at any rate with their chances greatly increased by a good training. Everything from overall to licence has been paid for them, and meanwhile they have been living with their families, drawing the "dole", and enjoying the material benefits of membership. Here the scheme works as a Training Centre and attracts men who might refuse to go to a Government Training Centre. No objection can be raised against young men being drawn into the scheme on that basis.

With regard to the middle-aged men, one marked feature seemed to be the preponderance of men with restricted employability. The scheme has, in that age group, attracted the "residually unemployed", the men with a psychological kink, with obvious symptoms of nerves or with physical disabilities. The placing value of these men was in many cases so low that in that respect they could unhesitatingly be ranked with the old men,[1] and in one important point they have one advantage over the older men as members of the scheme, in that they are parents of small children. The benefits of the scheme are greater for members with large families and accordingly with greater need for the goods produced by the Society. The scheme is therefore working, so to speak, on a natural "family allowance" system. Of the 261, only 15 were single men. Of the 246 married men, there were only 16 without children. Nine out of ten members were married men with children, and about half of these—107—had three or more children. Forty-seven members had five or more children. The total number of children in families where the allowance is supplemented by the scheme is about 665. This "family allowance" system is largely responsible for the influx of middle-aged men. As we showed elsewhere,[2] it is precisely among these age groups that poverty is most widespread. To raise the material standard of life is therefore a particularly necessary and socially important undertaking for these age groups. An addition of, say, 8*s*. 6*d*. a week to their weekly income, which seems to be a fair estimate of the real value of the scheme for a family man with two or three children,

[1] One of them had been sent by the Employment Exchange Manager himself, surely a sufficient proof that nothing can be said against the membership of middle-aged men of "poor placing value". This is the only case of a member having been sent by the Exchange. The usual method is that of members introducing and recommending friends.

[2] Cf. above, p. 111.

is probably sufficient to bring most of them above the poverty line.

To make this extra provision for the children of these men is certainly not a less valuable job than that of absorbing the older men, and, considering their low employment value, the presence of large numbers of middle-aged men in the scheme does not seriously diminish its value. But it is necessary to stress this fact because the description of the scheme as for "elderly men" might suggest that the members are exclusively men over, say, 50. There is no restriction of age over 35, although "preference is given to married men over 38".

It is not easy to assess the material benefits to the members. The average purchases by members of agricultural products are shown below, shop and scheme prices being contrasted:

TABLE LXVI

	Shop price	Subsistence Production Society price
7 quarts milk	4*s*. 1*d*.	1*s*. 9*d*.
1 doz. eggs	1*s*. 10*d*.	1*s*. 2*d*.
1 lb. bacon	1*s*.	6*d*.
½ lb. ham	10*d*.	5*d*.
1 lb. jam	5*d*.	2½*d*.
3 lb. beef	3*s*.	1*s*. 9*d*.
12 lb. flour	1*s*. 11*d*.	1*s*. 4*d*.
4 lb. tomatoes	2*s*.	10*d*.
20 lb. potatoes	10*d*.	6*d*.
Mixed vegetables	1*s*.	6*d*.
	16*s*. 11*d*.	8*s*. 11½*d*.

The difference between the shop price and the scheme's price per week for a member widens from 8*s*. as shown to 12*s*. to 13*s*. if things like coal, bread, pies, scones, shoes, etc., are taken into account. The usual figure at which the members themselves put the advantage from the scheme is about half that figure, 5*s*. to 7*s*. The two statements are not incompatible. Part of the saving to members consists not in that "their money goes farther", but that they buy better quality goods than they would otherwise have bought in shops. Of perhaps even higher value than the actual saving in money is the direction of choice which membership of the scheme implies. For the families of nearly all the members it has meant the transition from the use of tinned milk to fresh milk, a great gain in health for their families, or from the Lancashire diet of fish and chips, ready-made meat pies and potato cakes to a varied meat-plus-fresh-vegetables diet.[1] From the way in which the members talk about this change in their standard of life, it seemed that the sense for the dietary and also the aesthetic superiority of good food has been awakened. Even if the material benefit of the scheme ceased, it is probable that the members would spend their allowance in a better way and get more real value out of it than before.

The members of the scheme form a co-operative working community based on mutual trust. The benefit which the individual member derives from the scheme is not in a rigid way bound up with his contribution to it. There is no efficiency bonus of any kind; there is as we have seen a "family allowance system"; there is no rigid check on attendance, and no limitation of sales according to hours worked. Any member has unrestricted access to the full range of goods produced so long as he "does a reasonable share of the work each week in the opinion of his fellow members". The number of working hours is different in various units, and in various sections of the same unit, and also different for various seasons; it is fixed not by the managers of the scheme, not even by the General Committee, but by the committee of each unit (five to seven members, drawn from the various sections). The scheme is therefore only workable because, and so long as, there is the general willingness in each section not to "shirk" work and benefit from the work of others, but to contribute proportionately to the general pool. A break-

[1] The average weekly purchases of a member include $1\frac{2}{3}$ lb. tomatoes, $1\frac{1}{4}$ lb. peas, $\frac{3}{4}$ lb. cabbage and carrots, $\frac{1}{2}$ lb. cauliflower, swedes and sprouts, $\frac{1}{4}$ lb. beetroot, celery and beans. Parsnips, onions, and marrow have not caught on.

down of this mutual trust between the many various sections of the scheme would spell the end of the whole. And the constant temptation must be realized in order to appreciate the smoothness with which any major friction has been avoided and the way in which any attempt at "shirking" has been nipped in the bud. How tempting, for example, for the section of the outlying agricultural unit not to put in extra work to renew the defective wire round the cabbage fields through which the hens from the poultry section come and damage the cabbage! It does not make any appreciable difference to them, since sufficient cabbage is sent round every day from the main vegetable growing section. Undoubtedly this mutual trust is there, though it has sometimes to be invoked by persuasion and reminders that efficient work benefits not only the whole but through the whole the individual member himself. Such reminders are, e.g. the fixing of potato prices at the beginning of the cropping season on a sliding scale according to yield per acre:

Yield per acre	Price per lb. to members
x	y
$x+1$	$y-1$
$x+2$	$y-2$
$x+3$	$y-3$

Another aid to efficiency is exemplified by a graph fixed to the doors of the garage workshop, showing the saving in cash expenses of the Society that can be effected by economic use of petrol, and by describing past progress and failure in this direction. Here Subsistence Production methods make use in the same way as both capitalistic and socialist production of the "team spirit"; but more important seemed the atmosphere of mutual trust, which keeps alive among these unemployed men the spirit of industrial co-operation, where the efficiency and even the safety of each one is dependent on the work of his fellow-workers, a harmony which even in private industry is often rather a voluntarily obeyed tradition than one enforced by supervision. The number of members and the distances separating the units mean that to each member most of the others are not known personally, and with the expansion of the scheme this mutual trust is based more and more on the effect of co-ordination by the organizers and the General Committee than on personal confidence in the other members. In this way co-operation within the scheme is becoming more and more similar to the general "unseen" co-operation within industrial society; and this is, as we have seen in a previous section,[1] an indispensable source of personal content, independence, and social prestige to the English worker. Where it succeeds in reviving this, the scheme gets deeper in its treatment of unemployed men than an unemployed club can hope to do. "There are 1,500 people depending on me", said one of the members proudly.

The tendencies are to develop this working community into a living community, but not much progress has been made in that direction. Family parties on the lawn were, naturally, a great success, but evening classes are only just about to be started in co-operation with the Workers' Educational Association and their success is still uncertain. A Sports Club has just been founded, and the charge of 1*d.* a week for the Sports Club is a "statutory" deduction for each member. These "statutory deductions" (there is also 1*d.* a week for the Hospital) are another way in which industrial traditions are preserved by Subsistence Production. But the organization of leisure and of a community life apart from work is a task which has not yet been tackled, and is so far considered as side-tracking the main preoccupations of the scheme, which are practical and quasi-industrial. But in restoring to the unemployed members of the scheme much of what they had lost when they lost their job, in material and spiritual values, and giving them in addition some things which they have never had before, the scheme is an indication of what voluntary agencies can do for unemployed men.

The scheme is backed by a small band of men who believe in the future of the principles on which their work is based, and for

[1] Cf. p. 150.

whom their work is not an eight-hours-a-day job, but who have sacrificed tempting prospects elsewhere, and to whom the improvement of their work is of paramount importance in their thoughts all the time. We have indicated some of the difficulties and of the achievements, as they were seen by one of us. But it is certain that the scheme holds promise for the future.

A NOTE ON THE FINANCE OF THE WIGAN SUBSISTENCE PRODUCTION SOCIETY

If we try to calculate the cost of the Wigan experiment, there are four qualifications to be made. The first, which applies to almost all voluntary work, is that, of the gains of the scheme, not all are calculable in terms of money; the gain to society in increased employability of the members—not to mention such intangible factors as happiness and contentment—cannot be measured in terms of money. The second is that the scheme has had to cope with great external difficulties, and that the necessary capital expenditure has been higher than what might be possible under more favourable conditions. The third is that the Wigan scheme is a first experiment in subsistence production with its special technical and managerial requirements, and that the capital expenditure includes that experience which has to be bought once,[1] but which is a non-recurrent cost item and should best be put down as an "overhead cost" of society. The fourth qualification is that the scheme has been designed to accommodate 500 members and is capable of doing so with only slight additional capital and administrative costs. So the scheme, if we compare its cost with the benefit derived from it by the actual members is like an industrial enterprise in a depression, working far below capacity, with every prospect of rapidly increasing profit as the scale of operations increases.

With these qualifications the finances of the scheme may be summarized as follows. Up to the summer of 1937, a capital expenditure of about £60,000 has been incurred on the Wigan scheme, covering land, buildings, improvement, machinery, equipment, live and dead stock, tools, transport vehicles and development. Allowing 5% for wear and tear on the capital, and £5,000 for the annual cost of

[1] A proof of this is the second scheme in Monmouthshire where the experience gained during the first experiment has borne fruit. In the view of expert observers, this has resulted in a substantial reduction of cost.

administration,[1] the annual social cost of the scheme would seem to amount to £8,000. Against this we may set the benefit derived by the 260 members, which has just been shown to be in the neighbourhood of 12*s*. weekly or £31 per annum for each member over and above the running cash cost of production. The total surplus arrived at in the scheme works out, on this basis, at £8,060. This means that with the present membership, the scheme just balances, if (*a*) the labour of the members is not counted as a cost factor (which it is not, from a social point of view, because the members of the scheme are not deflected from any other productive activity), and (*b*) no interest is exacted on the original capital (which is, as a matter of fact, not exacted because it has been brought together by donations, principally from Lord Nuffield). On this basis the scheme is—on an economic calculus from the point of view of society—just "worth" the replacement of its capital equipment, but would not be preferable to relief.

It is estimated that a scheme run for 500 members would require an additional capital expenditure of £10,000, and may also involve an additional annual increase in cost of administration and supervision of £1,000 per annum. On this basis, the annual costs of the scheme would be £9,500, the total benefit over cash costs of production would be £16,120 if the benefit to each individual member were the same.[2] On this reckoning, a "full" scheme would show a handsome surplus, amounting to £13 per annum per member. The surplus would actually be sufficient to pay a full commercial rate of interest on the working capital at the rate of 5 %, and still leave a surplus of over £3,000 per annum, equivalent to £6 per annum per member. On this basis the scheme ceases to be a "charitable" proposition and becomes an act of "public works policy" on which any socially responsible body could embark on economic grounds, although the surplus per member, at the rate of 5*s*. weekly, would still be low, and as "public works policy" the scheme would not rank as a very tempting proposition.

[1] The amount which has to be spent on supervision and administration has been shown by experience to be higher than was at first theoretically considered necessary.

[2] Actually, it would probably be slightly higher, for the increased scale would make it possible to open up new lines of production.

(*b*) THE VOLUNTARY MOVEMENT AND ISOLATION: THE LINCOLN PEOPLE'S SERVICE CLUB

One of the most remarkable of the voluntary schemes is the People's Service Club in Lincoln, and we discuss it here because it is one of the few definitely successful experiments that have been made in dealing with the "residual problem". Its distinctive feature is that it attempts much more elaborate constructive work than any of the clubs in areas of residual unemployment that have been discussed so far. The organizers are not content to make provision to keep the unemployed man off the streets while he is out of work. They start from the assumption (which we have seen to be particularly true of a prosperous place) that he has dropped out of the community and that something positive is needed to bring him back, and the characteristic of the Lincoln clubs is thus an atmosphere of activity that is quite exceptional.

The organizers are working then on the assumption that one of the chief needs of the unemployed man is the restoration of some sense of "function in the community". It must somehow be made possible for him to do something which was needed by somebody, something that would bring him back from his isolation. There were thousands of jobs that needed doing, but were not economic, the provision of toys for poor children, of comforts for invalids and old age pensioners, the equipment of new playgrounds and of nursery schools. All these things would be useful if they could be provided, but the demand for them never became economic. To provide them, therefore, would not mean competition with the local tradesmen or local labour. The greatest care has been taken throughout that this condition should be observed. There has been criticism from some trade unionists, but there has also been help from others, and the close identification of the People's Service Club with the working-class movement has been the best answer to such criticism as has taken place. One of us, who spoke with a considerable number of men connected with the scheme, found that the idea that nothing should be done which might in any way conflict with Trade Union principles was foremost in the minds of nearly all. He found too that the idea of community service has "caught on". The originators of the scheme had an infectious enthusiasm for it, and in the last resort success is no doubt due to the fact that they were prepared to devote themselves to it, heart and soul, over a long period. Good organization, by itself, is worthless in schemes of this kind in comparison with such enthusiasm, and they stand or fall largely by the personal qualities of those who carry them out.

At the same time, methods have been carefully worked out to keep the idea of service constantly alive. Any projected plan of service is discussed fully at meetings of the welfare committee which take place week by week, and this committee, consisting as it does of the leading members of the club, is thus constantly reminded of the character of the work that is being done, for they have to consider whether it is meeting a real need and whether the need is likely to be met in some other way which makes it unjustifiable for the club to meet it. There is a rule that when any large undertaking is contemplated for an outside organization (such as the playground equipment that has been made for the Rhondda or for Page Bank in County Durham, or the sets of tables made for the Dockland Settlement Day Nursery or the Peckham Nursery School) representatives of the organization should first pay a visit to the club, so that the transaction should be on a personal basis. When the job is done, a deputation is elected from the clubs to make the presentation personally, and where things have been made for the City of Lincoln they have been on several occasions formally accepted by the Mayor at a public meeting. Several of the men specialize on work for individuals, old age pensioners, or invalids in hospital. In these ways the men who do the jobs come into contact with those for whom they are done, and get the sense that their work is worth doing and is appreciated by others.[1]

[1] This idea of community service has been followed in many clubs and the list of such services rendered to the community by the clubs is impressive. But in most places it is not the central idea of the clubs, and many club organizers told us that, though it worked for a time, they had not been able to maintain it.

The woodwork and metal workshops and the boot repairing shop in which children's shoes (and a pair of shoes a month for each member) are repaired, are the focus of the club's activities. The atmosphere in these workshops is business-like and friendly. The register of attendance in the boot repairing shop shows that two-thirds of those interested in that particular activity, about forty men, regularly attend twice a day. One or two only out of perhaps thirty men with whom one of us talked in the various workshops complained that they were not allowed to make articles for themselves often enough, and that their wives would be reconciled to the club more easily if they could sometimes bring home something for the household. The answer to this complaint is that anyone can make what he likes for himself at the evening classes, that a certain number of the toys made before Christmas are given to members for their families, but, most important of all, that once the principle of members making things for themselves (except within strictly defined limits) is allowed, the atmosphere which is of primary importance may be destroyed.

Other clubs which have done "service work" have often found it difficult to keep it going, and at Lincoln continuity depends on the right atmosphere having been created by an effort, constantly maintained over a relatively long period. It does not now appear in any way forced, though no doubt if new schemes were not forthcoming fairly often, enthusiasm would tend to decline. There has been achieved at Lincoln a feat which might well have been thought impossible, and has indeed been called impossible in some places where it has been tried elsewhere, but it has only been achieved as the result of an immense amount of personal influence.

The other distinctive characteristic of this scheme is its success with the difficult cases who are the real hard core of unemployment. This is a significant thing, for the problem of providing anything but shelter for these difficult cases has been given up in despair by most organizations that have tackled it, and they have said that there is no solution; that it is not possible to arouse interests in men of this type, and that nothing constructive can be done for them.

The Lincoln scheme, unlike many others, was constructive in origin. A large number of clubs in the larger towns, formed in the depth of the slump, were originally planned to provide men with shelter and some small degree of comfort to "keep them off the streets". The Lincoln clubs originated with a Workers' Educational Association class, and they have always believed in the possibilities of constructive work. It is this which is no doubt responsible for the record which the clubs have in refitting men for employment, without of course giving or claiming to give any sort of vocational training.

TABLE LXVII. LINCOLN PEOPLE'S SERVICE CLUB

Year June to May	Active membership in the course of the year	Active membership at the end of the year	Left for employment
1933–34	271	162	*c.* 70
1934–35	237	147	68
1935–36	227	120	86
1936–37	158	104	53

The proportion of those who have "left for employment" is very high. The figures suggest at once that the membership of the Lincoln clubs is not by any means confined to the "hard core" cases, but it is equally certain that at present the club is dealing, among others, with a high proportion of such cases, the sort of men whom we visited in Deptford and whom we claimed there to represent the residual problem.[1] A few typical cases of men with whom one of us talked during visits to the clubs may be given. There was first a number of men in the upper-age group, including one or two old age pensioners, like a skilled craftsman, aged 68, living with a married daughter, his income being 10*s*. old age pension, supplemented by 6*s*. from the Public Assistance Committee, who spends all day nearly every day working in the workshop. Another elderly case was one of those "men with a grievance", who bear a grudge against the world because they believe they have been unreasonably treated.

[1] See above, pp. 57 *seqq.*

This man lost his job six years ago while another man, eight years older than himself and with other means of support, employed by the same firm in the same capacity, was retained. There were several who were physically unfit, a skilled metal worker, aged 50, single, going blind. He too spends most of his day in the workshop and can turn metal by the feel, provided the job is not too fine. He is learning Braille and has become one of the most active members of the educational class. Another man, wounded in the spine during the War, who has not had ordinary employment since, also works regularly in the woodwork shop. Then there is the "poor industrial material", poor at least from the placing point of view, but not necessarily poor if a wider view is taken. One typical instance is a general labourer, middle-aged, who had only had six weeks' work (Council relief work) since 1922, a man who says that "why he does not get work is that 'he's always across the foreman'". "I'm never right and we always have words about it. In the army too I was always getting into trouble and I spent most of my time in India in prison." A French polisher, aged about 40, gassed in the War, and who has severe bouts of bronchial asthma, is another such case; or an upholsterer, who broke his apprenticeship to go into his father's business which afterwards failed. He is rather small and (even after the "Second Appointed Day") he is a Public Assistance Committee case. Or lastly there is a young man of 26 who learned a trade but was temporarily blinded from the effects of wood dust in a workshop where conditions were evidently bad. He was blind for six months, and though he was cured, his thick glasses and record of industrial disease obviously make it very hard indeed for him to get back to work. His appearance is exceptionally neat and he wants work desperately. The one thing that has "kept him from going mad" is to be able to work day after day in the woodwork shop of the club.

This summary of a few cases met in the Lincoln People's Service Club workshops will give some indication of the social task it is carrying through. Not the least among its achievements is the way in which it has been able to introduce men, by way of the workshops, to new kinds of education for which in other places they would be regarded as completely unsuitable. The result in intellectual attainment, of course, varies, but the personal results, in giving men a new status, new interests, and a new feeling of self-respect, are infinitely more important.

The purpose of this short account of the Lincoln Experiment is to show its distinctive features, and we will not, therefore, discuss those that are not so distinctive. One of its objects is to provide "social recreation for its members", and it evidently succeeds in doing so. It has a Dramatic Group, an active Women's Section, and has a "holiday rest home", in which families who need holidays most are allowed a fortnight's holiday during the summer, provided by the social service of the clubs.

"Service", as it is understood by these clubs, depends on fresh inspiration if it is not to flag. The organizers of the scheme believe that it would be a help to themselves, and to others who do similar service work, if there were more frequent opportunities for an exchange of views as to what might be done. There is a strong case for this, and if the men themselves were given the opportunity to assist in discussions of this kind it would no doubt provide valuable additional stimulus. A grant of money recently made to the club made some "missionary" work possible, and several club representatives went to Sunderland and elsewhere to discuss social service. It may be suggested that a more effective form of missionary work would be to introduce club leaders from other places to the Lincoln workshops. If they could stay in Lincoln and work for a month side by side with men who have been "brought up" on the scheme, they could hardly fail to feel the atmosphere that exists there.

A word must be said briefly about the finance of the scheme. Its annual turnover is comparable to that of a large Liverpool club (about £1,000, as compared with £900 for the Hood Street Club in Liverpool, 1935–36). The main difference is that at Lincoln something like half the annual expenditure is on materials, which in their manufactured form of course represent a substantially larger sum going to help the infirm, or the aged, or the community in general. To put it in other words, those who have helped to maintain the Lincoln club have made possible the work that it does for individuals and for the community, and have helped to contribute to that impressive list of services which it has done and amenities which it has provided. Our view is, however, that the contribution the club has made to the lives of the men themselves is of inestimably greater importance, and the high proportion of men returning to work represents value for money. The experiment is indeed one of the most encouraging things that have come out of the voluntary societies' efforts to help the unemployed.

On the other hand, the experiment is not one which can be repeated elsewhere, except in so far as others with a like enthusiasm for the idea of community service can be found. Community service is capable of becoming a popular ideal if it is continually fostered by people with enthusiasm for it and a belief in it, but it is their qualities much more than those of the ideal itself which are infectious. Like all work among the unemployed this stands or falls by the quality of person devoted to it, and it is thus people with ideas rather than people to fit ideas, whom those responsible for starting any service schemes among the unemployed have to seek.

IV. THE FUTURE

(a) THE CLUBS AND THEIR FUTURE

The account given of the "voluntary movement" in the six towns of the sample shows it confronted with two different types of situation demanding different treatment. There is the situation of an area where the unemployment percentage is considerable. That a man is out of work in such a place tells us nothing of his social status or his industrial quality, and a club for unemployed men therefore may be an institution of the same social quality as others which include members of all sections of the working class. But in a prosperous place the fact that a man has been out of work for a long time—unless he is elderly—does suggest that his industrial value is not high; or else that unemployment or other circumstances in his environment have so affected him that he finds it almost impossible to force himself back to work.

It follows, then, that in the first type of place what the unemployed club can do is to make it possible to use an opportunity, but an opportunity which in some measure the employed man shares with the unemployed. Men out of work are men with rather more time to spare than men in work, but if we are concerned with provision for leisure it must be recognized that this provision is needed for those who are working as well as for those who are not. Where unemployment has affected the man who is normal as well as the man who has some handicap, it is in many instances possible (as the work of the clubs has shown) to make constructive use of the opportunity which enforced leisure provides. In some places the clubs have been so successful (among a certain active section) that there is a possibility of the movement fostering a "little renaissance" in craft work, academic study and discussion, music and drama; and this is not something that might come of it in a century, but something—as those who have seen some of the drama festivals run by the club movement in the North of England would be ready to say—that is already coming into being here and now. In some places this tentative growth of a communal culture is new, as it is in Crook. In others, like the Rhondda, the clubs are maintaining a tradition that has long existed, for we have seen that the "community culture" of the Rhondda was at one time intimately associated with the churches and chapels there. If these had been still at the height of their influence when unemployment struck the valleys, there might have been no need of the unemployed clubs, for the first community centres of South Wales were these organizations. But the decline in the coal trade came at the same time as a decline in church-going, not so marked, perhaps, in Wales as elsewhere, but in most industrial areas leading to a rapid fall in the effective membership of churches and chapels, and rapid changes in the character of the beliefs of those who remained. This change in attitude, coupled with the effects of financial depression, has inevitably brought a slackening in the cultural influence of the old institutions. The question is whether the new can carry on something of the tradition which they established? If they can, they will have justified their existence over and over again.

Three things make it difficult for the clubs in the Special Areas to do this. One is the loss of leadership owing to transference or to the revival of local industry; another is the difficulty of making an organization formed for unemployed men into an organization for the community; and the last, much more important, is that, for a movement to achieve anything like the results which these religious organizations achieved, it must have something more to it than friendship and social opportunity. One of the Labour leaders in this country is reported to have said recently: "When your unemployed clubs can give these men something like a religion, we shall be interested in them." This expresses what is the real difficulty of the movement, but a difficulty that is in some places, in some degree, being surmounted.

The situation in Crook at the present time well illustrates the first two at least of these difficulties and we may consider it in detail for a moment to show them. The improvement in the employment situation during the last twelve months has resulted in important changes in the centres. Between 1932 and 1936 the unemployment register in Crook and district fell by over 2,000, nearly 50%, but the numbers remaining were sufficiently large to provide an adequate basis for an active membership. During the twelve months ending May 1937, the unemployment register has fallen by another 500 to about 2,500.

As a disproportionate share of the decline in unemployment has taken place in the Helmington Row area the effect on the Helmington Row Centre has been serious. This centre, which has always been a young man's centre, has lost its chairman (aged 25), its secretary (aged 26), and several members of its committee (in the twenties and early thirties) during the last few months. Some of these leaders have found work in other parts of the country, and are permanently lost to the centre;

others have obtained work at Brancepeth Colliery, from which the old Bowden Close coal is now being worked, and though they are able to continue in membership of the centre, they have had to resign their positions as officials and committee men, and this tends to diminish their interest and active participation in centre activities. It is significant that, whilst the average age of the old committee at Helmington Row was only 29, the average age of the new committee is 49. The actual membership of the club has suffered considerably as a result of industrial transference. Some thirty members have been lost during the last six months. But most members who obtain work in the neighbourhood keep on their membership. There are now 63 employed men who are members of the Helmington Row Centre, out of a total membership of 158. The question arises whether a centre governed by middle-aged and elderly unemployed men will continue to attract the growing number of employed younger men and, if not, what is going to be the effect of the change on the character of the centre.

The position at Stanley is rather different. The centre has a large membership of men of all ages, though men in the thirties and forties predominate, and although about 40 members (mostly between the ages of 25 and 40) are now employed, the officials and committee men (average age 42) have remained more or less unchanged. But there is every prospect of considerable changes in the near future. The Wooley pit is now being opened and 200 to 300 men will probably be taken on, chiefly from Stanley. The proportion of employed men in the Stanley centre is bound to rise considerably and, unless the present practice of excluding employed members from office and committees is altered, the result will again be what is, in effect, a community centre for employed and unemployed alike being managed by a group of elderly unemployed men.

The Crook (West Road) Occupational Centre has had a membership fairly representative of all adult age groups, though men between 30 and 40 have predominated. Owing to a shortage of accommodation, employed workers cannot be admitted and members who obtain employment have to leave. In actual fact, very few members have obtained employment recently, with the exception of a number of young transferees, and not many are likely to be affected by the re-opening of the Wooley pit. The centre is likely, therefore, to remain an occupational centre for unemployed men of all ages, with a stable but slowly ageing membership.

The Sunniside centre is essentially an unemployed old man's centre. The percentage of unemployment in Sunniside has for some time been considerably less than in the rest of the Crook district (about 13 % in May 1937), and those who are still unemployed tend to be the older men and the less satisfactory young men. But membership of the centre is still confined to the unemployed. Members, as well as committee men and officials, have to leave on obtaining employment. The average age of membership is now well over 40 and that of the officials and committee is over 50. Many of the members would like to admit employed men, but the officials and committee, who appear to have settled down to more or less permanent unemployment, are anxious to maintain the centre as an exclusive club for the privileged class, the unemployed, to which they belong.

In these four clubs, then, are exemplified some of the present tendencies; difficulties due to transference, the re-employment of members leading in some instances to their leaving the club, in others to the club changing its character and extending its membership to employed and unemployed alike, the rising average age of members, the tendency of a committee of unemployed men to remain in control, and so on. One of the most troublesome of them is the cleavage between employed and unemployed such as is implied in the Sunniside situation; though if what has been written earlier about Blackburn is considered, it seems that in some places, beyond this, there is what is probably a yet more fundamental cleavage of class, not easily noticed at first by the outsider, but seen to be, once it has been noticed, of central importance.

It will not do to attempt to force a policy on the clubs. Some of them, if we are right, have sufficient vitality to be already changing to meet changing needs, and they are those which, if they have not succeeded in providing a religion, have provided a next best to it in the sense of active purpose and corporate life that they have created. Many such clubs may become community centres for the community as a whole; and there are big tasks for such clubs to carry out. Others will equally certainly fail to adjust themselves to the change, and will ultimately become nothing more nor less than social centres for the elderly unemployed. It is worth emphasizing that provision of this kind can be in itself valuable, and has possibilities for development and experiment. Men over 65 can be included to enlarge the experiment's scope, and to give interest and some degree of comfort to these men is to do social work which is not spectacular, perhaps, but is of real importance. But it is also dangerous. For what is needed, if anything effective is to be done for the middle-aged and younger men, is something more alive and active. The provision of rest and recreation carries with it the risk of pauperization so that even with these "old men's clubs" the sense of purpose and life must somehow be preserved, if the movement is not as a whole to be discredited, and avoided by those who are the true leaders in local society. More than one instance of this has come within our experience—clubs that have gradually shed their active members, have become little more than a shelter which the "respectable" will not use, and have so brought disrepute on the movement as a whole in their district.

It is certain that the existence of a settlement which is in close touch with local needs makes adjustment and modification to meet new situations much easier and much more effective, and will be a source of great strength to the recreated centres, but it is only the settlement which has become an organic part of the life of the district that can hope to do this, that can keep in touch naturally with the leaders in the clubs and can make itself aware when their interest is flagging, encourage new blood and stimulate by the suggestion of new activities. To create leaders in the clubs is one of the jobs which a settlement can do, and the success of the club movement in the Rhondda is certainly based largely on this. The forming of *ad hoc* settlements will not necessarily strengthen the movement, unless a real demand already exists for them, or unless men and women with something akin to inspiration can be found to run them.

If they can get help of this kind, there seems to us to be no good reason why, in districts where there are not "class" distinctions between workers of different grades, the unemployed clubs should not become community clubs. Without this help, they will probably fail. The sooner the change takes place the better, for there are already traces in the Special Areas of the unemployed clubs making it difficult for a man to bring himself to take available work ("I believe I could get back again really, but I am so happy as it is. I have got so much to do in the club"—as a man in a club in the North of England expressed himself to one of us), and these will be much more likely to disappear when the club is serving employed and unemployed indifferently. That there should be any danger of an unemployed club keeping a man unemployed may seem an anomaly. It is a real danger, as those who have to do with the clubs know, and until this change takes place, the danger will still be there.

The thing can be done. In many places this distinction between employed and unemployed is being overcome, and some clubs are becoming community centres, though in others resistance is strong. And whatever problems it solves, this development may create in some districts a serious financial problem unless the basis of "adoption" changes, for the reason for adoption has been the desire to help the unemployed. We touch on this point again shortly in a later section.

What we may reasonably hope that the "voluntary movement" may produce, then, in areas where there has been heavy industrial unemployment, is a system of institutions which make it possible for the worker's leisure, whether he is employed or unemployed, to be spent in a way that makes him set a far higher value on it than he has ever set before, and brings into activity interests and powers that have remained dormant. The existence of settlements will make possible the fostering of such institutions, providing advice, inspiration, and teaching, and organizing contacts between one and another. And the regional house like Coleg Harlech or Wincham Hall is the natural apex of such a system where the worker, employed or unemployed, who has exceptional possibilities, may get the exceptional opportunity of developing them. That the unemployed clubs in areas of industrial unemployment may be the beginning of this growth is due simply to the fact that there alone has unemployment permanently affected all types of workmen, and that their membership has included therefore some men of exceptional quality. But for anything like this to come into being will take time, as it will need money, and personnel, and until the opportunities which the situation offers are more widely understood, neither is likely to be forthcoming.

In prosperous districts the unemployed club is entirely different in character. It is unthinkable that it should turn into a community centre; and to imagine that the establishing of community centres will solve the difficulties of the unemployed is to begin at the wrong end, for one reason why men are unemployed in prosperous places is that they have dropped out of the community and cannot make the effort to struggle back. They will certainly keep as far from a community centre as they keep from most institutional life under present conditions.

Nor will a social club for the unemployed work the miracle. It will give them a sort of community life, but life only within the unemployed community such as we saw happening among the younger men in Leicester or in the "cellar" clubs of Liverpool. Such a society will give them the feeling that unemployment is normal and that work is not worth doing, and at any rate under present conditions where unemployment brings with it necessarily so much harm, it would be disastrous to foster this feeling.

What is needed, at least for the younger and the middle-aged man, is something with a more active character; something that will prove to an unemployed man that he can work, and that he is a useful member of society. There are probably various ways by which that can be done, but there is one essential to all of them, someone with a sympathetic and also a forceful personality who will use the whole of it in the effort to help them. It does not so much matter what bee he has in his bonnet, as long as the bee is big enough. He must have enthusiasm, conviction and devotion. Given such a personality, the thing can be done—if money is forthcoming to finance it. But it is probably expensive, far more expensive than the job of providing clubs and centres in the Special Areas, which can largely run themselves, need ever be. And it is difficult. We believe that the Lincoln experiment and a few others (such as the centre in East London mentioned on p. 284 above) represent the most satisfactory attempts that have hitherto been made in this direction, so far as we have been able to discover, and with both of these one of the most noteworthy factors is the record of those who have got back to normal employment. One other may be added, though it does not come within the scope of our problem of long unemployment—the "Homes of St Francis" of which there are now several in England. These homes certainly represent the most effective effort that the Church has made to deal with this particular type of social problem. They have, like every other institution worth anything, their failures, but they also have their great successes; and it is those same qualities of enthusiasm, conviction and devotion behind them that are responsible. The tramp from the local workhouse finds himself treated on terms of equality, housed, fed, and taught a trade. He discovers that someone cares about him, and cares enough not only to subscribe money (though this in itself is very valuable and often represents real sacrifice) but to spend his life in trying to do something about it. Along lines such as these (if at all), the residual problem can be solved.

None of this, of course, is to question the value of establishing community centres in prosperous districts. It means only that they cannot in any way affect the residual problem as it exists at present in such places. They are concerned with the interests and the leisure of the normal worker, and if they succeed in capturing his loyalty and his imagination, they will be able to play an even greater part in his life when industrial depression returns and the "normal" man is again out of work. Indeed, until these or something like them are provided, any period of depression will lead to that hasty and inadequate improvisation such as the last slump brought with it, and in that way the provision of community centres in prosperous areas has a close bearing on unemployment. But the residually unemployed demand—except in the case of the elderly man who is not really unemployed but retired—specialized treatment, and it is certain that a community centre, in the sense in which the term is generally used, is not the institution to provide it.

(*b*) STAFFING AND FINANCE

If the account we have given of the club movement, and the suggestions which we have made about its future in the previous section are accepted, it means that something which is of permanent value, but which is different in character and purpose from what was envisaged when the clubs were started is gradually coming into being through them. On this view we may call the clubs "experiments in social organization for developing personality", and as the results of the experimental stage begin to crystallize, there are several important issues which will have to be faced. Our account must have made it clear that in our view the clubs that already have what might be called permanent survival value are only a relatively small number, and that considerable modifications will probably have to take place in the form and purpose of the rest if they are to be permanent; but that this number represents a new and original contribution which it may be hoped will be the beginning of a much more comprehensive movement. If this is so, several important conclusions follow. It means that we ought to begin to think in terms of a permanent organization. Both in staffing and finance the "movement" at present is temporary in character, and this is obviously a handicap to progress. It means that jobs in "social service" have no security of tenure behind them, and that no one who is responsible for the direction of social service work can look ahead more than a few months.

With regard to the first of these two issues, that of staffing, we understand that the organizations concerned are already giving it careful consideration. One or two points, however, may perhaps usefully be stressed. Our contacts with those who are doing field work have shown, if there was any need of showing, what great opportunities for personal work of an outstandingly useful and rewarding kind are offered by it. But it is, as much as any profession could be, a vocation, and efficiency or ambition are no substitute whatever in it for selflessness. Until the nature of the possibilities is more widely known, the chances of attracting the right men and women into it will be smaller than they ought to be, considering its promise.

Yet, however much emphasis is placed on the necessity for something akin to inspiration, it is no good expecting men who have family responsibilities to take up such work, unless some reasonable security is offered them. This involves not only some assurance of the permanency of the jobs concerned, but also, if possible, some pensions scheme. Until these are provided, social service will be a profession that many who might do well in it will have to refuse. The salaries paid in some places are still very low, and the authorities can hardly expect to attract really good men if they are not prepared to pay more than £200 a year. Good local committees have recognized this, and prefer wisely to put their money into men rather than into buildings. Security of employment would be more easily attainable if there were a greater degree of co-ordination among the various departments of social service than is at present possible, and there would be a strong case for treating them as a single whole, not only for purposes of salaries and pensions but also to reach some degree of interchangeability.[1] This does not necessarily mean that salaries ought to be standardized, though it might be well to fix certain minimum rates. There is something to be said for allowing a fair degree of elasticity in view of the great variety in character of the jobs concerned. At present many appointments

[1] The idea that some Civil Servants concerned with social problems might be seconded from time to time for social work of a voluntary kind is well worth consideration. A close liaison between official and unofficial effort is obviously essential, and this might be a good way of bringing the two together. It is already happening unofficially and the results are valuable to both sides.

are made in a somewhat casual way, and there is reason to think that the field is often not as good as it might be if the profession were regarded rather more as a whole.

Some people have evidently drifted into social service because they have no special qualifications for anything, and this is not the best introduction to it. We have had no means of judging whether the diploma courses in Social Service offered by some of the Universities are the best preparation for this particular kind of work, but several Wardens of Settlements emphasized the view that what was needed in addition was "experience, it did not matter what form it had taken". They felt that the man or woman who went into social service, after working for a substantial period on some perhaps quite different line, was far better equipped than those who went into it straight from the University. Others said that the most important part of training was a period of temporary service under a Warden of long experience, and it has been suggested that the provision of bursaries which make the extension of this arrangement possible, would be a great contribution to the solution of the difficulty of providing adequately trained staffs.

Because this work is of a peculiarly exacting kind, there is much to be said for organizing it in such a way that a "sabbatical year" is possible from time to time. A complete change of environment may be of the greatest value to those engaged on such work, while at the same time fresh contacts with social workers in other parts of the country, or abroad, can provide the new stimulus and inspiration which is one of the main requirements for the effectiveness of what they do. If endowments could be provided to make this possible, they would be undoubtedly a source of strength to the movement as a whole. Clearly all these things depend on the recognition that a permanent service is being created.

One suggestion which has been made seems to us to be worth full consideration, the suggestion that social service needs an "episcopacy". At present the central organization is to a very large extent preoccupied with administrative detail. Many of those who are working in the field said how warmly they would welcome the visits of experienced people who could talk over their problems and methods in a general way without having to spend their time dealing only with immediate details. It is not casual visitors who are wanted, but rather those who can spend perhaps several days in a place giving help and encouragement. This is a task in which men and women of ripe experience, who have recently retired from routine work of one kind or another, might be most valuable. They would obviously need to be chosen with great care, but they might make a most useful contribution to the movement. Especially while experiments are still being carried out in many different places, there is pressing need for thinking and advice, and for comparison between one scheme and another. It must be done, if at all, in a leisurely way, and an interminable rush from one club to another, collecting and confusing superficial impressions, is not what is wanted.

Signs of the makeshift character of the movement in its early stages are as apparent with its finance as with its staffing. Unemployment, and particularly long unemployment, was a new problem, or at least a problem more keenly felt than ever, within a community that had not the time to evolve settled methods of dealing with it. Institutions that were deeply concerned about unemployment but had also to concentrate on other tasks had neither the men nor the hold over unemployed people to step into the gap; an extension of ordinary charitable activities was not only inadequate but also impracticable as the ordinary requirements were at the same time swelling and straining the existing provisions to the utmost.

The need was well defined. The task was national. But with unemployment everywhere it was clear from the beginning that the main direction of any policy would have to be in the hands of regional bodies acquainted with the industrial and social conditions of their region, and also able to devise appropriate methods for eliciting a maximum of voluntary local financial help for the centres. These regional associations—twenty of them—have remained the administrative mainstay of the movement, and their financial contribution is by no means negligible even now, £11,000 being raised annually directly by the

Regional Councils, and in many cases the Councils have also been instrumental in the success of many a local committee's or club committee's appeal for financial help. The financial status of the Regional Councils has been considerably raised by the appointment of the Commissioner for the Special Areas whose grant to the National Council for Social Service is, naturally, reserved for the Special Areas and is largely administered by the five Regional Councils in the Special Areas of England and Wales. Models of this type of "strong regional body", which is the main source of financial support to the local clubs and also of specialized services and advice, are the Community Service Council for Durham County and the Tyneside Council of Social Service. On the regional bodies devolved more or less naturally the provision for the specialized club services, such as skilled instructors, which individual clubs or even town councils often could not afford. The Commissioner also made a considerable direct grant to one of the Regional Councils for new premises.

Where strong local town councils or—as in South Wales, the Valley Settlements—are intermediaries between the regional body and the individual clubs and where they are instrumental in supplying specialized services, they command both a number of voluntary contributions and also some direct access to the public purse, thus attaining a high degree of financial independence. Thus the Commissioner for the Special Areas in England and Wales made, in the year ended September 1937, grants towards the capital expenditure and maintenance of five Settlements amounting to over £18,000.

The smallest individual financial unit is, of course, the club. In our description of the movement in the six towns of the sample we have already seen how different are the growths which this common term covers; if we take only the Rhondda and Liverpool clubs, the former may be described as nearly a spirit without a body, the latter typically a formidable body but not always inhabited by a spirit. In financial terms this means that the one is a hand-to-mouth organization, resembling in this way one of the innumerable local slate or Christmas clubs, whereas the other may be a large-scale and complex financial enterprise. The financial dependence of the one club may be restricted to the gift of some books and a wireless, a share in the advantages of wholesale buying of leather and timber, and the free supply of skilled instruction for the club leaders at a Settlement or Residential College. The other club may have a financial sub-committee of the Management Committee, the building fund may have been brought together by the co-operation of five or six different bodies, the permanent Warden may draw his salary from outside the movement, there may be a substantial "special grant" for expansion, adaptation and equipment, there may be paid instructors in the club, several at a time, and even the maintenance and running of the club may be subsidized by "principal subscribers" and benevolent friends. There are clubs where membership means "giving something for nothing", and there are clubs where membership means "getting something for nothing", or for very little, for the member's contribution is generally a compulsory feature. We do not feel that the spirit of a club and its human success is conditioned entirely, or even mainly, by economic position. The ideal of a "poor" club, where the men are proud of the wooden hut they have built themselves, on ground levelled by their work, where they are masters, bowing only to the decisions of their acknowledged friends and experts or the majority of their fellows, is in itself neither a more nor a less valuable part of the permanent contribution of the club movement to community life than the ideal "rich" club, sufficiently well endowed to give the unemployed the best opportunities for technical and educational instruction that can be offered in our present state of knowledge, in well-equipped surroundings, with possibly something akin to the discipline of working life and a standard of work which is attractive even to the craftsman type of worker who would rather do nothing than be responsible for primitive and inferior work.

Club work was necessarily planned on a local basis, and it was further soon discovered that money which would not be forthcoming for an idea would be forthcoming for an actual club, for a concrete experiment, for the men in a particular locality. Elsewhere we have tried to show some of the effects of the system of adoption. But in a comparison of adoption and other systems of finance it should not be forgotten that adoption has in the first stages of the movement not been just a different method of financing, but that it has increased enormously the total money available for the work which is to be done. What is more, by mobilizing the latent good will of the community and its sense of responsibility towards the unemployed, this method of financing has contributed to the furtherance of that ultimate ideal which the movement has as a whole: in the best cases, where the adopting body was a local firm or corporation, it has led to a definite and personal association between the unemployed members and the staffs of the adopting body. In these cases the method of financing clubs by organizing direct and regular assistance to individual clubs has at the same time been one first step in a direction in which the movement is now beginning to march, and which is indicated by the term "community centres". It is a paradoxical fact that while in some small way the financial device of adoption has contributed to a development away from "segregation" of the unemployed in special clubs, in another sense it is an obstacle. The movement has in its early years been very largely built on these voluntary local contributions, to the extent of £65,000, during the financial year ended in March 1937. These funds have come through the special appeal of unemployment and the desire to "do something about it". It is difficult to imagine the idea of "social centres" or "community centres" exercising a similar appeal. Indeed, in the last few years of falling unemployment, there has been a marked decline in these voluntary funds. This decline, which has been made good by the activities of the Commissioner for the Special Areas, has amounted to a shift. The movement which in the beginning was predominantly voluntary has become, as far as finance is concerned, a mixed statutory-voluntary one.

Here we touch the vital problem in the finance of the movement. We saw that there was the local voluntary effort, working through the Regional Councils, Town Councils, and Club

Committees. The statutory local contributions, namely the local Education Committee grants for certain "qualifying" activities, were insignificant compared with the voluntary efforts. The addition of club work among the unemployed to the statutory system for dealing with unemployment, introduced obviously an essentially different type of work, for which the Ministry itself both for administrative and psychological reasons was not fitted. On the other hand it was clear from the beginning that the financial help of the Ministry was indispensable and highly desirable. Thus the financial status of the Central Body for the club movement—the National Council for Social Service—has been largely built on the administration and allocation of the public money going into the movement. Of the grants and expenditure made by the National Council, amounting to about £126,000 during the twenty-seven months from January 1935 to March 1937, about £80,000 or 64% was from the Ministry's fund.

This financial structure of combining local voluntary effort on a regional basis with a national body entrusted with directing public money into the proper channels has been successful from every point of view. The contact between the statutory and the voluntary agencies has been fruitful for both parties. There has been no question that the acceptance of a Government grant meant deflexion from a voluntary character. Perhaps never before in the history of public administration has public money been handed over to an unofficial body with fewer restrictions and conditions, with no cause for regret and little reason to suspect a misuse of the taxpayers' money. From the Ministry's point of view the grant has been payment for the undertaking of a difficult job—particularly in the first stages of trial and error—a job of value and significance for the community as a whole but with a close ultimate relevance to its own departmental work: a payment for having it done for them by an organization free from official responsibilities; a payment for the great financial and moral voluntary resources enlisted by the movement on this job; a payment for the opportunity of studying the difficulties of this kind of work, observing its natural tendencies, and remaining free all the time to decide when and where to step in. The taxpayer can rest assured that he has struck a very reasonable bargain.

The grant has meant a substantial addition to the movement's resources, the establishment of a central fund which can even out the inequalities of local contributions, specially useful where general impoverishment did not admit of a self-supporting local movement. It meant capital expenditure on hundreds of new centres which could maintain themselves or could be maintained on voluntary funds, but could not afford the initial capital expenditure for building and equipment. It meant a rise in the quality of the work that could be done in the clubs, for it meant the Residential Colleges where the leaders in the clubs could get better and more intensive instruction than could be given in a club. It meant also contact with the official mind and the application of official knowledge and experience to the movement, the introduction of official "tidiness" and the prevention of a chaotic muddle as a result of the healthy local variety, with nobody knowing what the other was doing. So it was certainly a reasonable bargain for the movement, all the more so as no sacrifice of principle was required.

There seem, then, to be two main factors that have to be considered in relation to the future financing of the movement. The first is the possibility that, in a year's time, the Special Commissioner's position may be substantially modified by a revision of the Act which governs it, or may even cease to exist. How important that will be for the voluntary movement can be realized from the fact that many of the South Wales Settlements owe their existence, substantially, to the grants made to them from the Special Commissioner's fund, as has been mentioned above. The Settlement with which the sample brought us chiefly into contact is indeed an exception, but many of the newer settlements would be in great difficulties if support from official funds was not forthcoming; and if this means that their Wardens will have to undertake, in addition to work that is already exacting, the task of raising large sums of money, their position will be impossible. How then are the Settlements and other social organizations in the Areas which are largely supported by the Commissioner's money to continue if this grant should be withdrawn?

The second factor which is already to some extent operative is the decline of adoption, and the reason for it. In some instances adopting bodies are beginning, with the revival in employment, to wonder whether the money they are subscribing is still a vital necessity. It was much easier to "make the case" for extensive private contributions to unemployed clubs when unemployment was at its height than at a time when it is decreasing, and when some of the clubs supported by such money are becoming clubs for employed as well as unemployed. For though, in our view, these clubs are doing work that is more valuable, its character is of a kind that does not lend itself easily to the "compassionate appeal". While it ought to be possible, then, to continue to raise money on compassionate grounds for clubs in areas of residual unemployment, money for the community centre type of club may have to be found in some other way; or rather, where possible, adopting bodies will have to be "educated" to see the value of supporting an effort which is cultural and is not simply confined to making temporary provision for the unemployed.

There will almost certainly have to be found, therefore, large sums of money in the not very distant future, if the movement is to continue. One thing which is abundantly clear is that they will not be found until the character of the movement is made explicit. People like to know how the money which they give is going to be used, and they are justified in wanting to know it. And it is unlikely that enough will be forthcoming, without State assistance, for the work to develop as it should. Voluntary subscriptions will always be an essential if new experiments are to be tried as they ought to be. But it looks as though the State, which is already, through the local education authorities, making a substantial contribution to the work of the clubs and settlements mainly by the provision of instructors, ought gradually to enlarge that responsibility as the work itself comes to justify such a change. When that happens it is a first necessity that the greatest possible degree of independence and freedom should be preserved. The analogy of the Government's contributions to the club movement during the first few years proves that the maintenance of a large measure of freedom is not incompatible with financial support from the State, and the way in which State contributions are paid to certain voluntary associations (such as the Workers' Educational Association and the Y.M.C.A.) for adult education provides a fair parallel. It is obviously desirable that, with this movement, too, the grant should come centrally, through one or other of the voluntary bodies concerned with it.

Our survey of the work done by the voluntary agencies for the unemployed ends therefore with a question. Can it become the foundation for a new system to be built, in which men will find opportunities to develop new interests, and new friendships through them? Unemployment has shown how great is the need for such a system; how hitherto the worker has been given little chance, and perhaps left little time, for developing his personality beyond the range of his work and of his family. Long unemployment, accompanied by any measure of insecurity, will always make it more difficult for him to use such chances fully, but if he has formed interests deep enough, and friendships close enough, when he is employed, they will stand the strain of unemployment. And they will be able to make it, unless it is drawn out too long, a time of recreation, and a time of hope.

Appendix I

RESIDUAL AND INDUSTRIAL UNEMPLOYMENT

One obvious difference between men affecting their way of life, their outlook, and their personal and economic problems is their Marital State. The following table contains for the sample date in November 1936 an estimate of the numbers of men, made for each age group separately, who are either (*a*) married and living with their wives, or (*b*) single, widowed, separated or divorced, and it brings out at once one of the differences between residual and industrial unemployment:

TABLE LXVIII. ESTIMATED MARITAL STATE

	South and Midlands		Wales and North (outside Special Areas)		In Special Areas[1]	
	(*a*)	(*b*)	(*a*)	(*b*)	(*a*)	(*b*)
Very young and young 18–34	3,300 (67 %)	1,600 (33 %)	24,100 (60 %)	16,100 (40 %)	15,300 (56 %)	12,300 (44 %)
Middle aged 35–44	4,000 (69 %)	1,800 (31 %)	17,700 (85 %)	3,000 (15 %)	17,600 (74 %)	6,300 (26 %)
Elderly 45–54	6,200 (56 %)	4,900 (44 %)	13,000 (72 %)	5,100 (28 %)	19,200 (74 %)	6,700 (26 %)
Old 55–64	12,700 (56 %)	10,200 (44 %)	16,500 (64 %)	9,400 (36 %)	15,700 (68 %)	7,500 (32 %)
All long-unemployed men	26,200 (58 %)	18,500 (42 %)	71,300 (68 %)	33,600 (32 %)	67,800 (67 %)	32,800 (33 %)

(*a*) = with wives; (*b*) = single, widowed, separated, divorced.

A comparison of the proportions of men living with wives and without, shows that, for the age groups over 35, there is a much lower proportion of men living with their wives in the South with residual

[1] Of England and Wales, that is, Durham and Tyneside, South Wales, and West Cumberland. The total number of long-unemployed men there at the date of the sample—100,600—is a safe estimate based on official figures given by the Special Commissioner for July 1936. The table, as far as the Special Areas are concerned, is based on the sample data in Crook and the Rhondda.

unemployment than in Wales and the North with their mainly industrial unemployment.[1] This suggests that there is a connexion between marital state and residual unemployment, in that there is more residual unemployment among men living on their own than among family men. Figures can only state this fact, and they do not show us which is cause and which effect: Is this residuum recruited from those low grades which fail both to succeed in industrial life and in personal life by founding a family? Or is it an element of unsociability in this group? Or does a man who lives on his own deteriorate more rapidly once he falls out of work, and is he thus more likely to remain in the queue? Or does he relax in his search for work more easily than does the family man? Or is it simply the result of heavier emigration of unmarried men from areas with industrial unemployment? The sample visits suggested that it is something of all these factors rather than any single one of them.

For the men under 35, it is significant that among the residual element there appears to be a higher proportion of married men, and we shall not be far wrong if we take this as an indication that wherever a young man in the South and the prosperous parts of the Midlands fails, for any considerable time, to find work, this is not due to any absolute difficulty in finding work, but is a question of low wages.[2] Even men of very low industrial quality find it easy to get work if they are in a position to accept what is a living wage for a young single man; the young family man, however, has difficulties when he has to insist on the higher wage appropriate to his circumstances. And the table thus suggests that the risk of long unemployment for the young family men in the South is definitely higher than the extremely low figures (1 and 2 per 1,000) which have been shown to be ruling for the young men as a whole. The impressions gained from visits suggest too that some of this surprising difference is due to the fact that young men, instead of improving their industrial quality, will often break an apprenticeship and rush into early marriage, perhaps influenced by the fact that the new unemployment allowance

[1] It should be added here that perhaps the percentage of men *not* living with their wives is slightly overstated, mainly in the highest age group, because it is partly based on conditions in Deptford which has the attraction of the L.C.C. lodging-house for lonely old men. This does not, however, explain the full difference, and it is, moreover, offset by a compensating factor in the North and Wales, where Council relief work and Special Commissioner's schemes which were counted as breaking long unemployment for the purposes of the sample, tended to favour family men and thus leave the sample with a high proportion of the category (*b*).

[2] This is discussed in detail above, pp. 193 and 201.

exceeds the old apprentice's or assistant's wage, and thus they will permanently spoil their working chances.

The preceding table showed separately the numbers of long-unemployed men, at various ages, and divided the family men from the others, in those districts with very little unemployment where the unemployed man is comparatively isolated (South and Midlands), in districts with a fairly high degree of unemployment though with the great majority of men working (North and Wales, outside the Special Areas), and in districts with widespread unemployment and little industrial hope for the unemployed (the Special Areas). These are key figures which, though not hitherto available, are indispensable for seeing in their quantitative proportion the various problems with which both the State and the voluntary agencies dealing with unemployment are faced. For many of them can be stated in terms of these three determinants: age, marital state, district. The solitary old man in a prosperous place--and there are 10,000 such men—is one definite problem for the Club movement. The unmarried young man in the Special Areas is the main object of transference policy, and the table shows their number to be still in excess of 12,000. Family transference, the policy for the middle-aged family men there, has to reckon with over 17,000 men. The process of getting the young man under 35 in the South into employment by individual placing is one which concerns 5,000 men. How many elderly men in the North who are continuously out of work could accept low wages for a probationary period because of their family status? The table suggests a figure of 5,000. The elderly family man outside the prosperous South is the object of many Social Service Schemes, Allotment Schemes, and Subsistence Production. Their number is 13,000. And there are other problems too: that of securing well-paid jobs for the middle-aged family men, who would otherwise lose by getting work and would not cover their basic needs; that of compulsory training for the young single man; these problems can be seen in their numerical dimensions.

The lesson of this analysis is important: the problem of the long-unemployed man, even if we consider it separately only with these three most important distinctions—age, marital state, and degree of unemployment—tends immediately to show innumerable facets, each with an entirely different set of issues raised, each of them important in numbers, but none of them overwhelmingly important so as to have a claim to be considered as the "dominant" problem in long unemployment.

Maintaining the fundamental division of the long unemployed

between the "residual" and the "industrial" groups, we may now proceed, with the help of the sample, to assess the importance of both sectors from the industrial point of view as potential labour reserve. The assessments on which the following information is founded have been made as a result of the visits to the men who happened to be caught in the net of our sample. Legally, any man in receipt of Unemployment Assistance, as were all the men in our sample, must be "fit and available for work". The question of "availability" also raises the problem of those unemployed for psychological rather than physical reasons, and this is dealt with in other parts of this Report. Here we deal with "fitness"—bodily and mental fitness. This investigation is not made superfluous by the legal qualification mentioned above. There are various degrees of fitness, and various degrees of restriction. There is indeed no hard and fast borderline between an "employable" man and an "unemployable" man, and, apart from this, under the pressure of economic conditions and social necessities, the statutory agencies have pursued deliberately the policy of putting a generous interpretation on the "capability" clause.[1]

The "industrial value" of a man will be different according as to whether we consider his present value for immediate re-employment or his ultimate value after suitable preparation and care. The immediate value is that which is decisive for private industry carried on for profit, on which most of the men must depend for re-employment. The most important consideration there, if we neglect for a moment the small group of men who do not come up mentally to the minimum standards of industry, is the present physical state of a man. And this is the criterion which is used in Table II.

The first thing this table shows is that of the total of 250,000 long-unemployed men in England and Wales at the end of 1936 only just over one half, some 130,000, were free from restrictions as to their immediate employability for ordinary industry, while there was a body of some 50,000 men at the other end of the scale who were definitely unacceptable to industry in their present state, the majority of them having some "obvious physical defect". Some light has been shed on this state of affairs in other parts of this report, which deal with standards of life and the mental and physical consequences of prolonged unemployment.

The second is that residual unemployment contains a substantially

[1] This is evident from the fact that, on the Ministry of Labour's own assessment, some proportion of the persons recorded as unemployed were classified as unemployable (in several samples of the register).

TABLE LXIX.

	Immediately eligible for re-employment under normal conditions		Immediately eligible for re-employment under great pressure or abnormal conditions only, e.g. lower wages	Not immediately eligible for ordinary re-employment		Total
	Very fit	Fit	Out of condition	Unfit	Obvious physical defects	
Residual Long Unemployment						
Numbers	4,700	26,900	26,900	5,600	13,200	77,300
	31,600			18,800		
Out of 100 in that group	6	35	35	7	17	100 %
	41			24		
Industrial Long Unemployment						
Numbers	13,700	86,400	42,100	11,800	18,700	172,700
	100,100			30,500		
Out of 100 in that group	8	50	24	7	11	100 %
	58			18		
Total	18,400	113,300	69,000	17,400	31,900	250,000
Out of 100	7	45	28	7	13	100 %
	52			20		

lower proportion of men who are immediately acceptable for re-employment, though it must be borne in mind that the majority of the men in this residual group live in the South and Midlands, where abnormal conditions, such as a pronounced scarcity of labour, may lead to a lowering of the standards by which industry determines acceptability. The difference between the two groups may fairly be taken as an indication that a poor physique is one of the factors behind residual unemployment.[1] Even in the group of industrial long unemployment, however, there is a substantial proportion (18 %) of men who are in their present state not acceptable to industry,

[1] Part of the difference is due to the higher proportion of elderly and old men among the residual group, where the state of physical fitness will be shown to be lower; but even after "standardizing" the figures, i.e. allowing for the age factor, there remains a genuine difference between the two groups.

representing over 30,000 men, and an even higher number of men who will be rejected as long as there is a plentiful supply of fitter men in the North and in Wales. Among that half of the long unemployed which alone represents an effective labour reserve (from the point of view of industry run for profit), the vast majority—100,000 men—owe their unemployment to industrial depression and economic friction. In particular, the effective labour supply among the wholly "residual" men in the Midlands and South is further reduced from some 44,700 long-unemployed men to some 18,400 fit men. It is clear that the concentration of long unemployment in certain parts of the country will become even more marked if we consider the men with standard industrial value among them. We saw that out of 100 long-unemployed men 18 live in the South; but for the men with high industrial value, this low figure is further reduced to 14.

Comparisons with other assessments, which have been made by investigators with a different outlook and possibly on different standards, are dangerous. But there is one comparison at this point which cannot be omitted, though it is made with every reservation. Two sample studies of Physical Health of the unemployed on the register, made by the Ministry of Labour in February 1931 and October 1934, left no doubt that there had been a considerable deterioration:

MEN

	1931	1934
Physique good	73·5	66·0
fair	23·3	29·2
poor	3·2	4·8

At the same time there was a marked difference between the short unemployed (on Insurance), the men on "transitional payments" as they were called at that time, and the Non-claimants, most of them Public Assistance cases.

MEN: 1934

	On insurance	On transitional payments	Non-claimants
Physique good	75·5	59·9	46·5

The second of these groups, the men on "transitional payments", are the group to whom we must look for a comparison, for they are the forerunners of the Unemployment Assistance Board register from which our sample was drawn. In the two years following the Ministry of Labour sample, the proportion of men with good physique has further diminished from 59·9 to 52%. Whether or not the two groups were enumerated on a comparable basis cannot be decided definitely. There is some reason to believe that the Ministry's standard has been stricter than that applied by the present investigators, and the change during the past two years would in that case be more considerable than the difference between the two figures just mentioned.

A valuation of the industrial and social usefulness of the long-unemployed men, which is suggestive both of the prospects of the long-unemployed man and of the appropriate "treatment" for him, may be made by considering his potential, instead of his present, industrial value. In making it, we have taken into consideration physique, intelligence, and employment history as it appears in our records, and the estimate is based on the picture of the man which they give. It was not specifically noted at the interviews themselves. For such a valuation, temporary obstacles which might easily be removed by refitting, good food, exercise, the mental effects of work and security, and perhaps some indulgence at the earlier stages of re-employment are discounted. Regarded from this social angle, many more men are employable ultimately, if not immediately: there may be serious restrictions on their employability on ordinary work for ordinary working hours at an ordinary working pace or at an ordinary wage, though they may still be useful at some special job. Quite apart from such men, there are of course some for whom no employer can be expected to have any use at any type of job. Again it seems useful to give separate figures for "residual" unemployment of the type and amount found in the South and Midlands (but "magnified" for the whole country, because it is underlying industrial unemployment elsewhere).

Thus we find that, taking this new standard, the number of potentially fully efficient workers among the long unemployed is increased from 131,700 (just over one-half) to 160,000 (just under two-thirds). 30,000 men, on our estimate, might be reclaimed for industrial society, in addition to those who are fully employable under present conditions, although it is, for the majority of them, not likely that they will have a chance to get back without some special measures. The number of "totally rejected" is brought down considerably in this new estimate, from nearly 50,000 to under 14,000—an indication that even the men with a "poor placing value", the unfits, and the men with physical defects, are by no means to be judged utterly unemployable. The real number of unemployables on this analysis (in which the possibility of a considerable margin of error must be

TABLE LXX.

	Fully employable	Employability restricted Mentally	Employability restricted Physically	Unem-ployable	Total
Residual Long Unemployment					
Number	40,000	7,700	23,500	6,100	77,300
		31,200			
Per 100	52	10	30	8	100
		40			
Industrial Long Unemployment					
Number	120,000	5,100	40,000	7,600	172,700
		45,100			
Per 100	69	3	23	5	100
		26			
Total	160,000	12,800	63,500	13,700	250,000
		76,300			
Per 100	64	5	25	6	100
		30			

admitted) would be comparatively small. This analysis strongly supports the Board's practice of keeping on the register the "unfits" and the "men with physical defects". A substantial number of these men might be reclaimed.

The composition of the two broad groups, the "residual" and the "industrial", is again seen to be significantly different. Even on this long view, only one-half of the residual group are fully employable, but over two-thirds of the industrial group. Only for one-quarter of the fully employable men is the problem that of residual and personal unemployment (including the age factor); in three-quarters of all cases it is an industrial problem. From Table III it can be seen also that a mental handicap is an important factor making for residual unemployment. One-tenth of the men that are (or would be) unemployed even if industrial prosperity were to return generally and if transference from declining to expanding industries were successfully carried through, do not mentally come up to the standard required by industry to-day, a standard which, incidentally, is constantly rising. The difference as between the two groups is much more marked among the mentally handicapped than among the physically handicapped, an indication that industries in times of prosperity and expansion will look to the physically slightly disabled men as a reservoir of labour rather than to the men with a low mentality.

The extent to which the long-unemployed men should really be regarded as "on the labour market" will be found, on reasonable standards, to be somewhere between these two figures of fully acceptable men; the "short view" figure of 130,000 and the "long view" figure of 160,000. The standard which seems most appropriate to present conditions is this:

"Any fully employable man in the South and Midlands up to 64. The men with physical restrictions up to 54.

"Any fully employable man in the North and Wales outside the Special Areas up to 54, and any man with physical restrictions up to 44.

"Any fully employable man in the Special Areas up to 54, but no one, in the Special Areas, with any restrictions of employability."

On this third standard we find, on the basis of the sample, that the total number of long-unemployed men who may be considered as on the labour market is 153,100, a figure between the two reached before as the number of fully acceptable men. This figure can perhaps be claimed to be a realistic count of the "labour reserve" among the long unemployed. It would mean that the long-unemployed men are separated into two broad groups, one group of over 150,000 (60%) who must still be considered as on the labour market, and one of just under 100,000 (40%) who must be considered as outside the ordinary labour market. In other words, there are about 100,000[1] long-unemployed men in England and Wales who, on any standard which takes into account economic realities, must be considered as outside the ordinary labour market. Some implications of this fact for the men concerned, as well as for the agencies working for them and for the community are apparent in the earlier sections of this Report.

The total proportion of long-unemployed men which has just been defined as outside the labour market is 40% of all men, but varies as between the three parts of the country which have been distinguished according to the degree of unemployment in them. In the South and Midlands, on our estimate, 31 out of 100 are outside the labour

[1] To this must be added, on a conservative estimate, some 15,000 men who have been long unemployed, but have not qualified for the receipt of Unemployment Assistance.

market, 33 in the North and in Wales outside the Special Areas, and 49 in the Special Areas. What this means is that the generally higher degree of fit or employable men, which has been shown to exist among the unemployed in districts with industrial depression, is more than offset by the inferior economic prospects in those districts as recognized, conservatively enough, in the standard used. One-half of these men with no appreciable chance of a return to industrial society are concentrated in the Special Areas.

TABLE LXXI. MEN OUTSIDE THE LABOUR MARKET

Where?	Who?	How many?	Of 100 long unemployed	Per 1,000 workers
South and Midlands	Unemployables, mentally insufficient, men over 55 with physical restrictions	13,900	31	3
North and Wales, outside the Special Areas	Unemployables, mentally insufficient, men over 45 with physical restrictions, all men over 55	34,100	33	12
The Special Areas	Unemployables, mentally insufficient, men with physical restrictions, all men over 55	49,200	49	58
England and Wales	—	97,200	40	11

A further step will give an idea of the waste inflicted by long unemployment. It has been shown that, industrially speaking, this waste is smaller than the aggregate figures would lead one to suggest, at least if we do not go behind the present state of affairs and attempt to see to what extent men are being reduced to the lower grades of employability by unemployment itself. We cannot deal here with this difficult question, with which the present investigators came in contact not less than other students in this field. But a fully employable man may still be of very different potential value, according to the grade of labour he might be fitted to perform with satisfaction to himself and to the community. A man with physical handicaps may still be a more useful worker than others who are vigorous and fit, if his industrial experience, intelligence and steadiness qualify him for a superior and responsible type of work. The question is, therefore, in what type of work, if any, would the best use be made of the unemployed man's personal qualities and inclinations? The answer, as estimated from the sample, is given, both for the residual and the industrial group, in the following table:

TABLE LXXII. SUITABILITY FOR VARIOUS KINDS OF WORK

	Skilled	Heavy	Light	No work	Total
Residual Long Unemployment					
Number	4,500	20,600	37,700	14,500	77,300
Of 100	6	27	49	18	100
Industrial Long Unemployment					
Number	20,700	89,100	43,900	19,000	172,700
Of 100	12	52	25	11	100
Total	25,200	109,700	81,600	33,500	250,000
Of 100	10	44	33	13	100

This table, apart from showing us the extent of the waste of men who might be skilled workers—over 25,000 of them—or of men who might do heavy work—over 100,000 (together more than one-half of the long unemployed belong to these industrially most valuable types)—is useful in giving a clear idea of the different type of men unemployed in prosperous areas, and the "industrial" long-unemployed queues. In the first group, less than one-third of the men are capable of skilled or heavy work, whereas in the second group the proportion is nearly two-thirds. For the men capable of skilled or heavy work, the problem is predominantly one of industrial unemployment (81%; only 19% in the residual group), but for the men incapable of these types of work, the problem is a residual as well as an industrial one (55% in the industrial group, 45% in the residual group).

The other important distinguishing factor, apart from the two types of long unemployment, is that of age. The sample shows that not only from the point of view of social policy, but even from an industrial point of view, the waste involved in long unemployment of younger men is considerably more serious than in the case of the older men.

The figures are as follows:

TABLE LXXIII

	Total number	Fully employable	Employability restricted	Unemployable
Very young or young	72,700	60,600	11,400	700
Per 100	100	84	15	1
Middle-aged	50,400	34,800	13,500	2,100
Per 100	100	69	27	4
Elderly	55,100	31,700	19,700	3,700
Per 100	100	58	35	7
Old	71,800	32,900	31,700	7,200
Per 100	100	46	44	10
All	250,000	160,000	76,300	13,700
Per 100	100	64	30	6

The connexion between age and industrial employability is very striking. Of the youngest age group, more than five-sixths are fully employable, among the old men less than half. There is a marked difference in age between the fully employable men (where the figures tend to fall in the higher ages), the group with restricted employability (where the figures rise steadily), and the entirely unemployable men (where they rise rapidly).

TABLE LXXIV. AGE DISTRIBUTION OF GROUPS WITH VARYING EMPLOYABILITY

	Of 100 fully employable men	Of 100 men with restricted employability	Of 100 unemployables
Very young and young	38	15	5
Middle-aged	22	18	15
Elderly	20	26	27
Old	20	41	53
Total	100	100	100
Average age about	39	51	55 years

It has already been shown that the totally unemployable men are only a very small part of the queues, and also a small part only of that proportion of the queues which must be considered as outside the labour market if economic realities are taken into account. Of this small number, of some 13,000 to 14,000 men, more than half are old workers over 55, an important qualification of the significance of the aggregate figures. The number of men under 45, who can be considered as entirely outside the labour market on personal grounds, is exceedingly small (some 3,000) and it is the men with some restriction on their employability (some 25,000, half of them under 35), who raise the real problems for the treatment of these younger men, such as the problems of refitting, special placing, reservation of light jobs, or wage subsidies.

On the other hand, the proportion of men mentally below the standard required by industry did not vary significantly as between different ages, being 4½ out of 100 men under 35, 6 in the middle-aged group, 5 in the elderly group and 6 in the old group. The absence of a rise in this type of restriction of employability which is in contrast with the marked rise in the other types, is remarkable and perhaps disquieting. For, considering that we have just seen that a higher proportion of mentally insufficient men is a distinguishing feature of residual, as opposed to industrial, unemployment, and that the proportion of this residual group is much higher among the older ages, we are forced to the conclusion that there are comparatively more mentally unstable and insufficient men among the younger unemployed; which means almost certainly that it is much more difficult for the young man of low mental grade to get a job now than it was formerly, when quickness was not perhaps so necessary as it is now, and when there was no "dole" as an alternative to low wages. At the other end of the scale, however, we find that the number of men of the higher grades of intelligence, fully up to good workers' standards, or better, was found to be rather higher among the younger men.

	Out of 100
Very young men	65
Young men	64
Middle-aged	62
Elderly	59
Old	58

It is perhaps not altogether wrong to see in these figures the traces of continued progress in education. The sample seems to indicate therefore that there are more young men in both the higher and lower mental grades of employability, compared with the older ages where mental qualifications are less widely scattered and more uniform, or at least, are more difficult to estimate in an interview. The marked difference in employability as between various ages is entirely due not to mental differences, but to differences in physique, by which the men in the sample have been classified with regard to their ultimate employability.

TABLE LXXV

	Outstanding physique	Good average physique	Doubtful physique	Sub-marginal physique
Of 100 young and very young men	24	51	22	3
	75		25	
Of 100 middle-aged	7	54	32	7
	61		39	
Of 100 elderly	7	41	39	13
	48		52	
Of 100 old men	4	38	42	16
	42		58	
Of all long unemployed in England and Wales	11	46	33	10
	57		43	
Numbers	27,300	114,700	83,400	24,600

The average age of the "upper tenth", the men with outstanding physical qualifications, is 31 years, of the lower tenth with a physique below the margin even desirable for normal light work it is 53 years.

Not less important are the differences between the status of men of different ages in a "reconstructive" analysis of the kind that has been undertaken above for the residual and industrial types. The following analysis distinguishes between various types of work, which these men could do with the greatest satisfaction to themselves and the highest value for the community.

Again the trends shown by the figures are unmistakable. The proportion of men who should be capable of the two higher types of work decreases steadily from five-sixths to less than one-third. On the basis of half a point for light work, one point for heavy work, two points for skilled work, we find that 100 men of various ages are worth the "efficiency unit" points given in Table X:

TABLE LXXVI. RECONSTRUCTIVE ANALYSIS

	Suitable for skilled work	Heavy work	Light work	No work	Total
Very young and young	11,000	49,600	10,600	1,500	72,700
No. per 100	15	68	15	2	100
	83				
Middle-aged	5,000	28,700	13,100	3,600	50,400
No. per 100	10	57	26	7	100
	67				
Elderly	4,900	24,800	18,100	7,300	55,100
No. per 100	9	45	33	13	100
	54				
Old	6,100	15,400	32,700	17,600	71,800
No. per 100	8	21	46	25	100
	29				
All	27,000	118,500	74,500	30,000	250,000
No. per 100	11	47	30	12	100

TABLE LXXVII. "WORTH" OF LONG UNEMPLOYED IN VARIOUS AGE GROUPS

	"Efficiency units"	Efficiency time units (see below)
Young and very young	100	100
Middle-aged	85	56
Elderly	75	30
Old	45	6
Average	79	—

Actually the concentration in the younger age groups of the social waste involved in unemployment is infinitely higher than that indicated by the efficiency unit count. For not only is the younger long unemployed capable of performing more valuable types of work, but he is also capable of performing them for a much longer time. The second column attempts to measure this factor by multiplying the efficiency units with the number of years during which their services can be performed. The enforced idleness of the 11,000 potential skilled workers under 35 among the long unemployed is a loss to the community which is, quite apart from human and social values, immense and actually immeasurable.

Appendix II

THE CASE RECORD CARD

NOTE (p. 414). In the space above General Remarks on the left-hand side a record of the usual wage was made. The Employment Record was obtained, where possible, for the last five years. A suggestion was made at the outset that men should be asked about the kind of employment they took immediately after leaving school, but this suggestion was dropped in deference to advice that it would prove impracticable. At a later stage in the visits when considerable experience of interviewing had been acquired, it was revived, with satisfactory results, and there is every reason to think that if details of this were required in some future investigation, they would be obtainable.

In the completed cards the "Unemployment Record" was not used. In so far as this unemployment record was not easily deduced from the Employment Record given immediately above, but attempted to secure additional information, it was found in practice to be unobtainable.

NOTE (p. 415). It was originally intended that a separate record should be kept showing leisure interests and activities, but this was possible only in a very limited number of cases.

The paragraphs marked "Industrial Transference" and "Industrial Training" were intended for a record not of a man's suitability for transference or training, but of his attitude towards them.

THE PILGRIM TRUST UNEMPLOYMENT ENQUIRY

CASE RECORD CARD

HOUSEHOLD CIRCUMSTANCES:

No.	Sex	Age	Rel.	Occupation or Status	Earnings	U.A.B. Allowance	Other Unemployment Relief	Other Social Income	Other Income
A									
2									
3									
4									
5									
6									
7									
8									
				Total					

GENERAL REMARKS:

Family Debts:

Rent: Rent Arrears

Contracted Payments

Meals Away

Travelling Expenses

Net Family Income

EMPLOYMENT RECORD:

	Dates Commencing	Dates Leaving	Occupation	Nature of Job	Place of Work	How Obtained	Reason for Leaving	Remarks
1								
2								
3								
4								
5								
6								
7								
8								
9								
10								

UNEMPLOYMENT RECORD:

	Date	Period	Form of Assistance	Complaints; Technical Offences, etc.
1				
2				
3				
4				
5				
6				
7				
8				

TABULATION

Appearance:

Health:

Health of Family:

Family Relations:

Domestic Standards:

Domestic Economy:

Children's Prospects:

Employability

Attitude to New Employment

Industrial Transference

Industrial Training

Social Institutions:	Membership Before	Membership After	Attitude
Trade Union			
Church			
Workmen's Club			
Friendly Society			
Co-op. Movement			
Adult Education			

Unemployment Welfare Schemes:

Amenity Schemes

Land Settlement

Allotments and Small-holdings

Poultry Schemes

Unemployed Clubs

Leisure:

Appendix III

THE STATE AGENCIES AND THE LONG UNEMPLOYED

The unemployed men in our sample were men who had worked in an insurable occupation and earned less than £5 a week. An "insurable occupation" meant until recently practically any kind of occupation in industry, commerce and distribution (except railways), but not agricultural occupations or personal service.[1] During employment such a man was a compulsory contributor to the Unemployment Insurance Scheme: this meant that his employer had to buy a special stamp on his behalf for every week during which (or part of which) this man was working for him, and to attach this stamp in the man's employment book which was in his care. Of the price of this stamp, 1*s.* 6*d.*, one-half came out of the employer's pocket, and the other half was kept back out of the man's own weekly or daily wage. The amount paid for his stamps was transferred to the Unemployment Insurance Fund. The Treasury added another 9*d.* for every 1*s.* 6*d.* received by the sale of stamps. Thus, as long as he was working, the stamps accumulated regularly in his book, the only blanks being for periods of illness, or for holidays—if there was a continuous week's holiday—or for periods of strikes and lock-outs. A single day's work meant the acquisition of a stamp.

When any of these men who were included in the sample was discharged, he was handed his employment book and went to the Employment Exchange to fill in a form, in which he claimed his contractual right to be indemnified for the loss of his job by the payment of a certain amount of money (determined by the composition of his family), just as anyone with an insurance policy will claim indemnification for the loss of a ship or a suitcase or a registered letter. The stamped employment book was his insurance policy. Nothing was however payable for the first six days after he filed his claim.[2] During this time his claim was examined, and finally he was found to

[1] Since our sample was taken, the circle of persons eligible for both insurance and assistance has been considerably widened.

[2] If he fell out of work to-day, he would only have to wait for three days.

be "eligible", that is to say, there were not too many blanks in his last employment books, and he had not thrown up his last job of his own accord. After being found to be "eligible" he was paid every week the contractual amount due to him, an amount reckoned as just sufficient to maintain him and those dependent on him. This payment was independent of his financial situation, and if there were any earnings, savings, pensions or other income in his family, in addition to the insurance payment, that made no difference to his right to receive it. His financial position was no more the concern of the clerk behind the Exchange counter than the clerk's affairs were his. On the other hand, if for some special reason the money paid out to him was not sufficient to keep his family from want, there was nothing but to turn to that last resource of Public Assistance, the old Poor Law. Apart from this experience, which he is very unlikely to have had, the only occasion when his affairs ceased to be his own business was when he had to "sign on", that is to say to attend at a certain hour in the morning (during normal working hours) at the Employment Exchange to show that he was not working then, or too ill to be "available" for any work he might find for himself or to which he might be sent by the Exchange. The fact that his employment book, which an employer has to stamp, is deposited with the Exchange was in itself a sufficient guarantee against his finding regular employment with a law-abiding employer while he was getting the insurance payment, but he might have gone off for a holiday instead of looking for work, or he might have earned his living by pushing a barrow, or he might have been working "black" for a low wage.[1] He was also expected to be "genuinely seeking work". This meant not only following up all jobs for which he was sent by the Exchange and doing his best to get them, but also making reasonable efforts on his own initiative. The payments were not to enable him to retire from industry for a time. "Signing on" and "looking for work" were the two things he was not free to do or to leave, and on which he was

[1] A recent official enquiry carried out in Aberdeen and Glasgow showed that in certain casual occupations the regulations were being extensively evaded. If a man says he has no employment book, he can be engaged on condition that an emergency book is taken out. It was found that in one Exchange area in Glasgow out of 2,044 books issued in 1936, 1,971 had apparently fictitious names. The men for whom these books were taken out were actually working, but evidently were drawing unemployment insurance or assistance as well. It is possible that several instances in the Liverpool sample in which it was suspected that the man was working, were of this kind. For particulars see *Port Labour in Aberdeen and Glasgow*, H.M. Stationery Office, 1937.

liable to be questioned. Of the money he was drawing, a certain part came from the public purse or other people's pockets, and during the depression it was the major part of his payment. But that did not diminish his status or his right to this payment, any more than any man's status suffers from having struck a lucky bargain with an insurance company, getting out of it more than he had paid in premiums, or from making a contract with a State-subsidized insurance company.

When he had been getting these payments for six months his rights under the insurance contract were exhausted and unless he happened to have a respectable pile of regularly stamped employment books, the payment from the contract was cut off. He was informed that he had ceased to be a "claimant" and if he wanted any further money he had to become a humbler "applicant", filling in a new form. What he then applied for might have had different names, according to the date of his application. It might have been called "Extended Benefit", or "Transitional Benefit" or "Unemployment Assistance" (which is what it is called to-day.) But beneath changing names and changing rules as to how the amount of money to be given was to be determined, the character of the payment remained the same: it was made in recognition of the fact that, although he had exhausted his contractual rights, he was in a different position from other persons who for some personal reason have exhausted or lost their contractual rights to a share in the social product of society, and are left to the charity of their local community.

He has remained a "claimant", for as long as he passes the various tests prescribed, he can be reasonably sure of his money and can defend himself against what he thinks is an unjustified interpretation of the rules to his disadvantage. But he has become an "applicant" in so far as the money he is living on is now clearly other people's money, given to him not in fulfilment of a contract, but only in fulfilment of the social responsibility to help the needy. And to the "genuinely seeking work" test and the "fit and available for work" test, there is now added a "family means" test. He is now compelled to state to the Unemployment Assistance Board's officer his own and his family's financial resources. There is also a "needs" test. Investigators come round to his home at fairly regular intervals and on special occasions—when he has made an application for some more money—and they try to form an idea of his requirements and living conditions. If he has kept by the rules, he has nothing to fear from these visits, as they can result in an addition to his allowance if he seems very hard up, but not in a decrease in it if he seems to manage fairly well.[1] He may have benefitted from this new test in money or other help, or he may not have benefitted from it. He may resent these visits as representing the lowering of his status or he may positively welcome them as a sign that the community takes an interest in him and as an opportunity for talking and "getting things off his chest". But the fact remains that stepping down from being a "claimant" to being an "applicant" has brought with it, in addition to the previous test, which did not touch more than the fringes of his life, two additional tests touching two vital spheres; the family income and its composition, the home and its requirements.

This has been the sequence of events for the majority of men in the sample, though there is a group of men for whom the intermediate stage of "claimant" between a worker and an "applicant" was omitted because the stamps in their employment books were too few to be a valid insurance policy.

[1] Except in the few cases where the visit of the investigator reveals household expenditure obviously incompatible with the revealed financial circumstances and, by tracing hidden resources, leads indirectly to a reduction in the applicant's allowance.

Appendix IV

MONEY REQUIREMENTS

Money Requirements according to Mr R. F. George's Standard, based on the London price level of July 1936. Excluding Rent.

Ages	Male	Female
	A. Food	
Over 70	4*s.* 1*d.*	4*s.* 1*d.*
14–70	6*s.* 9*d.*	5*s.* 9*d.*
6–14	5*s.* 5*d.*	5*s.* 5*d.*
Under 6	3*s.* 10*d.*	3*s.* 10*d.*
	B. Clothing	
Over 70	7*d.*	7*d.*
16–70	11*d.*	8*d.*[1]
Under 16	7*d.*	7*d.*

C. Cleaning materials and light

Families with one person	6*d.*
" two persons	8*d.*
" three "	10*d.*
" four "	1*s.* 0*d.*
" five or more persons	1*s.* 3*d.*

D. Fuel

Families with four persons or less	2*s.* 11*d.* (1¼ cwt.)
" five " more	3*s.* 6*d.* (1½ cwt.)

No provision is made for any expenditure other than the items shown above.

[1] In Mr George's standard he has reckoned the needs of single women between the ages of 16 and 30 as 1*s.* 0½*d.* We have not adopted this modification.

Appendix V

STATISTICAL TABLES

A1. AGE DISTRIBUTION OF SAMPLE BY PLACE: MEN ONLY

Age	*18–24*	*25–34*	*35–44*	*45–54*	*55–64*	TOTAL
Deptford	2	4	13	20	53	92
%	2	4	14	22	58	100
Leicester	1	8	13	21	46	89
%	1	9	15	23	52	100
Liverpool	27	70	68	52	56	273
%	10	26	25	19	20	100
Blackburn	2	18	47	23	33	123
%	2	15	38	19	26	100
Crook	3	29	31	27	29	119
%	3	24	26	23	24	100
Rhondda	15	52	55	66	54	242
%	6	22	23	27	22	100
Whole sample	50	181	227	209	271	938
%	5	19	24	22	30	100

A2. NUMBER OF DEPENDENTS BY PLACE: MEN ONLY

Dependents	0	1	2	3	4	5 or more	TOTAL	Dependents per 100 applicants
Deptford	47	26	11	3	4	1	92	84
%	51	29	12	3	4	1	100	
Leicester	29	30	8	5	3	12	87	172
%	33	34	9	6	4	14	100	
Liverpool	74	49	51	29	27	43	273	225
%	27	18	19	11	10	15	100	
Blackburn	43	39	12	16	4	9	123	145
%	35	32	10	13	3	7	100	
Crook	20	36	30	17	5	11	119	183
%	17	30	25	15	4	9	100	
Rhondda	77	68	44	24	10	19	242	154
%	32	28	18	10	4	8	100	
Whole Sample	290	248	156	94	53	95	936	171
%	31	26	17	10	6	10	100	

A 3. ENGTH OF UNEMPLOYMENT BY PLACE: MEN ONLY, EFFECTIVE RECORDS

Length of Unemployment	*1–2 years*	*2–3 years*	*3–4 years*	*4–5 years*	*Over 5 years*	TOTAL
Deptford	20	19	3	7	2	51
%	39	37	6	14	4	100
Leicester	17	16	15	11	26	85
%	20	19	18	13	30	100
Liverpool	51	51	41	48	56	247
%	21	21	16	19	23	100
Blackburn	12	9	13	15	51	100
%	12	9	13	15	51	100
Crook	9	9	7	6	77	108
%	8	8	7	6	71	100
Rhondda	25	38	25	41	100	229
%	11	16	11	18	44	100
Whole Sample	134	142	104	128	312	820
%	16	17	13	16	38	100

A 4. INCOME COMPOSITION BY PLACE: MEN ONLY

Income Composition	Mainly or wholly Unemployment Relief	Unemployment Relief supplemented by other income[1]	Unemployment Relief only supplementary to other income[2]	TOTAL
Deptford	53	15	22	90
%	59	17	24	100
Leicester	50	15	23	88
%	57	17	26	100
Liverpool	200	45	33	278
%	72	16	12	100
Blackburn	60	33	26	119
%	50	28	22	100
Crook	80	27	10	117
%	68	23	9	100
Rhondda	170	34	38	242
%	70	14	16	100
Whole Sample	613	169	152	934
%	66	18	16	100

[1] i.e. U.A. 50 %—75 % of total income.
[2] i.e. U.A. under 50 % of total income.

BY PLACE, MEN ONLY

Economic Level[1]	In Deep Poverty	In Poverty	On Subsistence Level	A little above the Poverty Line	Well above the Poverty Line	In Moderate Comfort	TOTAL
Deptford	10	11	18	14	30	7	90
%	11	12	20	16	33	8	100
	23		36		41		
Leicester	14	12	13	15	22	12	88
%	16	14	14	17	25	14	100
	30		31		39		
Liverpool	84	49	33	48	54	10	278
%	30	18	12	17	19	4	100
	48		29		23		
Blackburn	13	13	22	26	33	12	119
%	11	11	18	22	28	10	100
	22		40		38		
Crook	10	14	18	30	38	7	117
%	9	12	15	26	32	6	100
	21		41		38		
Rhondda	28	21	33	41	76	43	242
%	12	9	13	17	31	18	100
	21		30		49		
Whole Sample	159	120	137	174	253	91	934
%	17	13	15	18	27	10	100
	30		33		37		

[1] For details of this classification, see p. 109.

A6. FAMILIES BELOW THE "GEORGE" POVERTY LINE: INCOME COMPOSITION BY PLACE, MEN ONLY

Below Poverty Line	Families wholly dependent on Unemployment Relief (%)	Unemployment Relief supplemented by other income (%)	Unemployment Relief only supplementary to other income (%)	All families (%)
Deptford	37	7	—	23
Leicester	34	40	8	30
Liverpool	61	24	6	48
Blackburn	37	9	4	22
Crook	30	18	—	21
Rhondda	28	9	3	21
Whole Sample	41	17	3	30

A7. PHYSICAL STATE, BY PLACE: MEN ONLY, EFFECTIVE RECORDS

Physical State	Fit or very fit	Out of condition	Unfit or obvious physical defects	TOTAL
Deptford	21	30	23	74
%	28	41	31	100
Leicester	42	26	17	85
%	49	31	20	100
Liverpool	141	66	19	226
%	62	29	9	100
Blackburn	64	25	15	104
%	61	24	15	100
Crook	80	8	18	106
%	75	8	17	100
Rhondda	115	40	51	206
%	56	19	25	100
Whole Sample	463	195	143	801
%	58	24	18	100

A8. EMPLOYABILITY, BY PLACE: MEN ONLY, EFFECTIVE RECORDS

Employability	Fully employable	Restricted		Unemployable	TOTAL
		Mentally	Physically		
Deptford	39	5	21	4	69
%	57	7	30	6	100
Leicester	39	10	25	8	82
%	48	12	30	10	100
Liverpool	168	11	42	13	234
%	72	5	18	5	100
Blackburn	68	5	27	2	102
%	67	5	26	2	100
Crook	54	5	22	6	87
%	62	6	25	7	100
Rhondda	144	5	67	11	227
%	63	2	30	5	100
Whole Sample	512	41	204	44	801
%	64	5	26	5	100

A9. EMPLOYABLE QUALITY, BY PLACE: MEN ONLY, EFFECTIVE RECORDS

Potentially suitable for	Skilled work	Heavy unskilled work	Light unskilled work	No work	TOTAL
Deptford	3	22	34	15	74
%	4	30	46	20	100
Leicester	6	19	41	14	80
%	8	24	51	17	100
Liverpool	38	127	41	24	230
%	17	55	18	10	100
Blackburn	12	43	23	10	88
%	14	49	26	11	100
Crook	6	42	32	6	86
%	7	49	37	7	100
Rhondda	19	112	63	29	223
%	9	50	28	13	100
Whole Sample	84	365	234	98	781
%	11	46	30	13	100

A 10. DOMESTIC STANDARDS, BY PLACE: MEN ONLY, EFFECTIVE RECORDS[1]

Domestic Standards	House		Furniture		Clothing			Management		
	Clean	Dirty	Good	Bad	Good	Medium	Bad	Good	Medium	Bad
Deptford	55	6	52	8	Figures insufficient			23	—	2
%	90	10	87	13				92	—	8
Leicester	41	9	29	11	31	19	9	18	7	6
%	82	18	72	28	53	32	15	58	23	19
Liverpool	166	32	131	42	22	12	30	74	21	15
%	84	16	76	24	34	19	47	67	19	14
Blackburn	70	9	55	11	10	3	9	12	15	6
%	89	11	84	16	45	14	41	36	45	18
Crook	97	5	80	8	24	19	10	38	17	5
%	95	5	91	9	45	36	19	63	28	9
Rhondda	162	26	154	30	12	15	29	44	3	3
%	86	14	84	16	22	27	51	88	6	6
Whole Sample	591	87	501	110	99	68	87	209	63	37
%	87	13	82	18	39	27	34	68	20	12

[1] Owing to the obvious difficulties of comparison, these figures are put forward with reserve. There are technical reasons for thinking, for example, that the figures may underrate domestic standards in Leicester, as compared with other places. The proportions within each category, for each place taken separately, have much greater claims to accuracy than comparative figures between places.

A11. ATTITUDE TO NEW EMPLOYMENT, BY PLACE: MEN ONLY, EFFECTIVE RECORDS

Attitude to New Employment	Still thinking in terms of work	Beginning to accept state of Unemployment	Adjusted to state of Unemployment	TOTAL
Deptford	22	27	20	69
%	32	39	29	100
Leicester	19	44	24	87
%	21	51	28	100
Liverpool	81	91	56	228
%	36	40	24	100
Blackburn	27	31	35	93
%	29	33	38	100
Crook	27	40	18	85
%	32	47	21	100
Rhondda	45	91	55	191
%	24	48	28	100
Whole Sample	221	324	208	753
%	29	43	28	100

B1. NUMBER OF DEPENDENTS, BY AGE: MEN ONLY

Dependents	0	1	2	3	4	5 or more	TOTAL	Dependents per 100 applicants
Age 18–24	33	5	12	1	—	—	51	63
%	65	10	23	2	—	—	100	
25–34	50	23	47	28	16	17	181	201
%	28	13	26	15	9	9	100	
35–44	46	30	34	36	18	61	225	285
%	20	13	15	16	8	28	100	
45–54	62	61	37	18	14	17	209	166
%	30	29	18	8	7	8	100	
55–64	101	127	28	9	5	—	270	85
%	37	47	10	4	2	—	100	
ALL AGES	292	246	158	92	53	95	936	167
%	31	26	17	10	6	10	100	

B2. INCOME COMPOSITION, BY AGE: MEN ONLY

Income Composition	Mainly or wholly Unemployment Relief	Unemployment Relief supplemented by other Income	Unemployment Relief only supplementary to other Income	TOTAL
Age 18–24	31	7	13	51
%	62	13	25	100
25–34	148	16	17	181
%	82	9	9	100
35–44	146	47	29	222
%	66	21	13	100
45–54	113	49	47	209
%	53	24	23	100
55–64	174	50	46	270
%	65	18	17	100
ALL AGES	612	169	152	933
%	66	18	16	100

B3. AVERAGE AMOUNTS OF FAMILY INCOME, BY AGE AND SOURCE OF INCOME: MEN ONLY

Total family income	Unemployment Assistance of man in our sample and other Unemployment Relief	Other Social Income from Social Services of all kind	Earnings and Income from Capital, Savings	TOTAL FAMILY INCOME
Age 18–24	24*s.* 2*d.*	5*s.* 3*d.*	10*s.* 1*d.*	39*s.* 6*d.*
%	61	13	26	100
25–34	29*s.* 4*d.*	2*s.*	4*s.* 3*d.*	35*s.* 7*d.*
%	81	6	12	100
35–44	30*s.* 11*d.*	3*s.* 3*d.*	6*s.* 10*d.*	41*s.*
%	76	8	16	100
45–54	26*s.* 10*d.*	3*s.* 1*d.*	12*s.* 7*d.*	42*s.* 6*d.*
%	63	7	30	100
55–64	24*s.*	1*s.* 7*d.*	8*s.*	33*s.* 7*d.*
%	71	5	24	100
ALL AGES	27*s.* 3*d.*	2*s.* 8*d.*	8*s.* 2*d.*	38*s.* 1*d.*
%	72	7	21	100

B4. ECONOMIC LEVEL MEASURED BY THE "GEORGE" STANDARD, BY AGE: MEN ONLY

Economic Level[1]		In Deep Poverty	In Poverty	On Subsistence Level	A little above the Poverty Line	Well above the Poverty Line	In Moderate Comfort	TOTAL
Age 18–24		4	11	9	12	10	5	51
	%	8	21	18	23	20	10	100
		29		41		30		
25–34		48	28	25	36	36	8	181
	%	27	15	14	20	20	4	100
		42		34		24		
35–44		67	44	29	34	30	18	222
	%	30	20	13	15	14	8	100
		50		28		22		
45–54		30	15	30	33	76	25	209
	%	14	7	14	16	37	12	100
		21		30		49		
55–64		10	22	44	59	100	35	270
	%	4	8	16	22	37	13	100
		12		38		50		
ALL AGES		159	120	137	174	252	91	933
	%	17	13	15	18	27	10	100
		30		33		37		

[1] For details of this classification, see p. 109.

B5. ECONOMIC LEVEL MEASURED BY THE "GEORGE" STANDARD, BY INCOME COMPOSITION: MEN ONLY

Economic Level[1]		In Deep Poverty	In Poverty	On Subsistence Level	A little above the Poverty Line	Well above the Poverty Line	In Moderate Comfort	TOTAL
Income Composition: Families wholly or nearly wholly dependent on Unemployment Relief		142	101	114	122	126	8	613
	%	23	16	19	20	21	1	100
		39		39		22		
Families with supplementary other Income		14	14	17	41	60	23	169
	%	9	9	10	24	34	14	100
		18		34		48		
Families where Unemployment Relief is only supplementary Income		3	5	6	11	67	60	152
	%	2	3	4	7	44	40	100
		5		11		84		
ALL FAMILIES		159	120	137	174	253	91	934
	%	17	13	15	18	27	10	100
		30		33		37		

[1] For details of this classification, see p. 109.

B6. "STOP" WAGE[1], BY AGE: MEN ONLY

"*Stop*" *wage*	Lower Decile 90 % of men above	Lower Quartile 75 % of men above	Median 50 % of men above	Higher Quartile 25 % of men above	Higher Decile 10 % of men above
Age 18–24	16*s.*	25*s.*	32*s.*	45*s.*	50*s.*
25–34	32*s.*	40*s.*	45*s.*	50*s.*	60*s.*
35–44	40*s.*	45*s.*	50*s.*	55*s.*	60*s.*
45–54	40*s.*	45*s.*	50*s.*	55*s.*	65*s.*
55–64	40*s.*	45*s.*	50*s.*	57*s.*	65*s.*

[1] See p. 203.

B7. UNEMPLOYMENT ASSISTANCE BOARD ALLOWANCE, AMOUNT IN SHILLINGS AND PERCENTAGE OF AVERAGE STOP WAGE[2]

	Lower Decile 90 % of all men above	Lower Quartile 75 % of all men above	Median 50 % of all men above	Higher Quartile 25 % of all men above	Higher Decile 10 % of all men above
Age 18–24	14*s.*	15*s.*	24*s.*	29*s.*	29*s.* 6*d.*
%	41	44	71	86	87
25–34	17*s.*	26*s.*	29*s.* 6*d.*	34*s.* 6*d.*	38*s.*
%	38	58	61	77	84
35–44	17*s.*	27*s.* 6*d.*	33*s.* 6*d.*	41*s.*	44*s.*
%	34	55	67	82	88
45–54	17*s.*	17*s.*	26*s.*	32*s.*	38*s.* 6*d.*
%	33	33	51	63	75
55–64	16*s.*	17*s.*	26*s.*	26*s.* 6*d.*	32*s.*
%	32	34	52	53	64
ALL AGES	16*s.* 6*d.*	21*s.*	28*s.*	33*s.* 6*d.*	37*s.*
%	34	43	57	68	76

[2] Men with appreciable other sources of family income are excluded.

B8. PHYSICAL STATE, BY AGE: MEN ONLY, EFFECTIVE RECORDS

Physical State		Fit and very fit	Out of condition	Unfit and obvious physical defects	TOTAL
Age 18–24		23	13	6	42
	%	55	31	14	100
25–34		107	33	7	147
	%	73	22	5	100
35–44		123	44	33	200
	%	62	22	16	100
45–54		94	63	33	190
	%	50	33	17	100
55–64		122	66	54	242
	%	50	27	23	100
ALL AGES		469	219	133	821
	%	57	27	16	100

B9. EMPLOYABILITY, BY AGE: MEN ONLY, EFFECTIVE RECORDS

Grade of Employability		Fully employable	Restricted		Unemployable	TOTAL
			Mentally	Physically		
Age 18–24		34	1	8	—	43
	%	79	2	19	—	100
25–34		134	8	14	2	158
	%	85	5	9	1	100
35–44		131	11	39	8	189
	%	69	6	21	4	100
45–54		104	9	54	12	179
	%	58	5	30	7	100
55–64		106	13	88	23	230
	%	46	6	38	10	100
ALL AGES		509	42	203	45	799
	%	64	5	25	6	100

B 10. EMPLOYABILITY, BY AGE AND PHYSICAL CONDITION: MEN ONLY, EFFECTIVE RECORDS

Employability: Physical Strength		Good average or above	Doubtful	Insufficient	TOTAL
Age 18–24		25	10	2	37
	%	68	27	5	100
25–34		114	30	4	148
	%	77	20	3	100
35–44		109	58	13	180
	%	61	32	7	100
45–54		86	69	23	178
	%	48	39	13	100
55–64		89	89	34	212
	%	42	42	16	100
ALL AGES		423	256	76	755
	%	56	34	10	100

B 11. EMPLOYABILITY, BY AGE AND INTELLIGENCE: MEN ONLY, EFFECTIVE RECORDS

Employability: Intelligence		Good average and above	Doubtful	Insufficient	TOTAL
Age 18–24		24	12	1	37
	%	65	32	3	100
25–34		89	43	7	139
	%	64	31	5	100
35–44		105	54	11	170
	%	62	32	6	100
45–54		99	62	7	168
	%	59	37	4	100
55–64		117	77	10	204
	%	57	38	5	100
ALL AGES		434	248	36	718
	%	61	34	5	100

B 12. EMPLOYABILITY QUALITY, BY AGE: MEN ONLY, EFFECTIVE RECORDS

Potentially suitable for	Skilled work	Heavy work	Light work	No work	TOTAL
Age 18–24	6	29	6	—	41
%	15	70	15	—	100
25–34	23	102	22	4	151
%	15	67	15	3	100
35–44	18	103	47	13	181
%	10	57	26	7	100
45–54	16	81	59	24	180
%	9	45	33	13	100
55–64	20	51	108	58	237
%	8	21	46	25	100
ALL AGES	83	366	242	99	790
%	11	46	31	12	100

B 13. DOMESTIC STANDARDS, BY AGE: MEN ONLY, EFFECTIVE RECORDS

Domestic Standards[1]		House		Furniture		Clothing			Management		
		Clean	Dirty	Good	Bad	Good	Medium	Bad	Good	Medium	Bad
Age 18–24		27	9	26	5	6	2	4	11	2	3
	%	75	25	84	16	50	17	33	69	12	19
25–34		114	19	98	20	20	14	12	37	13	5
	%	86	14	83	17	44	30	26	67	24	9
35–44		141	27	103	31	22	20	23	51	27	13
	%	84	16	77	23	34	31	35	56	30	14
45–54		123	17	93	29	22	15	24	51	10	6
	%	88	12	76	24	36	25	39	76	15	9
55–64		177	17	133	26	32	18	24	59	11	11
	%	91	9	84	16	43	24	33	72	14	14
ALL AGES		582	89	453	111	102	69	87	209	63	38
	%	87	13	80	20	39	27	34	68	20	12

[1] See note to Table A 10. It is probable that the comparative figures for different age groups, given here, are considerably more reliable than the comparative figures for different places.

B 14. ATTITUDE TO NEW EMPLOYMENT,[1] BY AGE: MEN ONLY, EFFECTIVE RECORDS

Attitude to New Employment	Still thinking in terms of work	Beginning to accept state of unemployment	Adjusted to state of unemployment	TOTAL
Age 18–29	39	38	31	108
%	36	35	29	100
30–39	50	93	37	180
%	28	52	20	100
40–49	42	75	39	156
%	27	48	25	100
50–59	67	78	45	190
%	35	41	24	100
60–64	23	40	56	119
%	19	34	47	100
ALL AGES	221	324	208	753
%	29	43	28	100

C 1. ATTITUDE TO NEW EMPLOYMENT,[1] BY OCCUPATIONAL STATUS: MEN ONLY, EFFECTIVE RECORDS

Attitude to New Employment	Still thinking in terms of work	Beginning to accept state of unemployment	Adjusted to state of unemployment	TOTAL
Status of worker				
Minor commercial	13	11	8	32
%	41	34	25	100
Skilled	23	25	18	66
%	35	38	27	100
Semi-skilled	113	172	112	397
%	28	44	28	100
Unskilled	65	110	58	233
%	28	47	25	100
Submarginal	4	8	12	24
%	17	33	50	100

[1] For explanation of the three categories used, see p. 144.

C2. ATTITUDE TO NEW EMPLOYMENT[1] BY DEGREE OF FITNESS: MEN ONLY, EFFECTIVE RECORDS

Attitude to New Employment	Still thinking in terms of work	Beginning to accept state of unemployment	Adjusted to state of unemployment	TOTAL
Degree of Fitness				
Very fit	11	34	15	60
%	18	57	25	100
Fit	111	147	92	350
%	32	42	26	100
Out of condition	53	98	57	208
%	26	47	27	100
Unfit	9	24	21	54
%	17	44	39	100

C3. ATTITUDE TO NEW EMPLOYMENT,[1] BY EMPLOYABILITY: MEN ONLY, EFFECTIVE RECORDS

Attitude to New Employment	Still thinking in terms of work	Beginning to accept state of unemployment	Adjusted to state of unemployment	TOTAL
Degree of Employability				
Fully employable	152	203	98	453
%	34	45	21	100
Handicapped	48	99	76	223
%	21	45	34	100
Unemployable	6	15	22	43
%	14	35	51	100

[1] For explanation of the three categories used, see p. 144.

C4. ATTITUDE TO NEW EMPLOYMENT,[1] BY DOMESTIC STANDARDS: MEN ONLY, EFFECTIVE RECORDS

Attitude to New Employment	Still thinking in terms of work	Beginning to accept state of unemployment	Adjusted to state of unemployment	TOTAL
Domestic Standards				
Management:				
Good	63	93	40	196
%	32	48	20	100
Ordinary	25	21	17	63
%	40	33	27	100
Poor	10	10	14	34
%	29	29	42	100
House:				
Clean	167	231	125	523
%	32	44	24	100
Dirty	18	28	32	78
%	23	36	41	100
Furniture:				
Good	133	188	90	411
%	32	46	22	100
Bad	26	43	33	102
%	26	42	32	100
Clothing:				
Good	31	42	23	96
%	32	44	24	100
Medium	16	37	10	63
%	25	59	16	100
Bad	25	33	25	83
%	30	40	30	100

[1] For explanation of the three categories used, see p. 144.

C5. ATTITUDE TO NEW EMPLOYMENT[1] OF THOSE ABOVE AND BELOW THE "GEORGE" POVERTY LINE: MEN ONLY, EFFECTIVE RECORDS

Attitude to New Employment	Still thinking in terms of work	Beginning to accept state of unemployment	Adjusted to state of unemployment	TOTAL
Economic Level				
Below the George	160	223	149	532
Poverty Line %	30	42	28	100
Above the George	62	102	57	221
Poverty Line %	28	46	26	100

[1] For explanation of the three categories used, see p. 144.

INDEX

CAMBRIDGE: PRINTED BY W. LEWIS, M.A., AT THE UNIVERSITY PRESS

Titles in This Series

1. H. L. Beales and R. S. Lambert, eds. MEMOIRS OF THE UNEMPLOYED. 1934
2. A. L. Bowley and Margaret H. Hogg. HAS POVERTY DIMINISHED? 1925
3. Marian Bowley. HOUSING AND THE STATE 1919–1944. 1945
4. Henry Noel Brailsford. SOCIALISM FOR TODAY. 1925
5. H. N. Brailsford, John A. Hobson, A. Creech Jones, and E. F. Wise. THE LIVING WAGE. 1926
   bound with
   R. Palme Dutt. SOCIALISM AND THE LIVING WAGE. 1927
6. BRITAIN'S INDUSTRIAL FUTURE. 1928
7. A. M. Carr-Saunders and D. Caradog Jones. A SURVEY OF THE SOCIAL STRUCTURE OF ENGLAND & WALES. 1927
8. G.D.H. Cole. THE NEXT TEN YEARS IN BRITISH SOCIAL AND ECONOMIC POLICY. 1929
9. G.D.H. Cole and M. I. Cole. THE CONDITION OF BRITAIN. 1937

10. Hugh Dalton. PRACTICAL SOCIALISM FOR BRITAIN. 1935
11. Ronald C. Davison. THE UNEMPLOYED: OLD POLICIES AND NEW. 1929
12. M. P. Fogarty. PROSPECT OF THE INDUSTRIAL AREAS OF GREAT BRITAIN. 1945
13. Arthur Gleason. WHAT THE WORKERS WANT: A STUDY OF BRITISH LABOR. 1920
14. Wal Hannington. THE PROBLEM OF THE DISTRESSED AREAS. 1937
15. John Hilton. RICH MAN, POOR MAN. 1944
16. J. A. Hobson. THE ECONOMICS OF UNEMPLOYMENT. 1922
17. S. G. Hobson. NATIONAL GUILDS AND THE STATE. 1920
18. E.M.H. Lloyd. STABILIZATION: AN ECONOMIC POLICY FOR PRODUCERS & CONSUMERS. 1923
19. C.F.G. Masterman. ENGLAND AFTER THE WAR. 1922
20. The Pilgrim Trust. MEN WITHOUT WORK. 1938
21. G.C.M. M'Gonigle and J. Kirby. POVERTY AND PUBLIC HEALTH. 1936
22. Sir George Newman. THE BUILDING OF A NATION'S HEALTH. 1939

23. THE NEXT FIVE YEARS: AN ESSAY IN POLITICAL AGREEMENT. 1935

24. Sir John Boyd Orr. FOOD, HEALTH AND INCOME. 1936

    bound with

    Sir John Boyd Orr and David Lubbock. FEEDING THE PEOPLE IN WAR-TIME. 1940

25. OUR TOWNS: A CLOSE UP. 1943

26. Eleanor F. Rathbone. THE DISINHERITED FAMILY: A PLEA FOR THE ENDOWMENT OF THE FAMILY. 1924

27. William A. Robson, ed. PUBLIC ENTERPRISE: DEVELOPMENTS IN SOCIAL OWNERSHIP AND CONTROL IN GREAT BRITAIN. 1937

28. William A. Robson, ed. SOCIAL SECURITY. 1943

29. B. Seebohm Rowntree. POVERTY AND PROGRESS. 1941

30. E. D. Simon. HOW TO ABOLISH THE SLUMS. 1929

    bound with

    E. D. Simon. REBUILDING BRITAIN—A TWENTY YEAR PLAN. 1945

31. John Strachey. REVOLUTION BY REASON. 1925

32. Richard M. Titmuss. POVERTY AND POPULATION. 1938

33. Richard Titmuss and Kathleen Titmuss. PARENTS REVOLT. 1942

bound with

Richard M. Titmuss. BIRTH, POVERTY AND WEALTH. 1943

34. George Walworth. FEEDING THE NATION IN PEACE AND WAR. 1940

35. Whiting Williams. FULL UP AND FED UP: THE WORKER'S MIND IN CROWDED BRITAIN. 1921